D0934124

BERNT BALCHEN
Polar Aviator

CARROLL V. GLINES

SMITHSONIAN INSTITUTION PRESS
Washington and London

To Bernt Balchen's Carpetbaggers
and the crewmen of the Ve Do It Squadron
who braved Norway's wartime skies

© 1999 by Carroll V. Glines

Copy editor: Debbie K. Hardin
Production editor: Ruth Spiegel
Designer: Janice Wheeler
Cartographer: Rod Eyer

Library of Congress Cataloging-in-Publication Data
Glines, Carroll V., 1920–
    Bernt Balchen : polar aviator / by Carroll V. Glines
        p.   cm.
    Includes bibliographical references and index.
    ISBN: 1-56098-906-8 (alk. paper)
    1. Balchen, Bernt, 1899-1973.   2. Air pilots—United States—Biography.
    3. Explorers—United States—Biography.   4. Arctic regions.   5. Antarctica.
    6. Aeronautics—Flights.   I. Title.
    G585.B3G58   1999
    919.8'04'092—dc21
    [B]   99-20698

British Library Cataloguing-in-Publication Data available
Manufactured in the United States of America

⊗ ♲ The recycled paper used in this publication meets the minimum
requirements of the American National Standard for Information Sciences—
Permanence of Paper for Printed Library Materials ANSI Z39.48-1948.

Contents

Foreword

Bernt Balchen is one of the least recognized public figures in America, yet he was a hero to individuals the public called heroes. He was a leader of those who called themselves leaders. He was a person who managed to remain mostly anonymous to the public despite the honors he received throughout his lifetime.

He never sought fame; rather it seemed to seek him. He sought challenge and in doing so found his role in life. He sought excellence and won international acclaim. He believed in freedom and fought for it in the uniforms of three nations.

As a flyer he had few peers. It was Balchen the famous names sought out when they launched expeditions across oceans and uncharted continents. He was the first to fly above the South Pole and the first to see both Poles from the air.

Balchen the man was much like Balchen the hero. Fame and honors had little apparent effect on him. He managed to retain his low profile because he never took himself that seriously.

He became an explorer because he possessed the flight and navigation skills few men had in those early days of aviation. He was an arctic expert because his life was tied to the arctic and survival was the only way of life there.

He became a Norwegian resistance hero because his homeland needed him. He fought as a Finnish soldier in World War I because he understood that if Finland fell, Norway would follow. He was a friend to everyone—to the mechanic on whom he depended to change his spark plugs or a king who could cut red tape with a prime minister who stood in his way when he had a job to do.

He professed not to be a public speaker but could speak without notes on the future of aviation or the need for air power.

Adversity was not unknown to Bernt Balchen. Within the space of minutes he was congratulated by a president in the White House and handed a summons ordering his deportation as he left the grounds.

He became a colonel in the U.S. Air Force, drove out Nazi weather stations from Greenland during the war, rescued airmen downed on the Greenland ice cap.

He was outspoken and hated sham and pretense. His candor won him enemies, and the Senate never promoted him to star rank.

Balchen's friend, Lowell Thomas, paid fitting tribute: "He was the last of the great Norsemen."

George L. Weiss,
   Lieutenant Colonel, U.S. Air Force (Retired)
   Former Pentagon Editor, *Armed Forces Journal*

Acknowledgments

Of the many pilots who represent the Golden Age of Flight, Bernt Balchen is further distinguished: educated, modest, artistically talented, and with flying skills far more proficient than his contemporaries. To my delight, he kept excellent notes, diaries, sketches, and correspondence files throughout his life. These were judiciously distributed to archives throughout the country after his death by his widow Audrey, who has a keen appreciation of the historical significance of her late husband's accomplishments. I am greatly indebted to her for providing continual encouragement and extensive background knowledge.

I am also indebted to the Royal Norwegian Embassy, the curators at the National Archives and Library of Congress in Washington, D.C., the Air Force Museum, and the Ford Museum for their cooperation. Especially helpful was archivist Joseph D. Caver of the Air Force Historical Research Agency at Maxwell Air Force Base, Alabama, where most of the Balchen files of military significance are located. And I am grateful to Dr. Raimund E. Goerler, director, and Bertha L. Ihnat and Laura J. Kissel, archives assistants at the Byrd Polar Research Center at Ohio State University, for their efficiency in providing the Richard E. Byrd files for review. Thanks are also owed to Duane J. Reed, chief of Special Collections at the Air Force Academy, Colorado Springs, Colorado, who filled in gaps related to Balchen's contributions to the Air Force. Bruno A. Yoka, who served on the Greenland Coast Guard patrol during World War II provided interesting information about operations there. H. V. "Pat" Reilly, executive director of the Aviation Hall of Fame of New Jersey, sent valuable background on the *Atlantic* flight and the French museum at Ver-sur-Mer.

Because many of Bernt Balchen's activities during World War II were classified top secret and the participants on the missions he led were sworn to maintain that secrecy until several years ago, there was reluctance on the part of a few to respond to queries. However, I am indebted to Col. Robert W. Fish and two dozen members of the 801st/492nd Bomb Group and Balchen's Ve Do It Squadron for providing anecdotes, information, and photographs about that phase of the air war. Knut Hagrup, former president of Scandinavian Airlines System (SAS), also provided invaluable history on the airline. Signe Balchen, cousin of Bernt Balchen, sent photographs, as did Lars Gyllenhaal, Oyvind Aaonevik, Kjell Agren, and Torbjorn Olausson. Ornunf Thune and Toril McGowan provided valuable translation services.

My appreciation is also extended to Fred W. Hotson, past president of the Canadian Aviation Historical Society, for providing background and photographs about Balchen's pioneering days in Canada. Fred Schempf furnished information about the 10th Rescue Squadron; Lowell Thomas, Jr., also provided information about Balchen on the record-setting round-the-world flight on which they were passengers. The superb artistic ability of Rod Eyer to produce excellent maps is also very much appreciated, and my thanks are also extended to him for locating rare photographs.

Sincere appreciation is extended to Smithsonian Institution Press for continuing—through its History of Aviation series—to honor the men and women who led the way in developing aviation.

Introduction

When Walter J. Boyne, former director of the Smithsonian's National Air and Space Museum and distinguished aviation writer, was asked to describe Bernt Balchen, he said Balchen

> was one of the most important and least written about pilots of his era. An intelligent man and a brilliant pilot, he suffered from a flaw unknown to almost any other aviator of the day except Lindbergh—he was modest. He has received far less acclaim than he deserves, and his modesty was in fact the reason that he endured some ignominious treatment which a lesser person would have rebelled against.[1]

Although two Balchen biographies, written long before his death, and his ill-fated autobiography have been published, they did not reveal his many accomplishments over a lifetime or tell of what I believe were the disgraceful actions of Adm. Richard E. Byrd to discredit him. The time has come to give overdue credit to Balchen and disclose the dark side of a national hero who thrust a fraud of alleged discovery on the world.

I first met Balchen in the Pentagon in the early 1960s, when he was there as a consultant, as he was searching for an office that had been moved without notice to another location. I offered to help him and we found the new office together. We chatted amiably as one would with a next-door neighbor and I felt as though I had made a new friend. The next time I met him was in Alaska in 1972 commemorating the 25th anniversary of the establishment of the Alaskan Command and honoring those of us who had served in the command previously. Balchen, unpretentious and unassuming as ever, was recognized happily by everyone as if an Alaskan who had just come home after a long absence.

I published a book titled *Polar Aviation* in which I excerpted a story about him. I hoped that some day I would be able to write his biography and began collecting background information. After completing biographies of the Wright brothers, Jimmy Doolittle, and Roscoe Turner, in addition to other works on aviation, the time to begin came in 1996. Fortunately, Balchen kept copious notes and files during most of his life and, thanks to his wife Audrey, they are preserved in a number of accessible locations, mainly the Library of Congress, National Archives, the Air Force Academy, and the Air Force Historical Research Agency.

As the Balchen life story began to emerge during the hundreds of hours of research, the true worthiness of this unique Norwegian American came into ever sharper focus. He was a walking encyclopedia on arctic and polar exploration, and a daring pilot, engineer, scientist, artist, and visionary. He had a unique understanding of geopolitics and the art of one-on-one negotiation; his communication skills in several languages were exceptional. His ability to plan and put those plans into action were without peer. He could not only describe a course of action succinctly but also make precise maps and engineering drawings to accompany his words. And perhaps most surprising was his poetic, artistic nature that was expressed through the hundreds of sketches of arctic, antarctic, and Norwegian scenes he translated into beautiful and now very valuable watercolor paintings. He was the right man at the right time.

What follows is the life story of Bernt Balchen. His kind will not come this way again.

1·Spitsbergen

The dirigible looked like a giant gray whale as it slowly nosed out of the mist on 7 May 1926 at Kings Bay, Spitsbergen, which is located halfway to the North Pole from Norway. The *Norge* was en route with a mixed crew of Italians and Norwegians to fly to the Pole and on to Alaska, an unprecedented voyage for an airship of more than 3,000 fog-bound and icy miles.

Among those waiting for the dirigible's arrival from Italy under the guidance of its builder and pilot Col. Umberto Nobile, an Italian army officer and airship expert, were Roald Amundsen, a renowned Norwegian explorer and leader of the expedition, and Lincoln Ellsworth, a wealthy American who had shared a hazardous, unsuccessful flight to reach the North Pole with Amundsen and four others in open-cockpit seaplanes the year before. The financing for the venture was furnished by the Aero Club of Norway, Ellsworth, the Italian government, and bolstered by contracts with the press and motion picture producers.

The *Norge* had left Rome on 29 March 1926, made stops at Pulham, England, and Oslo, Norway, then flew to Leningrad, Russia. It remained there two weeks for maintenance and loading of supplies before proceeding to Kings Bay. It had covered 4,700 mi. by the time it arrived at Spitsbergen.

Amundsen and Ellsworth had reached Kings Bay on 12 April. Aboard the *Norge* were 16 men, many of them on leave from their respective military services. Included was Royal Norwegian naval air force captain Hjalmar Riiser-Larsen, second in command of the expedition. Waiting among the workers and ground crew was Lt. Bernt Balchen, a graduate of the naval air force pilot school at Horten, Norway. The handsome

25-year-old had arrived earlier at Spitsbergen with 50 others on the supply ship *Knut Skaaluren*. He was selected to join the *Norge* crew by Riiser-Larsen and had been granted leave to make the flight because of his expertise with engines and his reputation as a hard worker.[1]

Spitsbergen's location for this and other arctic air operations was ideal. It was the closest natural setting on the edge of the polar basin for an aerial attempt on the North Pole. It had been the launching place for Salomon Andree in a balloon and Walter Wellman in a dirigible in their attempts in 1897 and 1907, respectively. Coal had been mined there since 1910, and the mining camp had workshops, a store, and a dozen wooden houses near a coal dock on the bay. Amundsen, well-aware of what was available in terms of support, sent a ground crew to the site in early 1926 to build an open-roofed hangar and mooring mast in time for the *Norge*'s arrival.

Amundsen's decision to use a dirigible, although it was considerably slower than fixed-wing aircraft, was made because it could stay aloft longer than any heavier-than-air craft. The semirigid airship was 348 ft. long, powered by three Maybach engines, and held 550,000 cu. ft. of hydrogen, which gave it a lifting capacity of more than 20 tn. The standard fuel load enabled it to fly 3,600 mi.

Meanwhile, the near success of the Amundsen flight to reach the North Pole the year before had spurred others interested in being first to attain that goal using the airplane. One of them was Lt. Comdr. Richard Evelyn Byrd Jr., a 1912 graduate of the U.S. Naval Academy who had gained some brief arctic flying experience with the two-plane aviation unit of the Donald MacMillan Expedition in northwest Greenland in 1925. His father had been an assistant U.S. attorney general under President Woodrow Wilson. His mother was a direct descendant of Lord Delaware. His two brothers were Harry Flood Byrd, a governor of Virginia and later a U.S. senator, and Thomas Byrd, who was an apple farmer in the Winchester, Virginia, area.

In 1916, at the age of 28, Richard E. Byrd Jr. received medical retirement from active duty as an ensign because of a leg injury suffered at the Naval Academy, which was later aggravated by a fall aboard a ship. However, he was given an unprecedented opportunity to continue on active duty as a retired reserve officer and complete pilot training at Pensacola, Florida, during World War I. He was promoted to the retired reserve rank of lieutenant commander in June 1924 by special act of Congress.

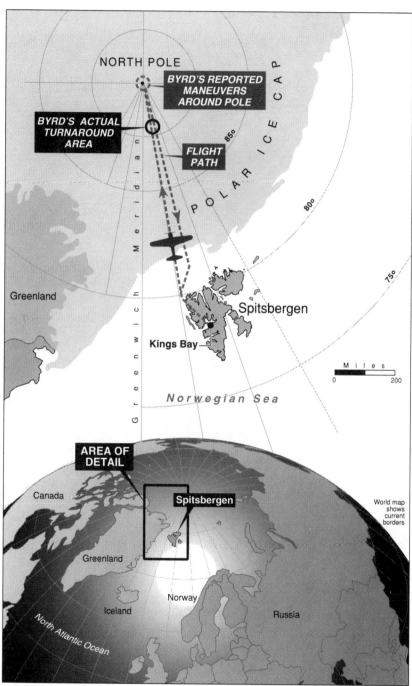

Map 1.

It was Byrd's experience—albeit limited—flying over Greenland the year before that had inspired him to consider a flight in a fixed-wing aircraft to the North Pole. He talked over the possibility with Floyd Bennett, who was a noncommissioned officer designated as a naval aviation pilot in October 1920 and who had been Byrd's pilot on the Greenland flights. Bennett was a competent mechanic as well as an excellent pilot who respected Byrd's planning abilities and strictly observed the officer–enlisted man relationship. Apparently, he had valued the experience of the 1925 Greenland expedition and had no reason to decline the invitation to accompany Byrd on his next adventure. Byrd's rationale for a polar flight was that he "might discover some new land or unexpected scientific phenomena" and "accelerate public interest in aviation."[2] Of course, there was certainly also the compelling desire to be the first to reach the Pole by air and thereby achieve worldwide acclaim.

Byrd's family connections enabled him to contact a number of wealthy individuals who financed his effort. Nearly $100,000 was raised from Edsel Ford, Vincent Astor, John D. Rockefeller Jr., Rodman Wanamaker, Dwight Morrow, and other nationally prominent businesspeople. The *New York Times* and the National Geographic Society also made substantial contributions through contracts for future articles.[3] Byrd and Bennett were granted leave from the Navy to put their plan into action as a private enterprise.

In four months of frantic activity, accompanied by much publicity, the plans turned into reality. Byrd, Bennett, and a crew of 50 volunteers selected from hundreds of inexperienced applicants departed New York harbor on the 3,500 tn. coal-burner SS *Chantier* on 5 April 1926. Aboard was a donated six-months' food supply and a dismantled Fokker F-VIIA/3m trimotor plane donated by Ford, named the *Josephine Ford* in honor of Ford's three-year-old daughter.[4] Also stowed aboard was a single-engine, two-seat Curtiss Oriole plane, named *Richard the Third* by Byrd's men after his son.

The *Josephine Ford* was Anthony H. G. Fokker's first trimotor aircraft. The 35-year-old Dutchman was noted for the World War I fighter planes he designed and manufactured for Germany, and had proved that his plane designs were equal to or better than those of the British and French. This huge craft, with three Wright 220 hp air-cooled engines, had room for two pilots and more than 10 passengers. It had been manufactured in Holland and made a perfect score to win the Edsel B. Ford Reliability Trophy the year before. These tours, held from 1925–1931, were efficiency competitions that gave airplane builders an opportunity to demonstrate their latest models around the country. Ford purchased the plane in the fall of 1925 for a reported $40,000 and made it available to Byrd for his Pole flight. In addition to the standard 200 gal. fuel tanks in the wings, two tanks had been installed inside the fuselage, each holding more than 100 gal. If more was needed, gasoline could be added in flight from 5 gal. cans.

Fokker had seen the potential publicity value of the flight and had stipulated in the sales contract that the name *Fokker* was to be displayed in large letters on both sides, on the leading edges, and under the wings of the plane so the name could be seen from any angle and there would be no doubt of its manufacturer.[5]

The *Chantier,* under command of Capt. Michael J. Brennan, arrived in Kings Bay on 29 April. It had come to Spitsbergen from New York via Tromso, Norway, and was anchored about 300 yd. offshore. Four of the ship's lifeboats were tied together and large planks laid across them so that the supplies and plane parts could be off-loaded. The planes were wrestled off the ship with great difficulty and at great risk to the people involved and pulled to the shore using the *Chantier's* lifeboats as a pontoon bridge. Byrd knew they were taking a great risk if a wind developed but decided that he had to get his people and equipment ashore somehow or return to the States as "ignominious failures."[6] The Fokker, newly equipped with skis, was nearly ready for flight when the *Norge* arrived on 7 May.

The single-engine Curtiss Oriole, also equipped with skis, was to be used as a search plane if something should happen to the Fokker and for taking aerial motion pictures for news and publicity purposes. After a short engine warm-up for the Curtiss Oriole, U.S. Navy lieutenants Alton N. Parker and Robb C. Oertell took off for a test flight around Kings Bay. When they were preflighting it, they had heated the oil but not the engine, so the overloaded oil pump stripped its gears and broke. They landed immediately when the oil pressure dropped to zero. The pump was removed and taken to Amundsen's machine shop in the dirigible's hangar for repairs, where Balchen made a new set of gears for it. He instructed Parker and Oertell on handling the engines in subfreezing weather and emphasized that the engine had to be covered with a tarpaulin and the whole engine heated, especially the oil pan, before attempting to start it.

Amundsen's ground crew had been surprised to see a rival party ap-

pear with a giant plane that was going to challenge the famous Norwegian's dream. Although the Norwegians were cordial, many must have
viewed Byrd as an unwanted challenger to their national hero.

To be the first to fly to the North Pole would mean world celebrity.
When Byrd saw the preparations that had already been made for the
Norge by Amundsen and his crew, he was aware that his rugged com-
petitor knew full well the dangers and challenges of the arctic. When the
aircraft were safely ashore, Amundsen met with Byrd at a cordial lunch
on 2 May 1926. Also there with Byrd were U.S. Navy lieutenants Oertell,
who would handle the fuel supplies for the flight, and George Noville,
acting executive officer. Standing respectfully aside was Bennett, whom
Byrd would depend on to do the flying while he navigated.

Amundsen had brought Lt. Balchen to the meeting to bring to the discussion his experience of hundreds of hours of flying in arctic weather
conditions. "There was an air of friendliness immediately," Balchen recalled later. "We didn't meet as competitors but more or less as collabora-
tors in an attack on the polar regions—an attack by two vehicles of the air,
one lighter, one heavier than air. Amundsen offered the facilities of the coal
mine quarters and the cooperation of the members of his expedition."[7]

Balchen was immediately impressed with the quiet, intent Bennett. He
spoke softly and seemed shy in the company of his commander. Bennett
had some seaplane experience but had never flown an aircraft with skis
and was very interested in learning how an airplane behaved on them.[8]

After the meeting with Byrd, the Amundsen group returned to prepare
for the *Norge*'s departure. At this point it was clear that a sharp antago-
nism was developing between some members of the two rival groups that
was fueled by the newspaper correspondents covering the flights. Each
wanted their respective leaders to be first to the Pole. However, Amundsen stressed to his crew that the flight of the *Norge* was to be a transpolar
flight and the North Pole was just one of the checkpoints they were to
pass on the flight to Alaska. He and his group would take their time with
their preparations, Amundsen decreed, and help the other camp when
needed.

Balchen was a fixed-wing pilot and curious about the Byrd crew's
preparations to get the Fokker ready for flight. It was immediately obvious to him that none of the Byrd mechanics had any experience with ski-
equipped planes. He watched Oertell laboriously wax the skis on the
Fokker with black shoe polish, an endeavor Balchen knew to be a waste
of energy. The skis seemed too weak for the weight of the aircraft and

had probably been designed by engineers with no previous knowledge of ski-flying and the stresses imposed on a ski-equipped aircraft.[9]

In his memoirs, Balchen wrote,

> Now in the arctic if there is one thing we know it is this: that the hard crystalline snow, at this time of year, acts like sandpaper, and even if wax gave a sliding surface, it wouldn't last long. Our experience in Norway with both racing skis and airplane skis has taught us to use an entirely different preparation, a mixture of pine tar and resin burned into the wood with a blowtorch. I described this to Oertell, but he said there was no time to change, because the test hop was due at noon.[10]

Balchen shrugged and went back to his task that day in the machine shop making a new driveshaft for a tractor. He heard the Fokker revving up for takeoff on a test hop and then heard the engines' roar stop abruptly. Amundsen rushed into the shop and said that the Byrd plane had broken a ski. He asked Balchen to help repair it. The *Josephine Ford* had jolted roughly over the snow hummocks, suddenly spun to one side, and plowed into a snow bank. One ski had shattered and its attaching strut was bent.

When Balchen reached the plane he knew what had happened. The skis had refused to let go of the snow. The weight of survival gear, extra fuel, and the friction of the skis were too great to enable the Fokker to gain flying speed. Skis had never been attached to a plane as large and heavy as the Fokker and had not been tried out before the plane left the United States. Balchen, experienced in operating aircraft in all types of arctic conditions, knew what strength and flexibility were required for skis on large, heavily loaded planes. Both skis were badly split and could not be repaired. There was a spare set of skis on the *Chantier,* but they would not be any better. The spare set could be strengthened with strips of hard wood such as ash or hickory, but there was no wood like that available anywhere at Spitsbergen. Balchen suggested they take a look at the *Chantier*'s lifeboat oars.

Some heavy oars were promptly brought ashore, over the objections of the ship's captain. The ship's carpenter cut the blades into strips and attached them onto the new skis. The bent landing gear strut was straightened and Balchen helped fit the skis. A mixture of pine tar and resin was burned into the skis with a blow torch, as Balchen had previously recommended.

The plane was ready for a final test hop later that day. A ramp of snow was built at the takeoff point so that the plane would gain a little extra speed by heading downhill. It started slowly down the takeoff area but it faltered as Bennett tried to gain speed, and the tail never left the ground. The plane had to be lightened, so about 300 gal. of fuel and 100 lb. of souvenirs were off-loaded. Bennett was then able to take off and made a successful two-hour test flight.

All appeared ready for Byrd's departure at midday on 8 May after a report was received that a high pressure area signifying good weather was developing over the entire polar area and was expected to last about 48 hr. It was a Sunday, and because Amundsen would not allow his crew to work on the Sabbath, they all watched as Byrd's men topped off the plane's wing tanks with fuel. The temperature was barely above freezing, and there was slush everywhere.

Byrd and Bennett climbed aboard and Bennett started the three engines. When they were warmed up, Bennett pushed the throttles forward but the aircraft did not move. He kept blasting the engines and when the plane finally jarred loose, it moved ahead only a few feet, too slowly to attain takeoff speed. Bennett shut off the engines. Byrd and Bennett climbed out and looked at the skis. Byrd beckoned to Balchen and asked what was wrong.

Balchen explained that when the temperature rises just above freezing, which it was then, the snow becomes sticky. The only thing to do is wait until the later hours when the snow freezes hard again and then the icy surface will make a takeoff possible.[11]

The suggestion made sense to Byrd, and shortly after midnight Greenwich time when the sun was low on the northern horizon and the temperature had dropped, Bennett started the Fokker's engines. Balchen had stayed up that evening and watched as Bennett began the take-off roll. When it was airborne, he reached in his shirt pocket, retrieved a small notebook he always carried, and made an entry in his extremely small handwriting: "9 May. Jo. Ford, B and B, depart Kings Bay, 0037."

Balchen watched with mixed emotions as the plane headed northward and gradually faded away over the horizon. At Amundsen's direction he had given the rival team valuable advice and assistance that had enabled the Americans to finally get off first without further mishap. He felt a keen loyalty to Amundsen, his mentor and fellow compatriot. If Byrd succeeded in reaching the Pole first, Balchen would be a prime factor in destroying the chances for Amundsen to have the honor.

Amundsen and Ellsworth had heard the plane depart. Amundsen told Balchen later, "I was glad they were off and I hoped they'd be back safely. It meant a lot to us that they would have a safe return. If something happened, we would have had to abandon our plans for the transpolar flight in order to instigate a search and if possible a rescue with the aid of the *Norge*, which would have cruising rates and ample facilities to conduct such an operation."[12]

Amundsen's crew, a little dejected, went about their work to get the *Norge* ready for flight. Contrary to what most historians have reported, the thought of a race was not uppermost in Amundsen's mind; he had a broader objective. Although he admitted it would have been an honor to be the first to fly over the North Pole, his experience had taught him that thorough preparation was the key to success, and he refused to push his crew to exhaustion. Riiser-Larsen explained, "For Amundsen the North Pole was not the goal. We had been up there the year before to 88 degrees North and beyond. Amundsen's dream for many years was to explore the total stretch across the Polar Sea of which two-thirds of the distance lay between the North Pole and Alaska. If there had been a race, it had been well within our power to get off before Byrd."[13]

The great Norwegian explorer explained this to his crew and restored their morale by telling them that even if the Norwegian–American–Italian team was not first to reach the Pole, it would be helping to establish a greater aviation milestone by helping the *Norge* complete the world's longest flight on its transpolar trip to Alaska.

Balchen's job was to check the condition and weigh every piece of personal equipment, food, and survival gear that was to be loaded aboard the *Norge*. Balchen was never content to be idle when his job was done, so when off-duty he gave ski instruction to the Italian members of the airship's crew on the mountains behind the camp. Most of them had never been on skis before, and it was Amundsen's order that every crew member and ground helper must have some skiing experience in case they were selected for the flight and the dirigible was forced down. Amundsen at age 54 set an example by skiing 10 or 15 miles a day to stay in shape.[14]

While Amundsen and his crew were at dinner on the evening of 9 May an Italian worker rushed in, shouting, "She come! They here!" Amundsen led the rush to greet the Fokker as Bennett circled the settlement; the whistle on the *Chantier* screeched and brought the crews from both expedition camps racing to the airstrip.

When Bennett set the plane down smoothly and brought it to a stop,

Amundsen opened the plane's door. As Byrd emerged, Amundsen gave him a smothering bear hug of congratulations accompanied by kisses on both cheeks. He also kissed and hugged an embarrassed Bennett. Ellsworth extended his hand and congratulated his two fellow Americans. Balchen, standing outside the crowd of well-wishers, reached in his shirt pocket for his notebook and made another penciled entry: "9 May. Jo. Ford returns Kings Bay 1607."

Strangely, no one asked either Byrd or Bennett if they had reached the Pole. It was assumed that they had as Byrd's crew hurried forward and hoisted the two airmen on their shoulders. They rushed them to the *Chantier*, where Byrd made an announcement over the ship's radio to the world that he had reached the North Pole and that he was the first person to do so.

The Fokker had been gone exactly 15 hr. 30 min. when it had been predicted that the flight would take at least 17 hr., with an estimated 21 hr. of fuel aboard. The distance to the Pole and return was 1,330 nautical mi. (1,529.5 statute mi.). That meant the average ground speed of the plane had to be 85.8 kn or 98.67 MPH to cover that distance. Balchen thought about these figures briefly and then dismissed them from his mind. He had flown a number of different aircraft but not a trimotor Fokker. He thought maintaining an average ground speed of nearly 100 MPH for that distance with the load it carried and with heavy skis attached was indeed excellent.

These simple figures would have an impact on his life far beyond what he could have imagined. They would embroil him in an unpleasant controversy that would much later become front-page news all over the world. They would influence his future adversely, cause him to be denied a coveted promotion, and follow him to the end of his life and beyond. They would cause geographers and historians to delve deeply into their significance and the historical claim they represented. And they would eventually tarnish the image of Byrd, a U.S. Navy admiral and national hero who had created his own aura of greatness.

While the Byrd party celebrated on the *Chantier* and the news was radioed to the world that this aviation "first" had been achieved, Amundsen's crew continued loading the *Norge*. When the preparations were almost complete, Amundsen's weight limitation figures, confirmed by Nobile, showed that the giant airship would be overloaded. Balchen and two other crew members had to leave the ship at the last moment to lighten her. There would be only 16 men aboard and Nobile's pet terrier Titina.

Balchen was disappointed as he watched the others file aboard the *Norge*. At 0850 on 11 May Nobile ordered the restraining ropes cast off, and the giant dirigible rose slowly and majestically upward to begin an aerial voyage of incredible distance.

As the sound of the *Norge*'s engines faded and the ghostly whale-like form glided slowly from view over the northern horizon, enthusiasm quickly drained from its ground crew. They returned to their respective tasks, waiting for news of the flight and the order to begin to dismantle their camp when the *Norge* reached Alaska.

After the *Norge* left, Bennett made several local flights in the Fokker, most of them with Balchen as copilot. Balchen was impressed with the Fokker's performance and commented that it was one of the nicest planes he had ever flown.[15]

When Balchen and a group of Amundsen's people were watching the Fokker being dismantled the next day, Byrd, Noville, and Bennett approached and asked what Balchen thought of the plane. He said he was enthusiastic about it. Byrd then said he was going to make another expedition to Greenland the next year, and asked Balchen if he would like to go along.

"Ja, you bet," Balchen answered promptly. Byrd then asked if he would like to go back to the United States with him until the expedition was ready. Balchen said he would if he had permission from his commanding officer at the naval aircraft factory at Horten, and from his superior officer who was there at Spitsbergen, and if he could get official leave from the navy.[16] Balchen asked how he could live in America, and Byrd told him not to worry about that because Bennett would need a copilot. If that did not work out, Byrd promised to find a job for him.

It sounded like the opportunity of a lifetime to see America and work with a man who had just proven himself a leader and had apparently accomplished a feat that many others envied. Balchen was flattered; Bennett, obviously pleased, stood by with a great grin on his face.

Word came to Spitsbergen that the *Norge* had reached the Pole at 0125 on 12 May. This was followed later by a message from Alaska via Norway: "NORGE ARRIVED TELLER ALASKA ELAPSED TIME 71 HOURS COMPLETING FIRST CROSSING OVER POLE EUROPE TO AMERICA."

Teller, a hamlet of 55 inhabitants on the extreme west coast of Alaska, was about 50 mi. northwest of Nome. There had been no injuries reported on the landing. The gallant airship was deflated and dismantled, never to fly again. Amundsen could now claim that he was the first person to have seen *both* poles. The *Norge* had taken the expedition successfully over an estimated 3,180 mi., two-thirds of it an unexplored frozen arctic region.

Balchen immediately wired Norway requesting additional leave and was granted a year off from the Norwegian naval air force to travel with the Byrd contingent to America. He packed his rucksack containing his naval uniform, some ski clothes, an extra pair of shoes, and some winter clothing. He slung his rifle and skis over his shoulder and climbed aboard the *Chantier,* where a scowling Capt. Mike Brennan confronted him.

He was tired of the group of ignorant landlubbers he had taken aboard in New York, and he confronted Balchen about his background. He was not very interested in his flying experience but asked if he knew what a compass was and if he could hold a ship's wheel. Balchen's three-word reply became a lifetime phrase that he would add to many English sentences that required his consent or approval: "Ja, you bet!"

Brennan was impressed and signed the smiling blond on as the ship's quartermaster, a navy designation for the person in charge of the ship's steering apparatus. Balchen was assigned the first watch as the ship departed through the ice floes to the open sea toward Norway on 20 May 1926. The last thing he saw in Spitsbergen was the *Norge's* mooring mast, now a symbol of Amundsen's realization of his goal.

The young Norwegian, who spoke English with a slight accent, was immediately accepted among the strange assembly of Americans with mixed occupational backgrounds. "They are always laughing good-naturedly at my clumsy Norwegian English," he wrote in his autobiography,

and when I say, "Ve do it," or "Ja, Ja, you bet," they slap their knees and ask me to say it again. Soon the whole ship is saying, "Ve do it, ja." I have much trouble with American slang, I have studied only Oxford English, and this is like trying to understand Lapp, almost. But I learn pretty quick to say, "Get out the lead from your pants!" just like an American, and I teach them in turn how to say "Skaal!" when they lift their glasses and clink the rims together.[17]

The trip took the *Chantier* down the Norwegian coast, and Balchen wondered when he would see Norway again. The first stop was England, where Byrd and Bennett were treated as conquering heroes. They were wined, dined, photographed, and interviewed for the next six days. Although Byrd accepted most invitations, there was one invitation that he declined without adequate explanation. He had been invited to speak at a dinner sponsored by the prestigious Royal Geographical Society but turned it down, although he was a member. He had a brief meeting with Sir Arthur Hinks, the society's secretary, but Byrd showed him no documentation of his flight. This apparent rebuff left many British scholars cautious about giving him credit for his claim without some kind of proof in the form of a navigator's log. Byrd held a press conference and announced that he was planning to submit appropriate evidence to the National Geographic Society on his return to America.

Byrd had been reluctant to show any evidence to the British, but he made detailed plans to ensure that he would receive public recognition of his claim in his own country. He had retained Harry A. Bruno, an aggressive public relations and advertising specialist, to plan a tumultuous welcome on their arrival in New York. Byrd and Bruno exchanged many radio messages to coordinate the arrangements, which would begin with a ticker-tape parade. Byrd sent a radio message to the Navy Department in Washington, D.C., requesting an officer to meet the *Chantier,* obtain the charts and logs of the polar flight, and take them to the Secretary of the Navy. The Navy was then to submit them to the National Geographic Society for review by an examining committee consisting of scientists it considered experts.

Balchen, Bennett, and the members of the ship's crew, being of little interest to the press, took the opportunity to visit the London sights. Guest passes to the Royal Aero Club were given to them, and it was there they learned from a London newspaper that the Italians did not believe that Byrd had reached the Pole and that the *Norge,* under their countryman's command, did. Balchen saw Bennett read the report, slowly crumple it, and throw it into a waste basket.

Polite skepticism was expressed in the *Tribuna:* "We await confirmation," an editorial stated. The *Impero,* a rival Rome newspaper, expressed doubts about the scientific significance of the American's flight: "Byrd flew over a zone already visited by explorers, while the Italian-Norwegian expedition will visit a huge, unknown zone between the North Pole and North America."[18]

The Italians were not the only ones to doubt Byrd's claim. The first public doubt was expressed by Odd Arnesen, a correspondent for the

Aftenposten, a Norwegian newspaper. He had radioed his office in Oslo on 10 May 1926: "BYRD OVER CROSS BAY. AFTER 15½ HOURS OF FLYING TEN MINUTES LATER THE TWO COURAGEOUS FLIERS LANDED IN GOOD CONDITION. THE FLIERS THEMSELVES IN-SIST THEY WERE OVER THE POLE BUT ON THE BASIS OF THE TIME THEY COULD HARDLY HAVE BEEN THERE. PROBABLY NO FARTHER NORTH THAN AMUNDSEN."

A newspaper in Copenhagen quoted an unnamed Danish explorer as saying, "We must remain skeptical until more exact information is at hand. The utmost that Commander Byrd will be able to prove is that the distance he has flown agrees with the known distance between Kings Bay and the North Pole. At best, he may possibly be able to prove that he was within one hundred kilometers of the Pole."[19]

As the *Chantier* left England for New York, Balchen stood his 8 hr. watches at the wheel and when not on duty performed routine chores as Captain Brennan directed. Balchen and Bennett had many chances to chat about flying, and the two slowly cemented a friendship through long discussions about what they wanted to do in the future. They both agreed that they wanted to fly to the arctic together.

Byrd was seldom seen, because he worked alone in his cabin. In his book *Skyward* he professed to be stunned by the world's enthusiastic re-action to his flight. He wrote,

> Before the *Chantier* had steamed many miles toward home, I began to realize that we had stirred up something by flying to the Pole. First there were radios of congratulation and good wishes. Then radios of inquiry. And finally, radios that literally ordered me to do things I had never even dreamed of doing, couldn't do if I wanted—such as make a speech at three different banquets, to be held in three different cities on one and the same night. I felt rather stunned about it; but, of course, greatly appreciative.[20]

Balchen was beginning to have doubts about his decision to go to Amer-ica when Bennett joined him on deck one day. Neither looked forward to the commotion that would probably be awaiting Byrd, and both admit-ted they were uneasy in crowds.

The long hours on watch gave Balchen the chance to think about the past and his future. He must have wondered what was going to happen to him when he arrived in America as an immigrant who would be recognized immediately by his strong Scandinavian accent. If Lt. Cmdr. Byrd could not keep his promise of a job and the expedition to Greenland did not take place, he would have to return to Norway and perhaps be criticized for helping the Americans win the honor of being first to the Pole. Answers would come soon enough.

2 · The Lad from Tveit

The invitation to go to America seemed full of interesting possibilities. "I want this more than anything in my life, to see the big new country across the ocean, to pioneer the new skies," he wrote in his autobiography. But when the ship sailed past Norway en route to England, he took a long last look at the shoreline in the distance and "wondered when I would see it again."[1]

Balchen was born in the village of Tveit in the Topdal Valley, a few miles northeast of the city of Kristiansand at the southern tip of Norway. It was the home of 300 hardy souls at the beginning of the twentieth century. Their main business then was farming and lumbering. A river bisects the valley, which is surrounded by rocky hills and lush stands of spruce, pine, and oak. The river was, and still is, noted for its excellent salmon and trout fishing.

It was here that Dr. Lauritz Balchen decided to establish his practice and minister to the physical ills of the people in the neighboring area. Dr. Balchen married Dagny Dietrichson, a member of a prominent Norwegian military family. Her uncle was Maj. Gen. Olaf Dietrichson, commander of the large army post at Kristiansand.

Dietrichson was from a family of nine children. After her father died when she was three years old, her mother was unable to take care of her, so she was sent to live in Nysen with her uncle, who provided her with a very comfortable lifestyle in a relatively sophisticated community, compared to the rudimentary life in the village of Tveit.

The transition to becoming the spouse of a country doctor in a small town was difficult for her. She was not used to roof-high snow drifts that kept her housebound during the harsh, dark winters. The often lengthy absences of her husband making house calls in remote areas added to a growing feeling of loneliness and discontent. Into this setting on 23 October 1899 came the couple's first child, a blue-eyed, blond-haired boy they named Bernt after his grandfather, who was a sea captain and ship owner in Kristiansand. Bernt was followed by two sisters: Marie (called Mia) and Dagny, named after her mother.

As the months went by, the young Mrs. Balchen became increasingly depressed in her isolated life. Her husband spent ever more time away from home. Too often the weather prevented his return or he felt obligated to stay with seriously ill patients during extended periods of their convalescence. In addition, she was frustrated when she found that many of his patients did not pay their bills and he refused to press them for payment.

The discontent finally led to divorce, and she left the children with their father. She subsequently married Capt. Olaf Harlem, a dashing army artillery officer stationed in Kristiansand. Bernt was only four years old at the time. The job of taking care of the three children fell to nanny Magny Olsen, a teenager. The doctor became particularly concerned about Bernt who was thin and frail; his mother's absence was a severe psychological blow to him.[2]

At age five Bernt became the object of his father's attention and was taken everywhere on house calls, which included skiing, to which his father introduced him at age six. They went into the hills behind Tveit, and his father taught him how to maneuver, jump, and race on skis. He also taught him how to make a snow burrow for himself and survive if he were caught out in a sudden snowstorm. Another of his father's favorite exercises to keep fit was putting the shot, a 16 lb. sphere of iron that is thrown for distance in competition. When his father practiced, Bernt would roll the shot back and then gradually, as he grew stronger, pick it up and deliver it to his father. The relationship between the two blossomed.

A good friend of the young Bernt was a retired sea captain named Tobias Olsen, who ran a small general store that was a meeting place for townspeople. Olsen taught him practical things like knot-tying, catching fish with his hands, and how to use small boats and make rafts.

As a result of his father's love of the outdoors and Olsen's teachings, young Bernt resolved that his future and vocation would somehow be connected with the outdoors. In 1907 he started grammar school in Kristiansand, where his father had sent him because the schools were better and he could experience a more cosmopolitan lifestyle. He lived with his mother and stepfather on the army post and learned to ride horses, drill with the troops, shoot on the rifle and pistol range, and attend army maneuvers and field exercises. He was made a mascot of an artillery battery and given a small tent to use during extended maneuvers.

This was a time of family upheaval for the three Balchen children. Mia joined Bernt, their mother, and stepfather, while Dagny went to live with an uncle. As a result of this separation, Bernt seldom saw Dagny. Mia remained close in Bernt's affection all his life.

Kristiansand did have more to offer: It was a city of 12,000 civilians and about 6,000 army and navy personnel. Bernt entered high school there in 1913 and suffered the next tragedy of his young life. His father had answered an emergency call from a patient on an isolated farm many miles from Tveit and made his way on skis through a raging blizzard. Exhausted when he returned, he caught pneumonia and died before another doctor could be summoned. He was 43.

Shocked by his father's death, Bernt gave minimal attention to his schoolwork and turned to resisting authority in the classroom through mischievous pranks. His undoing came after a number of misdemeanors when, to taunt the school superintendent, he removed the doors from all the stalls in the boys' bathroom and hid them. When the superintendent threatened to have the entire class remain two hours after school for the rest of the winter until the culprit confessed, Bernt stood up and admitted the wrongdoing. To his surprise, instead of a minor inconvenience of some kind, the punishment was expulsion until the next school year.

Bernt turned to his grandfather Balchen, then 74. He revered the white-bearded old gentleman for his worldly experiences and confessed what he had done and asked his grandfather if he could get him a job on a ship that would take him to New Zealand, which was as far away as he could imagine. He had heard that the farming was good there and that he could make a fortune. His grandfather refused, saying that because he wanted to make a living at farming, he would get him a job on a farm owned by the Kongsgaard family. Before he could realize what had happened, he arrived at the Kongsgaard's with a mandate from his grandfather to obey the family's orders.

Bernt realized within a few days that the never-ending repetition of farm chores was not what he wanted to do for the rest of his life. However, he stuck it out for eight months and returned to school heavier, taller, and stronger. He had been toughened by the hard work and discipline imposed by the farm family and began the school year with a different attitude. He surprised everyone when he applied himself to his studies, with emphasis on mathematics, history, and geography. By Norwegian law, all students had to study English during the last two years of their required seven years of schooling. Those who elected more schooling were required to learn more English plus French, German, and higher mathematics.

Bernt's great-uncle, gruff General Dietrichson, proved to be a stabilizing influence during this period, and he introduced Bernt to the famous explorers of the day who came to visit. Most prominent in his memory were Fridtjof Nansen and Roald Amundsen. The latter was a dinner guest at Bernt's home when Bernt was entering his teenage years and the lean, tall man with the large, hawk-like nose made a lasting impression on Bernt. Amundsen had an immense gusto for life, and as the first person to reach the South Pole he was the idol of nearly every Norwegian child.

Bernt was introduced, and the famous explorer asked him what he wanted to do with his life. Bernt replied that he wanted to go on polar expeditions and hunt seals and polar bears as his hero had done. "Then you must keep on skiing and camping and get in real good trim, beside getting good marks in school," Amundsen told him. "You must learn about previous expeditions and benefit from their experiences, and be thorough and well-prepared in all respects. Above all, you must learn to take care of yourself, to obey and give orders and to work with others."[3]

Bernt remembered that first meeting,[4] and vowed to follow the advice of the world's most experienced polar explorer. He was inspired by the idea of a life of freedom in the outdoors, and he would develop further his interests in mathematics, history, forestry, and science throughout the rest of his school years. He graduated from high school at Kristiansand in 1916.

It was the skiing after school each day during the winter that led to competitions that he enjoyed most. He began to win ski jumping and racing contests in competitions in which he represented Norway against the skiers of a dozen other nations. His interest in getting more speed and greater distance in jumps led to his making and working on skis in the school's wood shop. He learned about the qualities of the various woods and the best ones that should be made into skis, a knowledge that would prove to be especially useful in the years ahead. Woodworking and wood carving became a lifelong hobby.

Bernt's love of nature, sensitivity to his surroundings, and appreciation of form and color found expression in his growing skill as a self-taught artist. He captured in detailed sketches and watercolors the life around him. A sketchbook made at age 15 vividly portrays in detail and color his world—the marvelous forests, animal and bird life, scenes of the military base, skies, his home at Tveit. This skill and great natural talent developed in later life and he became a recognized painter of spectacular watercolors.

Bernt went hunting and fishing in the summer months. He killed game only to eat and during his entire life never collected hunting trophies of any kind. He took up weight lifting, shot putting, and bicycling, which gave him an unusual sturdiness for his age.

The handsome youth was interested in all things mechanical, and owned his first motorcycle at age 16. His competitive spirit in cycling enhanced his unusual stamina. He entered races and became a champion in southern Norway in 1917. He learned to box, and his stocky, muscular physique led to matches with older, heavier opponents. He later said boxing helped cure a quick temper, not only in the ring but in real-life situations.[5]

Bernt's interest in boxing earned him an invitation to join the Sparta Club, where he mastered the subtle tactics of boxing and became amateur welterweight boxing champion of southern Norway. During the high school summers, Bernt worked in lumber camps. He spent his spare time fishing, hiking, and camping alone in the forests.

Communion with nature convinced Bernt that he wanted to attend the forestry school at Moseby, Norway, where he received engineering training, and it was here that he found that he had mathematical skills he previously had not known he possessed. The stiff curriculum also included science, botany, geology, and map reading, and, of course, much work in the forests. He graduated second in his class of 16, and was hired by the area forestry service at Kristiansand. This was fortuitous because the Sparta Club was nearby, which enabled him to enter more boxing matches. He had risen out of the welterweight into the light heavyweight class.

It was now 1917 and World War I had been raging in Europe for three years; however, the fighting had not yet involved Norway directly, although the threat was always there. Although Norway had managed to maintain its neutrality, half of the country's ships had been sunk by German submarines, and there was a continuing anxiety of impending war among the young men of the country. Norwegian men were subject to conscription, and Bernt's number had not yet been called. Uncertain about what he should do—volunteer or wait until he was called—he sought advice from his mother's uncle, the blunt, tell-it-like-it-is Major General Dietrichson, who recommended that he join the French Foreign Legion. He gave Bernt a letter of introduction and wished him well. Bernt boarded a troop ship for France and entered the real military world of close-order drill, forced marches, and rifle marksmanship. He found himself among tough former street fighters of a dozen nations who drank heavily and brawled for the fun of it in their off-duty time. After six weeks of intensive training, Bernt and his new companions were transferred to near Verdun, where they would soon get into the fighting.

Just as his unit was ready to go to the French front, Bernt had to report to his company commander. He was informed that he had been called up for service by Norway and would have to return there immediately. Bernt sailed for home and was sworn into the Norwegian army at Honefoss as a private on 10 September 1918. His recent military service was soon apparent to those in charge, and he was selected for the artillery officers' training school at Kristiansand. Shortly thereafter, the war in Europe ended with the Armistice on 11 November 1918.

The threat of war was not over for Norwegians, however. Tiny Finland was being invaded by Russian troops and needed help from its Scandinavian neighbors to ensure it maintained its independence. Hundreds of Norwegians traveled there to fight with the White Army of Finland; Norwegian army officer trainees were permitted to take leave and volunteer. Balchen was among them. Along with several hundred other Norwegians, he hurried to the recruiting station at Kemi, Finland, to enlist as a private in the White Army under Field Marshall Karl Gustav Mannerheim. Balchen was immediately put on a ski patrol and promoted to sergeant. He made a number of night reconnaissance and infiltration patrols, and after two months was transferred to the cavalry.

The Finnish commanders decided that a massive cavalry charge was required to dislodge the Russians from their trenches near Sortavala. The Finns formed into battle lines on their mounts and lunged ahead. Armed with a saber, Balchen spurred his horse onward with the rest, and as he neared the trenches his horse stumbled and fell. He vaulted over its head and sprawled on the ground amid other fallen horses and men. He struggled to stand just as a Russian soldier took the opportunity to ram a bayonet into his thigh and abdomen. Balchen tried in vain to pull out his pistol and shoot his attacker. It was the last he remembered until he awakened 24 hours later in a hospital bed. After the Russian position had been taken, he was found barely alive on the battlefield among the dead.[6]

Balchen's wounds were serious. He was told his days as an athlete were over, but he was not convinced. He told the doctors he was going to achieve a goal he had been training for before he went to Finland: He hoped to compete in the 1920 Olympics in Antwerp as a member of Norway's boxing team. When he was released from the hospital, he returned home, recuperated, completed his officer training, and was commissioned as a lieutenant in the reserve in September 1919.

His term of required service was over, and he wondered what he was going to do next. He drove a bus during the period of a bitter railroad strike and got into some rough encounters with strikers, but his skill as a boxer enabled him to survive unscathed.[7] He continued to work out at the Sparta Club and won three boxing championships and two wrestling matches. He was a formidable contender in the heavyweight class and hoped to prove it when the time came for competing for the Norwegian Olympic team in boxing, wrestling, and skiing.

Throughout the years Balchen had a continuing passion for working on mechanical things, from watches and farm equipment to motorcycles and automobiles. He talked about his interests with his cousin Leif Dietrichson, a Norwegian navy pilot, who immediately encouraged him to apply for navy flight training, something he had not considered.[8] The thought of piloting an aircraft intrigued him, but he doubted he would be accepted, having already completed his required military training in the army. But Dietrichson persisted and wrote a letter of recommendation to accompany his application. While he waited to see if he would be accepted, Balchen demonstrated that he was truly Olympic material. In a four-day period, he competed in two ski races, two boxing matches, and two wrestling matches. He placed in the ski races, won both boxing matches, and one of the two wrestling matches. He then fought three more boxing bouts, winning all of them, and followed up with a wrestling tournament, in which he placed second.[9]

Meanwhile, the appointment for naval flight training came through and Balchen resigned his army reserve commission. Although he was now a newly appointed naval cadet, Bernt hoped that he would be granted leave to continue to compete for a spot on the 1920 Olympic team, but Admiral von der Lippe, chief of the Norwegian naval air force, refused his request. He gave Balchen a choice: Be a pilot or a boxer. Disappointed at having to decide on one or the other, Balchen made his choice. He would be a pilot.[10]

Balchen began his flying career at the Naval Air Training School at Horten in early 1920. The first winter and spring were spent in ground-school studying elementary aerodynamics, engines, meteorology, and navigation. He began instruction in small trainers and soloed that summer after 4½ hours of dual instruction. He immediately began to build up his flying experience in land and seaplanes. On a solo flight one day in a Sopwith Pup, the thrill of having that much power in his hands was too much to be wasted at high altitudes. Flying over the drill field where one of his uncle's field artillery batteries was drilling, the temptation to impress the ground-bound troops was too great to resist. He made a low pass over the drill field at full throttle. The horses and caissons stampeded in every direction; the band abandoned their instruments and fled for safety. He stayed aloft until he was nearly out of gas, then returned to face the wrath of his uncle.[11]

Balchen graduated first in his class despite this transgression and received his naval air force wings at age 20 in September 1921. Regulations required that he spend the next two years on a probationary status before receiving a commission. Meanwhile, because there was no flying during the winter months, he was put on furlough and spent his time hunting.

When flying was resumed in the spring, Balchen took the opportunity to make flights to different areas of Norway, practicing dead reckoning and contact navigation. He flew in and out of the fjords and inlets, along the ragged coast and upward to the mountains where he studied the glacier floes, the uninhabitable plateaus, and the far reaches of the forested areas. He visited cities he had not seen before: Narvik, Tromso, and Bodo in the far north, and the ports of Stavenger, Trondheim, and Bergen. He spent his ground time in the shops at Horten working on engines and repairing planes. He exhibited a special interest and expertise in repairing, installing, and experimenting with aircraft skis, gaining experience that would become extremely valuable in the years to come. In addition, he was appointed as a flying instructor.

In late 1922, when flying was canceled again because of the winter weather and the young flying officers were furloughed, Balchen could not stand to be idle and decided to return to his first love: the forests. He enrolled in the Advanced Forestry School at Harnosand, Sweden, to add to his store of knowledge and skills, and received an advanced degree in forestry engineering in 1923.

When the two-year probationary period was over, Balchen received his commission as a flight lieutenant on 1 January 1924. He reported for duty at Horten on 1 May. His life as an arctic aviator had officially begun. His first adventure would involve Roald Amundsen, his personal hero.

Amundsen, born of a Norwegian shipping family in 1872, was one of the best-known explorers of the arctic by 1925. He had gone to sea as a young man in the early 1890s. He had been caught in the ice pack during an exploratory and scientific expedition to the antarctic and drifted for a year in the Bellingshausen Sea before breaking clear. In June 1903 he captained a small sailing sloop searching for the north magnetic pole and the elusive Northwest Passage. He entered Davis Strait on the Atlantic side of the continent and emerged three years later in the Bering Sea on the west.

Amundsen—tall, shaggy-haired, and craggy-faced—proved that he was a man of unusual persistence who had a passionate desire to explore uncharted territory. He was self-confident of his own powers of endurance. One of his personal goals was to be the first person to reach both Poles. On 14 December 1911, after traveling nearly 2,000 mi. roundtrip by dog sled from his base, Amundsen and four companions reached that first goal—the South Pole. When airplanes became more reliable, he believed they would enable him to cover many miles of polar terrain in minutes instead of weeks. In 1914, at the age of 40, he earned the first pilot's license in Norway and began making plans for a flight to the top of the earth.[12]

World War I delayed Amundsen from pursuing his goal. Then financial difficulties prevented making any definite plans. His lecture tours in Europe and America did not provide much more than subsistence money. However, Lincoln Ellsworth, an adventurous American philanthropist, had met Amundsen and knew of his plans. He called on the famous Norwegian in early 1925 and agreed to provide the money to buy two German-designed Dornier Wal (Whale) flying boats then being built in Italy. Amundsen selected two Norwegian pilots—Hjalmar Riiser-Larsen and Leif Dietrichson (Balchen's cousin)—and two mechanics—Oskar Omdal and Karl Feucht—to operate the planes. Their plan was to land at the North Pole and pool the balance of fuel in one plane to provide sufficient range to continue across the unexplored area between the Pole and Point Barrow, Alaska.

After five weeks of preparation at Kings Bay, Spitsbergen, the six men departed on 21 May 1925. Both planes were forced to land 136 nautical mi. short of the Pole after 7 hr. of flight. One of the planes was damaged beyond repair on landing; a successful takeoff of the other was uncertain.

The four men spent the next 26 days stranded on stretches of open water surrounded by numerous ice floes. There was then no thought of trying to continue toward the Pole. For several days the six men hauled cans of gasoline from the damaged plane to the other and moved tons of snow to clear a runway; they then all piled into the one plane. Eight unsuccessful attempts were made to take off. Finally, Captain Riiser-Larsen managed to get the plane airborne and headed for Spitsbergen. En route, with fuel running low, Riiser-Larsen landed in an ice-filled sea. They saw a small sealing vessel, taxied toward it, and persuaded the captain to tow the aircraft to Spitsbergen.

Before the planes had left Kings Bay, Amundsen insisted that no rescue flights be sent to search for his party unless two weeks had passed without a message from him. However, when there was no word after 24 hours, the Norwegian government began making plans for a search by air in case their most famous national hero needed assistance. When the two weeks had passed with no word, Balchen, along with two other pilots, volunteered. Two seaplanes were placed on a ship and transported to Spitsbergen. The planes were offloaded and the pilots were about to begin flying northerly search patterns, just as a small sealing vessel eased into the harbor. On the deck were a half dozen grimy men: It was Amundsen and his crew. When the six men came ashore, Amundsen approached Balchen with his hand out. "I remember you," Amundsen said. "You told me you wanted to be a great discoverer and go on an expedition with me. You see, I don't forget."[13]

3 · Introduction to a New World

The *Chantier* made the trip to New York from England two days ahead of the time the welcoming party had anticipated. When Captain Brennan announced that they were off Sandy Hook, New Jersey, Byrd ordered him to remain offshore. It was a Thursday and the reception committee wanted the arrival to take place on Saturday, when the largest crowds could be expected to turn out. Two days later the ship moved into New York Harbor and arrived at noon.

Airplanes zoomed over the ship, tugs and small boats, flags flying, blew their whistles and rang bells, red fireboats pumped streams of water skyward in welcome. Balchen was impressed at the way America greeted its new national hero.[1]

As the ship neared its assigned dock, Balchen saw the overwhelming masses of people waving and shouting. It was a Saturday and extra thousands were able to witness the historical event; hundreds of police held the street open in front of the dock. Confetti and ticker-tape poured down from the tall buildings. When the gangplank was lowered, Grover Whalen, the city's official greeter, walked aboard, followed by a dapper mayor Jimmy Walker. They explained that the parade down Broadway would start at Battery Park. Walker and Whalen strode down to the dock with Byrd and Bennett in tow, and the crowds cheered in a rising crescendo. Byrd was dressed in his naval uniform and Bennett in civilian clothes as they began their walk at the head of the parade. Looking back, Bennett saw Balchen watching from the railing of the *Chantier* and motioned for him to follow with the members of the expedition. Balchen shook his head negatively. Byrd had told him that because he was not a member of the expedition he should not take part in any of the welcoming activities. He waved back, took out his pocket diary, and made an entry: "20 June. Arr. N.Y., 1200."[2]

Byrd and Bennett were accorded the biggest welcome since the victory parade of returning troops after World War I. A blizzard of paper rained down as they walked from the Battery to City Hall. Crowds filled the sidewalks from curb to curb, and the police had difficulty keeping the streets clear for them. Three hundred distinguished citizens and politicians of New York followed on foot. There were welcoming speeches, after which Mayor Walker handed medals to Byrd, Bennett, and other members of the expedition.

Meanwhile, it was reported from Washington, D.C., that a committee of experts had been appointed to study Byrd's reports and navigation figures and after studying them for a few hours had certified that his claim to have reached the Pole was valid.

On 23 June 1926 President Calvin Coolidge presented Byrd with the National Geographic Society's Hubbard Gold Medal in Washington, D.C., before an enthusiastic crowd of 6,000 distinguished guests representing the highest levels of government and the sciences. "We cannot but admire the superb courage of the man willing to set forth on such a great adventure in the unexplored realms of the air," the president said. "His deed will be but the beginning of scientific exploration considered difficult of achievement before he proved the possibilities of the airplane."[3]

The Hubbard Medal was also awarded to Bennett "for his distinguished service in assisting and in flying to the North Pole with Commander Richard Evelyn Byrd, Jr."[4] When Bennett learned that he and Byrd were to receive the nation's highest medal, he spoke briefly to Balchen about it. "I don't want to go down to Washington and get another medal for that North Pole thing," he said. Bennett did not explain what he meant and Balchen did not pursue the matter.[5]

Byrd returned to his hometown of Winchester, Virginia, where he was welcomed by hundreds of townspeople, led by his brother Harry F. Byrd, then governor. In the weeks following, the commander gave a number of speeches, and the public focus was always on him, while Bennett, the plane's pilot, stood stoically in the background.

Congress convened in December 1926 and enacted two special measures. One conferred the Medal of Honor on both Byrd and Bennett. President Coolidge broke a precedent by signing the citations personally. Each citation stated the award was bestowed "for conspicuous courage and intrepidity in demonstrating that it is possible for aircraft to travel in continuous flight from a now inhabited portion of the earth over the North Pole and return."[6]

The other measure promoted Byrd to commander in the naval reserve and Bennett to the grade of warrant machinist.[7] Both men were also awarded the Distinguished Service Medal and Distinguished Flying Cross by the U.S. Navy.

Whalen made an unexpected visit to Balchen aboard the *Chantier* while Byrd and Bennett were in Washington, D.C. Bennett had told him that Balchen had never seen New York and thought it would be nice if someone would take him on a guided tour of the city. Balchen was delighted, and the city's famous greeter showed him the major sights in his chauffeured automobile. Balchen gawked upward at the tall buildings as Whalen went into his tourist's spiel. When they passed Wanamaker's large department store, Balchen learned that Whalen was employed by Rodman Wanamaker to handle the store's publicity. Wanamaker had promised Byrd $30,000 to let the *Josephine Ford* be displayed there and also at the Philadelphia store to attract customers. To his surprise, Whalen said Balchen was to stay with the plane and answer questions from the expected large crowds.[8]

It took several days for the *Josephine Ford* to be moved from the ship to Staten Island for assembly. It was then towed to shore. Meanwhile, Byrd made arrangements for Balchen to stay as a guest at Miller Field on the island with the National Guard squadron, where he was welcomed cordially by the young pilots and was given pilot time in several of the top Army Air Corps fighters.

Balchen soon found himself standing alone with the Fokker behind a red velvet rope inside the Wanamaker store for many hours over the course of two weeks. Thousands of curious folks who had never been very close to an airplane or talked with a pilot asked thousands of questions, which Balchen tried to answer. He signed autographs and when young girls would titter about how handsome he was, he blushed and tried not to let them know he heard them.[9] His Norwegian accent, coupled with its slight British inflection, sounded as fascinating to the onlookers as their New York accent did to him. He said he felt like "a prize bull at a county fair" and blushed easily when young girls squealed with delight as he stammered something in Norwegian.[10] Blond, blue-eyed Balchen was the public image of a Viking and got more attention than the plane, which must have greatly pleased Wanamaker because it brought them in droves to the store.

The Fokker was next moved to the Philadelphia store and shown for another two weeks. Balchen continued to be embarrassed about the way the women—especially the teenaged girls—squealed with delight when he blushed and uttered something in Norwegian. However, Byrd had benefited from the displays of the *Josephine Ford;* his debt of more than $20,000 was paid off and he was free to make plans for his next venture. Those plans would include Balchen, but not as Byrd originally had said.

One of the people Balchen had met during the hectic days in New York was Harry A. Bruno, the public relations specialist Byrd had hired who had come up with the idea to display the *Josephine Ford* to help Byrd get out of debt. He had helped found an organization of male pilots in 1921 called Quiet Birdmen. Although QB meetings are anything but quiet, its members cherish the honor of membership because the talk is always of flying and they are totally dedicated to preserving the heritage of flight. Bruno invited Balchen to meet with them and was inducted in September 1926. It was at the QB meetings that he was able to meet some of the greats of world aviation, including military pilots such as Benny Foulois, Carl Spaatz, Ira Eaker, and Jimmy Doolittle. He also met Gen. Billy Mitchell, the famous crusader for air power who had been court-martialed for speaking out vigorously against superiors disagreeing with his views. Balchen learned later that Byrd had been a leading figure in defeating Mitchell's plans for a separate, independent air force after World War I and had testified against him during the court-martial. To counter this idea and ensure that the Navy would have its own air arm, Byrd had authored a bill that was presented to Congress that called for the creation of a Bureau of Aeronautics within the Navy Department. In congressional testimony, he said there was no reason for a third military department because it "would not only endanger the effectiveness of our national defense but increase enormously our national yearly expenditure." In his book *Skyward,* he bragged that Mitchell "was finally squashed" when he was court-martialed for insubordination.[11]

Balchen heard Mitchell's views about the future of aviation as a vital element of national power and was greatly impressed. Balchen began to form his own concept of geopolitics and the potential of the arctic as an aerial crossroads for world commerce.

One of the most important people in Balchen's immediate future was Anthony H. G. Fokker, known as "the flying Dutchman." He was noted for his hands-on approach to solving engineering problems but also for his explosive temper when displeased. He was impulsive and often erratic but also bright, inventive, and imaginative.

Fokker was born of Dutch parents on 6 April 1890 at Blitar, Java, and later educated in Holland and Germany; however, he never finished high school. Instead, he enrolled in an automotive institute at Zelbach, Germany, where he built his first airplane in 1910 and taught himself to fly. Two years later, at age 22, he established an aircraft manufacturing company at Johannisthal, outside Berlin. During World War I he provided the German air force with some of its most famous aircraft. Among them were the Dr.-1 triplane and the D-VII biplane, the latter regarded by many historians as the finest fighter of the war. He pioneered in the design and construction of aircraft using welded steel tubular construction and simplified cantilever wings.[12]

After the Armistice, Fokker was in a precarious position in Germany. The agreement at Versailles severely limited German aircraft production, which meant he would probably not be able to continue his work. In an amazing cloak-and-dagger move, he arranged to have the major part of his aircraft tools and equipment smuggled out of the country. Within six weeks he was in business again in Holland.

Fokker made his first visit to America in October 1920 and found that a number of his planes were being tested by the Army Air Service under the terms of the Armistice. Within two years six Fokker transport planes were delivered to the Army and a torpedo plane to the Navy.

In the ensuing years Fokker became an aggressive and successful exporter of transport planes from Holland. Particularly successful were monoplanes with enclosed cabins and cantilevered wings. Capable of speeds of more than 90 MPH, Fokker transports became world renowned for a series of record-smashing, long-distance flights and as the basic aircraft for KLM, the Royal Dutch Airline.

In the summer of 1925 Fokker settled in the United States and established a plant at Hasbrouck Heights near Teterboro, New Jersey. His first trimotor flown in the United States, the F-VIIA/3m, won the first place trophy in the 1,800-mi. Ford Reliability Tour of 1925. The purpose of the air tour was "to end the dominance of the military and the emphasis on thrills and stunt flying, demonstrate the reliability of travel by air on a predetermined schedule regardless of intermediate ground facilities."[13]

Balchen met Fokker at a Quiet Birdman dinner in New York City and realized that they had met before during a 1923 air show in Sweden where Balchen and his squadron mates had been putting on a flying exhibition. Fokker asked what Balchen was doing in America, and when he found that he was helping in the exhibit of the *Josephine Ford*, he gave Balchen his business card and told him that any time he showed up at his factory in Hasbrouck Heights there would be a job waiting for him.[14]

Balchen was delighted. Later, as Bruno was driving him to his hotel, he learned that Harry Guggenheim, director of the Guggenheim Fund for the Promotion of Aeronautics, offered to finance air tours by prominent aviators to make Americans more conscious of air travel and encourage business and industrial leaders to use aircraft for commercial purposes. Guggenheim asked Byrd to make the trip with Bennett, but Byrd said he had to return to his naval duties. He arranged for Bennett to go as pilot and Balchen as copilot and navigator.

No changes were made in the Fokker for the trip. It had the same engines as when it was manufactured in Holland. The wheels were the same the plane had before they were replaced with skis for the flight from Spitsbergen.

Balchen saw the tour as a unique opportunity to escape the city crowds and see the country he had heard about all his life. En route he learned that Bennett was from the old school of pilots who liked to navigate by flying at low altitudes so he could follow the railroad tracks, highways, and other visual landmarks. Balchen, on the other hand, had much experience with dead reckoning, which meant flying a compass course for a specified length of time, observing wind drift, and making appropriate course corrections. He had also become proficient at flying solely by the use of cockpit instruments at a time when few pilots had mastered the techniques. It was essential to Norwegian pilots because of the many days per year when the cloud level and visibility are below the minimum safe limits for contact flight.

The 40-city, two-month tour began in Washington, D.C., on 7 October 1926. Press kits with a description of the plane, its engines, and the story of its North Pole flight were prepared for local newspapers at each stop. The pattern at each landing became routine. There were the crowds at the airport, a hurry-up ride through the city, a Chamber of Commerce luncheon or civic club dinner, and a meeting with the local press. Bennett, not at all comfortable before an audience, was the featured speaker and spoke from a prepared script. He talked about the possibilities of commercial aviation and made an appeal for the support of airmail and improvement of airports. He emphasized that the *Josephine Ford* was not a unique experimental aircraft but simply a standard Fokker trimotor transport that had been modified to withstand the rigors of the arctic flight. He regularly began by apologizing in his opening remarks: "I am an aviator, not an orator."

Balchen always listened intently, glad that he did not have to speak. He was still very shy about his accent and unsure about his command of English before an American audience. En route between cities, Balchen kidded Bennett that he had heard the speech so many times that he had memorized it. Bennett, who never enjoyed the task, said, "OK, Bernt, if you think you know it so well, you give it at the next stop."[15]

The remark had been overheard by the others who would not let Balchen back out. That night at the usual dinner with local dignitaries looking on, Balchen began as Bennett always did: "Tonight, I tell you that I am aviator only, not an oriay-tor, you bet." Bennett broke into knee-slapping laughter and the audience roared. Afterward, he told Balchen, "From now on, you're the oriay-tor, Bernt. I'm only the aviator, you bet." Balchen, with his intriguing accent and unique manner of expression, thus became the after-dinner speaker for the rest of the tour.

The Balchen–Bennett friendship grew stronger during the two months, and Balchen learned much about Bennett's background. He was born in Warrensburg, New York, on 25 October 1890 and left school at age 15 to be an automobile mechanic. He enlisted in the U.S. Navy as an aviation mechanic, was trained as a pilot, and served as a Naval flight instructor during World War I. From 1920 to 1925 he was aboard the aircraft carrier USS *Richmond* and was selected by Byrd as one of the pilots for the 1925 MacMillan Expedition to the arctic. Bennett flew Byrd on three flights toward the polar sea from the base camp at Etah, Greenland. It was Bennett's piloting and navigational skills that induced Byrd to select him as the pilot for the North Pole venture. It became obvious to Balchen that Bennett did not like to talk about himself, especially about the North Pole flight.[16]

At one of their cross-country stops, Bennett suddenly asked, "How would you like to fly the Atlantic, Bernt?" Balchen did not know exactly what to say because the idea never occurred to him, but he answered with his usual, "Ja, you bet." Raymond Orteig, a French emigré and New York hotel owner, had offered a prize of $25,000 the year before "to the first aviator of any Allied country crossing the Atlantic in one flight, from Paris to New York or New York to Paris." The two discussed the possibility of borrowing or buying the Fokker from Edsel Ford to enter the race. Balchen took out the small slide rule he always carried with him and began to figure the plane's normal fuel capacity and the distance to be covered.

The idea excited both of them as they continued their trip. When they reached Washington, D.C., Bennett planned to have Bruno negotiate with Byrd and Ford for the loan of the plane. But their plans were not to be realized. When they returned to New York, Byrd directed them to fly it to Detroit where he was going to make a formal presentation of the plane to the Henry Ford Museum at Dearborn.

Both men were keenly disappointed by this sudden turn of events. The trip to Detroit was the plane's last flight. After they shut the engines down, Balchen took out the log book he had kept of the tour and asked Bennett, "Floyd, what do you get for the average cruising speed on these trips? Somebody might want to know that."

Bennett reached in his pocket for his notebook and began figuring. "I get about an even 70 miles an hour," he said.

Balchen's figures agreed. What Bennett knew and Balchen realized was that the average speed computation had great significance. The Fokker was the same plane with the same engines that Bennett had piloted toward the North Pole. The only difference then was that it carried a much heavier load and had heavy skis attached for the Pole attempt, which would have slowed it considerably below the average speed with the wheels attached. Neither man took the time then to divide the roundtrip distance between Spitsbergen and the Pole by the Fokker's average speed to determine the time such a flight would have taken. However, in notes made in 1949 Balchen said, "There was one thing that struck me quite soon and which strengthened in my mind all the time, that this aircraft had a performance even when cruising at a fairly high power rate far inferior to the speed which was needed to have contemplated or to have completed the flight from Kings Bay to the North Pole and back in the time stated or in the time they were away."[17]

Balchen's future seemed uncertain at this point, but he had that promise of a job with the Fokker company. He walked into the factory and asked for Fokker. Fokker, true to form, was in the shops in greasy coveralls, his bald head shining above his round face. When Balchen approached, he looked up, grunted a greeting, and asked bluntly in his strong German accent, "What you like to be here doing?" Balchen said he would like to work in the shops and observe the manufacturing techniques that Fokker used on all his planes. Fokker nodded assent and without further conversation dashed off to look for problems that needed immediate solutions.[18]

Balchen started working on the production line where several different types of single-engine and trimotor aircraft were in various stages of completion. He had been working there 10 days when one of the former that caught Balchen's eye was the Fokker Universal, a sturdy high-wing model with a cabin for four passengers and an additional seat in an open cockpit next to the pilot. He wondered if he would be allowed to fly it. Robert B. C. Noorduyn, vice president and one of Fokker's chief engineers, saw him inspecting it and asked if he would like to fly it. "Ja, you bet," he replied quickly.

Balchen instantly liked the Universal's flying characteristics. It was easy to control, did not produce a vicious stall, could carry a respectable load for its size, and could land in a relatively short distance. After several takeoffs and landings, he made out a pilot report as he would have done at his base at Horten after testing a new plane. He gave it to Noorduyn.

The next morning, as he donned coveralls to work on the assembly line, he was told to report to Fokker's office. Wondering if he was about to be fired, he walked in and was immediately confronted with an abrupt question from Fokker: "What did you do in the Norwegian air force before you here came?" Balchen replied that he was the chief pilot's assistant and test pilot at the Horten naval aircraft factory.

"Why you didn't tell me? You are test pilot here now."[19]

From that moment on, Balchen and "Uncle Tony" worked closely together. Both proved to be completely compatible, although of totally different personalities. Balchen admired the way Fokker's mind worked when confronted with a problem; Fokker liked the way Balchen would experiment and quietly carry out a possible solution, his trusty slide rule always at hand. Balchen described their relationship:

> Time never means anything to Tony Fokker, and this is one reason he and I get along so well, because to me too, when I have a problem I want to solve, it doesn't matter whether it is five o'clock in the afternoon or in the morning. Many a night we work in the factory long after everyone else has left, or spread out our work sheets on the living room table, in his home, or cruise over the weekend on his yacht, talking nothing but planes. Sometimes I think he never sleeps. Once I am

awakened in my boarding house at two o'clock in the morning by a bombardment of small stones tossed against my bedroom window. The landlady knocks at my door, frightened, and whispers, "There's some maniac outside. Shall I call the police?" Uncle Tony is standing below on the lawn, waving excitedly. "Bernt! Bernt! Come now!" he yells. "We go to the factory."[20]

It was an emergency as far as Fokker was concerned. Gold had been discovered in northern Ontario and the Canadian government had ordered six Fokker Universals for a 12-month project to make an aerial survey of the Hudson Strait, the stretch of seaway between the Hudson Bay and the North Atlantic. Planes were also in demand to transport miners and their equipment to new gold strikes. The problem was that few pilots had any experience operating the Universals on skis or floats and were having many landing accidents. When the skis were damaged, no one knew how to fix them or make new ones. Balchen's expertise was badly needed.

In the fall of 1926 Fokker ordered Balchen to take three mechanics and proceed to the Western Canada Airways (WCA) base at Hudson, Ontario. There the company's operations manager explained that two of their three Universals had crashed not far away but seemed repairable. He wanted Balchen and his crew to make them flyable and return them to Hudson. Balchen and his crew took dog teams to the planes and had them both repaired within a week.

Balchen made many flights to the gold mines at Red Lake, Woman Lake, and Gold Lake to relieve the WCA pilots. Prospectors paid premium prices to have themselves and their equipment hauled to where the strikes were, but the flights were often hazardous because of vicious snow storms and zero–zero ceiling and visibility. On one occasion Balchen was marooned for five days after landing on the ice of Hudson Bay during a blizzard. He had food for several weeks, plenty of arctic clothing, a rifle, a sleeping bag, and a primus stove. He had a mathematics book and his ever-present slide rule with him to work on math problems in the plane's cabin. He had learned from his father to be prepared for such eventualities and to be patient and wait until the weather cleared, as it always would.

Balchen was going to return to New Jersey in early March 1927 when he received a telegram: "AGAINST MY BETTER JUDGMENT HAVE LOANED YOU TO WESTERN CANADA AIRWAYS STOP HELP THEM ALL YOU CAN FOKKER."[21]

The company had contracted with the government to fly a survey party to Fort Churchill, several hundred miles north of Hudson. The contract called for the transport of 26 men and 14 tn. of equipment and supplies, including dynamite, to the harbor. Balchen was put on the WCA payroll and was to make flights from the end of the Hudson Bay railway line to Cache Lake, about 200 mi. south of Fort Churchill.

It was some of the roughest flying Balchen had done at this point. The temperatures were seldom above −45°F. All aircraft maintenance had to be done outdoors. The planes had open cockpits and there were no heaters inside the passenger cabins. The instruments would freeze up so that flights could be made only in good weather when the pilots did not need them to navigate. There was no radio, no weather service, no hangars, and no shops. The pilots camped in the open, often cooked their own meals, and serviced their own planes. Immediately after landing, the oil was drained so it would not congeal in the oil tank. When starting it again, the oil was then heated with a plumber's torch and poured back into the tank.

After one of his flights Balchen received a letter from Bennett that Byrd was having Fokker build a special trimotor plane to fly the Atlantic instead of making another expedition to the arctic. It would be the largest plane then flying in the United States. Balchen had seen the plans of this plane on the drawing board and predicted that it would be too nose-heavy to have both pilots, the navigator, and radio operator plus the latter's equipment and extra fuel tank up forward. He felt sure that Fokker would realize that and make the appropriate corrections.

Rodman Wanamaker had agreed to provide the plane on the condition that Byrd should attempt to reach Paris. He also stipulated that the plane must be named *America*. Bennett was to be the pilot and Lt. George Noville the radio operator; Byrd would be the navigator. Bertram B. "Bert" Acosta, barnstormer and racing pilot, would be the spare pilot. Byrd insisted he was not going after the Orteig prize and never entered his name. He had been advised by a number of aviators to fly a single-engine plane because it would be cheaper, simpler to operate, and probably have a greater cruising range. But Byrd wanted a multiengine plane that could carry a large load because it would "open the door to commercial transatlantic flights."[22]

Byrd did not tell anyone that he had really hoped to obtain a Ford trimotor with sufficient fuel capacity to make the Atlantic trip, but Edsel Ford did not offer any encouragement that their planned new transport would be available. Besides, Ford did not want to deviate from the standard model then in production because of the expense of adding additional fuel tanks.[23]

When the ice on the streams began to melt in northern Canada in late April, the skis on the Universals were exchanged for floats and wheels and the WCA contract operation continued through the summer months until completion in late 1927. Western Canada Airways received a citation from the Canadian government stating, "Despite the distance from any prepared base, and severe winter conditions, the Fort Churchill operation was an unqualified success. The selection of this site as the ocean terminus of the Hudson Bay Railway was made possible by these flights. There has been no more brilliant operation in the history of commercial operation."[24]

During the five months that Balchen had flown for WCA, he had begun to like Canada, bush flying, and the men he worked with, and thought he might stay in the north country. However, when he returned to Fort Churchill there were two telegrams waiting for him. One was from Fokker and the other from Byrd. Fokker had completed the new trimotor plane for Byrd's transatlantic flight, but there had been an accident and there had been injuries. Balchen was to return as soon as possible.

The new Fokker had three Wright engines, more powerful than those installed on the *Josephine Ford*. Increased wingspan and new engines enabled it to lift 15,000 lb., about 3,000 lb. more than the *Josephine Ford*. Fokker had planned to make the first test flight alone. However, Byrd insisted that Bennett go as copilot and Noville as an observer. At the last minute Byrd decided to join them. He jumped in and crawled toward the cockpit. The flight ended when the Fokker nosed over on landing and was badly damaged.

Balchen returned to New Jersey and found Bennett was in the Hackensack Hospital in traction with a fractured right leg, an injured left arm, a skull fracture, and a punctured lung. He had nearly died, but the prognosis was favorable. Fokker was unhurt, but Noville suffered minor internal injuries and had recovered quickly. Byrd said his right arm had "snapped like a match stick" and he had set it himself on the way to the hospital.[25]

Fokker was furious with himself for letting Byrd persuade him to take the three of them along on a test flight. He had been warned that the plane might be slightly nose-heavy with the fuel tank in the mid-section of the fuselage. All four men had crowded forward into the plane's cockpit because the 800 gal. fuel tank took up the entire central portion of the fuselage and left no clear passageway to the rear. No ballast had been added in the rear to counter the weight of the four men. Apparently Fokker did not realize how much the plane was out of trim with four occupants up forward.

The plane had performed flawlessly on the climb and level-off but as soon as Fokker reduced the throttles for landing, the nose fell and he had difficulty maintaining control. He made one pass over the runway and knew he was in trouble. He went around at full throttle and began an approach. He came in as fast as he dared but even with the control wheel full back in his stomach, he could not stop the nose-down attitude when he reduced the throttles. The plane's nose propeller bit into the ground and the plane flipped over on its back. There was no fire because Fokker had cut the switches.

In writing about the accident later, Byrd claimed that the instant the wheels touched the ground he "saw Fokker rise and make frantic efforts to jump out. Bennett was trapped as Fokker occupied the only exit. There was no way Noville and I could even try to get out."[26]

Fokker was furious at this implication of cowardice and said, "Maybe Byrd was excited and imagined this, a description more worthy of a layman than a supposed technician. Anyone used to piloting would have known that I couldn't have tried to jump out. Naturally, this comment disturbed me, not because I feared what airmen would think—they would know—but because of what the ordinary reader might suppose."[27]

According to Fokker, what had actually happened was that when he felt the airplane turning over, he drew his legs back and held on to the left side of the cockpit. The center engine was pushed slightly to the right where Bennett was sitting and pinned him in upside down. Fokker had fallen out of the cockpit on his head.[28]

The accident was embarrassing to Fokker because it was widely reported and he felt that his reputation as an aeronautical engineer was suffering from the adverse publicity. He had his men quickly disassemble the plane and work around the clock to rebuild it. To overcome the extreme nose-heavy condition, the navigator's compartment was moved to the rear behind the fuel tank and a crawlway was provided under one side of the tank so that a person could slide back and forth on his belly.

Byrd spent much time planning the equipment to be carried on the flight. A wind-drift indicator was installed that could be lowered through a trap door in the belly of the plane behind the main fuel tank. Bennett had devised a switch that would cut off all three engines at once in case of fire, and a dump valve was installed to drain the main fuel tank quickly in case of difficulty on takeoff.

A long-range radio developed by the Naval Research Laboratory in Washington, D.C., was donated to Byrd; it was supplemented by a small waterproof transmitter with a kite to loft an antenna in the event of a ditching in the ocean. The emergency survival equipment included two inflatable rubber rafts, which were stowed in the wing, signal flares, a Very pistol, carbide drift flares, and three weeks' supply of food. About 150 lb. of mail were to be carried, the first official U.S. international air-mail from the United States to France.

The modification and repair work went on day and night at the Hasbrouck Heights factory, and Balchen made several test flights. On 12 May he flew the Fokker to Roosevelt Field on Long Island, which had been leased along with a hangar by Wanamaker for the Byrd flight. At adjacent Curtiss Field, he saw the planes of two announced contenders for the Orteig prize: the *Columbia,* piloted by Clarence Chamberlin and built by Bellanca; and *Spirit of St. Louis,* manufactured by the Ryan Company in San Diego, which was to be flown by a pilot named Charles A. Lindbergh.

In Paris there were two other pilots preparing for their flight in the opposite direction against the prevailing winds. They were Charles Nungesser, French World War I ace, and Capt. François Coli, a one-eyed veteran who was first to span the Mediterranean. Public interest grew daily in what was now a race to see who would be first to depart. However Byrd, the subject of much previous news coverage from his North Pole flight, was being mostly ignored in the media as reporters searched for others to write about. As one writer commented,

> The public was disinclined to accept the well-born Virginian as a hero. Byrd's military bearing and fastidious dress and manners set him apart from the masses. The Byrds of Virginia had dominated state and national politics for several generations, and their prominence made them suspect in the minds of the hero-seeking public, however, and despite his tremendous achievements, Commander Richard E. Byrd could not fill the public need, and the hero's mantle remained unclaimed.[29]

Although Byrd and Noville recovered quickly from their injuries, it was obvious that Bennett would not be released from the hospital in time to meet Byrd's mid-May departure. Fokker wanted Balchen to replace Bennett but Wanamaker resisted. The flight had to be made by an all-American crew. Meanwhile Acosta would replace Bennett as pilot. Balchen described Acosta as belonging to the romantic rather than the scientific era of flying. Tall, with a dark complexion and sharp features, "He was a 'killer' with women, and he liked his wine, women and song."[30]

As Byrd pondered this new problem in his New York City hotel, Balchen stayed at Roosevelt Field running fuel consumption tests. The main cabin tank was filled with increasingly heavy loads of water for ballast, and the dump valve was tested to ensure fuel could be released overboard if necessary. The final test was made with a total load of 15,200 lb., and takeoff was accomplished in slightly more than 1,500 ft. Balchen then turned the aircraft over to Acosta, who made a flight around the field and accepted it on behalf of Byrd.

It was now nearing the end of May and Byrd kept delaying the signal to get ready for the takeoff because of the unfavorable weather forecasts over the Atlantic. Meanwhile there had been bad news about Nungesser and Coli. They had left Paris on 7 May in their single-engine monoplane and headed into strong westerly winds. In the ensuing hours many reports were received of their progress, but they were all false. When they were overdue, many searches were made for many weeks by Americans and Canadians, but the plane was never found; the fate of the two famous French aviators remains a mystery.

The news that Nungesser and Coli had vanished cast a gloom over the backers awaiting the decision to launch their respective planes. Chamberlin ran gas-consumption tests on his *Columbia* and Byrd kept checking the weather with Dr. James H. Kimball, chief of the New York office of the U.S. Weather Bureau, without making a decision. The quest for the Orteig prize would continue, although Byrd still insisted he was not competing.[31] As proof of his noncompetitive status, Byrd did not object when Balchen helped the other entrants. He assisted both Lindbergh and Chamberlin to plot their courses.[32]

Acosta was originally scheduled to fly with Chamberlin, but after a disagreement with Chamberlin, Acosta had been invited to go with Byrd. Chamberlin selected Lloyd Bertaud to take Acosta's place, but they also had a disagreement so Chamberlin quietly approached Balchen to go with him in his Bellanca in Bertaud's place. Balchen declined because he was Fokker's chief pilot and felt an obligation to Byrd.[33] Chamberlin then selected Charles A. Levine, owner of the plane, to go along.

Fokker wanted Balchen to be the relief pilot on the *America*, regardless of his nationality, but Wanamaker insisted that the plane was to be piloted by Americans. Fokker felt that his reputation was at stake and he knew that Balchen had proven his blind-flying expertise by keeping to the round-the-States flight schedule in spite of the weather.

Acosta, who had broken the world's endurance record by staying aloft for more than 51 hr. a few weeks before, had never learned the basics of blind flying and wanted to fly only when he could see the ground. This became abundantly clear when Fokker, Acosta, and Balchen made a test flight from Roosevelt Field in minimum-visibility conditions. Balchen was flying as copilot in the right-hand seat; Fokker was sitting in the observer's seat behind them. Acosta was at the controls, and when they flew into clouds, Balchen suddenly felt heavy in his seat and saw the turn-and-bank needle on one side. He grasped the wheel quickly and Acosta dropped his hands in relief. Acosta confessed that he knew nothing about instrument flying.[34]

Fokker heard this exchange and took Balchen aside after they landed. They walked to a corner of the hangar, and Balchen knew Fokker was trying to control his anger. He exploded in German when they were alone and said, "You must go on this flight to fly the airplane on instruments! As you can see, Acosta will get them killed. If they have to wait for good weather so Acosta can fly all the way, the plane will sit here all summer. I will be laughed at by the whole world!"[35]

Balchen reminded him of Wanamaker's edict that only Americans could go on the flight. Fokker cursed and ordered Balchen to go take out citizenship papers. Typically, he walked away hurriedly without further discussion. As far as Fokker was concerned, he had just solved the problem.

Balchen wrestled uneasily with the thought of becoming a U.S. citizen. Would he be a traitor to his homeland if he applied for American citizenship?[36] What would his family think? If he would have to give up his commission in the Norwegian air force, what would his old flying friends say? If he failed to be successful in America, he would have burned that bridge behind him. He had grown to love the America he had seen, mostly from the air. It represented opportunities so far that he could not have imagined before Commander Byrd invited him to accompany him from Spitsbergen. If he did not apply for citizenship, would he be letting Fokker and Byrd down, the men who had given him these opportunities? To help him decide, he spent the evening talking with Georg Unger Vetlesen, an old family friend. Although Vetlesen had not yet applied for citizenship himself, he advised Balchen to do so.[37]

Balchen went to the Bureau of Naturalization and filled out the Declaration of Intention form. He was now officially committed to join the citizens of the New World at the end of the five-year waiting period.

In the plane's hangar at Roosevelt Field, preparations were underway to officially christen the *America* on Saturday 20 May with Whalen presiding for Wanamaker. The word PEACE was painted under a fuselage window and AIRMAIL was lettered on the vertical stabilizer. A large speakers' platform was erected in the hangar; flags and bunting were everywhere. Large American and French flags were placed behind the speakers' podium. Water from the Delaware River, at the site of Washington's crossing, was available for the plane's christening.

Balchen wondered if Byrd would announce the takeoff time during the ceremony. However, there were only a few mechanics in the hangar and there did not seem to be any evidence that there was going to be a takeoff soon. Balchen learned that Kimball predicted the weather was clearing over the Atlantic and visibility was improving in Paris. It was raining lightly and Balchen asked a mechanic if Chamberlin or Lindbergh seemed to be getting ready. When he was assured that Lindbergh had gone to the theater in the city and Byrd was still in his hotel, Balchen went to his cot in the corner of the hangar and fell asleep.

4 · The Flight of the *America*

At 0500 on 19 May 1927 at Roosevelt Field, Long Island, Balchen was awakened by Fokker opening the hangar door. He was shouting in German, as he often did when he was excited. "Get up! Get me quick some fire extinguishers. That young fool is getting ready to take off. Maybe he will have trouble!"

As Balchen rushed outside with Fokker, a light rain was falling and it was difficult to see what was happening through the mist. The *Spirit of St. Louis* had been hauled to the takeoff point and the lanky figure of Charles Lindbergh, carrying a bag of sandwiches and an insulated bottle of coffee, climbed into the cockpit.

Balchen watched as the plane started moving for takeoff. It was going frighteningly slow as it approached the end of the field. Slowly, the wheels lifted clear and the plane was quickly lost in the murk.[1]

Balchen returned to the hangar of the America Trans-Oceanic Company, where workers began arriving to complete the preparations for the *America*'s dedication the next day. As the hours passed, special radio bulletins reported Lindbergh's progress until he was over the Atlantic heading east, then no more was heard. Acosta, Noville, and Balchen wondered what Byrd's reaction was going to be.

On hearing of the latest reports about the *Spirit of St. Louis*, Byrd told the press again that he was not interested in competing for the Orteig prize and had received "thousands" of letters condemning him for delaying the takeoff. "Coward," one typical letter read. "I am sick of seeing your name. You are a disgrace to America. You have never had any idea of flying across the Atlantic."[2]

But Byrd said he would not be goaded into making the flight by an uninformed public that knew nothing about flying. He intended to go only when he decided the time was right. He was not concerned about Lindbergh taking off first and rationalized later that no one knew what a three-engine plane the size of the Fokker would lift or its cruising range, and they were going to find out.[3]

Fokker commented on Byrd's delay:

> I could never understand why he did not take off before Lindbergh. There had been the most interminable series of test flights it has ever been my grief to witness. They dragged on for days. It seemed to me that every possible excuse for delay was seized on. I began to wonder whether Byrd really wanted to make the transatlantic flight, which was basically hardly more than an elaborate advertisement.[4]

Acosta, Balchen, and Noville continued to make test flights in the Fokker. Meanwhile Byrd went to Tufts College at Medford, Massachusetts, to receive an honorary master of arts degree and was sworn in by a post office department official so the plane could carry official U.S. mail to France.

Despite the fact that Lindbergh appeared to be making steady progress, Rodman Wanamaker decided to go ahead with the dedication ceremony of the *America,* even though the audience was smaller than anticipated. After some opening speeches, Byrd laid out his notes carefully on the lectern. As he was about to speak, Harry Bruno rushed to the stage and handed him a note. Byrd read it and put his speech notes aside. He paused briefly, then said, "Ladies and gentlemen, Charles Lindbergh has landed at Le Bourget at 10:22 P.M. Paris time." The audience cheered mildly, respecting their belief that Byrd would be disappointed that he had not been first.[5]

Lindbergh had arrived at Le Bourget Airport on 20 May 1927 amid one of history's greatest mob scenes. He had made the 3,600 mi. trip in 33 hr. 39 min. Although Byrd claimed not to be disappointed by Lindbergh's success, he was upset by the mail and telegrams he received criticizing him for not getting away first. One man from North Carolina wired the following: "I just want you to know what you may not realize that you are the world's prize boob to get left at the switch as you did." Byrd countered such criticism by saying, "To delay a little did not hurt our flight; while to have gone might well have done harm to the fine work he (Lindbergh) was doing in cementing French and American friendship."[6]

While Lindbergh was being feted wildly in Paris, Clarence Chamberlin still planned to make a flight but refused to announce his destination. He called a press conference on 3 June and announced that he would take off early the next morning for a "destination somewhere in Europe." He and Charles Levine were airborne at 0604 and made a successful crossing. When their fuel was nearly exhausted, they landed in a muddy field in Eisleben, Germany. They had been aloft for 42 hr. 31 min. and had flown 3,911 mi., a world record for distance.

Back in America, the news was greeted almost as emotionally as Lindbergh's flight. Within three weeks, Americans had spanned the Atlantic nonstop a second time, and there was still the third crew waiting to make the assault on the great water barrier between the continents.

After Chamberlin's takeoff, Fokker's impatience with Byrd's procrastination grew to explosive proportions. Byrd still claimed that he needed ideal weather to cross the Atlantic. Favorable forecasts were issued three times and each time the aircraft was tethered to the top of the take-off incline ready to go. After the third cancellation, Fokker lit into Byrd and told him the delays were ridiculous and totally unnecessary. He said, "If you don't get going I will buy the ship back and get going myself! Instead of taking the first good weather, you seem to use every possible excuse to stall it off. I am sick and tired of it. It is a damned shame!"[7]

On 28 June an obviously very weak Floyd Bennett arrived at the field on crutches, escorted by his doctor, who said Bennett was in no condition to make the flight. Fokker took Bennett by the elbow and motioned to Byrd and Grover Whalen to follow them to a corner of the hangar. After a long discussion, Bennett approached Balchen and told him quietly that he was going on the crew as the relief pilot and mechanic.

Just after midnight on 29 June 1927, Kimball telephoned Byrd and told him that, although conditions were not ideal, he should not delay his departure any longer. Although there was a light low pressure area over the middle of the Atlantic that meant rain and poor visibility at midcourse, the overall winds were from the west, which would give them a boost in speed over the route. Byrd immediately called everyone to meet him at the field.

Meanwhile, the *America* was hauled to the take-off position at the high end of the earthwork ramp and a rope was tied to the tail skid and attached to a stake. When the engines were revved up to full power, the rope was to be sliced with an ax and the heavily loaded plane would charge down the ramp and thus accelerate.

It was still dark and a light rain was falling, but a small crowd had gathered, somehow alerted that the takeoff was imminent. Before boarding the plane, Byrd handed reporters a typed statement that rationalized the flight. "Whereas I am attempting this flight for many reasons," it said, "I hope our countrymen will appreciate the fact that my shipmates, Noville, Acosta and Balchen, are flying over the top today totally for the progress of aviation to which they are devoting their lives. There is, I realize, little glory in the undertaking. There are no prizes awaiting them."[8]

Byrd and the others climbed aboard to their assigned positions. Acosta warmed up the engines, with Noville in the copilot's seat with his hand on the fuel dump valve. Acosta nodded to Noville and pushed the three throttles ahead while the plane strained at the rope. Suddenly the rope snapped before it could be axed and they were on their way down the wet field. Balchen, in the rear with Byrd at the navigator's table, watched as the halfway mark passed with the tail skid still on the ground. As the end of the field came threateningly close, Acosta eased back on the control wheel. The plane left the ground momentarily and settled back to earth, then struggled valiantly into the air again. Everyone breathed a sigh of relief as the end of the field passed, cleared by only a few inches. Takeoff was recorded as 0524. After Acosta turned on course, Balchen pulled out his notebook and noted: "29 June, 0610. Setting course up coast line, compass 83½ degrees, wind S.W. Clearing."[9]

Acosta brought the Fokker to its initial cruising altitude of about 2,000 ft. He steered across the tip of Long Island and headed for Cape Cod. About an hour later, Noville gave up his copilot seat to Balchen and went back to the radio compartment. When they had been flying for about 5 hr. and were off the coast of Maine, Noville began to transfer gasoline from 5 gal. cans to the large center tank and dropped the empty cans through a trap door into the ocean. Passing Halifax, huge buildups of cumulus clouds loomed ahead and the landmarks underneath disappeared in the mist and fog. Their last landmarks were now obscured. When they estimated that they were over Newfoundland, Noville passed a note to Acosta and Balchen (it was too difficult to move forward because of the gas tank). It said the plane's engines were using excessive fuel, far above the consumption that Balchen had calculated on his test flights. Balchen was surprised and could not understand why this was so. Both

Byrd and Noville came to the cockpit and asked what Balchen and Acosta thought they should do. It would be extremely embarrassing to Balchen if all of his figures had been wrong. If they turned back, they would not find the fields in Newfoundland because of the fog. While they thought about it, Acosta had to get above the increasingly thick clouds and turbulence; the extra power to make the climb increased the gas consumption.

Balchen felt strongly that Noville was mistaken and told Byrd so. Acosta agreed and Byrd finally nodded approval as they headed east on a heading of 108°. When they could not escape the clouds, Acosta released the controls to Balchen, who began to fly solely on instruments.

Balchen was hungry and remembered that he had stashed some chicken sandwiches in a bag under his seat. He asked Acosta to take the controls while he groped for it with his head down. He suddenly felt that a heavy weight was pushing down on him with such centrifugal force that he could not raise his head. He realized that the plane was out of control in a steep downward spiral and looked up to see the rate-of-climb indicator pointing steeply downward, the turn-and-bank needle was to the extreme right, and the airspeed was passing through 140 MPH, then 150, and then 160. Balchen grabbed the controls, leveled the plane, and climbed through the clouds to 8,000 ft. Acosta sheepishly asked Balchen to do the flying through any clouds for the rest of the flight.[10]

Balchen flew the Fokker on course during the night, and the effects of fatigue began to set in. In the early morning he realized that he had not slept for more than 24 hr. Acosta could take over and at least keep the plane straight and level as long they were above a level cloud deck. Balchen stood up and stretched his numbed legs and arms. He crawled to the rear compartment and took a nap while Noville took his seat in the cockpit. Balchen returned to the cockpit after about 4 hr. of fitful sleep. The plane's engines droned on monotonously but faithfully. However, the exact position of the *America* was uncertain as it continued on the compass course of 108°. Not knowing the exact direction or strength of the winds, no one had any idea whether they had drifted north or south of it. Noville was unable to raise any ground or ship stations on the radio and turned his attention to the gas consumption. After a while he meekly passed a note to Byrd saying, "Made mistake in first estimate. Have enough gas to fly all the way."[11]

This was good news, but as dawn lightened the horizon towering cumulus clouds loomed ahead. Balchen took the controls and plunged the

Fokker into them. He climbed slowly to the plane's maximum altitude of nearly 15,000 ft. but was still mostly in the clouds. Light ice began to form on the wing and propellers.

At 1500 in the afternoon, Noville passed a note to the cockpit that he had made contact with a ship that reported good visibility and a ceiling of 1,500 ft. He did not know its location but at least it was a contact with someone down below, for which they were all grateful. Balchen reduced the throttles and glided down through the overcast to get into warmer air. He broke out into daylight over the ocean. Now able to use the drift indicator, Byrd checked the drift and found the wind was from the northeast, which probably placed them south of their intended course. Byrd did not give any course corrections, so Balchen continued to fly a compass course of 108°.

Apparently Byrd had been unaware of the drama that had gone on in the cockpit during the night when the plane momentarily spiraled down and did not know that Acosta had done none of the flying in the clouds. He noted in his logbook, "It is impossible to navigate. Only an aviator knows what it means to be 18 hours without seeing the ground or water underneath. Acosta and Balchen deserve great credit for their fine work during this critical period."[12]

James E. Mooney, a zealous admirer of Byrd who would disparage Balchen in later life, described Acosta's role quite differently and very incorrectly in a 1930 book:

> Bert Acosta, one of the greatest pilots in America, a man with a very strong constitution, nearly collapsed under the strain after piloting the *America* through nineteen hours of storm and fog. They ran into another storm which brought down torrents of rain. Bert Acosta was very fatigued after unbroken hours of flying a heavy plane through the densest of fog. The fog and rain covered the glass in front so that it was impossible to see, and for the same reason Acosta was unable to wear goggles. In a desperate effort to see, he opened the window on his left, peering through the open spaces facing a wing that was traveling over a hundred miles an hour. Filled with rain and sleet, it tore at his eyes and he was compelled to duck back into the plane every now and then for a minute or two and then peer out again. His commander stood behind him watching the instruments. He checked the compasses very frequently.
>
> "Acosta," he cried, "you are off the course. You are flying in a circle."

Acosta turned around, eyes swollen and red. He said, "I can't see, Dick. I'm going blind!" His voice was heard above the roar of the motors. The last bit of strength he had was gone. He fell from his seat to the floor. The burden of the work at the controls of that heavy ship and the terrible punishment of the rain and wind in his eyes were more than human endurance could stand up under. Balchen was called to the controls.[13]

There was no sign of land or smoke plumes from ships as the Fokker droned on in the late afternoon. Balchen assumed the wind had drifted them south of their heading but stayed on the easterly course. That way, he figured, they were at least bound to hit Europe somewhere between Spain and Norway.

The weather brightened briefly and Balchen sighted a thin, dark line ahead on the horizon. He identified it as the westernmost tip of France near the port of Brest, which put the *America* about 250 mi. south of course. There was haze and darkening clouds ahead as they crossed the shoreline. It was 1925 local time.

Noville picked up a forecast from Le Bourget that reported mist and drizzle, with a forecast of heavy fog that night. With all of Europe ahead of them, there were lots of places to land. Rome or Berlin were possibilities with the gas load that remained.

The radio became inoperative just after the French coast was sighted. Noville had been working on it but had accidentally ripped some wires out of the set while turning around in the tight radio compartment, and the radio was useless. Because they could not reach anyone, they did not know that Paris was now reporting heavy rain, fog, and a low ceiling at Le Bourget Airport.

While Balchen rested briefly, Acosta took his place. Byrd also went forward to the cockpit, ready to take the controls if the last few miles of the flight would be made in clear weather. He sat next to a very tired Acosta and decided they should fly up along the coast and then follow the Seine River toward Paris. This decision was a bad call as far as Balchen was concerned. He was familiar with the French coast and suggested that Byrd's plan would take two hours longer than if they set a course from Brest directly to Paris and could get there before dark. Byrd ignored the suggestion and ordered Acosta to "Fly as I've told you!"[14]

Acosta flew along the coast in the growing darkness to Rouen and it began to rain lightly. He called Balchen forward to take over the controls when he could not see the ground ahead and went aft. Byrd remained in the copilot's seat.

They reached Rouen at 2030 in light rain, and Balchen searched for the Seine River. Byrd got out of his seat and went to the rear. Balchen was left alone and followed the river in the deteriorating visibility. When he reached the eastern suburbs of Rouen, the rain increased and he descended to 1,200 ft. but knew he should not go any lower. He climbed immediately to 4,000 ft. on instruments and headed for Paris on a compass course he figured would take him somewhere near the city.

After flying for an hour and still in rain showers, Balchen eased the plane down cautiously, then circled hoping for a hole in the clouds, but he could see no lights on the ground. It began to rain more heavily and Balchen was still flying on instruments. He decided the only thing to do was to climb back to 4,000 ft. and head back to the coast where the ceiling was higher.

After about an hour and a half, he glided down and broke out of the clouds over water at about 1,500 ft. When he turned back toward the east, he could see lights and a shoreline, which he identified as Rouen. He set a course for Paris again and figured he was over the city in about 1 hr. 20 min. He let down to 3,000 ft., which was as low as he dared to go because he knew the Eiffel Tower was somewhere underneath, and still could not see anything. He had no alternative except to return to the coast again and hope the ceiling was high enough to make a landing.

The engines had performed flawlessly for more than 40 hr. of flying time, but now gas was getting dangerously low. Through the black night, whipped by storms, Balchen steered resolutely back to the coast. He communicated with Byrd by notes. One of Byrd's queries read:

"Are we going to crash?"

Turning around, Balchen shouted, "Hell, no! The flares—Get ready to drop the flares!"[15]

When Balchen figured he was over the coast again, he began a letdown. Lights began to emerge out of the murk and he headed for a concentration of them. Suddenly he passed an electric sign on the roof of a building that read DEAUVILLE. He knew then they were a few miles south of Le Havre.

By this time Balchen was not looking for a field. The only hope to get down with a reasonable chance to survive in the darkness was to land on an open beach or purposely land the plane in the surf off the shore while he still had some engine power and control of the aircraft. The latter action was especially risky because no one had ever ditched a trimotored plane. As he inched slowly along the coast, he saw the beam of a lighthouse cut through the mist and an open stretch of beach nearby. He flew over it at about 200 ft., but a group of fishing boats had been hauled up on the sand and there was no room to land safely among them. The only choice left was to ditch offshore close to the lighthouse. He motioned to Byrd, who nodded in agreement.

As Balchen turned to make a pass at low altitude, the right engine coughed briefly from fuel starvation but caught again. Hearing this, Byrd threw three carbide flares out the trapdoor, which Balchen saw as he came around for a final approach. They were burning brightly on the surface about 100 yd. apart. He could see the flares ahead and decided to level out on the first flare, set down on the second, with the third in front to judge the height above the water. Just before he flared out for the landing, he cut all three engine switches.

Meanwhile everyone had gone to their emergency positions. He was alone up front, and Acosta was sitting in the compartment behind him. Noville and Byrd were back in the navigator's compartment. After the plane hit, the landing gear sheared off and the plane came to a stop, resting on its nose in the water.

Byrd's description of the episode varies from Balchen's and leaves a far different impression of the sequence of events from the time Balchen returned to the French coast. Generously using the pronoun "we," Byrd wrote,

A decision had to be made. My big job now was to try not to kill anyone beneath us and to save my shipmates. The only thing to do was to turn back to water.

It would probably be difficult for the layman to visualize our predicament, tossed around in the inky darkness of the storm, drenched in rain.

I doubt if anyone could realize the strain of this part of the flight. We had no assurance that the plane could be landed safely on the water, but there was no chance of a safe landing on the land where we could see nothing.

Thus the decision to turn back did not carry safety with it. It meant that even should we find water we could not be certain of landing without disaster, because I never heard of anyone landing in the water when it was pitch dark and when the water could not be seen. We could not even be certain of landing a great plane like ours safely in the water in the daytime.

So, when we turned, we faced uncertainty ahead, but there was nothing else we could do under the circumstances that would give us any chance whatever to save the lives of the crew and to avoid endangering the people beneath us.

We set a course for the lighthouse we had seen. The wind might blow us off a bit in the darkness, but if the fog were not too thick there, we were confident of hitting it provided we were where we thought we were while over Paris. Much of the way we could see nothing beneath us, and we were flying so low that Noville had to pull in the antenna of his wireless to prevent it from hitting objects on the ground. Finally, when I thought we were near the lighthouse, I asked Balchen to get down lower. He was afraid of running into something but we had to take the risk. We emerged from the mists and there was the lighthouse ahead of us.

We then flew over the lighthouse and, by the quick flash of the revolving beacon, we could tell that we were over water and dimly distinguish the shoreline. We could not discern the character of the beach. It was still raining and dismally thick.

I wrote a note to my shipmates which I passed around with the flashlight which read: "Stand by to land." I knew there would be a hard bump.

We now dropped a number of flares as nearly in a line as we could, about 100 yards from the beach line. They all ignited, and although they made a light in a pool of darkness, we hoped we would be able to judge the distance of the plane above the water as we descended. Of course, if we could not judge it, we should go into the water at flying speed, which would smash everything badly, since water does not give much when hit hard.

The gasoline was running low, we must not wait for it to give out and be forced to land.

Balchen happened to be at the wheel. I gave the orders to land.

The wheels touched, and though the landing gear is secured to the plane with a tremendous factor of safety, it was sheared off, along with the wheels, with hardly a jar of the plane, as though a great knife had cut it, thus demonstrating the tremendous resistance of water when hit by a rapidly moving object. No one had predicted that.[16]

It had been a perfect night ditching—precise and fairly gentle, despite losing the wheels—in 10 ft. of water less than 200 yd. from the beach. The plane had been aloft 42 hr. 6 min. and had flown about 4,200 mi.

As the cockpit filled with water, Balchen released his seat belt and struggled to find the escape door behind him in the radio compartment. He pushed it open and emerged into the cool air. He was slimy with warm oil from the center engine's oil tank that was beneath his seat and had apparently spilled during the landing. He saw Byrd and Noville escape through the hatch in the rear. Acosta suddenly appeared behind them.

All four men had been deafened by the many hours of the engines' roar and could not converse except by shouting at each other and gesturing. Noville ripped the rubber life raft out of the top of the wing and inflated it with a pump. The others reached inside to retrieve what valuables they could, including a strong box containing a piece of the historic American flag made by Betsy Ross they were to present to the government of France and the sack of U.S. mail. They all climbed into the raft, paddled ashore, and carried the raft up on the beach. All but Balchen were hurting from bruises.

It was now about 0500 local time and still raining; there was no sign of life nearby. Wet, cold, mud-caked, and groggy from lack of sleep, they struggled toward a village about a mile away as daylight was breaking. A small boy on a bicycle suddenly emerged out of the darkness, took one look at the four unkempt strangers, and quickly disappeared without a word. Many houses had fences around them and the gates were locked. Although they knocked on several doors, no one responded. They climbed the hill to the lighthouse and banged on the door. A head appeared out an upper window and Noville tried in his schoolboy French to tell him who they were. Auguste Lescop, the lighthouse keeper, and his wife hurried to open the door and let them in. They were promptly given hot coffee and dry clothing.

After warming themselves and eating a hot meal, all four men went to bed. A short time later, with the sea at low tide, the lighthouse keeper spotted the *America* resting on the beach. He awakened Byrd and Balchen, who hurried to the beach to see the *America* sitting alone in the sand. The wheels lay 100 yd. down the beach. They walked to the plane and pulled more items out of the fuselage.

They had landed on the beach at Ver-sur-Mer in Caen Province, which would later be known as Omaha Beach to Americans and honored as

Gold Beach in recognition by the village of its liberation from German occupation on 6 June 1944.[17]

A few villagers arrived and helped them salvage what they could. One man loaned a set of tools and helped them remove the engines and the wing. The crowd increased and a few rushed in and carted away pieces of the plane as souvenirs. Someone with a knife carved the word AMERICA from the fabric of the fuselage and sold it to the owner of the Deauville Casino, who displayed it proudly above the entrance. P. J. Philip of the *New York Times* cabled his editor from Paris: "In Ver-sur-Mer there certainly is not a house which does not have some little piece of that plane to exhibit when the tale is told of how the village rose to world fame in a single night, and how, it must be said, it honorably rose to its role and showed a hospitality and kindness such as could not be surpassed."[18]

After the crowds finally dispersed from the beach, the wing, some salvaged parts, and the three engines were hauled inland by Fokker employees, crated, and sent to the United States. They were later reconditioned and sold to an airline.

Joseph Coiffier, assistant to the mayor of Ver-sur-Mer, arrived and extended an invitation to Byrd and Noville to sleep at the mayor's home, while Balchen returned to the lighthouse to stay with Acosta. That night all four were guests at a banquet in Caen. Byrd sent a cable to Rodman Wanamaker that night: "DEEPLY SORRY WE DID NOT REACH PARIS WILL REPORT DETAILS FORCED LANDING DARK NIGHT UNAVOIDABLE AMERICA WILL BE REPAIRED WILL DELIVER FLAG AND MAIL WHEN WE REACH PARIS."[19]

The next morning the four men took the train to Paris, where Byrd was welcomed as a hero by a crowd of hundreds of cheering Parisians at the St. Lazare Station. It was difficult for them to debark from the train and get in the waiting automobiles because of the crowd. The streets were jammed with people trying to get a look at the new heroes. The gendarmes were helpless to do anything and threw up their hands. The crowd pushed and shoved and rocked the cars so much that several windows were broken. It was impossible to drive, so the crowd pushed them down the street to the Hotel Continental, where rooms were reserved for the flyers. Women leaned in the car windows, grabbed them by the neck, kissed them madly, and smeared them with brilliant lipstick.

The *New York Times* reported the story of the flight and the arrival of the crew in Paris for several days with large headlines. Byrd was quoted extensively; Noville and Balchen also gave short interviews, which were published in a special edition. Noville gave Byrd credit for the decision to ditch and Balchen for making the safe landing: "I told the Commander my idea of the risk was about one in 200," he said, "but thanks to his choice of the sea for the descent and Balchen's wonderful piloting we had that one chance."[20]

Hearing this, Philip wrote his story under a subhead that read, "Balchen Stands out as Hero." He quoted Balchen as saying, "I have flown in far worse weather but none I disliked more. It bothered me not knowing where I was and having to keep on going."[21]

Byrd was met at the hotel by the head of the American Hospital in Paris, who found him so fatigued and nervous that he recommended Byrd forego the planned social affairs for a few days. Exhilarated by the reception, Byrd ignored the advice. Late that afternoon they were taken to the Élysée Palace, where Byrd presented French president Gaston Doumergue with the piece of the Betsy Ross flag and was made an officer of the Legion of Honor by Premier Raymond Poincaré. As far as the French were concerned, the flight was a huge success, especially so because they had saved the piece of priceless Betsy Ross flag and had delivered the important mail destined for prominent Frenchmen.

As the news of the flight spread around the world, cables of praise for Byrd poured in to the hotel; one of them was from President Coolidge: "YOUR FLIGHT TO FRANCE WILL ADVANCE OUR KNOWLEDGE OF CONDITIONS WHICH MUST BE MET AND CONQUERED TO MAKE TRANSOCEANIC AVIATION PRACTICAL AND SAFE."[22]

There was great elation among Byrd's Navy friends in the United States when it was announced that he had reached France successfully. Secretary of the Navy Curtis Wilbur sent a "well-done" message and then told the press that he would award Byrd the Distinguished Flying Cross for his superior feat of piloting and navigation.

The next few days were a blur to Balchen. He sent a telegram to his mother in Norway: "ARRIVED IN PARIS TODAY ALL WELL."[23] She had it framed and hung it over her bed. Byrd, Noville, and Acosta cabled their families in the States and Byrd prepared installments about the flight for the *New York Times.*

Byrd and Noville retrieved their starched white Navy uniforms from the hotel where they had been shipped ahead for the many receptions they anticipated if the flight were successful. Balchen and Acosta took a taxi to the Paris Wanamaker store to take advantage of the offer to supply them with whatever clothes they needed on arrival. None of the ready-to-wear suits would fit Balchen, so a tailor worked all night to make him a jacket and pants. "All the shoes I can find are pointed," Balchen wrote, "and the clerk wants to sell me a derby even; but I draw the line at that. When I see my own reflection in the mirror of the hotel lobby, I almost shake hands with myself before I know who I am."[24]

The welcoming ceremonies continued over the next week. Byrd laid a wreath at the Tomb of the Unknown Soldier and made a courtesy call on Mrs. Charles Nungesser, wife of the missing French flyer. Each crew member received the Gold Medal of the City of Paris. They also received medals from the Aero Club of Paris and the Paris chapter of the U.S. National Aeronautic Association. Medallions were presented by the cities of Calais and Dunkerque.

Balchen and the others met many famous French dignitaries, including Marshal Foch, famous French World War I general, and Louis Bleriot, first to fly across the English Channel in 1909. Balchen recalled one of the outstanding events as the reception hosted by the Federation Aeronautique Internationale (FAI), the organization that certifies world record flights, where they were presented honorary memberships by Clifford B. Harmon, pioneer American balloonist and aviator.

Fokker, grateful that the plane had functioned flawlessly and was not to be blamed for Balchen having to ditch it in the ocean, sent Balchen a radiogram saying, "GLAD TO KNOW THAT YOU DID YOUR STUFF AND THAT YOU ARE SAFE IN PARIS."[25]

Balchen had no way of knowing that the expressions of praise for his valiant role in the Atlantic flight addressed to him would apparently annoy Byrd the rest of his life. Because some original congratulatory messages directed to Balchen do not appear in the Balchen files but are in the Byrd Archives, it is possible that Balchen never saw or knew about them.[26]

Byrd, Acosta, Noville, and Balchen were taken to Cherbourg and boarded the *Leviathan* for the trip home on 12 July 1927. Chamberlin was also on board. The ship docked in New York a week later to a tumultuous welcome, comparable to Lindbergh's a few weeks before. It was the second New York ticker-tape parade for Byrd, with thousands of New Yorkers cheering their hero. The *America* crew and Chamberlin received the traditional New York welcome on the steps of City Hall from Mayor Jimmy Walker and Grover Whalen.

The *America* crew went to Washington, D.C., for a luncheon in the

White House with President Coolidge. On returning to New York they were honored with a dinner at the Astor Hotel, at which Secretary of the Navy Curtis D. Wilbur awarded the Distinguished Flying Cross to Byrd and Noville. Some boos and comments of protest erupted in the audience when Acosta and Balchen were ignored and did not receive the honor.

Walker asked Secretary Wilbur to explain to the audience, in response to the boos, why the two pilots had not received the award. He replied that the pilots were not members of the armed forces. However, Acosta *had* been a pilot instructor in the U.S. Army Air Service during World War I and Balchen was still a member of the Norwegian armed forces. Walker later requested an official explanation from the Navy, and the secretary explained that he could award the medal only to members of the U.S. Navy. In a magazine article, aviation writer C. B. Allen explained the requirements covering the granting of the Distinguished Flying Cross and took sharp issue with its denial to qualified individuals, including Balchen, while wrongly awarded to others, solely depending on peer and political pressures.[27]

Balchen was puzzled and embarrassed about the incident. He did not understand why he would not get it and did not know the Secretary of the Navy could make the award only to U.S. Navy personnel. He returned to his hotel and was surprised to find Fokker waiting for him. Fokker wanted to hear the story of the flight without any of the embellishments and misinformation that he had read in the papers. He was pleased to hear that the plane and its engines performed so well and asked when Balchen could return to work. "I'll be back tomorrow morning," he replied.

Fokker reassured Balchen that he would always have a job with him, but he understood that he had an obligation to Byrd and that he would always honor it. By this time the relations between Fokker and Byrd had deteriorated, beginning when Fokker had become so frustrated by Byrd's continual delaying of the Atlantic flight. Fokker was not pleased that many newspaper photographs showed his plane in the surf, which he feared would convey the impression that it had crashed there because it had malfunctioned.[28]

Byrd's version of the *America*'s flight dominated the news for weeks after their return. He claimed he knew exactly where they would hit land, "although we were still several hundred miles away."[29] He added later in *Skyward*, "While over the ocean, three hours before we reached France, we knew our position and course very exactly. When we found Paris smothered in fog we were able to navigate back to the coast, the only place we could make a safe landing and save our lives."[30]

When one reads Byrd's account of the flight it appears that Byrd not only navigated but piloted the aircraft for a great part of the flight, although there was no way he could have navigated or flown through the clouds, because he had never learned how to fly on instruments. And according to both his account and Balchen's, he was never at the controls alone at any time.

Balchen was grateful to Byrd for bringing him to the United States and giving him the opportunity to make the flight, and he never commented publicly about the truth of any statements Byrd made about the Atlantic flight. However, Fokker expressed his opinion about the *America's* flight in his autobiography, which was published in 1931. He praised Balchen for the flight's success and wrote, "Balchen took over both the navigation and piloting when they reached France and brought the ship over Paris in a deep fog. Byrd seemed confused and entirely lost; Acosta was a physical wreck; Noville by damaging his radio had destroyed his sole usefulness."[31]

As if to compensate for not receiving any formal recognition in the United States, Balchen was awarded a medal by the Mayor of Hoboken, New Jersey, for "the extraordinary heroism of your deed and the splendid contribution your flight has made to the history of aviation."[32] Whalen and Wanamaker expressed their gratitude to Balchen, saying his addition to the crew had virtually ensured the success of the flight.[33]

5 · Tragedy and Prelude to Triumph

For Balchen one of the most interesting interludes in the ceremonies in Paris honoring the *America* crew was a discussion with Byrd, who confided his desire to take another expedition into a cold-weather country. But it was not to Greenland, as Balchen had been told previously. Byrd said he wanted to be the first person to fly over the South Pole, just as he had been the first to fly over the North Pole. He wanted Bennett and Balchen to be members of the expedition he was going to organize.

Balchen was always ready for a new challenge, and he was excited about the possibility. The first question in his mind was what type of aircraft would be ideal for such a flight. He offered to visit the Fokker plant in Amsterdam to talk with "Uncle Tony's" engineers. Byrd agreed and Balchen, glad to escape from the celebrations in Paris, went to the factory and laid out the criteria he envisioned for a new or modified Fokker transport. It would have to operate on skis and carry a larger gas tank and payload over a great distance at a fairly high altitude. The engineers immediately went to work making detailed drawings.

On board the *Leviathan*, Byrd and Balchen discussed his visit to the Fokker plant and the specifications Balchen had left. They agreed that, in addition to the large plane, two single-engine planes should be included in the planning. They talked about the establishment of a base camp, ships to transport the aircraft and supplies to the antarctic, how to raise the planes from the ship to the ice cap level, the types and number of crew members needed. A myriad of logistical problems had to be solved to accommodate a large group of men who would have to be totally self-sufficient while living in an extremely isolated location for an estimated two-year period.

The name of Roald Amundsen kept coming up in the conversations, and it seemed logical that he should be consulted. Amundsen had more experience with food, clothing, and survival equipment in a harsh, cold-weather environment than anyone else through his arctic and antarctic expeditions, especially the latter, which had been a monumental, successful adventure. It was decided that Balchen should go to Norway and get Amundsen's expert advice.

Balchen went to Norway in August 1927. In a "To Whom It May Concern" letter, Byrd wrote that "Lt. Balchen is going to Norway as my accredited representative; he is authorized by me to make purchases in my name, and I will make payment on his purchases immediately upon presentation of the bill for said purchases."[1]

When his ship reached Bergen, Norway, for its first stop, Balchen was surprised to find a large crowd on the dock and the waterfront buildings draped with banners welcoming him home. His old squadron mates at the Horten air base flew a formation of planes overhead in salute. It was a glorious homecoming for Balchen, who thought he might be treated like an unwelcome stranger. "I would not exchange this greeting for all the parades up the Champs Élysées or Broadway, because the crowd is shouting my name, and these are my own people saying with their hearts, "*Velkommen hjem, Bernt!*" I have to look away for a moment and swallow hard."[2]

The ship stopped next at Kristiansand, where his mother eagerly awaited him at the ship's dock. Balchen then went to Oslo for a luncheon with the Aero Club of Norway and was awarded the club's Gold Medal. He was so overwhelmed that he found it difficult to respond.

The next day Balchen received a message that King Haakon VII wanted to see him at the Royal Palace. The monarch listened intently to Balchen's description of the Atlantic flight and of Byrd's plans to go to antarctica. The king was particularly pleased that Balchen was seeking the wise counsel of Amundsen and that Oskar Omdahl, who had been with Amundsen on his try for the North Pole, had also been invited to go on the Byrd expedition.

Omdahl and Balchen visited Amundsen at his home outside Oslo. They discussed the many requirements for the coming venture, and Amundsen recommended that Byrd establish his headquarters near Framheim, where he had had his base and where he believed there was the best average weather in the antarctic.

Amundsen recommended they obtain an old but remarkably sturdy sealing vessel, named *Samson*, which he had used in 1893 for an arctic voyage. He contacted the owners, found out what had to be done to make it ready, and obtained a price that Balchen approved.

They discussed proper clothing, and Amundsen sketched a parka he had designed that was based on a native garment with a hood sewed to it. This hood could be drawn tightly around the head with a drawstring. One special suggestion was that they enlist the services of Martin Ronne, then 68, a tailor and sailmaker, who had been to the antarctic with Amundsen in 1911 and had been invaluable in designing clothing worn on the long trek to the South Pole.

While Balchen was in Norway, Byrd had decided to take a new Ford trimotor to the antarctic instead of the Fokker, and had already secretly ordered it. Henry and Edsel Ford donated the aircraft for the expedition and added a substantial amount of money. The change was a complete surprise to Balchen and a stunning blow to Fokker, who insisted that Byrd honor the contract to purchase the new plane, which had arrived at the New Jersey plant from Holland. Fokker demanded that Byrd remove it from the factory immediately. As it had no engines installed yet, Byrd asked Ford to finance three engines so it could be flown to Dearborn for storage until sold.[3]

When he returned to the United States, Balchen found that the Ford had some distinct advantages over the Fokker, which was constructed with wood and fabric. The Ford was sturdy, all-metal, and could be more easily disassembled and crated for transport on a ship. Floyd Bennett and Balchen went to Detroit immediately in June 1928 to begin preparations for extensive flight tests. They flew a factory model trimotor, similar to the one Byrd was to get, to Grand Mere, Canada, and St. Albans, Vermont, for ski tests over the next six weeks. Afterward they gave the Ford engineers their assessment: The plane was unsatisfactory because it was underpowered with its three Wright 220 hp engines and could not carry a large enough load or reach the altitude necessary for the critical leg over the 10,000 ft. plateau to the Pole. The engines were not supercharged and the propellers were fixed-pitch when variable-pitch props were available for better fuel efficiency at cruising speeds. Further, the fuel consumption and altitude test flights were made with wheels; skis would cause a further reduction in speed and fuel efficiency. They recommended that a more powerful center engine replace the current one.

Bennett and Balchen laid out their requirements for special modifications and the extra tanks that the plane needed to make the 1,600 mi. roundtrip to the Pole from a base to be located somewhere in the Ross Sea area, as Amundsen had suggested. Arrangements were made to have the center engine replaced with a new 525 hp Wright Cyclone, which would satisfy the load and altitude specifications.

Meanwhile, Balchen returned to the Fokker plant and continued to test trimotor aircraft that were destined for the U.S. Marine Corps and Pan American Airways. He also tested some seaplanes for the Cuban navy and Universals for Western Canada Airways. Omdahl and Balchen worked together, but Omdahl was not happy at the Fokker factory. Against Balchen's advice,[4] Omdahl agreed to pilot Frances Grayson, a successful real estate businessperson, from Maine to Copenhagen, Denmark, in a Sikorsky S-38 amphibian. They were accompanied by Brice Goldsborough, who had installed the navigation equipment on the *America* and other transatlantic aircraft. The plane departed Roosevelt Field on Christmas Eve 1927 and was never heard from again.

On several aircraft transfer flights from Teterboro, New Jersey, to Canada, Balchen noticed that Bennett did not appear fully recovered from his accident. He seemed weak and was very pale. He dragged his injured right foot and had developed a habit of licking his lips nervously.

On a trip to deliver two Universals to Winnipeg, Canada, they stayed overnight in Chicago. Bennett seemed unusually quiet and told Balchen that he appreciated his encouragement during the days he was recovering from the accident and help getting him back in flying shape again. Bennett thought that Balchen had gotten a raw deal in the Byrd-directed news coverage of the transatlantic flight but said it would shock Balchen if he knew the truth about the North Pole flight. Bennett said he was sickened by what he knew. "This confirmed my suspicion from my knowledge about the performance of the North Pole plane," Balchen said later. "I thought of Amundsen, Ellsworth, and Nobile who, after all, were the first to reach the North Pole by air. By some kind of silent agreement, we never mentioned this anymore."[5]

After returning from this trip, they found that the Fokker had been outfitted with the three engines Edsel Ford had financed, and Balchen and Bennett flew it to Dearborn for storage. They then tested a ski-equipped Bellanca that Byrd had received gratis, but it did not meet the requirements they had set. It was also flown to Dearborn and sold.

When the Ford trimotor with the new center engine was ready, it was loaded with a set of skis that Balchen had designed, and he and Bennett flew it to Reindeer Lake about 200 mi. north of Le Pas, Canada. They stayed there for a week and, although the skis were satisfactory, they reduced the plane's performance so much that it firmly convinced them that the Pole flight could not be made without that more powerful engine in the nose. They returned to Dearborn and left recommendations for a few minor changes with the Ford engineers.

A number of transatlantic attempts had been made during 1927 and 1928 after the *America*'s flight; too many failed. One of the successful crossings in an east–west direction was made by the *Bremen,* a German single-engine Junkers W-33, flown by two Germans and an Irishman: Baron Ehrenfried Guenther von Huenefeld, and two pilots—Capt. Hermann Koehl and Col. James C. Fitzmaurice. The crew of *Bremen* departed Dublin for New York on 12 April 1928.

The *Bremen* ran into bad weather when it reached the North American coast. The plane drifted 400 mi. northward in the clouds because of strong southeasterly winds. When the plane ran low on fuel and finally broke out of the clouds in daylight, the crew expected to see some form of habitation below but saw only a forested, arctic landscape. They landed on the ice on a small catch basin at the top of an island in a space that was only about 700 ft. long with a stone wall at one end. It was only because of a fierce wind that the *Bremen* could land in such a short space without more damage than a deformed landing gear and a bent propeller.

The word was quickly radioed to North America that the first successful plane flight from Europe to the New World had been completed with a forced landing on Greenly Island, Labrador, about 800 mi. from Quebec. The world press now had another sensational aviation episode and a race began to get firsthand stories about the rescue of the stranded flyers and retrieval of the plane. The first to arrive at the scene were Clarence A. "Duke" Schiller, famous Canadian bush pilot, and Dr. Louis Cuisinier. Fitzmaurice was flown out to Murray Bay, Canada, by Schiller and told what had happened and what was needed to repair the plane so it could continue the flight.

In the United States, C. B. Allen suggested sending a large plane to help in the rescue. Herbert Bayard Swope, owner of the *New York World* and Allen's boss, ordered reporter Charles J. V. Murphy to the scene and asked Byrd to furnish the Ford trimotor and his two famous pilots for the trip. Byrd consented when Swope suggested that the publicity would probably stimulate more financial support for his expedition.[6] However, the antarctic plane was not yet ready, and a standard Ford trimotor transport was to be substituted. Bennett, Balchen, Murphy, and Tom Mulroy, Byrd's engineer on the *Chantier,* immediately flew to the Ford factory at Dearborn; both pilots had bad colds and Bennett remarked wearily, "We're a fine pair to go rescuing somebody else!"[7]

Edsel Ford noticed that both men seemed ill when they arrived and suggested they spend the day in the Ford Hospital while the substitute trimotor was being readied. Bennett complied, but Balchen knew how much work was required and wanted to be on hand. Mechanics worked all night transforming the plane from a standard passenger transport by taking out the wicker chairs and installing two large fuel tanks. Although weak and nauseated, Balchen loaded skis, spare parts, a propeller, two spare wheels for the *Bremen,* and cans of benzol, the special fuel that the Junkers used. Balchen and Bennett took off with the Ford for Murray Bay on 20 April in rain and poor visibility, accompanied by Murphy, Mulroy, and two mechanics. En route the plane's heater did not work well and everyone was very uncomfortable. Bennett, dressed in Balchen's leather flying suit (which he borrowed because it was warmer than his own) spent the time dozing while Balchen flew on instruments. When they broke out into the clear, Balchen could see that his friend was perspiring despite the cold and felt his forehead. It was obvious Bennett had a high fever. Balchen offered to return but Bennett said he would rather go on and would relieve Bernt in a little while. He fell asleep and Balchen continued to fly to Murray Bay.[8]

They arrived in the evening and landed on the ice of Lake St. Agnes on wheels. These were exchanged for skis and Balchen talked with Fitzmaurice and Schiller about the situation at Greenly Island. Meanwhile, Bennett was taken to a nearby farmhouse and put to bed. Murphy stayed with Bennett, and when Balchen checked later, it was clear that Bennett was in no shape to fly. When a doctor arrived, Bennett's temperature was more than 100°. Balchen told Bennett that he would fly to Greenly with Fitzmaurice as copilot and check on Bennett when he returned. However, he began to feel weak himself and wondered if he were catching whatever Bennett had.

"I don't know whether I'll be here when you get back," Bennett said. "But you go up and get them. And promise me one thing—that in case anything should happen, you will go to the Antarctic with Byrd."[9] Balchen promised he would and stood by while plans were being discussed to evacuate Bennett to a hospital in Quebec where he was later diagnosed as having lobar pneumonia.

Balchen bid Bennett goodbye and departed on 23 April for Seven Islands for refueling before proceeding to Greenly Island; aboard were Fitzmaurice, Murphy, and Ernest Koeppen, a German mechanic.

No landing strip existed at Seven Islands, so Balchen landed on a narrow strip of ice in the bay. A dog team delivered some fuel from a nearby village. While they waited, Balchen began to feel very weak, but planned to take off for the return flight that afternoon. The snow was sticky as the temperature rose above freezing. He knew he would not be able to get the plane airborne because of the sticky conditions, so remained in a small boardinghouse nearby until the early morning hours when the temperature fell below freezing.

The flight to Greenly Island took 5½ hr. When he circled the island and saw the large green wing of the *Bremen*, he wondered how they had managed a landing within such a small area. Balchen landed on the ice in the lee of the island where he met von Huenefeld and Koehl.

The task was to get their plane from its perch on top of the island to the ice below. People from the other side of the island arrived with dog teams. As Balchen supervised, the tail skid was tied to the dogs, and they hauled it downhill to the bay ice.

Meanwhile, Bennett's condition had worsened. Doctors made an urgent call to the Rockefeller Foundation in New York requesting serum be sent immediately. John D. Rockefeller Jr. and Harry F. Guggenheim located two types of pneumococcic serum at the Rockefeller Institute in New York. Lindbergh, who happened to be a guest at the Guggenheim home, volunteered to fly the vials to Quebec. He departed Curtiss Field, Long Island, in an Army observation plane and plunged through blinding snowstorms. But he was too late. Bennett had died at 1000 25 April 1928. Balchen learned of his friend's death the next day when a dog team brought a message from Mulroy: "FLOYD BENNETT DIED YESTERDAY."[10]

Bennett, one of the world's foremost aviators, had died at age 38; Balchen had lost his closest American friend. "I felt quite lonely up there," he said later.

Bennett's body was flown to New York and laid in state in his naval uniform at the 71st Regiment Armory. It was then transported to Washington, D.C., for burial with full military honors at Arlington National Cemetery and laid to rest near the grave of Adm. Robert E. Peary, famous arctic explorer, whose claim to have reached the North Pole in 1909 would, like Byrd's, be challenged in the years ahead.

Byrd announced that the plane he would use to fly over the South Pole would be named *Floyd Bennett* in his honor. An Associated Press news release commented that Bennett "had captured the admiration of the world and the love of all who knew him by his unassuming manner, his quiet courage, his lack of ostentation."[11] The airport, then being constructed at Barren Island, New York, was named Floyd Bennett Field and opened to flying in May 1931. That year, a permanent memorial was erected in Warrensburg, New York, Bennett's hometown.

There was nothing Balchen could do when he heard the sad news but transport von Huenefeld and Koehl while others got the German plane ready to fly. He flew to Murray Bay, where the Ford's skis were exchanged for wheels. It was announced that the fliers would not give interviews until they had paid their last respects at Bennett's funeral in Washington, D.C. Next morning, with the three *Bremen* fliers and Herta Junkers aboard, Balchen took off in poor weather conditions and had to fly close to the ground because of severe icing conditions in the clouds. He flew at progressively lower altitudes down the Lake Champlain Valley and the Hudson River. The clouds kept lowering and when he arrived at the Bear Mountain Bridge at New York City, he had no choice but to fly under it to get to Curtiss Field for refueling.

A big reception was planned for the *Bremen* fliers in Washington, D.C., and Bennett's funeral was scheduled at Arlington. Because it was doubtful that the flight could be made safely from New York, the three *Bremen* fliers left by train and arrived after the funeral but participated in a short memorial service at the gravesite the next day. Balchen desperately wanted to attend the funeral and departed later when the weather eased but had to turn back near Trenton, New Jersey.

The three returned to New York and were given a parade up Broadway and a reception at City Hall. Balchen was invited but was in no mood to participate. The loss of his valued friend was too much on his mind and he felt he did not belong among those celebrating the *Bremen*'s flight.[12]

On 2 May, the *Bremen* fliers returned to Washington, D.C., for a formal visit where they were greeted by President Coolidge at the White House, met Lindbergh, and were introduced at a session of the House of Representatives. A special bill was passed awarding each the Distinguished Flying Cross, the first such award to airmen who were not

American citizens. Balchen was puzzled when he heard about the awards but made no comment.[13]

Messages of condolence for Bennett to his family arrived from aviators and friends from all around the world. The unselfish act of assistance by Bennett and Balchen had received much attention in the world press. The German Reichstag voted to honor Bennett "for self-sacrificing and timely aid to Captain Koehl, Baron von Huenefeld, and Colonel Fitzmaurice in Canada at the cost of his life."[14]

The years 1927 and 1928 marked a period when airmen around the world were trying to set speed, altitude, endurance, and distance records and advance aviation by making improvements in aircraft that would set new marks. Many risked their lives in uncharted skies in search of gold and glory. Of those who tried to defy the odds by flying the world's largest oceans in 1927, thirteen had lost their lives in the Atlantic, seven in the Pacific, and five in preparing for transocean flights. But aeronautical technology was progressing rapidly. The proof was in the flights that were successful. Australian Charles E. Kingsford-Smith flew 7,300 mi. from Oakland, California, to Australia; two Italians, Arturo Ferrarin and Carlo del Prete, set a new nonstop distance record of 4,466 mi. from Rome to Brazil; a U.S. Army Air Corps officer, John A. Macready, set a new altitude record of 38,704 ft. The *Graf Zeppelin* arrived in the United States from Germany after a 111 hr. flight. Amelia Earhart became the first woman to cross the Atlantic by air.

One of the most notable flights in the spring of 1928 was made without much publicity. On 16 April Capt. George H. Wilkins, an Australian, with Lt. Carl Ben Eielson, an Alaskan bush pilot, had flown from Point Barrow, Alaska, to Spitsbergen. It was a sensational 2,200 mi. nonstop flight in a single-engine, ski-equipped Lockheed Vega cabin monoplane over barren polar wastes, most of which had never before been viewed by humans. Immediately afterward they began planning a similar venture in antarctica. Within the same year, the two became the first in history to fly over both polar regions. When Wilkins first announced his plans to go to antarctica and use an aircraft to make surveys, Byrd thought Wilkins might be planning a flight to the South Pole. Wilkins assured Byrd that he was only interested in survey work.[15]

The history of aviation in the antarctic is short compared to that of the arctic. The remoteness of the area, its lack of importance from a strategic and economic point of view, plus the greater difficulties involved in supporting operations there has contributed to this difference. The South Pole is located on a vast plateau more than 10,000 ft. above sea level at the center of an area of ice and snow as large as the United States and Mexico.

With the South Pole flight as his main objective, Byrd intended to sail south in September 1928 from New York through the Panama Canal to the West Coast before proceeding to New Zealand and finally to antarctica. He planned to establish his primary base at the Bay of Whales by late December on the western side of the Ross Ice Barrier near where Roald Amundsen had established Framheim, his 1911 base. This site was to be called Little America and was chosen because Amundsen had reported very few high winds in that area, an important consideration for flying. Several subbases or supply depots were planned toward the South Pole about 100 mi. apart, where the planes could land in bad weather to survive the fierce storms and be used as launching points for scientific exploration.

Byrd estimated that the expedition would cost more than $450,000, but he eventually collected more than $750,000, much of it because of the enthusiastic backing of Gilbert Grosvenor, president of the National Geographic Society. To downplay the South Pole flight as the primary objective, he stressed to all he contacted that the purpose of the expedition was scientific.[16]

Byrd operated from an office in New York at the Biltmore Hotel with an office manager, personnel director, secretaries, and clerks to keep track of the expedition's arrangements. Flying operations were established at the Army's Mitchel Field on Long Island, where Balchen tested the aircraft.

There were thousands of decisions to be made about personnel, scientific equipment, and supplies. They would be cut off from civilization for at least a year, and there would be no opportunity to make up deficiencies. There had to be specially designed arctic houses, a workshop for the scientists, a complete machine shop for repairs, and protection for the planes. Among the thousands of items needed were sleds, dogs, tents, clothing, sleeping bags, footgear, skis, food, radio equipment, and a large assortment of tools. Most important to accomplish the flight to the Pole was the selection of planes, lubricants, and gasoline that could function in the extreme temperatures that would reach to −75°F.

One of the air tragedies of 1928 occurred when Umberto Nobile attempted a flight to the North Pole in the airship *Italia* in May. He crashed onto the polar ice pack north of Spitsbergen, and the planes and men of seven nations joined in the hunt to find him and his crew. When Amundsen was given the message about Nobile, he immediately volunteered to lead an expedition to rescue him. On 18 June Amundsen and Leif Dietrichson, Balchen's cousin, departed Tromso, Norway, in a seaplane to begin the search. Amundsen and Dietrichson never returned. Nobile and some of his crew were rescued a month later.

While Byrd and his staff worked on the myriad details of seeking funds, acquiring equipment and supplies, and selecting personnel from the hundreds of volunteers who applied, Balchen was appointed chief pilot of the expedition and given *carte blanche* to organize the aviation division. He had thoroughly tested the Ford trimotor and had shaved more than 550 lb. of weight off its original construction as a civilian transport. He approved the selection of Harold G. June, a U.S. Navy chief petty officer and pilot, who was also a mechanic and an excellent radio operator. In June 1926 they loaded the Ford with 12,000 lb. of weight and took it up to 12,000 ft. in a 2 hr. test to ensure that it could clear the polar mountains.

Balchen and June also tested several other types of planes that were being considered to accompany the Ford. They chose a Fokker Super Universal with a 425 hp Pratt & Whitney Wasp engine as the utility plane for short reconnaissance flights; Byrd later named it *Virginia* after his home state. For aerial survey work, a Fairchild single-engine monoplane with the same type of engine was donated and christened *Stars and Stripes*. Both were fitted for skis and were flown to Canada for testing under stressful subzero conditions. A smaller, lighter plane made by General Aviation Corporation, nicknamed the "Pooper" by the pilots, was also donated, but this aircraft failed to reach the antarctic because it was too small and underpowered to serve a useful purpose.[17]

Balchen designed crates for the planes for shipment and compiled long lists of emergency survival equipment that he requisitioned from Canada and Norway. Balchen was an excellent draftsman, and he made engineering drawings for the planes' snow hangars, storage sheds, dog tunnels, and maintenance shacks, as well as detailed sketches as guides for prefabrication. He outlined how to make a roof of snow blocks, determine the height of snow excavation, height of the walls, the roof construction, and the incline needed to get the plane out of the hangar when ready to fly. His meticulous sketches proved extremely valuable.

Three mechanics joined the group, including E. J. "Pete" Demas, a young cabin boy who had been aboard the *Chantier* in 1926, Kenneth Bubier, and Benjamin Roth. For the flying crews, Dean C. Smith, a veteran airmail pilot, was recruited. Then Capt. Alton N. Parker, a U.S. Marine reservist pilot who had been flying with Transcontinental Western Air Express, was also approved. Army Air Corps Capt. Ashley C. McKinley, a veteran aerial photographer, was chosen to complete the flying contingent.

Byrd figured he would need about 40 or 50 men but realized he would be able to obtain only a few who would have had any experience in conditions of subzero cold and many months of darkness and light. Dr. Laurence M. Gould, a prominent geologist who would make mineralogical surveys, was named second in command. Dr. Francis D. Coman, a physician from Johns Hopkins Hospital in Baltimore, signed on as medical advisor and dietitian. The *New York Times* assigned Russell Owen, a reporter who had been at Spitsbergen, to follow Byrd's North Pole attempt. Two photographers were recruited to provide motion and still picture coverage.

Byrd decided to take a large contingent of 85 dogs, mostly Greenland huskies that had been donated, and persuaded two Alaskan dog drivers to go along. It was a wise move and the dogs contributed immeasurably to the success of the expedition. A Ford snowmobile with caterpillar treads was sent along to see how it would fare in the subzero cold. It was no match for the dogs, however, and eventually was abandoned.

Meanwhile, the *Samson* arrived from Norway at the Todd Shipyard in New York for renovation and outfitting. Balchen's uncle Captain Dietrichson was the skipper of a crew of Norwegians, mostly sealers.[18] The ship was renamed *City of New York* for the expedition. It was a barkentine of 515 tn., made of heavy timber about 34 in. thick. Over all was a sheathing of greenheart, a tough, slippery wood that would slide over ice and that could withstand the crushing of the ice. A small steam engine provided power to make a speed of about 6 kn when operated without sails.

When the equipment and supplies began to accumulate, it was evident that the *City of New York* could not handle it all. A larger freighter, the *Chelsea,* was provided and renamed the *Eleanor Bolling,* after Byrd's mother. But it was soon apparent that these two ships were not large enough to carry the mountain of equipment, supplies, food, the aircraft, and the spare parts that were being donated, very little of which was ever turned down. Magnus Konow, a Norwegian shipping and whaling magnate, was contacted and assigned two whale-factory ships named *Sir*

James Clark Ross and the *C.A. Larsen* to assist, with the understanding that they would also be used to search for and catch whales after being unloaded in New Zealand. The *City of New York* sailed from New York on 25 August; the *Eleanor Bolling* left Norfolk, Virginia, on 25 September, followed by the *Ross* with the dog drivers, dogs, their equipment, and 40 tn. of dog biscuits. All three transited the Panama Canal and headed directly for New Zealand.

The aircraft, gas, oil, and about 100 tn. of equipment and eleven of the expedition members, including Balchen, were loaded on the *Larsen* and departed Norfolk in mid-September. It stopped at San Pedro, California, where Byrd and others joined the expedition. The *Larsen* left San Pedro on 10 October 1928 and arrived at Wellington, New Zealand, on 5 November.

En route Balchen practiced celestial navigation to keep busy and extend his knowledge of the heavens in the southern hemisphere. Meanwhile, the *Ross* had taken the dogs to Dunedin where they were put on Quarantine Island until sailing for antarctica. The entire contingent moved to Dunedin, New Zealand, where everyone met for the first time in three months.[19]

The supplies at Dunedin filled two warehouses. Decisions had to be made over the next three weeks about what to take from the overabundance of supplies. Many uncertain factors and contingencies had to be considered in selecting what was needed. The essential items had to be loaded aboard the *City of New York,* plus the key personnel. It was thought that the *Eleanor Bolling,* although it had a metal hull, might not be strong enough to get through the ice pack but would go as far as it could. The *Larsen* and the *Ross,* after unloading, went to sea to seek whales and report their observations of the extent of the ice pack. This meant that the *City of New York* was loaded with hundreds of pounds of food, supplies, scientific instruments, and clothing. In addition, the Fairchild to be used for aerial photography had to be included and was packed in two crates. There was just room enough for these between the foremast and the mainmast. Alongside them were barrels of gasoline, oil, and components of several prefabricated houses. Eighty-five dog crates were stored aft along with 75 tn. of coal.[20]

The *City of New York* left Dunedin for antarctica on 2 December 1928. The ship was loaded well over the Plimsoll mark, the line that shows the safe depth to which a ship may be loaded. The *Eleanor Bolling* followed and had two missions: tow the *City* to the ice pack, and supply the *Bolling* with more coal when it got there. It would then return to Dunedin to bring down the two larger planes and the balance of the supplies. The *Larsen* would meet the *City* and take it in tow through the ice pack and leave when it reached the Ross Sea.

The *Larsen* was located on 10 December, and eight days later dropped the towline as the Ross Sea, relatively free of ice floes, appeared ahead. On Christmas day Balchen wrote in his diary: "25 December, 2400. Off Ross Ice Shelf."[21]

They had arrived at the northern edge of the ice shelf in front of the ice barrier and the next day made the first landing at Discovery Inlet. They sailed eastward along the face of this great ice cliff to the Bay of Whales, which was reached on 28 December. Balchen and others made a reconnaissance trip on dog sledges to look for a site for Little America. On 1 January 1929 they returned to the ship and the unloading began.

6 · To the South Pole

The ship *City of New York* eased into Discovery Inlet and inched up cautiously to the ice shelf under the precipitous sides of the Ross Ice Barrier. It was anchored by large iron hooks, and several men leaped off once it was firmly attached to the ice. They were eager for exercise, and strapped on skis to try them out. Balchen and fellow Norwegians Carl Petersen and Chris Braathen skied off to locate a site for Little America, but none could be found after skiing about 25 mi.

They reboarded and the ship was moved about 75 mi. along the Ross Ice Shelf to the Bay of Whales. Two dog teams, driven by Arthur Walden and Norman Vaughan, then took Byrd, Balchen, Petersen, and Braathen on a search for Framheim, the base site that Roald Amundsen had used in 1911. They sledged for about 15 mi. but could not find it and radioed the ship that they were making camp for the night. The next morning they scouted along the bay and came on an inlet, which Byrd promptly named Ver-sur-Mer after the *America*'s landing place in France. Nearby, they found a large flat area that all agreed was ideal for Little America. It had a good expanse for a flying field that would permit takeoffs in all directions. On New Year's Day 1929 the unloading began and the base building began.

By the middle of the month, the first prefabricated house was completed. One house was to be used as a mess hall and bunkhouse, another a work house for the administrative staff, and a third structure was to be used for storage and to accommodate a few of the men. Eventually, the camp would have a mess hall, gymnasium, blacksmith's forge, administrative room, garage for the Ford snowmobile, snow hangars for the planes, facilities for the dogs, equipment, and supplies, and three 60 ft. radio antennas.

To protect the houses from blowing away an excavation 5 ft. deep into the snow was made before the walls were put up. The two main houses were separated by about 200 yd. so that in case of fire in one of them or a break in the ice barrier the men would have some housing left. A tunnel, lined with food boxes and covered with canvas, was dug between the buildings to save everyone the discomfort of going outside. Storage rooms were made with blocks of snow and flat roofs so that drifting snow would blow off and not accumulate on top (because of high winds).

On 15 January the Fairchild FC-2W monoplane *Stars and Stripes* was uncrated and the engine warmed up. All three pilots flew it briefly, and on 27 January 1929 Balchen, with Byrd navigating and June acting as radio operator, flew east along the shoreline of the Ross Ice Barrier, where large mountain ranges had been reported by Amundsen in 1911. They found Scott's Nunatak protruding through the snow caps and then the Alexandra Mountains and King Edward VII Land.

Balchen described his first observations: "The barrier looked very flat from down below but as we got up, we could see that there were forces in motion there all the time. We could see pressure holes in the barrier, and sliding walls with pressure ridges. Nothing was stationary, something was taking place there all the time which would greatly influence the shape of the Bay of Whales."[1]

They ran into low clouds and snow squalls and turned south where other mountains loomed on the horizon. Flying closer, they saw 14 peaks sticking through the snow. Byrd named them the Rockefeller Mountains in honor of John D. Rockefeller, Jr., one of the chief contributors to the expedition. As Gould commented wryly, they were named after the signature on the $100,000 check.[2]

When they returned from the 5 hr. flight, they saw the *Eleanor Bolling* had just arrived from New Zealand with the Ford trimotor and the Fokker Universal and more supplies. The unloading proceeded very fast in the faint hope that the ship could make another supply run to New Zealand and back before the bay froze over. The unloading of the Ford and the Fokker was almost disastrous. As they were lowering the planes to the ice, a crack developed. The docking area suddenly split open near the barrier's edge and disintegrated. The entire slope sheared off part of the barrier and the ice broke up into three large pieces. Everyone put on life belts. The center section of the Ford lay on a broken ice fragment nearest the barrier, which began to tilt, causing the gap between the ice floe and the ship to widen gradually. Sides of aircraft boxes were quickly laid between the floe and the ship to act as a bridge. The plane's fuselage was then hoisted with a block and tackle up on the top of the barrier.

The planes were towed by dog teams the 4 mi. to Little America, assembled, and preflighted. The *Bolling* departed on 2 February for New Zealand after unloading its 440 tn. of supplies. There was little hope that the ship would return with the last of the supplies before the end of the month.

On 14 and 16 February Balchen and Dean Smith made test hops in the *Floyd Bennett,* and on 18 February Balchen, with Byrd and Lloyd Berkner as radio operator, took off for more exploration toward the east. Parker and June flew the Fairchild. When they ran into an overcast sky, the two planes turned southward toward the Rockefeller Mountains and in the southeast saw a high peak in the far distance that resembled the Matterhorn. They decided to return to base rather than fly toward it.

"Byrd told me to keep on an easterly course," Balchen recalled.

> We stayed on it and as we came right to the south of Little America, we had it on our right side and could see it about ten miles to the north. I asked Byrd where we were going. He said, "We're going home." So I said, if we're going home we have to turn back because Little America is behind us. He must have got his dead reckoning a little tangled up. If we had kept on going we would have wound up at McMurdo Sound. He wouldn't believe it but I insisted so he said, "All right, go home." We made a 90-degree turn and glided into camp.[3]

At this time the *Bolling* had to turn back from its planned return to antarctica from New Zealand because of the ice forming in the sea. On 22 February the *City of New York* departed, leaving Byrd and his 41 men on their own to spend the winter.

McKinley, the aerial photographer, was disappointed that he had not been asked to accompany June and Parker in the Fairchild. When it returned, he and Smith approached Byrd for permission to photograph the area to the east, because the weather was perfect for aerial mapping. Byrd reluctantly consented but asked them to fly along the barrier no farther than 75 mi., possibly because he was afraid they might discover something without him. They headed east and when they saw that the weather was also good to the southeast, they decided to photograph the Rocke-

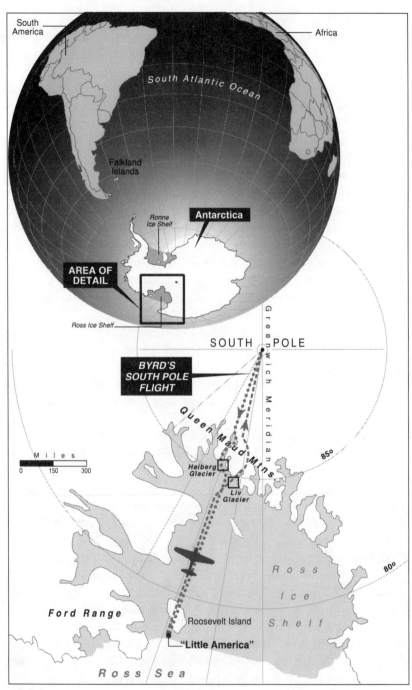

Map 2.

feller Mountains that Smith said "hardly deserve such a grand title as mountains; they are scattered cones of rock jutting up through the ice floor, none of them over a thousand feet high."[4]

Looking ahead, they saw a dark speck jutting from the horizon and decided to fly toward it while McKinley filmed it. It was a majestic mountain about 8,000 to 10,000 ft. high. They returned to Little America after 7 hr. of flying and told Byrd what they had done. With Balchen, Gould, and Owen looking on, Byrd asked Smith and McKinley to locate the mountain on a map. Smith tells of Byrd's reaction:

McKinley and I compared notes and conferred at some length.

"From our longitude here I'd say it lies pretty close to northeast by east, call it sixty degrees. I'd put it somewhere in here," and I drew a circle about thirty miles in diameter on the map.

Byrd spoke very seriously. "This is important. I congratulate you gentlemen on confirming my discovery. You have located this new land in almost exactly the same place where I saw it this morning."

"You saw it this morning?" exclaimed McKinley. "But you didn't say anything about it after the flight."

"No. I wanted to be sure before I announced it. But I did mark it on my map. Wait, I'll show you."

Byrd went into his room, closing the door behind him. We all sat mute. I caught Balchen's eye. He shrugged and rolled his eyes to the ceiling. Owen kept shaking his head, gently. Gould looked amused.

After about five minutes, Commander Byrd returned, spreading a map on the table.

"Here is the course of flight this morning," he said, pointing to a penciled line. "And over here is where I marked the new peak." He showed us a heavy cross, drawn with a softer pencil than the course of the flight itself. Sure enough, if transposed to my map his cross would fall close to the center of the circle.

"Now that you too have seen this mountain, I feel justified in announcing the discovery. I have decided to call the area Marie A. Byrd Land in honor of my wife. Russ, you are authorized to report this to the *Times*. Please let me check the story before you send it."

The commander shook hands with Mac, Lloyd and me. "Congratulations again on a splendid flight. This is a historic day."

McKinley and I walked together to the mess hall. "It takes keen vision to be a great explorer," he cracked. "You and I will never be great explorers."[5]

The photographs that McKinley had taken were excellent. When Gould examined them he was eager to make a geological survey of the Rockefeller Mountains, which had not been planned before. Gould persuaded Byrd that such a survey would justify the scientific purposes of the expedition. On 7 March two dog teams were readied to go toward the mountains about 140 mi. away. At the same time, Balchen, with Gould and June aboard the single-engine Fokker Universal, headed toward the mountains and landed. The plan was to establish a camp and keep the plane there until Gould had completed his survey. They parked the plane, piled snow blocks on the plane's skis to hold it down, threw ropes over the wings, attached them to the skis, and piled more snow on top. They erected a tent and put their personal equipment inside. It was too late for Gould to make theodolite readings, so they remained overnight in their sleeping bags. The next morning a high wind of about 60 MPH developed and the guylines attached to the plane's skis snapped. The wind had moved the plane a few feet, and as they shoveled frantically to put the weight of snow on the main and tail skis, it moved again. That was not enough so they tried to build a wall with blocks of snow around the plane.

The wind died down in the afternoon to give them a respite but picked up again, and the plane looked as though it was going to become airborne. Balchen went inside and found that the airspeed indicator registered a steady 60 MPH with gusts to 90 MPH. The blowing snow stung like needles as they struggled to tie the wings down. Each person took turns hanging on to the restraining ropes while another shoveled snow around the fuselage. By midnight, all three were exhausted and agreed that they should get everything out of the plane and dig down into the snow in case the plane was damaged or blew away. Meanwhile, the tent had been ripped and everything inside was saturated with snow. The wind shrieked for hours as they tried to rest in their sleeping bags.[6]

The wind died down the next morning and June tried to get Little America on the radio, but he got no reply. However, they heard his message and were not concerned at first. Balchen intended to fly back that night if the weather cleared, but it did not. After another night, the snow and wind increased and they spent still another day waiting. Balchen used the time sketching the mountain ranges they could see and associated them with the triangulation measurements Gould made.

On 14 March Balchen began to preflight the Fokker, but the wind had increased. Inside the plane the airspeed indicator showed gusts of 100 to 120 MPH. It was now too risky to get in the plane, and no one went inside it again. The snow that was holding the plane down eroded steadily. The men had no choice but to crawl into the tent and their sleeping bags and wait it out.

Balchen woke up first the next morning and saw the plane lying right-side up on the snow about a mile downwind. He decided to take a look at it. As soon as he started, a gust blew him off his feet and he was blown toward the plane at a fast clip on his back. He was able to brake himself near the plane and saw that it was so badly damaged it would never fly again. The landing gear had crumpled and the propeller had apparently been turning because the tips were curled forward and had hit the skis. Fortunately, the fuel tanks in the wings had not ruptured so there was fuel available if needed.

They were 140 mi. from Little America, and Balchen considered skiing back to the base but knew that Gould and June, inexperienced on skis, would never have been able to make it. They had a six-week supply of food, so they could wait until either the Fairchild or dog teams could be dispatched to pick them up. Finally, at dusk on 19 March they heard the Fairchild. They rushed out and laid out a "T" of orange flags to mark the wind direction. It was Smith, Byrd, and Malcolm P. Hanson, radio operator. Byrd decided that he, Gould, and Hanson would remain there while Balchen, Smith, and June would return to Little America. Smith and June returned later to retrieve the other three.

It had been a valuable experience and no one was hurt, but now only two aircraft were left. Many changes in plans were made to support the ground parties, including having one of the planes available for supply and rescue if necessary during their operations.

Balchen laid out a work schedule for the aviation section during the coming winter. He and his crew dug holes in the shelf ice for the Ford and Fairchild and then built hangars of snow blocks around them according to the plans Balchen had drawn previously. When the sun appeared for the last time on 17 April the men fell into a camp routine where all shared the housekeeping duties, including shoveling snow into the melter to provide water, hauling coal, and standing night watch. Everyone was to be at breakfast at 0800, have a make-it-yourself snack at noon, and dinner at 1700.

Radio communications were arranged every Saturday night so that expedition members could talk with their families. Some of the men gambled or played cards and backgammon; others spent their off-duty hours reading books from the 1,000-volume library or engaging in a hobby; Braathen, for example, painstakingly built a model of the *City of New York*. A few took classes at the "Antarctic University" from the specialists in geology, aeronautics, navigation, and radio repair. Balchen, June, and Smith taught aviation groundschool courses. McKinley lectured on aerial surveying. Parker decided to read the *Encyclopedia Britannica* starting with the first page of the first volume. Motion pictures were shown and on several occasions musical shows were staged spoofing the life they were forced to lead in their snowbound world. Every Saturday night at 2300, radio stations WGY, Schenectady, and KDKA, Pittsburgh, beamed programs directly to Little America.

Byrd kept to himself much of the time in his private room. The others were crowded together into more than a dozen small buildings buried in the snow and traveled between them through eight-foot-high tunnels like a group of moles.

Balchen had his own ideas about what to do with his time when he could not work on the planes. He rechecked the performance computations on the Ford, drew fuel consumption curves for the different phases of the Pole flight, and set up a cruising chart. He had taken articles and books on aerodynamics to prepare himself further as a test pilot when he returned to the States and continued to carry his small slide rule with him to work out math problems. He kept a book in his knapsack titled *Engineering Aerodynamics* by Walter S. Diehl in case he had to spend hours snowed in because of a forced landing or caught out in a blizzard when skiing. In addition, he always carried a small paint box and sketch pad.[7]

It was Byrd's custom to take short walks for exercise when weather permitted. He would choose only one individual to go with him and would have probing, confidential talks to inquire what they thought about others. Balchen took the opportunity, when he was invited on one occasion, to tell him that he was completely satisfied that they could make the flight to the Pole without any difficulty. The total fuel consumption should be about 51 gal. per hour if the pilot followed the performance charts.

Without thinking about what Byrd's reaction might be, he mentioned that he was thinking of making a performance chart for the Fokker used on the North Pole flight in case Byrd would like to have it for his files. It was the wrong thing to say. Byrd immediately flew into a rage and told Balchen to forever stay away from making any performance reviews of that flight. When he saw that Balchen had taken the slide rule out of his pocket, he said, heatedly, "Forget about that slide rule! From now on you stick to flying. I'll do the figuring!"[8]

Balchen tried to forget the incident but recalled his own calculations at Spitsbergen, the long flight around the country in the Fokker when he and Bennett had kept a careful engine log, and the revealing remarks made later by Bennett. With the reaction brought on by the appearance of his slide rule, he suspected that Byrd knew now that he also knew the truth.

Vaughan, one of the dog handlers who was asked to accompany Byrd on one of his walks, said that Byrd put his questions in such a way that he demanded Vaughan's acquiescence. Vaughan noted in his memoirs,

> His words left me with the distinct impression that if I did not agree to support him unreservedly and thereby become a member of his loyal legion, I would not be one of the boys. I think Byrd was afraid he would need to call on his men later to back up his claims of what had happened in Antarctica. It seemed important for him to know that if his critics tried to deny his achievements or disregard the data he had collected, we would stand loyally with him and tell the truth.[9]

One of the objectives Balchen had during the wintering over was to rebuild the fuel system on the Ford so that fuel could be pumped to either wing through a selector with hand pumps near the pilots' seats. This was done in the snow hangar, which had to be heated so he and the mechanics could work. Although outside temperatures were −40° to −50°, they could work in relative comfort with gloves and sometimes with bare hands as long as they were near a blow torch or heated metal parts.

Martin Ronne, the oldest man on the expedition, worked continuously on designing better clothing and on trail tents based on drawings Balchen made. They designed the Balchen–Ronne tent, which was later marketed in Norway for many years. Balchen and Sverre Strom built a sled based on one originally designed by Fridtjof Nansen, Norwegian scientist and statesperson, whom Balchen considered one of the greatest arctic explorers. He made a stress analysis of it and they overhauled the sledges to make them lighter and stronger. They were shortened by one section when Balchen's analysis took into account the dogs' capabilities, which had not been considered by previous sledge designers.[10]

Owen, the *New York Times* reporter, who had also been at Spitsbergen, was a keen observer of the men with whom he lived so closely. Always looking for colorful information about them to radio to his paper, he described Balchen at work:

> I ducked through a tiny hole into the igloo around the front of the Fairchild this afternoon and found the Chief Pilot and two mechanics trying to get the carburetor off. It was forty-five below outside, and at least thirty below in the igloo, although there was a gasoline blowtorch burning in one corner. There was a faint blue light shining through the top of the walls, and yellow shone through the canvas covering the roof. A small pit had been dug under the engine, and there was the Chief Pilot with bare hands, wearing his usual sunny smile, working away with tools that would have burned anyone else, they were so cold. Occasionally he would have to take hold of an engine strut to support himself, and when he got loose he would thrust his hand up past searing metal, unscrew it and take it out.
>
> "There, that is out," he would say, and smile, and walk over and put it down carefully on a piece of canvas. Then he would run his hands through the blue flame of the blowtorch once or twice and go back to his cold task.[11]

The sun made its appearance for a few minutes on 24 August to mark the end of the long winter darkness. Balchen described what he saw in an artist's terms:

> The horizon got redder and redder every morning as the sun was approaching. But this day, at high noon, we could see the gleam of sunlight coming in over us and streaking down from the north towards us. The barrier and the snow had a purple bluish glow, and we could see the rays of the sun striking down over the snow. We had some light scattered clouds over us. The lower side of them had gotten a golden glow from the sun rays coming over this rose red horizon to the north. Above in the zenith the sky was a turquoise cold blue. It was a sign for us to get ready for the coming season's activities.[12]

The antarctic winter of cold and darkness had taken a toll on the crew in different ways, as they each adjusted to the work they were assigned and how they chose to spend their off-duty time. After their walk together, Byrd seemed aloof toward Balchen. In an original first edition of his memoirs (which was destroyed by the publisher under circumstances that will be discussed in Chapter 15), Balchen commented,

> We have been living together half a year now and I still do not know
> Commander Byrd any better. Even in the confinement of Little Amer-
> ica, where the rest of us are drawn to each other more closely by the
> darkness and the homesickness, he has managed to hold himself apart.
> The men do not understand his cold detachment, so they go instead to
> Larry Gould with their various problems. You could put it this way:
> Commander Byrd is a commander but not a leader.[13]

As daylight increased, everyone began working overtime to meet Byrd's
schedule to make the Pole flight. Balchen saw a personnel problem developing among the mechanics and felt that their team spirit had dissipated.
They scowled at one another and made sarcastic remarks behind one another's backs. He came on three of them engaged in a violent argument,
each insisting that he alone was responsible for servicing the Ford. He explained that they were all assigned to both aircraft and their job was to
work together and help each other whenever they could. They then told
Balchen that Commander Byrd had taken them individually for a walk
and told each one that the responsibility for the planes rested on his
shoulders, and he should watch the others and report at once if they detected any disloyalty among them. Balchen let them know that he was in
charge of the aviation unit, that he reported to Byrd, and they reported to
him.[14] These frequent walks with individuals were a strong indication to
Balchen of Byrd's increasing paranoia and his obsession about loyalty, a
trait that would become more pronounced as time passed.

"Why does Commander Byrd continue to sow these little seeds of jeal-
ousy," Balchen asked himself.

> Is it a perverse amusement that leads him to pit one man against an-
> other? Harold June and Dean Smith and the other pilots have all been
> taken on these little walks of his, and Byrd has hinted confidentially to
> each of them that he will be the chief pilot over the Pole. Night after
> night I lie in my bunk, trying to understand him. There is no doubt
> that he is capable of brash courage, as he showed when he voluntarily
> risked his life in the rescue flight to the Rockefeller Mountains when
> there was no real need of his going, or the time he unhesitatingly
> jumped overboard to save a seaman from the icy Bay of Whales. Is it
> devotion to his men, and if so, how do you reconcile this with his dis-

trust of them? Is it a desire for public acclaim, then? Or does a deep-seated inferiority require him over and over to prove himself?

Sometimes I think it will be easier to solve the mystery of the South Pole than to find an answer to this man.[15]

Balchen confronted Byrd about his practice of telling individuals that he depended on them personally and quickly learned that Byrd did not like anyone questioning his leadership or personnel management. Others had similar confrontations with Byrd, especially Owen. Byrd insisted on cen-soring and rewriting Owen's dispatches to his paper to the point where Owen, in frustration, reportedly took to his bed for days at a time in a lethargic state.[16] Byrd never accepted the principle that an American jour-nalist was free to report what he observed and, short of war, did not have to submit his news reports to anyone for censorship.[17] To Byrd, not being allowed to approve Owen's dispatches to his newspaper was evidence of disloyalty—a trait he absolutely could not tolerate. Byrd is believed to have considered him the most disloyal of all those on the expedition.[18]

This anxiety about disloyalty led Byrd to form a secret brotherhood he called the Loyal Legion. Those invited to join were asked to sign an oath that they would not divulge the fact that it existed. An extract of one lengthy sentence in the oath stated,

> I will hold as confidential and sacred matter anything whatever con-nected with the Loyal Legion, nor will I, by any act whatever, make an effort to learn the names of the other members of the fraternity; that in case of disloyalty displayed in a crowd when you are present, I will act in response to a predetermined signal and a predetermined course of action; that I will strive just as faithfully after the expedition ends to maintain its spirit of loyalty and will oppose any traitors to it then, as now. In short, I . . . will protect this expedition against [traitors] from within."[19]

Those who signed the oath were reportedly implored by Byrd years after the expedition to destroy any reference to the Loyal Legion in correspon-dence. Balchen apparently never knew about the Legion, because the oath or the Loyal Legion is not mentioned in any of his writings or diaries. He may have been one of those that Byrd considered a "traitor" because he was concerned about Balchen's knowing that the Fokker had not reached the North Pole.

Byrd's aloofness and obvious feelings of insecurity bothered some of the men. Byrd valued his solitude, and he stayed in his room and maintained distance from subordinates. Ill at ease among the men, he usually passed on any rebukes or criticisms about someone's actions or decisions through Gould.

The supplies and equipment that were to be loaded aboard the *Floyd Bennett* for the Pole flight were carefully inventoried and weighed. Every item was weighed to the ounce, including not only the clothing, food, camera, and plane equipment but even such small items as scissors, toilet kits, towels, sheath knives, pocket compasses, watches, and pencils. The maximum takeoff weight of the Ford, its four-person crew, and cargo was figured at 15,300 lb. Of the cargo weight, 1,400 lb. was survival equipment consisting of tents, sleeping bags, sleds, skis, extra clothing, and food. Then there was the weighty photographic equipment that McKinley needed to make an aerial survey of the route between Little America and the Pole. It was a 1,600 mi. roundtrip between the two points, but it could not be made without refueling at some time during the flight. A depot of supplies and fuel would be established about 400 mi. south, directly on the flight path to the Pole.

It took about 10 days to dig the Ford out of the snow hangar and attach the wings. On 13 October 1929 Gould left with his nine-person geological party and five sledge teams of nine dogs each for the trek to survey the Queen Maud Range and look for minerals and fossils. They were to set up a series of small depots along a line pointing from Little America toward the Axel Heiburg Glacier at the foot of the Queen Maud mountains. The final depot would be the refueling point for the Ford on its return from the South Pole flight. Gould's party would also act as a radio station for weather reports and relay messages between the Ford and Little America.

Balchen designed a movable shed he called Noah's Arch, which was pulled over the planes' engines so they could be serviced out of the wind. When the Ford was ready, Balchen and Dean Smith made several load, speed, and fuel consumption test flights and confirmed that the average fuel consumption would be 51 gal. per hour at normal cruising speeds. This done, the first order of business was to use it to supply the depot at the foot of the Queen Maud Range. Byrd selected Smith as the pilot, June as copilot, McKinley as photographer, and himself as navigator. Balchen remained behind to handle radio communications at the base, along with Petersen.

The Ford left in good weather on 18 November. Meanwhile, Gould's geological ground party on dog sledges had made 200 mi. at a good speed of about 20 mi. a day, and Smith was able to follow the party's trail. Messages and cigarettes were dropped when they saw them below. Smith landed the plane at the foot of the range and the group set up the depot with supplies and fuel. They took off again and headed east. Balchen soon received a message at Little America that they were experiencing a very high fuel consumption and had decided to return to Little America immediately. They reported crossing a large area of deep crevasses about 120 mi. away, then suddenly went off the air.

After a couple of hours without any communication, Balchen decided to look for them with Petersen. The two loaded 20 five-gallon cans of gasoline and some oil in case Smith had landed out of gas. A large soldering lamp was added for heat to help start the engines. As Balchen took off, Petersen received a radio message from Joe de Ganahl, radio operator with the Gould trail party, that he thought they could expect to find that the Ford had landed in a very rough area with large snowdrifts and a rough surface. Knowing the approximate latitude of that area, Balchen felt sure Smith would be following the ground party's trail. He was right; they sighted the plane about midnight.

Balchen circled several times, lined up for the approach, and landed safely despite huge ice ruts. Smith had made a miraculous landing in the heavier Ford across heavily corrugated ridges with deep furrows channeled in the hard ice and was very lucky not to have cracked up. Balchen found Byrd and the others tired and dirty in their tent; McKinley had slipped while trying to drain oil from one of the engines and was covered from head to foot with oil. The *Floyd Bennett* was indeed out of gas and the group was very pleased that Balchen had thought to bring extra fuel.

After the plane was refueled, Balchen and Petersen offered to help get the engines hand-cranked, but Byrd assured them that they could take care of it themselves, so Balchen took off for Little America to await their return. Hour after hour went by and the Ford failed to show up. After 17 hours without any radio communication with the *Floyd Bennett*, Balchen and Petersen took off again in the Fairchild with another 100 gal. of gas, oil, a stepladder, and tools in case some engine malfunction had developed. They vowed they would not return to Little America until the Ford was in the air. They landed near the plane and found it in good condition but everyone was thoroughly fatigued after many hours of cranking. They had started one of the engines but could not start the other two. After trying for several hours, they were so tired that they had drained the oil from each engine and went to sleep.

Balchen took the booster coil from the Fairchild's engine and had all three of the Ford's engines going within an hour. After Balchen checked the engines thoroughly, Smith, Byrd, and the other two climbed on board hurriedly and took off. They apparently were so eager to get away that they took off without cleaning up the materials they had left. Balchen and Petersen loaded the tent, sleeping bags, five pairs of skis, and unused supplies aboard the Fairchild and tried to take off. Balchen ran up the Fairchild's engine briskly but could not get the tail ski free. Petersen got out to shake it loose and Balchen started to taxi as slowly as he dared while Petersen ran alongside and hauled himself in on top of the pile of sleeping bags. The Fairchild bumped and smashed on the uneven surface so violently that Balchen was afraid the skis would be badly damaged, but eventually the plane lifted off. Balchen remembered that experience as "one of the roughest takeoffs I ever had."[20] Petersen recalled the two trips to rescue the Ford as the most interesting part of the South Pole expedition.[21]

After his return to Little America, Byrd, obviously in a bad mood, invited Balchen for one of his walks. Byrd asked why the Ford had such high fuel consumption and Balchen said he would go over the whole engine installation to find out the cause. Then Byrd asked why they had not been able to start the Ford's engines and why Balchen had not instructed them in cold weather starting procedures. And why was it that Balchen could start the engines when no one else could? Balchen had no answer except that they had not heated the engines properly before being cranked up.[22]

What Balchen found during his inspection of the engine was that one of the Ford's fuel pumps had developed a leak underneath the pilot's seat, which June had tried to fix in flight with chewing gum and heavy tape. The mechanics also discovered several small leaks in the fuel lines, connections, and pumps that were promptly repaired. Because the mechanics worked for him, Balchen thought Byrd blamed him personally for the fuel leaks that had caused the forced landing. Instead he asked, "How is it you always do the right thing? Why do I always have to come back to you? I made up my mind a long time ago you would never be my pilot, but now I have no choice. You will fly to the South Pole with me."[23]

Balchen was surprised; he thought Smith would be chosen because he had made the rehearsal flight. If it had not been for the fuel consumption incident on the return flight from the depot, several also thought Smith would have been chosen. Smith wrote in his autobiography:

> During the winter Byrd had told us he would attempt to apportion the important flights among Balchen, Parker and me. June had relinquished any first-pilot flying in order to act as co-pilot and radio operator. Each pilot must have prayed he'd be the one to get the polar assignment. But all of us knew that Balchen was almost certain to get it. Although of the three, I had the most flying experience, any of us should have ample skill to make the flight, and Bernt had by far the greatest survival skills. Disappointed as I was, this was the sensible choice.[24]

Balchen was pleased at being selected; his only regret was that he and Floyd Bennett would not make the trip together. Balchen believed that Smith was especially hurt by the decision, "But as my friend and as a man he took it fine."[25]

After checking the three engines and the gas lines, Balchen took the plane for a test hop and found the gas consumption was exactly as he had said it would be: 51 gal. per hour. He reported that the plane was ready for the flight to the Pole whenever the commander wanted to go.[26]

On Thanksgiving Day, 28 November 1929, the geological party radioed a weather report to Little America: "Perfect visibility. No clouds anywhere."[27] The time had come for the epic flight. The crew consisted of Byrd as navigator, June as copilot and radio operator, McKinley as photographer, and Balchen as pilot. Mechanics checked the plane over for the last time. Five-gallon gas cans were passed hand-to-hand by a line of men to a mechanic on the top of the wing who poured them into the wing tanks. Others helped load the equipment. The top of the fuselage gas tank was covered with sleeping bags and the aisle was filled with a dismantled sled, skis, ropes, and a tent, plus 1,200 lb. of personal and survival gear and enough food to sustain life for six to eight weeks if they were forced down. The total weight was at the absolute maximum load for a safe takeoff. At the last minute Byrd insisted that an additional 250 lb. of food be added "just in case." To Balchen's dismay, two large white canvas bags were hastily thrown into the cabin.

Balchen told Byrd they were now overloaded. Either food or fuel would probably have to be dumped overboard when they got to the Queen Maud Mountains to climb up to and clear the plateau. Balchen told the crew loading the plane to place the two food bags on top of the pile of equipment near the door so that they could be easily thrown out if necessary.

When all was in readiness to accomplish Byrd's fundamental reason for being in the antarctic—that is, fly over the South Pole—Byrd and McKinley with his photo equipment took their places in the rear; June crept forward over the equipment to his radio station. Balchen gave the *Floyd Bennett* full power, and they headed for the South Pole. The weather was ideal. After nearly 5 hr. they passed over the geological party and dropped messages, some chocolate, and cigarettes.

Balchen started climbing after passing over the trail party and headed toward the mountains to search for the best route to the polar plateau. The top was thought to be about 9,500 ft. above sea level, which meant that the plane would have to climb to an altitude of 10,000 ft. to get over it safely. Balchen climbed slowly up the long floor of the glacier, fighting heavy downdrafts and vicious turbulence. As he approached 8,500 ft., with the engines at full throttle and the rate-of-climb indicator at zero, the Ford's ceiling had been reached with the load they had and was approaching a stall. The extra 250 lb. was too much. It had to go and Balchen shouted to throw out one of the 125 lb. bags.

The Ford rose grudgingly to 9,500 ft. but no more. He ordered the second bag out and he slowly coaxed the plane up to about 9,700 ft. The turbulence was severe as the plane approached the surface of the glacier, but Balchen expected to get some updraft at the top and barely managed to get the Ford to clear the flat polar plateau stretched ahead. He had to fly at full throttle for about 1½ hr. to maintain the altitude above the surface. He was grateful that the engines ran faultlessly.

In his memoirs, Balchen gave more details about the approach to the Pole:

> According to my dead reckoning, we should be at the Pole in another fourteen minutes. I send a message back to Byrd on the trolley cable that connects the cockpit with the navigator's compartment. Fourteen minutes later, at 1:14 in the morning, Byrd sends a message forward on the trolley for June to broadcast to the base: "We have reached the South Pole."
>
> We make a circle in the direction which would be westward, except that here everything is north. The trapdoor behind me opens, and Byrd drops an American flag on the spot, weighted down with a stone from Floyd Bennett's grave, and we turn north again. I am glad to leave.

Somehow our very purpose here seems insignificant, a symbol of man's vanity and intrusion on this eternal world. The sound of our engines profanes the silence as we head back to Little America.[28]

Byrd composed a radio message that represented the accomplishment of his dream: "My calculations indicate that we reached the vicinity of the South Pole. Flying high for a survey. The airplane is in good shape, crew all well. Will soon turn north. We can see an almost limitless plateau. Our departure from the Pole was at 1:25 P.M."[29]

As he looked over the vast wasteland of ice and snow, the ever-present artist in Balchen reacted to his surroundings as they eased down the Axel Heiberg Glacier instead of the inbound route up the Liv Glacier they had flown. Looking down on the glacier flowing from the polar plateau in the sun, he said it was one of the most beautiful sights he had ever seen. He was impressed by "the green blue shadows, the cold colors and the dark brown and black sandstone of the mountains, on the steep, rocky sides, and far out in the north the dull turquoise blue sky with wisps of clouds."[30]

The depot at the foot of the Queen Maud Range was easily located and they landed beside the supply cache at 0445. They dumped 200 gal. of fuel into the wing tanks and left for Little America about 0600.

They arrived at the base at 1008, with about 75 gal. of gas left— enough for about 1½ hr. of flying. Just as Balchen had computed, the average consumption on the flight had been 51.7 gal. per hour. The total flying time was 17 hr. 34 min. out of the 18 hr. 43 min. they had been gone. (The extra hour and nine minutes were spent on the ground refueling.)

The entire group of expedition members was lined up and cheered as Balchen brought the *Floyd Bennett* to a halt. As the four emerged from the plane, they were picked up and carried to the mess hall for a celebration.

Balchen had been sitting so long that he was stiff and sore. He slipped out of the mess hall quietly and went skiing for a couple of hours with Strom and Braathen.

Balchen reviewed the flight in his mind while everyone was celebrating. As on the flight across the Atlantic, Byrd had not taken a single sextant shot to ascertain that they had actually reached the South Pole. There are no significant landmarks that identify the vicinity of the South Pole, so it was determined solely by Balchen computing the speed and the time that the aircraft had flown and estimating when the aircraft *should* have arrived over the southernmost point on earth.

Nevertheless, the day was a supreme one in Commander Byrd's life. The *San Francisco Chronicle* summarized that "a wonder-surfeited world can still feel a tremendous thrill" at Byrd's feat. President Herbert Hoover declared it a magnificent Thanksgiving Day gift to the nation after the stock market crash of the month before. The president immediately dispatched a radio message to Byrd:

> I know that I speak for the American people when I express their universal pleasure at your successful flight over the South Pole. We are proud of your courage and your leadership. We are glad of proof that the spirit of adventure still lives.
>
> Our thoughts of appreciation include also your companions in the flight and your colleagues, whose careful and devoted preparations have contributed to your great success.[31]

Byrd also received messages of praise for his achievement from Army and Navy officials, diplomats, governors, and members of national and international scientific and geographic societies. While Byrd was basking in the triumph, a bill sponsored by Virginia Sen. Claude Swanson was whisked through Congress without roll call or debate and was signed by Hoover on 21 December 1929. Byrd was promoted by this special legislation directly from commander to the rank of rear admiral on the retired list, skipping the rank of captain. He had risen in retired rank from lieutenant to rear admiral solely through political promotions in only six years. The nation was waiting for him to return home to receive more honors in person.

Several more short survey and mapping flights were made in the Ford and Fairchild in December and January, including one flight during which Byrd sighted a mountain chain in the distance that he named the Edsel Ford Mountains. However, he planned no major flight to examine them. The prime reason for the expedition had been achieved and the planes had served their purpose.

After the Pole flight, Balchen offered Byrd all the records from the flight test of the Ford and analysis that he had made prior to the epic flight, but Byrd said he had no use for them. For reasons he never understood Balchen was completely cut off from any activities in camp after the flight. He was sent out on sled trips measuring crevasses and then was put in charge of a camp on the other side of Floyd Bennett Bay, where supplies to be returned to the United States were accumulated. Byrd had honored Bennett soon after the expedition arrived by naming the bay and harbor after him. Though hurt by Byrd's sudden, unexplained attitude toward him, Balchen said nothing. He was content to be physically active and made several sled trips along the barrier to pass the time awaiting the arrival of the ships to take everyone out.[32]

Gould and his team returned to camp on 19 January 1930, having completed 1,500 mi. of sledging. Smith piloted the last flight in the Ford in late January with June as copilot. When the end of January had passed and no ship had arrived the men became anxious. Smith wrote in his autobiography that there was "an undeclared mutiny" and "the atmosphere in camp was tense and ugly."[33] Balchen later told a magazine writer some of the men were drunk and disorderly and threatened to "get" Byrd, who had locked himself in his quarters. Balchen was concerned and offered to tangle with anyone who made a move against their leader. He reminded the men that mutiny was a crime and persuaded them to return to work.[34]

This episode was apparently unknown to Byrd, and Balchen found himself still cut off from activities at the camp. It was getting colder each day and the men were concerned that they might have to stay another year if the *City of New York* could not get into the Bay of Whales.

"As far as I was concerned," Balchen said, "I would not have minded at all staying another year; it would have suited me just fine. I had lots of things to do. I had books to read and more I wanted to learn. I liked the climate and I liked my work. We had enough fuel so we could do considerably more flying the next year. But that was not in the cards."[35]

The *Eleanor Bolling* was unable to get through the unusually thick ice but the *City of New York* arrived in the Bay of Whales on 18 February. It was hastily loaded and departed for New Zealand 26 hr. later. The planes could not be taken and were anchored securely with snow blocks. It was hoped they could be used on Byrd's next expedition, which he was already thinking about and which eventually took place in 1933–1935.[36]

By any standard of that era of exploration, the expedition had been a great success. Byrd had organized it, obtained the funds and supplies, and led the expedition. The planes had flown more than 7,000 mi. and the expedition's crews had seen nearly a quarter million square mi. of the continent that no one had ever seen, most of which had been photographed and mapped by McKinley. Despite the potential hazards, not a person had been lost or severely injured. No one had suffered a mental breakdown or had become ill from nutritional shortages. The expedition had pioneered the use of aircraft, radio, and electricity in the antarctic and thus helped bring polar exploration into the age of advanced technology. When asked in subsequent years about the significance of Byrd's first antarctic expedition, Balchen said it provided experience and knowledge about equipment and survival procedures and cold weather requirements for humans and machines that were vital later in saving lives.

7 · Fame and Misfortune

The ship *City of New York* arrived in Dunedin, New Zealand, on 10 March 1930, where receptions, speeches, and dinners marked the beginning of an extended welcome for the expedition members. Some of them left the group and returned by passenger ships to the States. Byrd left on the *City of New York* from New Zealand for Papeete, Tahiti, and arrived on 12 April. Balchen followed a week later with the *Eleanor Bolling,* which remained in Tahiti about four weeks for repairs after weathering a typhoon in the South Pacific. From Tahiti the ships sailed for the Panama Canal Zone.

When the *Bolling*'s first mate became ill before departure, Balchen replaced him and took over the ship's navigation. He had continued to practice celestial navigation at Little America and made hundreds of observations on the trip to the States. The *City* arrived at Panama on 14 May and the crew was greeted with a huge celebration. Byrd attended several receptions and then headed for the interior to write an article for the *National Geographic*. He was visited by *New York World* reporter Charles J. V. Murphy, who would later ghost-write *Little America,* Byrd's book about the expedition.

The *Bolling* arrived a week later, and Balchen and Dean Smith visited France Field, an Army Air Corps base on the Atlantic side of the isthmus, where they were invited to fly the pursuit planes stationed there for canal defense.

Both ships went through the canal and left Panama on 3 June. They were scheduled to arrive in New York on 19 June, a date that Byrd and his backers had decided would be best to give him a rousing hero's welcome. They arrived off the Atlantic coast on 16 June and slowed down.

When the ships entered the harbor on 19 June, fire boats escorted them to the dock. Dozens of vessels, flags flying and whistles blowing, trailed behind. Military and civilian planes and the Navy's dirigible *Los Angeles* circled overhead. A large fleet of convertible Packards waited at the dock to take the expedition members up Broadway through a storm of paper and half a million cheering spectators. It was Byrd's third ticker-tape parade, an honor that has never been duplicated. Speeches by Mayor Jimmy Walker at City Hall and others followed. When Walker saw Balchen he said, "Balchen, you here again? Seems all I do is greet you here on the steps of City Hall!"[1] The entourage then proceeded to the Biltmore Hotel, where they were ushered to a crowded reception and luncheon. A banquet was held that evening and the day's activities were covered by the fawning press. The *New York Times* devoted the first six pages of the next day's editions to the welcoming festivities.

When Balchen settled into his hotel room, he called Tony Fokker, who came immediately. His first question to Balchen was, "How soon can you start working for me?" Balchen replied he was ready immediately and Fokker put him on the payroll as of the beginning of June, although the month was more than half over.[2]

Before he could begin working, however, there were more receptions and dinners. The Byrd family and the expedition's members went to Washington, D.C., by train on 20 June and were whisked to the White House to meet President Hoover. As the group left the White House, a large group of reporters outside the front gate, pads in hand, were waiting to interview Byrd. A man approached Balchen from out of the crowd and asked if he were Bernt Balchen. When Balchen said he was, the man handed him an envelope and quickly walked away. Inside was a subpoena to appear at a deportation hearing at the Bureau of Naturalization. It stated that he was in the country illegally and therefore would be deported to Norway. He had violated the five-year residence requirement by leaving the country to go to the South Pole with Byrd. C. B. Allen, one of Balchen's reporter friends, on seeing what Bernt was reading, took the letter and passed it around to the others.[3]

There was much furious scribbling and the reporters dashed away with their story for the day: One of Byrd's men was going to be kicked out of the country for going to antarctica! The injustice of deportation under these circumstances was immediately broadcast and headlined in the next editions. The Bureau of Naturalization was contacted for comment and the reply was that the law would not permit the bureau to give Balchen citizenship credit for his absence based on the assumption that Little America was American soil. A bureau spokesperson said that assumption would be a "trespass on international questions" where it had no sanction.[4]

Balchen returned to his hotel in shock, wondering what to do. He assumed that there would be no problem because he had been invited on an American expedition to the antarctic and had sailed under the American flag with an internationally recognized American leader. As the day's events whirled around in his head, the telephone rang. The caller spoke rapidly in a high-pitched voice and Balchen could barely understand the New York-accented English. It was New York Rep. Fiorello LaGuardia saying, "It's a Goddamn outrage," and announced he would introduce a special bill in Congress giving full credit for his absence in antarctica and added that "a bunch of my 'Scandihoovian' friends in the Senate are going to back it."[5] He invited Balchen to bring the subpoena to the Capitol, where Balchen met Sen. Henrik Shipstead from Minnesota and Rep. Andrew Furuseth from California, both of Norwegian descent, who vowed to do something about it.

Because the law was firm about the residency requirement, there was only one thing to do: Draft a bill that would give Balchen and any others so affected full credit for their absence toward citizenship. The bill was passed in both houses without opposition.[6]

Meanwhile, the National Geographic Society awarded Byrd a Special Gold Medal of Honor for the expedition's accomplishments, as he had already received the Hubbard Medal, the organization's highest award. Gilbert Grosvenor, the society's president, hailed the expedition as "one of the most comprehensive, dramatic, and productive explorations of modern times."[7]

Byrd returned to New York, where he received a gold medal from the Aeronautical Chamber of Commerce at a banquet on 25 June; the other members of the expedition received silver medals. At a later banquet a Distinguished Flying Cross was given to five flying members of the expedition—Byrd, June, McKinley, Parker, and Smith. Balchen was told he was ineligible because he was not a citizen and was not a member of the armed forces of the United States. It was the third time that he was denied the decoration for flying achievements, and Balchen later admitted it was quite humiliating to him.[8] Subsequently he learned that Carl O. Petersen, the radio man who had flown with him on the flight to rescue the Ford, also received the award. He was a civilian without any military background. No explanation was ever given.[9]

The round of receptions, luncheons, and dinners continued and culminated in a dinner given by New York governor Franklin D. Roosevelt at the governor's mansion in Albany. Many of the expedition members were taken up the Hudson River by a Navy destroyer. Balchen declined the invitation.

Instead, Balchen reflected on his antarctic experience with Byrd and jotted down some revealing notes that have never been disclosed before:

> I am just sitting taking an account of certain happenings over the past couple of years, and I am trying to get some things hooked together so they can make sense to me and fit into my evaluation of events and the direction they sometimes have taken without any logical explanation that would satisfy me. The leader of the expedition now just promoted to the rank of Rear Admiral US Navy (Ret) whom I have come to know quite well since I met him in Spitsbergen nearly four years ago has more than once puzzled me with his Dr. Jekyl/Mr. Hyde appearances.[10]

Balchen made notes about Byrd's life, from his birth in Winchester, Virginia, to his command of an aviation unit on the 1925 Donald MacMillan expedition to Greenland for about three weeks in the summertime. Balchen noted that Byrd's longest flight away from the base was 107 mi. and all flights were made in amphibians from open water.

Byrd's next venture was with the expedition to Spitsbergen, where he lived on the ship the whole three weeks they were there.

> With a total of some forty days in the Arctic in the summertime, he was considered the greatest expert on Arctic aviation before we left for the Antarctic. It had many times caused me difficulties when we were planning for this trip to smooth out some inane statements made by him in front of other people about the cold weather operations we were facing down there. Public adulation and undeserved know-how can be very difficult and many times dangerous when decisions have to be made on these bases on subjects which can determine the whole safety and outcome of an undertaking.
>
> I had admired his ability to get the expedition together and to meet people and to get funds out of them for his expedition. I have not known anyone who could equal him there. He was a great organizer and promoter—one of the best I believe our country has seen. His years in Washington must have stood him in good stead. His connec-

tions in the top offices could not be equaled by any. He several times said to me, "There is not a thing that I cannot get from my government." That was also obvious to me when I saw the ease by which he got commissions to become officers for men who had been with him and with no military background. His power in this and affiliated fields completely flabbergasted me many times. He knew the doors and he had influential support for all his requests. The way his [promotion to Admiral] came through was ample proof.

In my estimate he was not an outdoor man. He had no interest in hunting, fishing, camping or skiing. He was one of our most consistent visitors to the gymnasium; he took calisthenics and kept himself in good physical condition through set-up exercises. His light build and muscular structure indicated a man not used to the outdoors.

His drive to go on these expeditions where he never went on any trips by foot, skis or dog team was puzzling. When asked why he did not go out he would complain of different ailments that would prevent him from taking any exercise.

The only reason that was left for me to find as a motive for these trips and to be the great Arctic traveler was publicity and notoriety. There was never a situation [discussed that he didn't respond], "On one of my previous trips to the Arctic, I had the same thing happen to me."

For a leader he is too prone to listen to gossip and flattery. This many times makes it difficult for those of us who head the different departments to discharge our jobs with undue interference.

In all the years that I was together with him on ships and down in the Antarctic I never saw him practice shooting the sun or take celestial observations, or at any time try to figure out the ship's position during our travels. It has always been necessary for me to continually practice my shooting the sun or other celestial bodies with the sextant during the years when I did my work in navigation. Routine is a very essential thing when doing aerial or ship navigation. His dead reckoning ability never impressed me from what I actually saw of him.[11]

A welcoming reception honoring Balchen was held at Teterboro, New Jersey, on 2 July 1930. Byrd sent a congratulatory message that was read to the audience. In view of the aloofness Byrd had demonstrated during those last days in antarctica, Balchen was surprised for once again Byrd showed what Balchen viewed as his incomprehensible two-sided personality. He acknowledged Balchen's contributions to the North Pole flight for showing us how the Norwegians burn into the skis a mixture of tar and resin which greatly increased their efficiency. The whole world knows the great job he did on the trans-Atlantic flight when he landed the plane in the water at night without injuring any of the personnel.

> His ability is many-sided. You know how he can pilot, but he is also an excellent mechanic and aircraft engineer and constructor, and I selected him as a senior pilot and in charge of the aviation branch of the expedition because I knew of no one in the whole world I would rather have with me in that position.[12]

Balchen was tired of all the receptions and dinners and was happy to work for Fokker again flight testing new aircraft and working on aerodynamic problems. General Motors Corporation had become the dominant owner of the company by having acquired 40 percent of the shares of Fokker Aircraft Corporation in May 1929 and changed the name to General Aviation Corporation. In the fall of 1930 Eddie Rickenbacker, then vice president in charge of sales for General Aviation, asked Balchen to demonstrate one of the new single-engine Fokker F-12s for a wealthy Texas oil tycoon. They cruised over New York City at a fairly high altitude and were over the East River when the engine quit. The nearest airport was Newark, New Jersey. Balchen put the aircraft in a long glide, ducked between some smoke stacks, inched over some tall buildings, and made a smooth dead-stick landing (landing without engine power) at the airport. It was a close call. The Texan's face was drained of color and his hands shook. Sensing what had happened, the Fokker sales representative rushed up in an automobile and whisked the man away. "He probably explained to him that I had shut the motor off on purpose to show him what the plane could do," Balchen said later.[13] The sale was made.

The problem was that a vacuum had been created in the fuel tank that prevented fuel from getting to the carburetor. Balchen repaired it and took off for Teterboro Airport. That day, 18 October 1930, Bernt Balchen, at the age of 30, married Emmy Alvhilde Sorlie, 22, a Norwegian from Oslo whom he had met previously in New York City. They subsequently rented a duplex in Hasbrouck Heights, New Jersey, where Bernt Balchen, Jr., was born to the couple in October 1931.

The nation was reeling in the effects of the Depression during the winter of 1930–1931 and the aircraft industry was in the doldrums. Balchen was laid off. To produce some income Balchen announced in January

1931 that he was planning a world-circling flight in a Fokker and would attempt to beat the time of 21 days the German dirigible *Graf Zeppelin*, piloted by Hugo von Eckener, had taken in September 1929. Balchen believed he could do it in six days. He contacted several newspapers for financial support but the offers were insufficient to cover expenses. He dropped the idea and had to look elsewhere for personal income. In February 1931, the New York, Philadelphia, and Washington Airway Corporation (also known as the Ludington Line) needed pilots. He was hired as a relief pilot flying trimotored Stinsons.

On 23 May 1930 Congress authorized special Byrd Antarctic Expedition Medals for its members "to express the high admiration in which the Congress and the American people hold their heroic and undaunted services in connection with the scientific investigations and extraordinary aerial exploration on the Antarctic Continent."[14] No presentations were held. The medals were mailed in July 1931 to each recipient but Balchen's address was not known at the time so his medal was sent to Byrd, who forwarded it to Balchen in care of the Fokker company. It was enclosed with a form letter from Byrd that he sent to all those who were not U.S. citizens. The letter said it was the first time a medal of this kind had been given to those who were not American citizens, and added, "I trust that you will like the United States and that you will always make it your home."[15]

A few days earlier, Balchen had received a strange, rambling personal letter from Byrd reminding Balchen that they had been friends a long time and that he had

> done nothing but praise you throughout the country in my lectures, my articles and my book. I have been loyal and true to you publicly and privately.
>
> I am well aware that some people, for whom I have done a great deal, have by subtle and unfair methods attempted to convince you of many things derogatory to me. I am not willing to believe that they have succeeded because I think you have too much intelligence and too much loyalty in your makeup to be turned aside from the facts and the truth by ambitious and envious people who have based their friendship with me not on loyalty of manhood but on a basis of money.
>
> I believe in you and appreciate greatly that you have not allowed these people to twist you, with their subtle methods, around their fingers by tempting you with a prospect of money and more fame, at the

same time trying to pull me down thinking that in so doing they can pull others up. I don't believe these people are the real friends of yours they profess to be. They are thinking of themselves more than they are of you. . . .

This gang I am speaking of never seeks any place to give me credit but thinks up all kinds of things to criticize me, most of which are unjust. Of course I am not perfect. I have many faults. But I have tried to play the game and I know in my heart I have done so.[16]

Balchen did not know what prompted such a strange letter and did not respond.

On 18 March 1931 Balchen went to New London, Connecticut, to make a speech to a local civic club. While there he received a telephone call from Merian C. Cooper, a director at the RKO movie studios. He said that the *Viking*, a sealer based at St. Johns, Newfoundland, on which a movie team was traveling to make a documentary, had exploded in the ice north of Newfoundland. He had scant information about the accident but feared the worst. The group of about 20 people was under the direction of Varrick Frissell, son of a prominent New York physician who was a friend of Cooper's. Cooper had talked with Juan Trippe, Pan American Airways president, and had obtained permission to use one of the airline's twin-engine Sikorsky S-38s to try to locate the ship. He asked Balchen if he would make the flight. His answer: "Ve do it."

The aircraft was stored in a hangar at the Boston airport and had not been flown for a year. Cooper arrived with Randy Enslow, who was to be the copilot.

While Bernt worked on the plane to install an extra fuel tank, more information about the ship became known. There were 123 people aboard the *Viking* and about 100 of them had walked about 10 mi. across the river ice to an island and spread the word about the disaster. Inexplicably, the entire movie team was missing.

Balchen and Enslow flew the Sikorsky to St. John, New Brunswick, where they had to remain overnight because of the weather. Next day they flew to Cornerbrook, Newfoundland, and landed in the bay. One engine was malfunctioning because two spark plugs were badly fouled. Balchen had no spares. To solve the problem, he cleaned them and put one in each engine. "The engines were kind of shaking," he said, "but it was an emergency so it was the only way we could run."[17]

Balchen flew over the mountains of Newfoundland and out over the heaving ice pack to try to locate any survivors. There had been a snowstorm after the explosion, which covered anything left on the ice floes.

Balchen and Enslow searched the area for many hours during the next three days at about 100 ft. and found nothing and no one. If anything had happened to the engines at such a low altitude, they would have crashed among the ice floes. "The fate of those lost people was at stake," Balchen said, "so we had to do our utmost and disregard normal safety precautions."[18]

They were reluctant to leave but they knew there was no hope that anyone on the ground could have survived the bitter cold without proper clothing or any survival equipment. They flew the amphibian from Newfoundland to the East Boston Airport, where an unpleasant surprise awaited Balchen. Collector of Customs Wilfred W. Lufkin fined him $500 for making an unauthorized landing at Boston without first obtaining permission from the Commissioner of Customs in Washington. Balchen was an alien coming from a foreign country and had not landed at an airport designated to process aliens. To get the fine remitted he would have to submit a petition to the Secretary of the Treasury. Balchen was shocked and told the press that he had never experienced difficulty before when landing at American airports from Canada or Newfoundland. He assumed that because his flight was well-covered in the world press he would not be required to file a reentry petition. But because the law stated that the East Boston Airport was not a designated port of entry, Lufkin said he had no choice but to levy the fine.

Cooper, Trippe, and Lewis Frissell, father of the missing Varrick Frissell, contacted the press and exerted their considerable influence on government contacts. The fine was later remitted. The missing people were never found, dead or alive.

Balchen was approaching the time when he could file for his naturalization papers. The previous December a bill was introduced in Congress to confer American citizenship on Balchen and 12 other members of the Byrd expedition. However, the Department of Labor objected and the newspaper reporters centered on Balchen as the most famous of the group to interview for their stories.

Raymond F. Crist, U.S. Commissioner of Naturalization, said the government would have to offer an objection to the granting of citizenship until Balchen completed a full term of uninterrupted residence within the territorial limits of the United States. "We have no alternative but to refuse Balchen citizenship," he said. "[However] if the court should see fit to construe Balchen's stay in Little America as legal residence within the United States, that will settle the question."[19]

Congressional pressure was put on the Labor Department, and two days after the papers carried the story, Balchen was advised that he could present his petition for citizenship papers to a federal judge in Hackensack, New Jersey, and expect to be a citizen within three months. Balchen went into court for a hearing on his petition for citizenship on 3 July 1931. The federal examiner reminded the judge that the law required a person to remain in the States for an uninterrupted five-year period but that Balchen had left the country not only to go to antarctica but Canada, Holland, and France as well after he had filed his first papers in 1927. "However, the government will leave this matter to your honor's judgment," he concluded.

Balchen was called forward and asked if all his flights out of the country had been made under the American flag. When Balchen answered strongly that they had been, his petition to file the final papers was approved. Balchen told reporters that he had wanted to become an American citizen from the moment he arrived in 1926 and learned of American ideals and opportunities. He and Emmy received their naturalization certificates on 5 November 1931.[20]

Balchen's responsibilities as husband and new father bore down on him heavily, as they did with millions of other men while the nation staggered under the blows of the Great Depression. He was able to obtain several charter flights for the Ludington Line and TWA, as well as test-flying assignments from Douglas Aircraft Company. He and Clyde Pangborn also flew F. Trubee Davison, a contender for the office of New York governor, around the state on a campaign tour.

Several times during that summer Balchen met with Lincoln Ellsworth, who was getting restless and talked about leading his own expedition to the antarctic. His father, who had been opposed to his exploration in the arctic, had died, leaving him free to use his inherited wealth to do what he pleased.

Ellsworth invited Balchen to Zurich, Switzerland, to talk further but Ellsworth still could not decide if he should go. Balchen thought the expedition would never take place, especially when the nation was in the throes of the Depression.

Also that fall Balchen received an invitation through Laurence M.

Gould to meet with George Palmer Putnam, grandson of the founder of G. P. Putnam's Sons Publishing Company, and his wife, Amelia Earhart, who had gained international fame in 1928 as the first woman to fly across the Atlantic. Although her husband insisted she was in command of the flight, she had been only a passenger. Wilmer L. "Bill" Stultz, the pilot, and Lewis E. "Slim" Gordon, the mechanic, were at the controls of the Fokker F-7 the entire flight.[21]

Earhart was unhappy with the fact that she was "only baggage" and "a sack of potatoes"[22] on the flight. She had not been invited to take the controls because she could not fly on instruments. At breakfast one morning she casually asked her husband if he would mind if she flew the Atlantic solo. If Putnam would back her financially, she could establish two aviation "firsts"—the first woman to make the trip alone and the first person to cross the Atlantic twice in a heavier-than-air craft.

Putnam, ever the publicity seeker, thought it was an excellent idea. He asked Balchen if he could teach her how to navigate and fly blind using instruments so she could make the flight. If so, he wanted the preparations kept secret so that she could back out if Balchen thought she was not ready. Balchen said it was "perfectly feasible"[23] and laid out a training plan. He flew to Newfoundland in February 1932 to take a look at the field at Harbour Grace from which some early flights had departed for Europe. He also looked at Stephenville as a possible departure point if her Lockheed Vega were fitted with pontoons. As an afterthought, he also visited Gander Lake in Newfoundland to see if it would be an adequate seaplane harbor for future operations, because transatlantic flying was at the stage where it was being discussed by several of the large airlines.

On returning to New York Balchen began to teach Earhart navigation techniques and instrument flying. The latter was of primary importance so she could fly through the clouds and fog she was sure to encounter. She was a fast learner and demonstrated that she could maintain a course on instruments even in turbulence. On 1 March Balchen flew her Lockheed Vega from the East Boston Airport to Teterboro. The Fokker factory was empty and the hangar that was used by the Curtiss-Wright Corporation was available, which gave them plenty of space to work. At this time, only one other person knew of the project: Edward Gorski, formerly a master mechanic for Fokker. The Vega had been repaired after an accident Earhart had at the Norfolk Naval Air Station in September 1930 and had been rebuilt into a Vega 5-B by the Detroit Aircraft Corporation. It had been used for flying by the Ludington Line between Washington and Norfolk. It was released to Balchen on 5 March 1932, and those who knew of the transfer assumed that Balchen was going to use it on an antarctic flight with Ellsworth, as had been rumored in the press.

Balchen and Gorski stripped the Vega, replaced the fuselage with one from another Vega, removed the wicker passenger seats, strengthened the fuselage with braces to carry a large fuel tank, added tanks in the wings to supplement the normal tanks, installed a new fuel-transfer system, and attached a new supercharged Pratt & Whitney engine. With a larger fuel capacity, the Vega could fly 3,200 mi.

Additional instruments were added and calibrated, including a drift indicator, two compasses, and a directional gyro. Balchen and Gorski made several test flights with the Vega loaded with sand bags to simulate the take-off weight. Because the landing gear might have been damaged on landing with the excess weight, Gorski dropped the sandbags over the New Jersey meadow lands. By mid-April the plane was ready and Balchen was satisfied that Earhart was qualified on instruments and sufficiently familiar with the plane to make the trip. Her plans had still not been announced and she carried on with her voluminous correspondence, lectures, and interviews without saying a word. When her secretary left on a vacation to South America in late April, she still had not mentioned it. Nor did she tell her mother or any other family member.[24]

Meanwhile, Earhart and Balchen mapped out the route she would take. She wanted to leave as soon as the plane was ready, but the weather over the Atlantic would not cooperate. She made frequent trips from her home in Rye, New York, to Teterboro, hoping for a favorable forecast from James Kimball, head of the U.S. Weather Bureau in New York, who had been told of her plan. On 17 May, while she was in the city to christen and get a ride in a new Goodyear dirigible, Kimball reported that the weather looked promising but not yet good enough. However, the reports from Harbour Grace were favorable two days later. She put on her flying suit and hurried to Teterboro with maps, a comb, toothbrush, and a can of tomato juice.[25]

Earhart met Balchen and Gorski, along with Gould and Putnam at the airport. No one seemed to notice as Balchen got into the pilot's seat and Earhart and Gorski crawled into the rear. They arrived at St. John, New Brunswick, to find that the word had already spread. "Lady Lindy" was going to dare to make the transocean flight.

The trio flew to Harbour Grace the next afternoon. Earhart went to a hotel to rest while Balchen and Gorski preflighted the plane. Balchen followed the weather reports based on ocean liner and London messages being relayed by Putnam from New York. They continued to look favorable, although storms were possible en route.

Balchen made up a flight plan for Earhart that included the best throttle settings at various altitudes and the course to fly based on the forecast winds aloft. On the morning of 20 May 1932, the fifth anniversary of Lindbergh's departure, Balchen called Earhart at the hotel to tell her that the time had come to take off. She obtained a container of soup from the hotel kitchen and took a taxi to the airport. Balchen briefed her on the weather, the course, and what precautions she should take. She asked if she could make it and Balchen assured her she could. She started the engine, checked the magnetos, nodded, and was off. As soon as she was out of sight, Balchen sent a cable to her husband: "AE TOOK OFF 712 NFLD PERFECT PERFORMANCE."[26]

Earhart made a wide turn over the city and out over Conception Bay, then disappeared in the twilight. Departure weather was fair but it slowly worsened, and four hours out of Newfoundland, she encountered a severe storm. Her altimeter malfunctioned and she could not tell her altitude above the ocean. Her tachometer iced up and the exhaust manifold on the engine cracked and began to vibrate; flames trailed from the engine. As she climbed to get above the weather, the wings began to ice up and the plane stalled and fell into a spin. She was able to pull out of it as the ice melted but was so close to the water that she could see the waves breaking below her. She held the predetermined compass course all night but had no idea of the wind direction. The weather gradually improved as her estimated time of arrival over the coast of Ireland approached.

To stay awake and alert, she drank the tomato juice and the soup. Then she noticed that the cockpit fuel gauge was broken and gasoline was dripping down the side of her neck. She no longer knew how much fuel she had left and decided that she should start looking for a place to put the Vega down as soon as she saw land.

The wind was from the southwest and had blown Earhart about 200 mi. north of her course, almost missing the northern tip of Ireland. When she saw the coast, she flew south over green fields and followed some railroad tracks looking for an airport. Finding none, she landed safely in a meadow near Londonderry, Northern Ireland. Although she planned to fly a maximum of 3,200 mi., she actually flew 2,026 mi. in 15 hr. 18 min. and had achieved the two aviation firsts that were her objectives.[27]

Earhart found a telephone and called her husband. She then cabled Balchen: "YOUR HELP MADE IT POSSIBLE THANK EDDIE TOO AE."[28]

Earhart left the Lockheed in Ireland to be dismantled and shipped home, and was given a hero's welcome with medals and banquets in England and Europe. She returned to the States to the fanfare reserved for other record-setting Americans. This included a meeting with President Hoover, the award of the National Geographic Society's Special Gold Medal, the first woman to be so honored. In her acceptance speech after receiving the medal she described instrument flying as a "significant step in aviation," and paid tribute to Balchen as her mentor.

Earhart was presented to a joint session of Congress, which voted to award her the Distinguished Flying Cross. Vice President Charles Curtis later presented it to her for "displaying heroic courage and skill as a navigator at the risk of her life." She was the first woman to receive this award. She had no military service.

After the Earhart flight, Balchen met with Ellsworth again and agreed to accompany him on the proposed transantarctic flight that had been rumored for months. At first, Ellsworth thought he would try to find a ship with a catapult so a plane could be launched without having to take off from the land, which would require a base to be established. This would enable him to make deep nonstop thrusts into the continent and be recovered by crane after each flight, but Balchen persuaded him to reject the idea because it would be too risky in seas filled with huge ice floes. He then planned to attempt a roundtrip flight across the antarctic continent between the Bay of Whales and the Weddell Sea. This was later rejected because of the logistics requirements in favor of a single transcontinental flight. Balchen recommended that a meteorologist should accompany the expedition. Ellsworth objected but finally gave in and a meteorologist was recruited.

Concurrently, Admiral Byrd was planning a second two-year stint at Little America to carry on more exploration and to build on his fame as the world's authority on antarctica. Balchen had decided that he would not go with the second Byrd antarctic expedition, even if asked. He felt that he had fulfilled his obligation and promise to Floyd Bennett and was not going to contend again with what he regarded as Byrd's strange personnel management style and paranoia about loyalty. He liked Ellsworth and thought it would be an interesting undertaking to help him organize his transantarctic expedition and make the unprecedented flight across the continent.

Despite his growing fame, Ellsworth was timid about the public attention he garnered. His shyness and avoidance of anything showy or seemingly self-promoting made him less newsworthy than Byrd, who always sought publicity and grabbed the headlines wherever he went.

Ellsworth remained very passionate about polar exploration. After the unsuccessful expedition to try to fly to the North Pole with Amundsen and the flight in the *Norge*, Ellsworth had decided that although the South Pole had been already reached by air, there were still nearly five million square miles of the continent that had never been seen by humans. He had no interest in reaching the Pole and hoped to make an accurate survey of an 1,800 mi. route across an uncharted region and thus provide a more complete picture of the world.

Rather than base the rationale for the expedition on a single flight across the continent, which could be interpreted as grandstanding, he planned to make several landings for surface observations.[29] Ellsworth had specified in Balchen's contract that they were to land "whenever necessary" on account of the weather or to make observations. It was these two words that were to be the basis for a later disagreement between them. The key word in the contract, as far as Balchen was concerned, was "necessary."

Ellsworth planned to take only one aircraft because he believed that by flying only in good weather and landing in time before any storms so that the plane could be lashed down, the plane would be safe from damage. A skilled pilot would thus prevent any accidents "and leave us in a position to walk away from the machine if it was necessary to abandon it." He also stated that two planes would require two or more pilots and other additional members, an extra cost that he did want to bear.[30]

Ellsworth enlisted Sir Hubert Wilkins, the famous Australian explorer, as his scientific advisor because Wilkins had already mapped and flown in both the arctic and antarctic. He had used early Lockheed Vegas and had persuaded Jack Northrop to produce a faster plane that would withstand subzero conditions. Balchen was given the task of overseeing its construction and was given a "To Whom It May Concern" letter by Ellsworth giving him "full authority to discuss in full the engine, airplane and airplane wireless requirements for the expedition and to draw up contracts for the purchase of such equipment."[31]

Balchen immediately ordered a Pratt & Whitney 500 hp Wasp engine for the plane and specified the type of propeller, fuel pump, and electrical requirements for a total engine price of $4,680. He went to the West Coast to discuss the engineering details with Northrop and was favorably impressed with the man and the company. He approved the purchase of a built-to-order Northrop Gamma 2-B at a price of $33,000.

The Gamma was an all-metal cantilever, low-wing monoplane, which the engineers claimed would have a top speed of 180 MPH. It pioneered the full-span, split trailing-edge flaps with "park bench" ailerons, and was reportedly capable of landing at the slow speed of 42 MPH. Fully loaded, it had a cruising range of about 1,700 mi. without extra tanks. The skis were to be interchangeable with wheels and pontoons.[32]

Ellsworth offered Balchen $800 per month to oversee the production of the aircraft until two weeks after the airplane was accepted from the manufacturers and stipulated,

> After that time it is planned to store the Airoplane [sic] until some time in 1933 when extensive practice flights will be made. During the interval it is understood that you will not participate in any unusual or hazardous flying and in consideration of this I propose to pay you a retaining fee of three hundred dollars per month until such time as practice flying is commenced. From that time until some time between February and April 1934 when the Expedition is expected to terminate, the eight hundred dollars per month will be resumed.[33]

Ellsworth also agreed to pay all of Balchen's living expenses when on expedition business. However, Ellsworth wanted no responsibility for any insurance or financial claims that might result from the expedition. Ellsworth, like Byrd, obtained financial assistance from contracts he made with the *New York Times,* the North American Newspaper Alliance, and the National Geographic Society.

Ellsworth had given Balchen *carte blanche* to lay out the specifications, follow the plane through production, and give it thorough flight tests to include ski operations in subzero conditions. The unusual requirements included increased fuel and oil tankage, ski pedestals, and special skis that were made of wood sheathed with metal. In addition to pilot and navigator, the plane had to be able to carry a cargo that would consist of a sledge, tent, two weeks supply of food, primus stove, photo supplies, snowshoes, a snow knife and shovel, radio, and portable generator.[34]

In California, after many conferences with Northrop and Don Berlin, chief designer, Balchen consulted Dr. Theodore von Karman at the California Institute of Technology to work out design difficulties that were encountered. Balchen was delighted with the chance to help design a new aircraft and take it through extensive tests.

Balchen labored alongside the workers on the production line. The plane, named *Polar Star* (now in the National Air and Space Museum in Washington, D.C.) was completed in August 1932 and ready for flight testing in October. In addition to Balchen's tests, a number of flights were made that fall by Edmund T. "Eddie" Allen and Frank Hawks to check fuel consumption and the plane's flying characteristics. In February and March 1933 Balchen, along with Chris Braathen, who was hired as chief mechanic for the expedition, flew the Northrop to Canada. They were joined by Wilkins. They changed the wheels for skis and tested them with the new type of ski pedals attached to the skis that Balchen had specified and helped design. They also tested new tents, skis, and trail equipment on trips into the Canadian bush. Some modifications were made on the plane and the engine for easier cold weather maintenance. When they returned to California in late March 1933 they were satisfied that the plane was ready for the trip.

Balchen flew the plane to New York to give it a long-range gas consumption test. Meanwhile Wilkins had been looking into getting a ship for Ellsworth and decided that one could best be obtained in Norway. In April 1933 Wilkins, Balchen, Emmy, and Bernt Jr. left on the SS *Stavangerfjord* for Bergen, Norway, with the plane aboard. Emmy and Bernt Jr. would stay in Norway with relatives while Balchen was in antarctica. After they arrived, the *Polar Star* was stored at the Horten Naval Station while Balchen and Wilkins searched for a ship to buy.

They found the 135 ft. 400 tn. *Fanefjord,* a sealer that could be manned with a small crew of 15. It had a long cruising range of 10,000 mi. with a diesel engine that could guarantee a speed of about 8 kn. When the sails were hoisted it could make 2 or 3 more kn. on average. The decisive factor was its large hold, which could be modified so the plane could be stored below deck. Balchen made a mockup of the plane's fuselage and had the ship's hatch modified. He found that the plane could be eased below by first raising it vertically and then sliding it carefully into place. It slipped in with 1½ in. to spare. The wings fitted easily alongside.

Capt. Baard Holt was selected as the skipper, and crew members were recruited from among experienced Norwegian volunteers, most of whom Balchen knew. All had experience in the polar regions, except the meteorologist and a young Norwegian physician named Berg. The only other American, besides Balchen and Braathen, was Walter Lanz, the expedition's radio operator.

The ship was loaded with food and supplies for 18 men for 2½ yr. Most of the supplies were donated by interested Norwegians; the clothing was the best they could obtain from Norway, Canada, and Alaska. The ship departed Norway on 29 July 1933 for the 18,000 mi. trip to New Zealand. Ellsworth renamed it *Wyatt Earp.*

The voyage from Norway was made via the Azores and Capetown, South Africa, and arrived in Dunedin, New Zealand, on 10 November 1933, where Ellsworth saw for the first time the ship and plane he had bought. Balchen remembered the trip for a special reason: He had an attack of appendicitis and had to have his appendix removed during the stop at Capetown.[35]

The Ellsworth party departed Dunedin on 10 December 1933 and headed for the base at Little America. The following day, Byrd's second antarctic expedition arrived in Wellington, New Zealand. The *Wyatt Earp*'s radio operator received a message that Byrd had told the press he had given Ellsworth and Balchen permission to go to the antarctic and that Balchen had his permission to fly there with Ellsworth.

"This didn't set too well with Ellsworth, Sir Hubert or myself," Balchen later said. "The same afternoon we met the pack ice at latitude 63:30 south and longitude 174 east, the farthest north the ice had been encountered. It gave us a foreboding that we would have something to fight."[36]

The succeeding days were almost too much to contend with. Heavy pack ice, huge drifting ice bergs, and high winds threatened to turn the ship into match wood. Balchen had an accident that nearly disabled him. His diary noted,

December 31st 1933: Watch from 12–4. Ice is very heavy now; the other watch hadn't moved hardly for the last two hours. We got into a little slack of ice. On backing up, the rudder hit a piece of ice. The wheel spun over and knocked me out. The spokes hit my right arm and three of them broke. It was a wonder my arm didn't. My left ear was split. I came to and crawled out and was taken down to bed. The doctor gave me some morphine which fixed up the pain. When I woke up the ship was lying still and it was not possible to get any farther. My arm is still without any feeling but I think a couple of days will fix me up. At 12 o'clock sharp we fired our guns, blew the siren and made as much noise as possible. The old year ceased to be and a new one arrived with a lot of things waiting for us. We were about the first people on the globe to celebrate New Year's Eve.[37]

The ship cleared the pack ice on 3 January 1934, arrived at the Bay of Whales, and moored on 8 June. Balchen and Braathen were eager to visit Little America and skied to look over where they had lived four years before. The radio towers were sticking out of the snow but the rest of the camp was snowed over. The rudder of the *Floyd Bennett* was sticking out of the snow so the two burrowed down to the cockpit and found everything just as they had left it, perfectly preserved by the extreme cold. As Balchen sat in the pilot's seat reminiscing about his flight over the South Pole with Byrd, he noticed something on the floor: It was his faithful slide rule that he had used so often and had lost. He picked it up and slipped it into his pocket.

Balchen did not want to waste any time getting the *Polar Star* airborne and had it unloaded and preflighted early the next morning. He and Braathen made two short test hops, then Balchen took Ellsworth on a 30 min. reconnaissance flight to the south and east of Little America. During the flight Balchen noticed something strange. There were very few seals around and very heavy pressure ridges had developed in the water areas. The general weather atmosphere seemed ominously unstable. In a very short time, the weather deteriorated into a total whiteout. They left the aircraft tied down about a mile from the edge of the sea. The ice around the ship was rising dangerously from the sea swells underneath and was breaking up. Balchen and Braathen, worried about the plane, skied to the site to move it back. Large cracks began appearing quickly in the 15 ft. thick ice beneath their skis. In less than 20 min. the bay ice was heaving and breaking up as far as anyone could see. Balchen hollered for help from the ship's crew to save the plane but it was too late. It was upended and the left wing, aileron, and skis were damaged beyond repair. However, they managed to get the plane onto an ice floe and anchored it down before returning to the ship. The next day, the captain was able to maneuver the ship next to the floe and the plane was carefully lifted on board.

The damage to the plane was extensive and could not be repaired. Because the flight across the antarctic was the major reason for the expedition, there was nothing that could be done but pack up and go home. The *Wyatt Earp* returned to Dunedin on 28 January 1934.

Ellsworth decided to have the plane returned to the factory in California for repairs and left for the States with his wife on a cruise liner. Balchen and the others loaded it aboard the tanker *Texaco South Africa,* whose captain had offered to take the men and plane without charge to San Pedro, California. The question in everyone's mind was whether or not Ellsworth would try again. However, by the time he reached the States, he announced that he was going to return before the year was over.

After the plane was repaired at the factory and tested, Balchen and Braathen learned that Ellsworth was going to attempt to fly from the other side of antarctica—from a base on one of the islands off the Palmer Archipelago, then south of South America across to Little America. The flight would be along the west coast of the Weddell Sea to its head, then, without landing, across the antarctic continent to the Ross Sea—a distance of 2,800 mi. Meanwhile, the *Wyatt Earp* would make its way to the Ross Sea and through the ice pack and around the shore line to the Bay of Whales to Little America, where it was to pick up the aircraft, Ellsworth, and Balchen.

The advantage in this plan was that the flight would be toward Little America and assistance would be available there on Byrd's arrival for his second expedition. Most important, they would be able to obtain frequent weather reports by radio from there and from Byrd's parties in the field, which would have been increasingly difficult if they were flying in the opposite direction.

When the plane was ready in California, Balchen flew it to the Edo Aircraft Corporation on Long Island to have floats fitted, as this time there might be a need to use them. Balchen tested the plane and the expedition crew went aboard the liner SS *Monterey* at Los Angeles on 25 July 1934. They left for New Zealand and arrived at Dunedin in the latter part of August.

The *Wyatt Earp* left Dunedin on 19 September 1934, with 17 men aboard. Ellsworth had decided to depart on the flight from Deception Island, located 600 mi. south of Cape Horn, South America. Wilkins had been there in 1928–1929 and had made flights from a runway he improvised on the beach. It probably could still be used provided the plane took off before the summer melting began.

The 3,000 mi. voyage to Deception Island was a rough one through vicious seas. The *Wyatt Earp* rolled badly in the month-long gale until it reached the smoother waters near the island. Although the sea became more tolerable, the weather did not. Wind-driven snow squalls hampered visibility, but the ship was finally eased into the harbor and docked.

It took a week to get the plane unloaded. When they got it ashore and assembled, Balchen primed the engine and turned on the starter but there was a loud bang. A connecting rod had bent and a broken knuckle pin had scored a cylinder. Of all the spare parts that had been put aboard the ship, there were no spare knuckle pins. They were on the list of parts to be supplied by the engine manufacturer, but they had not been packed. There was nothing else that could be done but to order extra pins from the States and have them shipped to southern Chile where they could be picked up by the *Wyatt Earp*. The pins were flown from the Pratt & Whitney plant and arrived just as the ship pulled into the harbor in the Strait of Magellan after an 1,800 mi. trip.

Meanwhile, four men—Ellsworth, Balchen, Braathen, and the meteorologist Dr. Holmboe—had chosen to remain at Deception. Ellsworth wanted to study the birds in the area and Holmboe made weather observations; Balchen and Braathen took the *Polar Star*'s engine apart. Balchen had enrolled in the Alexander Hamilton Institute's Business Course and spent much time reading the course literature and studying for the tests.

They were comfortably housed in the old whaling station, but the weather was disheartening with storm after storm descending on the island. The snow had melted very fast, so the chance to use the old runway was lost.

During this period, Ellsworth had an opportunity to observe Balchen at work. "The man's versatility was amazing," he said.

Besides being a good navigator and a pilot with few peers, he was a marvelous man on skis. On the trail, he was tireless. After he and Braathen had torn down the engine ready for repair, to find an occupation for himself he built a light sledge suitable to be carried in the plane. No Norwegian professional sled builder could have turned out a better job. Besides this, he was a good cook. He did the cooking for our little shore party on Deception Island, and we fared better even than at the hands of the Wyatt Earp's cook. Had he chosen a career in art, he would have been successful, for he could draw and paint like a professional. He made beautiful sketches of Deception Island and other scenes along the archipelago.[38]

When the *Wyatt Earp* returned three weeks later, Ellsworth decided to look for another place for a landing field farther south on the Palmer Archipelago. They finally decided to try Snow Hill Island, where an expedition from Sweden had wintered from 1901 to 1903. The old hut they had used was in good condition considering that it had been 31 years since the Swedes had left. The northeast part of the island was bare of snow and consisted mostly of sandstone and mud flats, which contained millions of fossils, proving that life had existed there millions of years before.

The plane was unloaded but it was more than two weeks before the weather would permit any flying. Snow, sleet, low ceilings, and fog covered the area. One day Balchen and Braathen went ashore to work on the plane and a snow storm came up that was so severe that the ship had to pull away and stand by in the bay. They were stuck in a tent for three days because they did not have time to get to the ship before it pulled out.[39]

Balchen and Braathen made a test and reconnaissance flight on 18 December and established radio contact with the ship. Weather reports had been received from Little America, where Byrd's expedition was now thoroughly ensconced, and they had similar bad weather there. Ellsworth was getting impatient and set a deadline. He said if they did not get off before 1 January they were going to pack up and go home. Balchen tried to convince him that they would get off whenever they had a chance of success and suggested shorter flights to explore Weddell Sea areas that had not been seen by humans.

Ellsworth was adamant that they had to make the flight before his deadline, but Balchen was just as firm that they could not take the chance of the weather closing in at Little America or closing in behind them so they could not return to their base. Furthermore, despite the contract, Balchen wanted a third man aboard if they were forced down, while Ellsworth felt strongly there should be only two so more fuel and survival equipment could be carried.

Wilkins and Balchen persuaded Ellsworth to wait a while longer and when the weather had cleared up there and it was reported by Byrd's meteorologist that it was reasonably good at Little America, Balchen and Ellsworth loaded their gear aboard the Northrop. Finally, on 3 January 1935, after several false starts when Balchen could not get the plane airborne because of the drifted snow and glazed surface, he finally inched the heavily loaded Gamma off the sticky surface.[40]

Balchen set the course for Little America, but they did not fly very far before they ran into a wall of bad weather. The tops of the clouds were above the plane's capability to climb over them, so he flew over the east side of Graham Land so that Ellsworth could at least see and make observations and sketches of some of the continent on that side. They flew over fjords, inlets, islands, and several mountains never before mapped. The flight lasted about 2½ hr. and covered about 400 mi. before Balchen turned back toward Snow Hill. Ellsworth was very displeased with Balchen's decision not to proceed through the weather. He thought they would land somewhere to wait out the weather and then continue, but Balchen felt they could be stranded for an indefinite length of time if they did. Besides, if they had an accident and the plane was not flyable, Balchen felt that he was physically capable of skiing to either Little America or their base but that Ellsworth was not. When they arrived at Snow Hill, Ellsworth vented his disappointment and stomped off to the ship.[41]

Balchen was unmoved by Ellsworth's appraisal of his decision. As Ellsworth stomped from the landing area to the ship, Balchen remarked to Wilkins, "Ellsworth can commit suicide if he likes, but he can't take me with him."[42]

Ellsworth later wrote,

Balchen grievously disappointed me, but that has not lessened my esteem for him. When the following year [on his next expedition without Balchen] our radio broke down and the world did not hear from me for two months, the magazine *Time* insinuated that I had deliberately silenced the radio to build up publicity for myself. One of the first to speak up in my defense was Bernt Balchen.[43]

Ellsworth remained keenly disappointed in the failure to make the transantarctic flight but rationalized the expense of the expedition this way: "It added five islands, three deep fjords, and several conspicuous mountain peaks to the sum of human knowledge about the Antarctic. There is satisfaction, to be sure, in having added the results of this expedition to the sum total of knowledge."[44]

On 11 January the *Wyatt Earp* left for Montevideo with the *Polar Star* through heavy pack ice, snow squalls, and fog. The ship was stuck in the ice for several days and was nearly crushed by ice floes that were 30 to 40 ft. thick. For one seven-day period, which Balchen considered the most harrowing of any of his experiences aboard any ship, the *Wyatt Earp* pushed, turned, backed up, and groped relentlessly through the jagged ice floes and towering bergs. It was nearly rammed several times, but after many frustrating days the gallant ship was finally able to get into clear waters.

En route to Argentina, Ellsworth announced that he planned still another trip the following October to accomplish his cross-continent flight.
Meanwhile, the *Polar Star* would be stored and the ship would be docked
at Montevideo until his return the next fall. He wanted Wilkins and
Balchen to head the party again; Balchen was offered a retainer of $300
per month until the expedition departed from the United States the
following fall. Balchen listened intently but told Ellsworth he had other
plans. He said he wanted to return to Norway and left the ship at
Montevideo.[45]

8·Prelude to War

A cablegram awaited Balchen in Montevideo from Hjalmar Riiser-Larsen, his former commanding officer in the Royal Norwegian air force: Five Norwegian shipping companies had formed Det Norske Luftfartselskab (DNL), an airline that would be managed by Rudolph and Thomas Olsen of the Fred Olsen Line and Thomas Falck of the Bergenske Steamship Company. Riiser-Larsen had been appointed a director and said they wanted to begin operations in May 1935. Would Balchen be interested in returning to Norway to help in its development?

Balchen cabled that he was *very* interested but had to conclude his responsibilities with Ellsworth first. He traveled to California and reported to Northrop and his engineers on the performance of the *Polar Star* in the antarctic climate and other matters of interest about the expedition, then sailed to Norway, arriving there the beginning of May 1935.

Riiser-Larsen met Balchen at the dock, and Balchen saw his wife and son for the first time in two and a half years. A meeting with the Olsen brothers soon followed. The Olsen Line, then one of the largest steamship freight lines in the world, had been founded by their father, a forward-thinking man who had instilled in his sons the necessity of keeping up with the continual improvements being made in transportation, especially aviation. There had been several previous attempts to start an airline beginning in 1927, but they had failed because of inadequate capital.

Because of its mountainous topography, Norway always faced difficulties constructing roads and rail lines, particularly along the coast; therefore, transportation between the major cities had usually been by ship. The same problem of topography applied to building airfields; as a consequence, Norwegian aviation was focused on seaplanes that required fewer facilities beyond a good harbor large enough for aircraft to land and dock. A national scheduled airline with land planes would require the support of the government for airfields, passenger, and maintenance facilities.

There were only about a dozen airfields in Norway in the mid-1930s; no seaplane stations existed except for a few small military bases, and none were strategically located. An airline would have to start from scratch, beginning with an inexperienced ground organization and minimal facilities. The first step, as Balchen saw it, was to visit the major cities and inform the townspeople that their cooperation would be needed if they were to have any scheduled airline service.

Riiser-Larsen and Balchen made a good team, with Riiser-Larsen running the office and Balchen supervising the pilots, inspecting facilities, and planning for the future. The equipment used during the first summer would be a German JU-52 transport on floats to fly between Oslo and Bergen and connect with the southern cities along the coast.

To make arrangements to accept the plane in the summer of 1935 Balchen went to the seaplane base at Travemunde, Germany, which was one of the Luftwaffe's main training sites for their Baltic Sea patrols. Balchen was surprised to see, despite the restrictions against building an air force as specified by the Versailles Treaty signed after World War I, some Heinkel bombers and Messerschmitt fighters on the airfield. He was received cordially by the Luftwaffe officers, who were not at all hesitant about admitting that it was a military base and that they were making a rapid buildup. He was allowed to examine several of the bombers and fighters and saw that they had many flying hours on them as evidenced by the worn rudder pedals and seats.

Balchen also saw Hitler Youth marching and drilling, singing, and goose stepping. Balchen sensed that something was going to happen.[1] Industries of all kinds were growing rapidly, buildings were being built everywhere and no one was out of work. But the German economy was shaky. Hard currency was needed and the German aircraft industry would give large discounts and rebates from foreign countries to get it.[2]

When he returned to Norway Balchen visited the American ambassador Anthony Drexel "Tony" Biddle and Norwegian government officials and gave them a lengthy report about what he had seen in Germany.

Deutsche Lufthansa began making daily flights to Oslo from Copenhagen, Denmark, with seaplanes. In 1936 DNL joined in a pool arrangement with the German and Swedish air operations, which Balchen viewed as a welcome arrangement at the time because it enabled Norway to be a part of the burgeoning airline industry in Europe.

Based on his transatlantic flight in 1927, observations of aircraft and airline developments in the United States, and discussions with leading aircraft manufacturers, Balchen was very interested in the long-range economic potential of transatlantic transportation. He felt that Norway should also be making plans to establish overseas international routes, and received a favorable reception for the idea from the DNL directors. He returned to the United States in January 1936 to find out what types of aircraft might be available and to look for an American partner to establish a transatlantic route. To his pleasant surprise, financial and airline leaders were willing to meet with him to discuss the idea. Pan American Airways officials were among those Balchen talked to, although none of those he contacted could make any commitments. However, he had a sudden, unexpected break. He met Postmaster General James A. Farley and brought up the subject of transatlantic air transport. At that time few thought that regular flights across the Atlantic could be sustained all year or ever be economical. Balchen disagreed with this and said he believed transatlantic flights would eventually be made year-round because of the aircraft and engine advances then being made. Farley was interested in his rationale, especially when Balchen said that DNL was trying to make contact with Pan American Airways for a Norway–United States route.

Farley listened intently, then said, "Bernt, you have something there and I think the Boss would like to have your opinion on these things. Can you come over with me tomorrow?"[3]

The next morning Balchen met with President Roosevelt in the White House and briefed him on his concept of a partnership to begin transatlantic operations. The president was extremely interested and asked Farley to have Balchen meet with the Norwegian minister and get authority from the two governments to negotiate an operational agreement between DNL and an unspecified American airline. A meeting was held 21 February 1936 at the Norwegian Legation.[4]

Norwegian minister to the United States Wilhelm Morgenstierne immediately authorized Balchen to appear before a congressional committee and received permission to enter into negotiations with Pan American to open a route to Norway. This was the first bilateral air agreement between the United States and Norway. Balchen then worked out a tentative agreement with Pan American in New York for test flights to take place during 1937 on a route from New York, to Reykjavik, Iceland, and on to Bergen, Norway. Pan Am would fly the first leg to Reykjavik, and DNL would fly the second to Bergen.

Balchen bought a twin-engine Sikorsky S-43 amphibian for the company and brought it to Norway by ship in August 1936. The 15-passenger S-43 was the ideal aircraft at the time, because it could operate with equal ease from European landing fields or from the harbors and fjords along Norway's mountainous coast line. Trial runs were made to London, Amsterdam, Stockholm, and other European cities with a Norwegian crew.

That summer DNL also chartered two trimotored Junkers JU-52 transports on floats. Balchen checked out the pilots, but the first one had a fatal accident on the route between Bergen and Trondheim when he flew in bad weather into a mountain four days after Balchen had cleared him to fly; all aboard were killed. Balchen led the rescue team in a futile search for survivors. He was furious when he learned, after checking the pilot's records, the cause of the accident: The pilot, against Balchen's many cautions during pilot briefings, had attempted to fly in the clouds on instruments when he had no blind flying experience.[5]

Several weeks later Balchen led a mercy mission and flew a doctor and nurses in the remaining JU-52 to a small village in a rugged, deep valley on Lake Loen at the head of the Nordfjord. It had been all but obliterated by an avalanche and a resulting tidal wave in the adjoining lake. It was a dangerous undertaking with the lake full of floating trees, houses, and debris. Balchen landed cautiously and taxied slowly to where the village had been literally torn from the hillside. Of the 128 people in the village, 90 had been killed. Balchen made several flights to evacuate the injured.

In June 1937 Balchen lost three dear friends—Chris Braathen, his wife Molly, and Arild Wideroe. They had been riding as passengers in a plane that had lost a wing, and all aboard were killed. And Amelia Earhart, with Fred Noonan as navigator, had disappeared between Lae, New Guinea, and Howland Island in the mid-Pacific while attempting a round-the-world flight. Balchen wrote in his diary: "There is an empty space in my circle of friends."[6]

In the interest of looking toward the east for possible DNL route expansion in the future, Balchen made a trip to Moscow in July 1937 to visit officials of Aeroflot, the Russian national airline, and discuss possible cooperation to exchange passengers, mail, and cargo. He had difficulty with the Russian officials on arrival because he was traveling as a Norwegian courier on an American passport. They confiscated the passport and would not tell him when it would be returned.

At the Moscow airport he saw evidence of a military buildup, with bombing planes parked in large numbers. He visited Prof. Otto Schmidt, director of the Polar Institute, who had just returned from an expedition to the North Pole. Schmidt, a brilliant scientist, had established a floating ice station, supplying it with Soviet four-engine cargo versions of the TB-4 heavy bomber. Four scientists remained there for nine months after the planes left.

During a dinner at the Swedish Legation, Balchen learned about the ingrained mindset of suspicion and mistrust that the Russians exhibited in their everyday lives. For example, according to one diplomat, if someone approaches you in Russia and says, "Hello, it's a fine day today," the average Russian reaction is, "What does this person mean by this remark? What is he up to for him to make such a comment? What does he want from me?" A veteran Norwegian diplomat told him about the "two truths" that guided the Soviets in all their dealings—one was for the ruling hierarchy and the other for outsiders.[7]

Balchen did not have a satisfactory meeting with any Aeroflot employee. When he asked to see the Aeroflot manager, he was told he was on vacation and it was not known when he would return. Balchen was followed everywhere he went, and during his absence from his hotel room his luggage was searched. It was obvious he would not meet any Aeroflot or government officials nor would it be possible to work with the Russians on any kind of cooperative venture. His passport was finally returned with the help of the Norwegian Legation.

The business of establishing a viable airline continued at a slow pace. Several more Junkers transports were purchased, and Balchen made several trips to Germany to buy spare parts. Traveling with a group of Norwegian officials to Berlin's Tempelhof Airport in 1938 after Hitler's invasion of Austria, he saw more than a hundred bombers lined up with machine guns protruding from the tails. One Norwegian member of the group remarked, "What in the world are they going to do with those?" Balchen replied that they were certainly not to be used for fishing trips but for war. The Norwegian asked, "For war against whom?"[8]

On this same trip Balchen witnessed a torchlight parade from the balcony of the Kaiserhof Hotel, with 250,000 people participating, and heard Goebbels and Hitler speak. (Balchen spoke German and was thus able to understand them.) Goebbels was a good speaker, Balchen said, who appealed to the German public. There was a catchy repetition in his speech that aroused the audience. Hitler followed and ranted about what he was going to do to his enemies and telling what a wonderful thing the Anschluss, the "union" or annexation of Austria, was and how Austrian industry was going to be built up, all with the help of the Reich.

"It was terrifying to see the masses and the power that propaganda and speech had," Balchen recalled. "When I heard the surge of voices, like an ocean, and saw the Nazi flags with the swastikas, and the torches and heard the *Sieg Heil*, it scared me. I realized then that we were up against an ideology that looked medieval to me."[9]

Balchen made a final trip to Berlin in May 1939 to discuss the possibility of obtaining military equipment and parts for DNL's JU-52 transports. While at the Adlon Hotel he had a chance meeting with Ernst Udet, famous German flying ace who was then in charge of German aircraft technical developments. He had visited the United States many times to demonstrate his considerable aerobatic flying skills and was well-liked by American pilots. Balchen had met him several times at air races and Quiet Birdmen meetings in the United States. Udet invited him to his apartment for cocktails and dinner. Udet said they might have a visitor later.

About 2200 Air Marshall Hermann Goering arrived. The ensuing conversation was about mutual aviation acquaintances and Balchen's trips to the polar regions. The conversation drifted to military aviation developments and eventually hit a sore spot with Goering. He suddenly exploded with anger when Goering and Udet began to discuss freezing the design of the Messerschmitt fighters and other warplanes ordered by Field Marshall Erhard Milch and Hitler. By the time the second bottle of brandy was opened, Hitler was no longer the Führer; he was demoted to *"der kleine Korporal"* (the little corporal).[10]

Balchen visited the Junkers factory the next day and was told that there were more than 20,000 workers there, with further increases planned. Stuka dive bombers were also being produced in great numbers. He traveled to Oschersleben and Balchen saw about 400 of the latest Messerschmitt fighters lined up on the airfield.

Balchen returned to Norway more deeply concerned about the possibility of war. It was clear that Norway was not prepared for any military confrontation with the Germans and should update their military forces as soon as possible. It seemed to Balchen the formation of an international airline alliance was more important than ever to connect Scandinavia with the North American continent.

At this time it was learned that British Imperial Airways was negotiating with Washington, D.C., authorities for transocean service rights. If a small nation such as Norway got an agreement with an American carrier, Great Britain's flag carrier would be at a competitive disadvantage. The British planes were not ready yet and Pan American/DNL officials were notified by American civil aviation officials that their flights would have to be postponed until further notice.

Balchen and DNL's board of directors were very disappointed. They realized that the only way to establish transatlantic air service now would be for a joint operation with the Swedes, Danes, and Finns. Denmark's Det Danske Luftfartselskab (DDL) and Sweden's AB Aerotransport (ABA) each already had an international network in place with routes to Berlin and Amsterdam, whereas DNL and Finnair (Aero OY) were concentrating on establishing domestic routes. At a meeting of executives of the four airlines it was decided that Balchen should return to the United States and present a case on behalf of all four to obtain cargo, mail, and passenger rights to and from Scandinavia. The official history of Scandinavian Airlines System (SAS) reported the developments: "Off Balchen went, and he quickly gained the results he sought. Thanks to his numerous aviation feats he was at that time more famous in the U.S.A. than in his native Norway. He had meetings with Secretary of State Cordell Hull, and he was equally well received by the heads of the federal postal and civil aviation authorities."[11]

Finland, on the brink of war with Russia, could not participate in these meetings. The other three nations agreed in principal that a direct route between Scandinavia and the United States would be operated by themselves or in a sharing agreement with a U.S. air carrier. In this climate of cooperation, the solution was to form what was initially called the Scandinavian Air Union.

During the Washington, D.C., meetings with aviation and postal authorities, Balchen was able to negotiate an agreement to have full rights for DNL to pick up traffic at Foynes, Ireland. Pan American inaugurated its first transatlantic flight on 28 June 1939 from the base at Port Washington, Long Island.

The international situation became more tense. The Norwegian government, now more worried about Germany's intentions regarding Scandinavia, sent Balchen back to Washington, D.C., with a military delegation to negotiate the purchase of updated military equipment and combat aircraft. He was also requested by the Finnish government (chief of the Finnish air force, General Lundquist) to assist in procuring fighter planes for Finland.

When German panzer forces invaded Poland on 1 September 1939, Pan American immediately abandoned its route to Ireland and flew to England via Lisbon, Portugal. On 3 September Prime Minister Neville Chamberlain announced that a state of war existed between England and Germany.

Hitler's aggression in Europe was now more threatening than ever to Norway. Riiser-Larsen joined Balchen in convincing the Norwegian government of possible attacks by Germany and that Norway must prepare to defend itself. When in Washington, D.C., Balchen called on his American military friends at the War Department and told them what he had seen in Germany and Russia. Balchen felt that they did not take his report seriously and told him they had better, more up-to-date information.[12]

On 7 November 1939 it was announced in Stockholm that Balchen the next day would fly the first plane on a new Stockholm–Oslo–Aberdeen, Scotland, route. The inauguration of the route was in the hopes that war would not involve the Scandinavian countries and they could remain neutral. However, they became deeply concerned when on 30 November 1939 the Soviet Union attacked a relatively inferior but fiercely determined Finland with 540,000 troops. The main defense was the 88 mi. Mannerheim Line, which held and caused massive Soviet casualties. However, the Soviets reorganized and a 900,000-person force overwhelmed the Finns, who suffered about 50,000 casualties out of 150,000 troops; the Russians lost an estimated 200,000 dead and 400,000 wounded. In view of these horrendous losses, the threat to the other Scandinavian countries from the Soviet Union now seemed more probable than an attack from Germany.

Balchen, in Helsinki when the war between Finland and Russia began, was asked to be a consultant to the Finnish Air Staff and agreed to do what he could in his unique position as a representative for Norway and now Finland. With their supplies low and no hope of replenishment, the Finns surrendered and the hostilities ended on 13 March 1940. The cost of peace to the Finns was heavy and bitter. The peace treaty caused Finland to cede 16,000 square miles of territory to the Soviet Union.

Balchen had been negotiating with American equipment manufacturers for the Royal Norwegian air force and placed a few contracts in

1939. As a result he was recognized as a valuable go-between whose signature on military orders was valid. It was now more imperative than ever that the deliveries begin as soon as possible. In addition to these new responsibilities, Balchen went to the United States just before Christmas 1939 to prepare for a meeting of the Scandinavian Airmail and Air Traffic Commission scheduled for January. Increasing numbers of telegrams began to arrive from Norway for Balchen in Washington, D.C., asking him to procure all kinds of war equipment and ammunition while he was making arrangements for the delegations of the commission to arrive. Meetings were arranged with the U.S. State Department with a renewed urgency to get an airline operation inaugurated into a neutral country. Bergen, Norway, was discussed as an entry point because it was north of the combat zones of Europe. Pan American Airways was again the airline of choice, and negotiations were reopened with their top officials.

A charter agreement was made with Pan American to provide service to Norway with a four-engine Sikorsky S-42 seaplane beginning on 7 June 1940. Meanwhile, the requirements for war supplies for Norway were increasing daily. Procurements were made through the Norwegian Military Commission, and they were completed by the end of March. The delegates from the Scandinavian countries returned home, leaving Balchen in the United States to handle the follow-up paperwork.

On 8 April 1940, while Balchen was on a yacht in New York harbor having lunch with the sales manager of the Goodyear Rubber Company, he heard a radio announcement that a German troop transport had been torpedoed off Kristiansand in southern Norway. Norwegians had saved many of the German troops from drowning and learned from them that their forces were planning to occupy Norway "to protect the country from an invasion by the British." The next day the German invasion of Balchen's homeland began.

Forty thousand German troops were ashore within three hours. The 20,000-person Norwegian force was no match for the overpowering Nazi war machine, but the terrain, the poor road system, and determined resistance from the population caused the Nazis to take sixty-two days to complete the occupation. British naval and ground forces that had come to help were outnumbered, beaten, and forced to withdraw on 8 June 1940. The Germans, cruelly and without warning, had broken a Norwegian peace that had lasted for more than 125 years. Thousands of Germans, who as children some 20 years before had been invited to the country to recover from starvation after World War I now returned to kill, capture, and enslave those who had treated them as their own children.[13]

When the news of the invasion of his homeland was announced in Washington, D.C., Balchen had sole authority over military contracts in the United States worth about $20 million. He also had the responsibility to carry out the charter agreements with the Scandinavian countries and Pan American Airways. However, the agreements were canceled and negotiations would not be resumed until the international situation cleared up.

Although the Norwegian forces had capitulated on 9 June 1940, Norway never signed a surrender document, nor were peace terms ever agreed on. King Haakon, his family, and top government officials had escaped two days before on a British warship and set up a government-in-exile in London. Other Norwegian government officials fled to the northern part of the country; some were able to escape by ship to England, Canada, and the United States.

Balchen, who held dual Norwegian and American citizenship, reported for duty with the Royal Norwegian air force at the Washington, D.C., office of the Norwegian minister to the United States. When Balchen presented Minister Morgenstierne a list of the contracts and commitments of the Norwegian government with U.S. suppliers, he was immediately empowered to negotiate "matters pertaining to aircraft ordnance and ammunition in connection with the question of the Norwegian Government's possible purchase of such materials in the United States of America."[14] It was indeed an unusual arrangement for an American with dual citizenship in another country to conduct such vital procurement actions on behalf of that foreign government, but it served to prove the confidence that the leaders of Balchen's homeland had in his integrity and honesty.

It was obviously a time of great confusion. No one knew what funds were available, and equipment made by a number of American firms was about to be shipped; all wanted to know where to send it and to be paid. Balchen called on the French–British Purchasing Commission in New York City and worked out a deal whereby the money would be loaned to pay the bills, with the equipment to be security for the loans. Shortly, however, the British and French wanted to buy the materials but Balchen would not agree unless he had authority from the Norwegian government-in-exile in London. He did not get it. Instead, he received instructions to go to Canada and negotiate with the Canadian government for a suitable place where a camp could be set up to train Norwegian pilots, mechanics, and soldiers, men who made their way by long, dangerous routes to join the Norwegian air and ground forces. The shortage of airfields in the British Isles, plus the fact that Norway had aircraft built in the United States being readied for delivery when the country was invaded, led to the decision to request Canadian facilities.[15]

Balchen found a welcome there where he was already well-known for his pioneer flights to Hudson Bay in 1926. Within three weeks of the German invasion of Norway Balchen had an agreement with the Canadian government that the Island Airport outside Toronto would be made available to build a training base that would be called Little Norway. Bernt immediately assisted in negotiating the initial contracts for construction.

Col. Oscar Klingenberg of the Royal Norwegian air force, then military attaché at the Norwegian Legation in Washington, D.C., was chosen to head the training schools. The camp officially opened to accept the first trainees on 10 November 1940 and the first fully trained Norwegian unit went overseas in April 1941 to Iceland. The initial all-Norwegian fighter squadrons arrived in England in June 1941.[16]

When building construction on the base was begun and high-ranking officers were on hand, Balchen returned to New York where he acted as air attaché, civil aviation representative, and recruiting officer. When more Norwegian officers arrived, Balchen turned over these liaison functions to the Norwegian Legation in Washington, D.C.

There were two Norwegians to whom Balchen believed Norway especially owed a debt of gratitude during this period of confusion. One was Georg Unger Vetlesen, who helped to organize the buildup of Little Norway and assisted people who had escaped the country to work for the government-in-exile. The other was Thor Solberg, who established an office in Washington, D.C., to deal with aircraft manufacturers and handle procurement affairs; both took on their responsibilities without pay.

In June 1940 Balchen's wife arrived in New York from Norway with Bernt, Jr., and the couple soon came to realize that they had come to a parting of ways. They agreed to separate and she left for Arizona. However, a divorce was not to become final until January 1948.

Balchen asked to get into action when it appeared that the administrative tasks were in capable Norwegian hands. He had met Clyde Pangborn, and they discussed their experiences together while at Teterboro. Pangborn was then flying as a contract pilot for the British Royal air force to ferry aircraft to the war fronts under the American Lend–Lease

Act. More pilots were needed, so Balchen asked for permission from the Norwegian air force to fly for the British. Permission was granted, and on 1 February they were selected to be the first pilots to ferry a new Consolidated flying boat (PBY) from San Diego to Manila for eventual British use at Singapore. They were to fly via Hawaii, Midway, and Wake Islands, to Guam, and the Philippines.

Balchen and Pangborn made three PBY ferrying flights across the Pacific together and returned via Pan American Airways Clippers. Although they had a high priority, they were not always able to get aboard without a few days' wait.

While waiting for the Royal air force to accept a PBY at Cavite in the Philippines in May 1941, the two visited Nichols Field, where some U.S. Army Air Corps friends were stationed. One was Lieutenant Lester Maitland, who had flown from the United States to Hawaii in a Fokker at the same time that Balchen had flown across the Atlantic in 1927. As they left Maitland's office preparing to go to lunch, a civilian approached Balchen and asked if he were Lieutenant Balchen. He showed his identification as an FBI agent and said that Maj. Gen. Henry H. "Hap" Arnold, chief of the U.S. Army Air Corps, had asked the Bureau to locate Balchen. The agent asked if he could reply to General Arnold that he could be found at Lt. Maitland's office. Balchen was puzzled but said, "Ja, you bet."

That evening, as the group of old friends gathered for dinner in Manila, the same agent approached Balchen and handed him a cablegram. The message was that Balchen was to report to the Norwegian and British embassies in Washington, D.C., as soon as possible and that he was to travel Priority 1 on Pan American at U.S. government expense.

Despite having the highest travel priority, it took 10 days for Balchen to reach Washington, D.C. He promptly reported to the Norwegian Embassy, then to the British Embassy, where the air attaché took him directly to General Arnold's office in the War Department building. He was greeted warmly by Arnold, whom he had met during his test work with Fokker. Balchen recalled,

He looked at me and said, "Bernt, where in the hell have you been? I've been looking all over the world for you for the last three months. Naturally, I thought I would find you in England but you turn up in, of all places, Manila. That's no place for you. Quit this fooling around and join this man's army; we have use for you here and we have a job that I think would interest you."[17]

Arnold then asked what his rank was and Balchen told him that it was flight lieutenant in the Royal Norwegian air force. "Well, we'll make you a captain right now. Go down the hall to see [Maj. Gen. Carl A.] 'Tooey' Spaatz."[18]

Surprised at this unexpected turn of events, Balchen left, and as he went into Spaatz's office, he met another friend, Maj. (later Maj. Gen.) Edward P. "Ted" Curtis, a World War I ace, then an aide to General Spaatz. Curtis recalled that when Arnold first summoned him,

> I went in and he said, "Where's Bernt Balchen?" I said, "Sir, I haven't the faintest idea where Bernt Balchen is." "Well, find him! Get him in; I want to commission him in the Air Force. I want to send him to Greenland," he said.
>
> So I eventually ran Bernt down. We got him in and he was quite willing to be commissioned in the Air Force. We went through the usual routine of getting him a physical examination, then Dave Grant, the Air Surgeon, came into my office and said, "You can't commission this guy. He's got the worst hernia I ever saw in my life, and if Hap tries to send him up to Greenland, the guy will die."
>
> "Well, what do we do about that?" He said, "You'll have to get it operated on." I said, "Fine. Send him out to Walter Reed [Hospital] and get him operated on." He said, "You can't send him to Walter Reed; he's a civilian."
>
> So I solved the problem by hiring Bernt as a consultant on the frozen north at 50 bucks a day or something like that, and we put him in one of the civilian hospitals in Washington, and got his hernia operated on.
>
> Then it developed that there was an Army regulation that you couldn't commission anybody until six months after they had a hernia operation. So we had to get General Arnold to waive that provision, and eventually got Bernt commissioned, and off he went.[19]

Balchen reminded General Spaatz that he was still a lieutenant in the Royal Norwegian air force and had to be officially discharged before he could accept a commission in the U.S. Army Air Corps. Spaatz told Curtis to take care of that formality, and as they walked away Curtis explained that Balchen was to go to Greenland as head of Task Force 8 and establish an airfield for servicing aircraft being sent from the United States to England under the Lend–Lease Act. The field was also to be used as a base for aircraft to patrol Greenland and the sea lanes and to act as a weather and radio reporting station.

Balchen was eager to join the U.S. Air Force, and when notified that he was released from the Royal Norwegian air force he relinquished his Norwegian citizenship as required to accept a commission (he heretofore had dual citizenship) and was sworn in to the U.S. Army Air Corps on 5 September 1941 as a captain, specialist reserve. At the same time Balchen was awarded the rating of command pilot based on his more than 6,000 hr. of flying time.

As commander of Task Force 8 he was now ready to tackle the formidable, unprecedented task of establishing the northernmost American military base in history. It was to be one of the most valuable links between the aviation resources of the United States and the battle zones in Europe.

On 12 September 1941 General Arnold wrote Balchen a personal letter that explained the importance of the task:

Dear Balchen:

No greater challenge to the pioneering spirit of Americans has ever been presented than the present vital necessity for the United States Army Air Forces to prepare themselves for operation in the Far North. The thin paths beaten in the snow by courageous explorers have been obliterated by time. It is up to us to establish detachments to serve as stepping stones to the far-flung areas we must reach.

To accomplish this task, we have hand-picked a small group of men with known qualities of leadership, of ingenuity, of initiative. You are part of this group. On you rests the success of our job. Upon your shoulders rests the burden of keeping us informed of the weather, ships which may pass through your area and the many other important incidents which will come to your notice or attention.

Communications and correspondence are sharply limited by secrecy which of necessity surrounds your mission. Do not feel, on this account, that you and the enlisted men under you are "forgotten men," or in any danger of becoming so. I have issued specific instructions that I be kept constantly informed of your activities, which are of the deepest concern to me.

I know your job is tough. I know, also, that your standards are high. We are depending on you.[20]

With this encouragement from the highest ranking Army Air Corps offi-cer, Balchen immediately set forth on a new endeavor wherein his past experience, talents, and intuition would be put to the ultimate test. Among his many qualifications for the task ahead was his engineering education and knowledge of arctic construction under the permafrost conditions expected, which he had acquired when he was stationed at Horten in Norway and when he worked with Amundsen at Spitsbergen. The location already selected by the War Department was a flat site at the head of the Sondrestromfjord in southwest Greenland, code-named Bluie West 8. Its corollary importance as a base from which spectacular rescues of air crews would be conducted was not anticipated.

9 · The Challenge of Bluie West 8

American interest in Greenland had been aroused as early as 1916 during treaty negotiations with Denmark. At that time Denmark agreed to sell the Virgin Islands to the United States for $25 million if the United States would relinquish all claims to Greenland based on the explorations of Robert Peary. Peary had loudly protested such an agreement because he foresaw that Greenland could be a valuable land link between Europe and the North American continent. However, the treaty was signed without consideration of Peary's viewpoint. Later, Gen. Billy Mitchell, famous U.S. air power advocate, reminded senators in congressional testimony in 1919 that if airmen had been consulted before it was signed, they would have advised against giving up American rights to northern Greenland because it "would form an ideal air base for commercial air traffic to Europe and Asia in case of war."[1]

Norway, Great Britain, and Canada were also interested in Greenland, and the debate continued until 1933 when the Permanent Court at The Hague decided for Danish sovereignty over the entire island. Thus from the days of Mitchell, the Army Air Corps planners and thinkers had advocated a defense of the United States by thrusting air forces far from U.S. shores. Originally this meant meeting any enemy invading by sea as far away as possible and was the basic rationale for production of long-range bombers. Under President Roosevelt, the concept grew to one of hemispheric defense, including Canada. As Hitler began his conquests in Europe, the danger zones enlarged when it was assumed that the German Luftwaffe would soon have its own long- range bombers. Iceland, Greenland, and Newfoundland could be stepping stones for German aggression across the North Atlantic to the East Coast of North America.

In August 1940 the governments of Canada and the United States announced the establishment of a permanent joint board to coordinate defense measures for North America. A 99-year lease agreement was made on 9 April 1941 with Henrik de Kauffmann, ambassador for the Danish government-in-exile, in which the United States would take over the protection of Greenland and, in return, be allowed to build bases on the world's largest island.

One of the first steps needed to aid the allies under attack or threatened directly was the removal of an arms embargo that had become effective in November 1939. This was known as the Cash and Carry law, which allowed warring nations to acquire arms within the United States by cash purchase. The U.S. Army Air Corps was then able to release combat aircraft to France, England, and other allied nations. Those destined for the European theater were dismantled and sent by ship. As the war progressed and German submarines became an increasingly active threat, the urgency to establish air bases in Greenland became more pronounced. If bases were established in Greenland and Iceland, it would be possible for planes with moderate range to be flown from the factories of the United States and Canada to the fighting fronts in Europe.

With the background of international interest in Greenland, the South Greenland Survey Expedition, consisting of diplomats, naval and army officers, and an observer from the Royal Canadian air force, left the United States in March 1941 and spent several months scouting the terrain in Greenland. In the late spring and early summer of 1941, small U.S. Army detachments were sent to establish and man communications and weather stations in Labrador, Baffin Island, Newfoundland, Greenland, and Iceland. Thirteen stations, eight on western Greenland and five on the eastern side, were scheduled to be constructed and staffed. At the same time, U.S. Army Air Corps planners decided on four locations where aviation units should be based as soon as possible; one of them was at the Newfoundland Airport at Gander Lake. This was because the latest German bombers had the range to fly from Norway to Newfoundland and then, with one refueling there, to New York. By stationing bombers at Gander Lake, American forces could patrol the approaches to the hemisphere, and prevent the establishment of Axis air bases on the continent or on Greenland, some 800 mi. to the north.

Disturbed by Hitler's successes in Europe, the air staff in Washington, D.C., made a study of future requirements to assist in expediting the transfer of aircraft to England. In a report to General Arnold in July

1941, the study recommended that a "staging airdrome" be established at Sondrestromfjord on the western side of Greenland. The study specified that housing should be supplied for 54 people plus accommodations for 70 transient ferrying crew members. A 5,000 ft. runway with parking ramp and a two million gal. aviation gasoline storage area would be required, and installation of a direction-finder station, aircraft radio range, weather station, and a large maintenance hangar were also recommended.[2]

In August 1941 Capt. Elliott Roosevelt, son of the president, then assigned to the 21st Reconnaissance Squadron in Newfoundland, was placed in charge of a survey team and ordered to make an extensive aerial survey of Greenland and Iceland. His candid report covered geographic, psychological, economic, climatic, combat, and communications information gleaned over a three-week period. Among his observations was his concern that although Greenland's defenses would be relatively safe from attack, Iceland was more vulnerable to enemy aggression, and the flow of aircraft to England could be interrupted if it were under German control. Roosevelt commented,

> The airports could be placed out of commission with the greatest of ease. . . . Because the British used Iceland as a rest camp for infantry troops after Dunkirk, a plan of defense has grown up which is extremely vulnerable and which leaves open the question as to whether too much reliance can be placed on Iceland as a ferry base of operations. . . . Terminal defenses for airports in the British Isles which are now used by the Ferry Command are ludicrous.[3]

Thinking of the political aspects of the ferrying operation, Roosevelt commented that there were "many Nazi sympathizers throughout Iceland amongst the native population" but the Icelandic press was controlled by the British. "Icelanders hate the British," he wrote. "At the present time they are on the fence regarding their attitude toward the United States occupying forces. The way the situation is being handled, in another six months the Icelanders will dislike the U.S. as fervently as they do the British."[4]

In his conclusions and recommendations Roosevelt stated, "If the U.S. Army Air Forces operate a ferrying of aircraft for delivery in the British Isles, they must control the weather and communications systems all the way to the British Isles, including the terminal point."[5]

The first movement of U.S. troops to Newfoundland had occurred in January 1941 when a small contingent arrived at St. John's to form the nucleus of the Newfoundland Base Command. The preparations for bases in Greenland were not as far along. Surveys made in the spring and summer of 1941 had failed to disclose any site immediately suitable for an airfield on the east coast, but a promising site that could be built most easily was found on a glacial moraine at the southern tip of the island at Narsarssuak, about 35 mi. northeast of Julianehaab. It was considered ideally located midway between Goose Bay, Labrador, and Reykjavik, Iceland, approximately 775 miles from each. It was given the code name of Bluie West 1 (BW-1). A base at this location would enable relatively short-range combat aircraft being ferried to make short hops from the factories in North America to the units in the British Isles. Work on this base had begun in July 1941 when an advance task force of engineer and general service troops arrived. It was designated the headquarters of the Greenland Command. By September Army engineers had constructed 85 buildings and 3 mi. of access roads and work had begun on the airfield.

Recognizing that another base was needed as a backup, a site was chosen farther north on the west coast near Sondrestromfjord just above the Arctic Circle and was code-named Bluie West 8 (BW-8). This was planned originally as an alternate base for aircraft moving from Goose Bay, Labrador, to Iceland during periods when bad weather made landings impossible at BW-1. However, the flying weather proved to be generally better along the alternate route through BW-8 and across the ice cap of central Greenland than to the south along the route through BW-1. A third base, named Bluie East 2 (BE-2), was established on the east coast near Angmagssalik, principally as a weather station. Because weather reporting was essential and because Greenland holds the key to forecasting the next day's weather in Europe, ten other small Bluie bases for weather reporting and communications were established and staffed along the east and west coasts of Greenland during mid-1941. They were also important for flying in Greenland because violent winds, called *williwaws* in Alaska and *foehnwinds* in Europe, can develop rapidly in a local area with a fury of up to 150 MPH.

It was this background of surveys and concerns for the ferry route that had caused General Arnold to seek out Balchen and use his expertise and knowledge to get BW-8 built and put into operation as quickly as possible. Balchen's initial task was to establish a basic construction plan for the base, specify the supplies needed and order them, have administrative and construction personnel assigned, make arrangements for shipping, and meet a September sailing date. Lt. Comdr. Charles J. Hubbard was loaned by the Navy; Dr. Francis D. Coman and Dr. Paul A. Siple, formerly on Byrd's antarctic expeditions, were called on to assist in provisioning for the base. Vilhjalmur Stefansson, leader of the Canadian arctic expedition of 1913–1918, was also consulted because of his experience in Greenland.

After beginning his work, first as a civilian then as an Army Air Forces captain, Balchen spent the next two hectic months carrying out the duties and responsibilities of an officer of much higher rank. In addition to being responsible for preparing runways, housing, and maintenance facilities he would also be the base commander with further responsibilities of patrolling the coastal areas and Danish settlements and acting as a communications link to transmit radio messages between U.S. forces in England and the United States. A letter of instructions was addressed to Balchen to emphasize the importance of his task:

The War Department recognizes the arduous duty and serious responsibility involved in this assignment. It is a duty which will require the highest degree of leadership and courage. The welfare of your men should be uppermost in your mind. Patience, humor and understanding must be carefully balanced with firmness. Every effort will be made to effect relief of the personnel in your detachment at the earliest possible time."[6]

Balchen did not have much information to go on in the selection of the exact site and layout for BW-8. Prof. William H. Hobbs of the University of Michigan Expedition had been at Sondrestromfjord in 1928 and established a base camp called Camp Lloyd. Bert R. J. Hassell and Parker D. Cramer had planned to refuel there on their projected 1928 flight from Rockford, Illinois, to Sweden to prove that new commercial air routes could be developed over the Great Circle route via the northern latitudes. They were unable to find Camp Lloyd, and made a crash landing. They were rescued by native fishermen and members of the Michigan University Expedition.

Donald MacMillan's 1931 flight from Boston to Labrador, Greenland, Iceland, the Faeroe Islands, and London proved how an air route could be established with a stop in Greenland. In 1933 Charles Lindbergh made a survey flight along the Greenland coast for Pan American Airways and believed the area at the end of the 115 mi. long Sondrestromfjord was a possible site for a future Pan American refueling base.

There was no doubt in Balchen's mind about Greenland's value to the overall scheme of getting aircraft to Britain. Balchen had visualized Greenland as a potential refueling stop in 1935 when he was head of operations at DNL because it would take advantage of generally prevailing clear weather and mild wind velocities, compared to any other route.

Despite the information from these early flights and surveys, Balchen felt that planning for a modern air field had to be based on aerial photographs taken a few months previously because of the ever-changing arctic ice fields. Laying out the various base facilities, ordering the construction materials, and planning the progress of the work depended on knowing the latest topographical features and information available.

Balchen learned that he would be assigned 70 Army specialists and about 700 civilian construction workers for Task Force 8 who had previous arctic or antarctic experience. They had to be volunteers but could not be told exactly where they were going except that they were going to a cold climate. Most of the workers hired were from Minnesota, the Dakotas, and other cold-weather states, selected for their experience with construction in subfreezing weather. The military men were hand-picked for their specialties.

Balchen's first meeting was in Washington, D.C., with an Army Corps of Engineers officer and the chief engineers from the two construction companies that won the contract. They were briefed on the urgency and special requirements of the project, now given top secret status. The number and size of barracks, dispensary, fuel storage area, warehouses, and vehicle and aircraft maintenance facilities were calculated and superimposed on the latest photographs. Army logistics tables were used to determine the long list of supplies needed, which had to be ordered from a number of manufacturing sources, all of which were being pressured by growing government demand for their products. Balchen had the highest priority from General Arnold for not only all the materials required but for the transportation to get them to the Brooklyn Port of Embarkation in time to meet a deadline for the departure of ships on 29 September 1941. Most of the critical materials had to be trucked from the west and midwest, and when he needed help to cut red tape or instill a sense of urgency into a company or organization that was dragging its feet, he called General Arnold's office and soon after resistance ceased. Because the whole project was classified top secret, only a few could be told why the special equipment or supplies were needed and their ultimate destination.[7]

The list of items requested included experienced dog teams. Balchen acquired 35 lively huskies from New Hampshire to fill this order. The kennel added two half-breed timber wolves, which turned out to be valuable additions as sledge-wheel dogs in the months to come. Sgts. Hendrick "Dutch" Holleman and Joseph Healy were assigned as dog drivers. They had already spent two Christmases away from home with the two Byrd antarctic expeditions and had become well-acquainted with isolation and the problems associated with it. They became two of Balchen's key personnel.

Balchen, inexperienced in the formal procurement procedures of the U.S. Army, ran into occasional road blocks when he could not divulge the reason why he needed items that were not standard. Building materials for housing were especially difficult to order. Balchen told of one encounter at the Corps of Engineers headquarters where he was told exactly what type of prefabricated house he could order but which Balchen said was unsatisfactory. He recalled,

> I was taken before a colonel who gave me a dressing down. He said, "Captain, that's what you're going to get." I said, "Colonel, that's not what I want." He nearly had a stroke from getting an answer like that [from a captain]. So, I said, "Will you just be kind enough to call General Arnold and he will clarify the situation for you, Sir."
>
> He so did. He told General Arnold that he had a very impertinent Air Force captain in his office who apparently didn't know very much about rules and regulations, and couldn't accept what he was going to get. Then his tone changed. He was holding on to the phone and said, "Yes, Sir." "Yes, Sir." "Yes, Sir." He turned to me and said, "Well, Captain, you will get what you want. I didn't know that this was such a special project."[8]

Procuring ammunition presented another problem for Balchen. He asked for a wartime allotment of ammunition from the Ordnance Department but a major intercepted his order and questioned why he needed a wartime allotment when there was no war. Balchen invited the major to call General Arnold's office. He was told to issue whatever Captain Balchen requested.[9]

In this fashion Balchen wound his way through the maze of the various government agencies that had control over what he needed. He found that many were living in a blissful, peacetime world of their own and were not moved to action until prodded by General Arnold.

Aircraft equipped for arctic operations were needed for surveys and patrol work, but ski planes were not available at the time. Balchen called his old friend Bob Noorduyn who, after leaving Fokker, had designed a high-wing single-engine plane that could be outfitted with skis, pontoons, or wheels for bush flying in the north countries. It was ideal for the work Balchen knew he had to do and he obtained one of the first models Noorduyn produced, which the Army Air Forces labeled the C-64 Norseman.

Recreational and educational needs were also addressed during the procurement process. Balchen knew well from his months in antarctica that everyone would need time off from the hard work that faced them, and relief from the cold, long arctic nights. In addition to novels and general interest nonfiction books, Balchen asked for polar literature that, when added to his own large personal library, amounted to about 600 volumes on the history of the polar regions. He procured a large assortment of games, puzzles, boxing gloves, footballs, and skis.[10]

Some of the things he could not get, despite General Arnold's *carte blanche,* included a collapsible Christmas tree and gifts for his men such as shaving and toilet kits, knives and clocks. He contacted Grover Whalen at Wanamaker's and explained the situation without revealing any classified information. He bought as many Christmas presents as he could afford with his own money and the balance was donated by Wanamaker. Three large crates full of Christmas gifts and decorations were delivered to the port by departure time.

Balchen and the main contingent of troops and workers left on the SS *Munargo* on 9 September 1941. Two cargo ships loaded with 50,000 tn. of construction supplies, lumber, cement, tractors, and trucks followed. The ships got underway in good weather and proceeded to Newfoundland and Labrador where the men saw their first icebergs. Balchen called everyone on deck and told them where they were headed. Three days later, the coast of Greenland with its jagged mountains and glaciers came into view.[11]

Preceded by the two cargo ships, on 9 October 1941 the *Munargo* steered into the fjord leading to Sondrestromfjord, where a pilot came aboard to take them through the narrow 1 mi. gap, which the natives call *Semiutak* (which means "cork" or "stopper"). The fjord is about 115 mi. long, moving in a northeast direction with mountains rising 7,000 ft. out of the water at the entrance. Farther on, the mountains are lower and there is a change in the geological formations from the sedimentary alpine formations to the rounded-off granite and glacier-like hills. After about 100 mi. the fjord widens and the Greenland ice cap can be seen in the distance.

The weather and the tides were factors that had to be considered when unloading the ships. Everything had to be unloaded over a 3,000 ft. wide mud flat, which was exposed at low tide; barges were used when the tides were high. Later, a channel was dredged through the mud and a small dock was constructed on the beach.

The first cooking facility on shore was a blacksmith's forge; a lean-to was built and the men could spend the first few nights ashore on the floor. Slowly but surely, with the men working in shifts around the clock, the camp took shape. Warehouses were built to protect the supplies, and a communications shack was erected to inaugurate BW-8's responsibilities to establish radio communications and report the weather.

Balchen's first major task was to select a suitable site for the airfield and see how closely it fit the plan they had made in Washington, D.C. Balchen, with Sergeants Hendrick Dolleman and Joseph Healy, and Capt. John M. McBride, the camp physician, made a trip inland about 9 mi. by dog sledge to the area that the aerial photos indicated might be the best place for a runway. They inspected the area and Balchen approved the site. The nearby mountains were ideal for antiaircraft defense batteries.

When he returned to the camp, it was clear that the heavy equipment, such as bulldozers and tractors, had to be put to work immediately making a road to the airport site. Surveyors laid out the area for a single runway 6,000 ft. long and 500 ft. wide. As long as the ground was frozen and snow-packed, there was no difficulty in leveling it for aircraft operations, but it was the permafrost that had to be reckoned with in constructing a large air base. Fortunately, Balchen had had some experience with it in Spitsbergen and Norway, but there were more lessons to be learned that Balchen would use to guide the construction of future air fields in arctic climates.

On 24 October Balchen sent a classified message to General Arnold stating that two buildings had been erected. By 9 November all the construction workers and soldiers were ashore and under cover. The days were getting much shorter now and work slowed as the temperature dipped. Much more equipment and supplies were needed and the requisitions were radioed with great urgency to Washington to meet the schedule to begin accepting aircraft. That urgency was suddenly enhanced on 7 December 1941 when the news was received that the Japanese had bombed Pearl Harbor.

Balchen immediately called his men together and told them that America was now at war with the Axis powers. He read excerpts from the Articles of War to them and explained what changes were necessary in the organization now that they were all subject to military law.[12]

BW-8 took on a new life as everyone worked continuously on a three-shift basis, seven days a week. "Came our first Christmas, and I saw what I had expected: faces around me expressing a quiet gloom," Balchen recalled.

There was no mail from home—the last had come in with the last ship; none would arrive until spring. The snow creaked under our shoes as we walked to the mess hall. On the door hung a gay Christmas wreath. As I opened it, a holiday atmosphere came towards me. Red and green garlands adorned the rafters. The Christmas tree, now put up in all its glory, stood in the middle of the floor, lit with candles of different colors and with a mound of packages underneath. The warmth, the smell of food, the expectant faces added to the feeling of Christmas. We had all spruced up in our Class A uniforms; the civilian workers had donned their best.

The table was laid with a white cloth. I suspect it had come from the hospital but asked no questions. Also from the hospital was a cup of Christmas cheer for everyone: a fruit cocktail with the function of hiding the taste of the other major component. The concoction was prescribed by the medics and approved by the Commanding Officer. It served the purpose well.

Master Sergeant Eugene Smith said grace, then I said a few words and we drank a toast to the President and to loved ones far away. Dinner left nothing to be desired: sweet pickles, celery, olives, chicken soup, and a giant turkey with all the trimmings. A hum of voices and laughter soon filled the room."[13]

Balchen made the first flight in the Noorduyn C-64 Norseman on 7 January 1942 after it was assembled on the ship. He took off from the bay ice, circled the area, and set it down on the fresh new BW-8 airstrip. He radioed General Arnold that the field could now be used in an emergency. A British Royal air force Hudson bomber was the first to land there on 14 March 1942 because of the weather at BW-1.

By mid-January, one hangar, camp buildings including the hospital, recreation hall, and machine shop were completed. But this progress was not accomplished without a price. The freezing temperatures caused frequent machinery breakdowns. When the temperatures varied from below to above freezing it was difficult to unload ships in the harbor because the ice piled up or was too thick to permit the barges to float cargo ashore. There was only a short time to get everything under roof, the supplies properly stored, and the radio station working before the last ship left.

There was no time for recreation, but the spirit of dedication to the construction effort that developed under Balchen's leadership was striking. His characteristic, "Ve do it!" became a motto that followed him through the rest of his military career. This can-do spirit was contagious and infected all who served with him. The civilian workers, making much more money than the soldiers, worked with them together genuinely as a team; when not on duty on Saturday nights, the civilians would hand out free beers. Balchen, promoted from captain to major on 1 February 1942, issued only one order for the civilians: no beards. He had long before found that thawing out a set of frozen whiskers can be very painful.

One evening, while talking with Captain McBride, the camp doctor, the name of Knud Rasmussen, the Danish–Eskimo explorer, came up, and McBride asked Balchen if he knew him. Balchen recalled a meeting with Rasmussen in 1927 in which he told of establishing a camp at Thule, a site farther up the west coast. Rasmussen was disappointed that neither Amundsen, Ellsworth, Nobile, nor Byrd had taken his advice to consider that site as a take-off point for their flights. He said Thule had excellent harbor facilities, much better than Spitsbergen, and a large flat area would make an excellent airfield for planes or dirigibles. Balchen recalled that General Arnold had mentioned that besides building the base at BW-8 Balchen was to look for other possible sites; he made a note to plan a flight in that direction and send his findings to Washington, D.C.

In the latter part of August 1942, during a lull in the BW-8 operations, Balchen decided to fly north to Thule to see about the possibility of building a base there. He found that it had everything that would make a good air base, as Rasmussen had said. Several long runways could be constructed and a good harbor would provide easy ship access. He made a lengthy report to General Arnold, the first ever made concerning Thule's potential as a major U.S. military installation.

The first air search of many to follow came shortly afterward when six construction workers decided to walk on the ice about 60 mi. down the fjord. A rumor had spread among the civilian workers that one of the supply ships had run aground on the return to the States, had been abandoned, and had about 10,000 cases of beer aboard. Two of the men returned after a few hours, saying that the other four had continued.

Balchen took off in the C-64, saw the other workers walking wearily back toward the base, and radioed their position to BW-8. They were picked up, extremely cold and tired, by dog teams and hospitalized. (They never found the beer.)

Although the construction of the base was being accomplished under top secret security, Lord Haw Haw, the Briton who broadcast Nazi propaganda aimed at English-speaking forces, featured BW-8 on one of his radio programs. He mentioned Balchen and described exactly where the base was located. At that time, Balchen's radiomen intercepted messages from a German radio station that was broadcasting weather information to German ships and submarines. The broadcasts were coming from somewhere in eastern Greenland, but the BW-8 operators could not identify the station's location. During this period when radio communications were so important, it was found that there were frequent total radio blackouts that came without warning and were thought to be connected to the displays of the aurora borealis. At these times it was impossible to contact the field only 8 mi. away from the base. The radio blackouts were sometimes so complete that when contacts were resumed, there were a lot of angry messages from Washington, D.C., about unanswered communications.[14]

With the responsibilities of command increasing daily, Balchen was promoted from major to lieutenant colonel in April 1942. In appreciation for the job he was doing despite the difficulties of the weather, supply shortages, and uncertain communications, he was promoted to full colonel in August.

The port at Sondrestromfjord had been closed from 12 January until 23 June, when the U.S. Coast Guard cutter *Northland* arrived. It signaled the beginning of the second construction season as ships began to dock with much-needed equipment and supplies.

In early June 1942 Balchen received a message that the first phase of Operation Bolero was to begin. Bolero was the code name used for the initial flights of aircraft to build up the U.S. Eighth and Ninth Air Forces in England, which would eventually support the invasion of the continent. Fully equipped combat crews and their aircraft would be passing through Greenland's two main bases en route to England in ever-increasing numbers. Fuel, maintenance, and rest facilities had to be fully operational. Balchen reported on 15 June 1942 that Bluie West 8 was ready to accept Bolero aircraft. On 26 June 49 B-17s, 80 P-38s, and 52 C-47s began their historic flights from Goose Bay, Newfoundland, to

England. The first wave of 18 B-17s took off headed for BW-1 and BW-8 but only nine reached their Greenland destinations safely. Six had turned back to Goose Bay, and the remaining three were forced down along the Greenland coast in bad weather on 27 June 1942. They had been trying to get into BW-1 or BW-8 but one had to ditch and the crew was later rescued from an island. The second landed in a small patch of meadow near a native village named Egedesminde north of BW-8. The plane stopped a mere 18 in. from a huge boulder that probably would have caused an explosion. Fortunately, no one was hurt.[15]

The third plane had been sending SOSs, but the signal bearings were unreliable at first. When they became clearer on the second day, Balchen found the plane sitting on the ice cap.[16]

There were 13 men aboard the B-17 named *My Gal Sal* and none were injured in the wheels-up landing. The pilot was Lt. Ralf Stinson, who took command of the situation. He had ordered the crew to saw off the propeller of the number 4 engine and idle it to keep the batteries charged so that the radio operator could maintain a listening watch and send homing signals for rescuers. Balchen dropped food and supplies, including a bottle of whiskey. Their only rations until then were about a dozen sandwiches and a carton of chocolate bars.

Balchen returned to BW-8 and took off in a PBY-5A amphibian with Navy Lt. Aram Y. Parunak of Patrol Squadron 93 as pilot to home in on the B-17's radio bearing. They looked for a landing area, preferably a "dimple" or lake, which often forms when snow melts during the summer thaw and collects in hollow places on the ice surface. They located such an area about 2 mi. long and 12 mi. away from the B-17. They returned to BW-8 for the dog drivers, Sergeants Dolleman and Healy, stripped the PBY of guns, ammunition, and oxygen equipment, and returned to the small lake. Parunak landed and Balchen and the others used a rubber life raft to go ashore through ice-filled waters with skis and snow shoes, a primus stove, manila rope, and emergency rations. The PBY took off for BW-8 just in time to escape a heavy fog while Balchen, Dolleman, and Healy set up a camp on the edge of the lake. Next morning a sleet storm developed that kept them immobile until late afternoon. Leaving Dolleman with the camp to set off smoke flares at intervals to guide them back to the lake, Balchen and Healy left for the B-17 on skis. It was hard going through slushy conditions. They encountered deep crevasses, which were often disguised by snow bridges that could give way without warning when stepped on. Roped together, the two soon found that they could not go any farther when the fog got so thick they could not identify the crevasses ahead. After Balchen fell into a shallow water-filled crevasse with his skis on, they returned to the lake. They left for the crash site again when the fog lifted.

Meanwhile Parunak had flown over the B-17 and dropped snowshoes, ropes, sleeping bags, emergency rations, and a message that Balchen and Healy were on the way. After Balchen's party arrived at the wreckage, they helped Stinson and his men get ready for the trek to the lake and cautioned them to take only their sleeping bags, twenty-four hours of rations, and essential items with them. However, a couple of the men slipped some weighty items into their pockets like cameras, electric razors, dress shoes, brief cases, and framed pictures.

The party set out roped together with Balchen breaking a trail in the lead. The group began lightheartedly on snowshoes but soon the trudging began to take a toll on those inexperienced in snow travel. The treasures that seemed so important began to be discarded as they plodded along wearily.

Parunak flew over and dropped a message warning that a storm was approaching. Balchen immediately ordered that no rations were to be eaten except in an emergency and no one was to discard his sleeping bag, no matter how much it weighed or how tired he was. It was essential that they get to the lake with as few rest stops as possible and Balchen urged, cajoled, and threatened to keep everyone moving. When they arrived at the camp at about 0500 the next morning most were so exhausted that they collapsed on the ground and fell asleep instantly. None seemed to want to taste Sergeant Dolleman's hot pemmican stew (made of a dried meat mixed with fat) that Balchen and Healy devoured with gusto. Parunak arrived in the PBY, and it took three trips to get the group back to BW-8. Three of the men had to be hospitalized for exhaustion. Shortly after the last flight, a deep crevasse opened up in the lake and it drained completely.[17]

Although it had not been mentioned as a corollary mission when Balchen was assigned to take command of BW-8, it was soon obvious that search and rescue operations were to take a considerable amount of his time and effort. Several days after Lieutenant Stinson's B-17 crew arrived at BW-8, Balchen received a message that Col. Robert W. C. Wimsatt, the new commander at BW-1, wanted to see him. When Balchen arrived, however, Wimsatt was missing. He had flown a North American AT-6 two-seat trainer on a local reconnaissance flight with a sergeant as passenger and had not returned. Balchen immediately began to search with other planes and found the AT-6 had crash-landed on a moraine of a glacier above a small lake northwest of BW-1. There were no signs of life, and the area was too small to land any type of rescue aircraft. Balchen returned to BW-8 and got a tent, sleeping bag, and some supplies and dropped them at the site, which was in a location with a steep wall along the glacier near some small "melt lakes." There was, however, a large lake on a plateau above the crash site about 10 mi. away where Balchen thought he could make an approach and landing in a PBY.

Visibility was poor with heavy fog and heavy rain; no plane could get near the area for three days. On the fourth day, Balchen, Dr. McBride, and a team of trained men from BW-1 loaded stretchers and first aid materials in the amphibian and set off for the large lake. Fog rolled in and they had to spend the night at the side of the lake. Balchen and McBride hiked to the edge of a shelf that dropped down a steep mountainside. With only a few feet of visibility ahead, they inched down to the rugged valley and came to a river that was too swift and broad to cross. They went upstream and finally found a place where they could wade across. McBride got severe cramps from the cold water, so they erected a shelter and fell asleep.[18]

When they awoke the next morning, the fog had lifted and they made their way to the AT-6. The sergeant was unhurt and popped out of the trainer's rear seat when he heard them shouting. Hearing voices, Colonel Wimsatt, who had been sleeping in a tent nearby, got out of his sleeping bag. He was in pain from a broken nose and jaw and McBride did as much as he could to make him comfortable. The four then hiked up to the glacier where the PBY crew was waiting with a rubber raft. Within four hours, Wimsatt was on his way by B-17 to Walter Reed Hospital in Washington, D.C., for recuperation.

To his pleasant surprise, Balchen later received a letter from the Army Adjutant General's Office in Washington stating, "The heroism displayed by you in Greenland June 27 to July 6, and July 14 to July 18, 1942, has been brought to the attention of the Secretary of War, and by direction of the President, under the provisions of the Act of Congress approved July 2, 1926, you have been awarded the Soldier's Medal."[19]

In addition to the C-64 Norseman he had ordered, Balchen was also able to call on Army Air Force and Navy aircraft, including Consolidated

PBY-5A amphibians for surveys, reconnaissance, and rescue missions. Balchen made surveillance flights to eastern Greenland and a number of Greenland villages. He also looked for evidence of enemy activity to the northeast across the ice cap and down the east coast at likely spots such as MacKenzie Bay, where the Norwegians had a radio station. No signs of enemy activity were found.

Balchen's problems on the ground at BW-8 became aggravated during the midnight sun period when it became relatively warm in the daytime and the effects of thaw set in. The roads became like a pig wallow and the prefabricated buildings on the permafrost exposed to the sun caused them to heave and sink. The only thing that could be done was to take the buildings down.

The solution came about by sheer accident, Balchen reported. They put up a refrigerator building for their frozen meats on a cement pedestal on top of a lot of gravel. The pedestal remained in place and the building did not heave and shift. From then on, the buildings were put up on a base of dry gravel where water would not penetrate. It was one of the most important construction discoveries that they made.[20]

Balchen was always conscious of the morale of his men and advised them to get acquainted with the area by taking local hikes to observe and appreciate the wild life. He issued an order that no birds or animals were to be killed within 3 mi. of the camp because the game knew they had a sanctuary there. The men captured three peregrine falcons and began training them, using falconry instruction books that Balchen had included in the library. Three ravens were also caught and trained, although they soon became a nuisance because they liked to collect anything shiny, including such items as military insignia that attracted their fancy. These birds became a principal morale factor as the men worked with them to see what they could train them to do.[21]

One of the first requisitions for recreational equipment that Balchen sent to the States included fly- and bait-casting rods, and most of the men took advantage of the opportunity on their time off. Fishing became one of the principal recreational and activities in the summer months at BW-8. When the patrol boats and icebreakers were able to go outside the fjord, Balchen sent out recreation parties, and about 500 lb. of cod could be caught in a couple of hours. The favorite fish was the arctic charr, a species that had become landlocked in the interior waters since the Ice Age.[22]

Herbert C. Stein, a meteorologist and cryptographer, recalls that Balchen would occasionally have the cook boil a couple of fish heads and serve them to him. Then, as those around him in the mess hall watched, he would comment on how good the eyes were as he picked them out to eat. Stein said that Balchen's knowledge of birds and flowers was "endless" and he knew them by their botanical and common names. "He always had a slide rule in his pocket to solve problems," Stein recalled. "His love was the sauna, especially when there was fresh snow to roll in. And he was not one for saluting, but always had a few words and a smile when he passed anyone."[23]

"He was not a loner," Earl MacDonald recalled. "He was too warm for that. But he was so far ahead of his time, he seemed alone. He was talking to me about space travel in 1942. And when he had a concept, it wasn't just an idea. He would tell you the economics, the material resources and the human consequences of it."[24]

Another activity that Balchen introduced was skiing. He insisted that everyone stationed at BW-8 learn to ski and led groups on skiing trips around the surrounding area. He made it a point to know each man personally and within a few weeks knew the capabilities and weaknesses of each of them. He gave talks about the history and geography of Greenland, with emphasis on survival techniques. He recruited passengers experienced in the arctic to tell of their experiences as they passed through the base.

By the end of Balchen's first year in Greenland, living conditions at BW-8 had become much more bearable, even enjoyable, and his concern for the welfare of his men kept morale high. They knew their respective jobs of supporting aircraft movements to and from the United States were important and appreciated.

10 · "War Below Zero"

When you fight the Arctic, you fight on the Arctic's terms," Balchen wrote in 1944.

On the trail you fight sudden thaws, and treacherous snow bridges that give way under your weight, and crevasses into which a driver and team of dogs may plunge and never be seen again. If you are flying, you fight icing conditions that overload your wings with tons of ice; you fight eccentric whirlwinds over the ice cap that rack a ship and drop it several thousand feet in a second; you fight the fog. Most of the times you win, but sometimes you lose, and the Arctic shows no mercy to a loser.[1]

This observation became abundantly clear to all crew members and passengers on aircraft that were forced down on the Greenland ice cap during World War II. Balchen and his fleet of search and rescue planes became their lifeline. Knowing that most airmen flying through BW-8 had never experienced severe cold weather, Balchen briefed as many crews headed to the war as he could and always concluded his talks with the assurance that, "If you go down, I will find you!"

In early June 1942 the rugged Norwegian began to prove what he said. Four B-17s were assigned to BW-8 for the purpose of making regular weather observation flights between Goose Bay, BW-8, and Iceland. A Lieutenant Teague was pilot of one of them and became lost and crash-landed while returning from Iceland to BW-8. He sent out Mayday calls, but the radio operators at BW-8 could not get bearings on him. All that was known was that he had landed on a flat gravel island, no one was injured, and they could see water to the west. Not knowing where to look, search planes went in several directions to no avail. Balchen flew a PBY to an area where he remembered seeing gravel flats south of Godthaab and found the B-17 undamaged where it had been marooned for a week. He radioed a ship belonging to the Greenland administration and steered it to an area near the crash site where the men were picked up. The plane was later gassed up and flown off. Later, an emergency field was built on the gravel flats and named Teague Field.[2]

A valuable lesson about survival rations was learned from this crew's experience that Balchen passed on to other crews during briefings at BW-8. Many would break open their survival ration packages during long flights for a snack, and when they needed them they had nothing left. The only food aboard Teague's plane was a case of grapefruit and a tin of spiced herring, which they had subsisted on for more than a week.

On 15 July 1942, two B-17s were escorting six P-38s across Greenland to Iceland and ran into severe weather. Hoping to land at BW-1, their alternate airfield, they received a radio message that it was fogged in. They were diverted northward to another auxiliary field, but the weather was reportedly no better. Postwar examination of German records revealed that these orders, intended to mislead the American crews, originated from the German radio station then in operation at Sabine Island.

The fighters were running low on fuel and taking on ice. Lt. Bradley McManus radioed that he was almost out of fuel and was going to have to land. He dragged the ice cap for several miles, found a smooth spot, and made a wheels-down landing. After rolling for 100 yd., the plane flipped over. McManus crawled out and waved to the other circling planes. Realizing that none of the planes had anywhere to go, they all landed wheels up in close proximity to each other. No one was injured beyond minor scratches; the eight planes had made the largest successful group crash landing in aviation history.

The 25 men hurriedly made camp and divided their rations, which were calculated to last 15 days. The B-17 radio operators made radio contact with an auxiliary field and gave their position based on the navigators' sun shots. They were near the east coast about 20 mi. within the interior of the ice cap. That night a storm closed in and they settled down to wait.

They made cooking stoves with the oxygen bottles, using supercharger oil for fuel and a parachute strap for a wick. For recreation they practiced target shooting with their .45s, destroying the bomb sights and other secret paraphernalia on the wrecked planes. They set up a battery-operated radio and were able to receive music from Iceland.[3]

A fleet of five rescue planes—two C-47s, two B-24s, and a PBY—dropped food and medical supplies. Eight days after their landing, Navy Lt. Frederick E. Crockett, the commanding officer of Bluie East 2, made his way to the site with a dog team. All the men were successfully evacuated and returned to the States.[4]

The rescues already made were examples of more to come, as a new winter descended on Greenland in 1942, which meant storms, darkness, heavy icing, and high winds. Concurrently, the traffic to Britain increased as the U.S. Eighth and Ninth Air Forces continued their buildup of fighter and bomber units. Most crews were completely inexperienced in cold weather operations, and when they went down they were exposed to the fury of the elements never imagined. Injuries always compounded survival problems and the possibility of being rescued alive. It was Balchen's philosophy that no matter what the odds, a search for downed planes would always be launched as soon as possible.

One of the most disappointing searches that Balchen experienced began on 5 November 1942, when a Douglas C-53 transport was flying across the ice cap from Iceland bound for BW-8 with a crew of six. When they radioed that they were lost, they were advised to go to BW-1, but the next time they were heard from, they said they had landed on the cap. Although they had given their position, it was erroneous because that would have put them down on the water. A large-scale search was launched immediately, but the C-53 could not be located. On 9 November, with no long-range aircraft available at that time, Balchen exercised his wartime rights as a military commander and ordered a TWA DC-4 off its route and used it to search for several days until bad weather grounded it. Despite an extensive search that went on for weeks in which Balchen participated for many hours of rough flying the C-53 was never found.

One of the search planes, a B-17 with a six-man crew, designated PN9E, was diverted from its flight to England to assist and departed from BW-1 on 9 November. It was also reported missing.

Balchen immediately began making 2 to 6 hr. search flights in a PBY across the ice cap for several days until nightfall, sometimes in good visibility, at other times in blowing snow, fog, and winds of more than 150 MPH. The severe turbulence threatened to shake the wings off his aircraft, and he had to call off the search for several days because of the severe turbulence.[5]

The lost B-17 was piloted by Lt. Armand L. Monteverde; his copilot was Lt. Harry E. Spencer. There were six other crew members aboard. One passenger, Sgt. Paul J. Spina, had broken his wrist and had severe lacerations; he had lost his gloves and shoes in the crash and his hands were badly frost-bitten. Another had a bad cut on his head when he was thrown through the bomber's plexiglass nose. Others were relatively uninjured but suffered from frostbite on fingers and toes. Although they were wearing winter flying clothes, they had no special arctic clothing or sleeping bags and no water. Their emergency rations were scattered all around the area in the snow. They wrapped themselves in their parachutes and a tarpaulin inside the fuselage and huddled together for warmth to begin a long wait.

Monteverde made a splint for Spina and made him as comfortable as possible. Lt. William F. O'Hara, the navigator, got snow in his boots when he was carrying Spina inside the plane but thought nothing about it and did not dry them out.

The next few days crept by with no let up in the wind and blowing snow. On the morning of 12 November the weather was clear and Spencer and O'Hara decided to walk toward the southeast to see if they could spot the coast to determine their position. They had gone a short distance when Spencer suddenly disappeared. He had fallen through a snow bridge into a 15 ft. wide crevasse that seemed to have no bottom. Fortunately, his fall was stopped by a block of ice. O'Hara called the others for help and Spencer was brought to the surface by the use of parachute shroud lines and harness.

That night O'Hara thought his feet were frozen and Monteverde massaged them until they softened up but were still dangerously off-color. Spencer's fall, Spina's injury, and O'Hara's new problem was an ominous sign.

Cpl. Loren E. Howarth, the radio operator, tried to get the radio transmitter and receiver thawed out and working, and after six days of trying he finally succeeded. With the help of Spencer and Pvt. Clarence Wedel, Howarth moved the radio into the navigator's compartment and used a life raft to keep the blowing snow out. Although he could now transmit SOS's and requests for bearings, he did not know what frequencies others might be listening on. He finally succeeded in finding a common frequency and was told that dog teams were being sent out to find them; the weather was impossible for flying.

Meanwhile, the tail of the fractured B-17, sitting on the edge of a crevasse, began to slip backward. The crew made ropes out of parachute shroud lines and tied these to the forward part of the plane, hoping it would hold the rear in place. They made a stove out of the bomb-sight case to warm their survival rations, which they estimated would last two weeks.

Balchen, when weather permitted, directed the search in the DC-4 without results. When Capt. Harry Hanson, captain of the TWA airliner, got impatient, Balchen radioed Washington, D.C., to inform TWA that their plane and pilots would be engaged in the rescue until Balchen could release them. And that would not be until the Air Force sent other aircraft suitable for search.

Balchen, with Hanson piloting, located the B-17 on 24 November, about 40 mi. from Bluie East 2 near Comanche Bay. He was shocked to see its tail hanging over the abyss and its fuselage broken in half at the radio compartment. He established radio contact and, seeing that they were in a dangerous crevassed area, ordered the men to stay with the plane where they had set up housekeeping and not move away unless they were roped together. Sleeping bags, fuel, food, clothing, and medical supplies were parachuted out and Balchen told them a ground party would soon be on the way.

When the DC-4 roared overhead, the able men poured out of the wreckage into the numbing cold and waved. They watched helplessly as the strong wind caught the parachutes and dragged the boxes far out of reach. Seeing this, Hanson made a run at about 200 ft. altitude and Balchen let additional rations, a primus stove, fuel, clothing, and sleeping bags free fall. Most packages fell within easy reach this time and all were retrieved by the next day.

Balchen's flight was the first of a number of missions scheduled to reassure and supply Monteverde and his crew. An attempt was made to reach the scene with a dog team but the deep, powdered snow on top of an icy surface was too much for them. Sleds were overturned and some of the dogs died when they fell into deep, dark crevasses. Another unsuccessful attempt was made by Lt. Max H. Demorest and S.Sgt. Don T. Tetley, who set out from the Atterbury Dome weather station on the ice cap with two motor sleds and tried to avoid the crevassed areas. At the same time the U.S. Coast Guard cutter *Northland* launched a small Grumman J2F-5 Duck, a single-engine amphibian, in heavy fog. Aboard the plane were Lt. John A. Pritchard, Jr., the pilot, and radioman Benjamin A. Bottoms. They managed to locate the B-17 and asked Monteverde if it was safe to land. Monteverde recommended against it, especially with wheels down. But Pritchard landed anyway and loaded two of the men who needed medical attention aboard and flew them to the *Northland*. Meanwhile, the TWA DC-4 flew over again with more food and clothing and radioed that the motor sleds were still en route.

Demorest and Tetley got within a mile of the B-17 but had to stop using the motorsleds because of deep crevasses. From there they skied carefully to the plane where they were greeted heartily. Afterward, they decided to go back to their sleds and try to get them closer to the wreckage. When they returned and were within about a 100 yd. of the B-17, Demorest and his sled suddenly fell into a crevasse and disappeared. Tetley shouted for help and Monteverde and others rushed from the plane to his side. They could see the sled about 150 ft. down, too far to reach, but did not see or hear Demorest. For the next two days they continually revisited the site and shouted repeatedly for Demorest but never received an answer. He was never found.

On 30 November Pritchard landed the amphibian again, but had to take off quickly before an approaching rolling fog that would soon cover the area. He took Howarth, the B-17's radioman, with him. Tetley, saddened by the loss of his lieutenant, pitched in to teach the remaining crew members how to make a room of snow blocks under the plane's wing and get better protection from the weather. He also acted as the radio operator and received a message from the Coast Guard cutter asking if Pritchard was still at the site because he had not returned to the ship. His plane was spotted four months later by an Army Air Forces (AAF) search plane near the coast where it had crashed against a mountain in heavy fog. Pritchard, Bottoms, and Howarth were never found.[6]

The fog was a precursor of much worse weather to follow, and the cutter had to leave the area. No planes flew over the B-17 for several days and, although not completely comfortable and on short rations, the men settled into a routine of simple chores.

O'Hara's feet were beginning to turn black with gangrene and had to have medical attention as soon as possible. On 7 December Monteverde decided that the only chance to save O'Hara's legs was if Tetley would take him to their home station on his motorized sled, accompanied by

Spencer and Wedel. Spencer set out in the lead on snowshoes to test for crevasses while Tetley drove the sled with O'Hara riding on it; Wedel walked behind. When they were about a mile and a half away from the B-17, Tetley thought they were out of the crevassed area and all could ride on the sled as he prepared to take it on a steep rise ahead of them. Spencer knelt down to take off his snowshoes; Tetley got off the sled on one side, Wedel came to the other. Suddenly, Wedel's weight caused him to break through a snow bridge into a crevasse. He tried desperately to clutch the side of the sled but his grip slipped and he was gone. Spencer and Tetley moved the sled and cautiously looked down into the bottomless split but saw nothing. They remained for two hours calling and watching but he was lost.

Rather than go back to the plane, Tetley decided to press on toward their base so O'Hara could get medical attention or he, too, would be lost. They proceeded cautiously and went about 6 mi. when the sled's motor stopped. An oil line had broken and there was no way to fix it. They set up a tent, which gave Spencer and O'Hara some protection; Tetley settled into a snow hole he made for himself.

All they could do now was wait. They had no radio and only three days' rations. Daylight was now lasting only about two hours. However, Capt. Kenneth H. "Pappy" Turner, an experienced former airline pilot assigned to BW-8 on temporary duty, found them while flying his B-17 and dropped supplies on 9 December.

The weather was impossible for the next two days, but when it broke Turner returned with more supplies. Spencer and Tetley began to improve their quarters, which was not easy in the cold. Corey Ford and Oliver La Farge explained how they survived:

It took about three hours to melt water and thaw out the canned foods for a meal, as everything was frozen solid. The stove required continual repair. Until the snow buried it hopelessly, they put in a good deal of time trying to get the sled into operation. Tetley, who was also the cook, rigged flare pots out of used tin cans, in which they burned kerosene. They usually got up in the dark around seven o'clock, cooked breakfast and went to work, then cooked dinner at five. They would sleep until midnight and then have a snack from their rations and coffee.

At first the diggable snow above the solid ice was so shallow that they could dig rooms only three feet high, in which they could barely crawl around. This was bad enough for the two who were able-bodied, but far worse for O'Hara, who was now very weak. They nursed him as well as they could, and they were deeply impressed by the way his morale stayed up and he did not complain.[7]

The days dragged on through Christmas but the morale of the three was sustained by Pappy Turner's flights when weather permitted. With the wind and snow worsening daily, using a sled to rescue them was impossible. A dog team started out but had to turn back after several days and barely made it back to the base, with only three dogs of the original 15 left. One of the men had to have three toes amputated and several teeth removed because of injury from the cold as a result of cold air sucked into the mouth during exertion.

In late December Balchen was called to BW-1 for a conference with Colonel Wimsatt, who had returned from the hospital, and Coast Guard Adm. Edward H. "Iceberg" Smith, commander of the Greenland Patrol, to discuss what more could be done to rescue the crew. Balchen proposed to make a belly landing on the cap with a PBY, but the Navy refused to dispatch one so a message was sent to higher headquarters in England. Permission was granted to send one with the stipulation that it be manned only by volunteers.[8]

Balchen polled the volunteers and selected Lt. Bernard W. Dunlop as one of the pilots, two radio operators, and a crew chief, plus Capt. P. W. Sweetzer, the medical officer at BW-1. The plane was stripped of armor plating and guns to lighten it and Balchen waited for the weather to clear. On 5 February he received a message from General Arnold, who expressed concerns about his making a belly landing: "Factory indicates forward bulkhead of PBY too weak for landing on snow."[9] Balchen was determined to proceed with the rescue attempt and replied that he was going to take the risk.[10]

Meanwhile, Balchen had ordered a small ski-equipped plane from the States, but its skis could not cope with the rough-snow terrain. A Barkley-Grow ski plane used in the Canadian bush was then borrowed from Maritime Central Airways of Canada and flown dismantled to BW-8. Jimmie Wade, one of the airline's top pilots, and Capt. John G. Moe, a navigator with the Air Transport Command, volunteered to see if they could reach the sled. However, they had a forced landing on ice-covered snow and spent a week struggling to survive before being rescued by native hunters.

The weeks dragged on, planes continued to drop supplies to the B-17 and the sled whenever possible, but the winter's ferocity made landings impossible and ground parties still could not be dispatched. In January during one of the PBY flights, Balchen was caught in a williwaw that he said was the closest he ever came to death in an airplane and could not understand how the wings of the Catalina could withstand such violent turbulence.[11]

The only consolation to the men left in the B-17 was that they knew at least 100 people were involved in trying to get them to safety. It was Balchen's job as BW-8 base commander to continue sending out available aircraft for the PN9E rescue, in addition to the other flight operations he had to conduct. He flew over the two stranded groups several times in January. Because O'Hara's life was in grave danger, his rescue was imperative and was given first priority. Balchen decided that nothing else had worked so they would make a belly landing with the PBY as he had proposed earlier.

On 5 February the weather was flyable and Balchen ordered a B-17 and another Catalina to accompany his PBY, piloted by Lieutenant Dunlop. After making a run at low altitude to inspect the area, Dunlop landed smoothly right next to the sled camp. Sweetzer checked O'Hara and found him seriously emaciated and weak. He weighed only about 80 lb.; Balchen carried him carefully to the plane. As soon as everyone was aboard, Dunlop pushed the throttles forward but the plane refused to move. Balchen knew immediately that the wing floats had iced up. He ordered the able-bodied men out of the plane and stationed two of them on each float to break them loose. They rocked the plane from side to side while Dunlop gave the engines full power. The plane broke free and Balchen told Dunlop to taxi slowly in a circle because to stop would cause it to freeze again. As the plane came by, one of the Catalina's crew and Dr. Sweetzer reached out and hauled the men in through the side window area one by one, and then the plane returned to BW-8. Spencer and Tetley were found only to be suffering from fatigue. O'Hara was evacuated to the States and had to have both legs amputated below the knee.

At the B-17, the remaining three men—Monteverde, Spina, and Sgt. Alfred C. Best—were being supplied as regularly as possible but were unable to communicate with the rescue planes. They did not know about the tragedy with the sled and assumed that it had returned to the base. If any notes had been dropped telling them about it, they were lost. Monteverde had developed severe pains in his legs and hands from the cold and could barely move. As a result, the rescue crews making the drops did not see any signs of life. A new danger they faced was the crumbling of the snow wall they had built against the winds. They could also feel that the plane's fuselage was slowly sinking into the crevasse on which its tail was resting.

It was not until Turner's B-17 dropped some mail and a walkie-talkie radio that the ensuing conversation was the first indication in many days that the three men below were still alive. However, there were more than three weeks of freezing, howling weather still ahead, and Best became seriously ill. Their food supply began to run low when weather prevented the planes from flying, and they ran out of candles. The only fuel for the stove was the plane's high-octane gas, which was poisonous and caused them to cough up black mucous for hours every time they used it.

In early March Turner returned overhead with the news that Balchen was going to land a PBY as close as possible to the sled camp where Tetley, Spencer, and O'Hara had holed up for so long and a dog team was en route to the B-17. On 17 March they saw and heard the dogs approaching and soon Capt. Harry L. Strong, Dolleman, and Healy arrived. Two days later, the six men made their way to the sled camp, which Monteverde called the Imperial Hotel because it seemed so luxurious compared to their B-17 "home." Meanwhile, Balchen and Dunlop, with the experience of one landing wheels-up on the ice with a PBY behind them, planned to pick up this group. They stripped the plane of unnecessary items and carried minimum fuel because they now had nine dogs and six more men and equipment to put onboard. On 5 April, a windless, warm day, they landed wheels up and loaded everyone aboard. But with the increased load, sticky snow, and no head wind, the PBY on its belly could not get airborne after three tries. The engines overheated and the right engine caught fire. They spent the night there and found that some of the auxiliary equipment on the right engine was burned; however the engine would run, although engine oil spewed out all over the fuselage. It looked like the plane might have to be abandoned. Even if it could take off, it could not do so with all the men aboard.

"Now we were in fine shape," Balchen recalled. "I found myself up there on the Ice Cap with eleven men. Fortunately, all could be transported, some on the sled with the dog team and the rest could walk. But we had about 80 miles to get to the weather station and that is a long walk at any time, particularly in the Arctic when you haven't been trained for it."[12]

The next day Balchen decided he, Strong, Dolleman, and Healy would take the dog teams and ski to the weather station, which he believed they could do in two days or less. Dunlop could then fly the three rescued men and his three-man crew back to Bluie East 2. Balchen told everyone his plan, and the next morning the men jerked the plane loose from the ice. Dunlop tried to take off with both engines running but could not make it on the first try. He tried a second time and finally disappeared in a cloud of snow. When safely airborne, he shut off the right engine's propeller to save the oil. All the taxiing and false starts had caused a heavy fuel consumption, and when they were 5 min. out from BE-2, the crew chief reported that the gas gauges showed zero fuel. Although it looked like a water or ice pack landing would be necessary, Dunlop decided to continue toward the field. He cut in the feathered propeller on the final approach but did not drop his wheels until the last few seconds; the main gear came down but the nose wheel did not. The plane nosed down when the air speed dropped and skidded easily on the tough keel without a scratch, just as the engines quit.

Balchen and the others left the camp site on skis with the dog sledge and headed eastward to avoid a heavily crevassed area. The going was easy for the first 5 mi., but the wind increased and the dogs could not keep their course. When the visibility cut down to about 15 yd. in blowing snow, they tethered the dogs and put up one tent. But the wind increased so much that they could not get the second one up. All four hunched together all night in the one tent. They left the next morning when the wind died down. They avoided more crevasses, and as they approached the coast Balchen was able to identify the coastline at Kjoegebugt. After traveling about 17 mi., as indicated on the sled's distance-measuring wheel, they camped that night in two tents but had to remain there from 10 April to 16, caught in another williwaw. They had radio contact twice a day with the ice cap weather station WYUV at Atterbury Dome, their destination, which first reported winds up to 100 MPH, which increased two days later to 125 MPH.

The storm finally abated on 16 April after six miserable days in the tents, during which they could converse only by shouting. The dogs had come through safely, and the four set out for the weather station through high snowdrifts and horrendous sastrugi (ruts) that made travel extremely difficult. They arrived at the weather station on 18 April to find it buried in about 25 feet of snow. Digging down inside, they found the seven weathermen safe and in good spirits despite having been there for about nine months. However, Balchen could not see how they could live any longer under those conditions. He promptly sent a message to the commander of the Greenland Base Command at BE-2 telling where they were and asked that the men be evacuated and replaced as soon as possible. One of the PBYs landed in the nearby bay and took everyone and the dogs to BE-2.[13] This was the last episode in the longest sustained attempt to save people in any theater.

Unfortunately, many of the subsequent rescue operations in Greenland are recorded mainly in the memories of participants because of wartime secrecy about operations in Greenland.

The world press found out about Balchen's "northland epic" despite the secrecy. Typical headlines read, "Noted Antarctic Hero Distinguishes Himself in Heroic Army Air Rescue" and "Bernt Balchen Is Hero of Epic Rescue." He was unaware of this until many months later when someone sent him news clippings.[14]

When Balchen arrived at BE-2, Colonel Wimsatt, who had returned to his post as Greenland's overall commander, showed him a top secret radio message from Washington, D.C. It said that on 14 March a German military party had attacked a Danish weather station on the east coast of Greenland at Eskimonaes. The Danes had stationed personnel there before the war and the government-in- exile had established the Northeast Greenland sled patrol, which was part of the Danish defense agreement with the United States. In the fall of 1941 U.S. Coast Guard commander (later admiral) Smith was put in charge of the Greenland Patrol and was responsible for organizing the Danish trappers and native people into a scouting force. They were hired by the U.S. Army to form sledge patrols along the east coast of Greenland as far north as 77° and report any signs of German occupation.

On 11 March 1943, three members of the patrol saw two figures in the distance fleeing from a hut on Sabine Island. They searched the hut and found two sleeping bags and a green uniform tunic with the Nazi swastika on the sleeve. As they searched for further evidence, they heard someone approaching; leaving the sledges and dogs behind, they fled on skis to the patrol station at Eskimonaes, 90 mi. to the south.

Using the abandoned dog teams and sledges, a party of Germans under command of Lt. Hermann Ritter and based at Sabine Island, arrived at

Eskimoneas on 24 March and fired on the camp with machine guns to give the impression that they were a large force. The Danes fled on skis with only their rifles and a radio transmitter, leaving their personal effects, ammunition, dogs, and three sledges behind. They made their way to another weather station on Ella Island and reported the information to the Greenland authorities. Meanwhile, the Germans placed the Danes' personal effects in one hut and burned down everything else. Ritter left a note:

> *March* 24: The U.S.A. protects its defense interests here in Greenland. We do the same also. But the administration on Greenland gave orders to capture or shoot us, and besides that you gave weather reports to the enemy. You are making Greenland into a place of war. We have stayed quietly at our posts without attacking you. Now you want war, so you shall have war. But remember if you shoot with illegal weapons (dumdum bullets) which you have at hand here in the loft of the radio station, then you must take full responsibility for the consequences, because you are placing yourselves outside the rules of war. Note we have put all personal effects of the hunters and all pelts in this hut, while we have destroyed the radio apparatus operating for the U.S.A. (Signed: *Commandant of the German Wehrmacht Detail in Eskimonaes*).[15]

Returning to his base, Ritter and his men came on three more Danish patrol members. Eli Knudsen driving the lead sled apparently did not hear Ritter's command to halt. One of Ritter's men leveled his rifle and fired, killing Knudsen instantly. The other two were relieved of their weapons, and Ritter took them to his home base on Sabine Island at Hansa Bay. On arrival he decided that Peter Nielsen, one of the Danes, should return alone to Sandodden, where Knudsen had been killed, and bury him. Nielsen did this, then continued to Ella Island to report.

Meanwhile Ritter ordered Marius Jensen, the other prisoner, to guide him to investigate a weather station that was reported to be at Mackenzie Bay. A few miles out of sight of the base, Jensen took advantage of a moment when Ritter was not in reach of his rifle and took him prisoner. Together they set out on an unprecedented 350 mi. trek south to Scoresby Sound, where Jensen turned his prisoner over to the American authorities. However, the news of the attack and Ritter's capture spurred the War Department to order immediate action. The Germans had established a radio station 60 mi. north of Eskimonaes and were sending their reports to Norway for use by the German submarines against Allied convoys en route to the Russian port at Murmansk. Strangely, the radio stations on either side had failed to detect the radio signals of the other, even though the Germans had been there from August 1942 until March 1943.

After the rescue of the Monteverde crew, Balchen proceeded to Bluie West 1 en route to his base at BW-8. Colonel Wimsatt handed him a message stating that the German base on Sabine Island was to be destroyed. It was signed by Gen. George C. Marshall, the top military leader. Wimsatt told Balchen that he (Balchen) was in charge of the mission.

Balchen checked the maps and then decided to go to Iceland to use the long runways at Keflavik, where bombs and other equipment were more readily available. He took the pilots and crews of two B-17s to Iceland when the weather broke on 7 May.

The distance from Iceland to the German base on Sabine Island and return is about the same distance as New York to Kansas City or London to North Africa. Extra fuel was put in bomb-bay tanks, so he could take only half loads of bombs. Just before midnight on 13 May, Balchen led the B-17s off and arrived over Eskimonaes about 0330. The base was completely burned out. Sled tracks were seen leading away, but they decided to bomb it anyway. However, the primary objective was the German base at Hansa Bay on Sabine Island, and the B-17s did not have enough range for such a long trip.[16]

Balchen returned to Keflavik and was assigned two B-24 Liberators, which had longer range; the B-17 Flying Forts, this time with the full bomb bay tanks, would be escorts. Trained gunners would be in position, because there had been reports that long-range German bombers had been seen along the Greenland coast, apparently from Norway.

The plan was to have the slower B-17s take off ahead of the B-24s. The latter would catch up with the B-17s about 95 mi. from Sabine Island. One of the B-17s would stand by with the B-24s while Balchen proceeded to Sabine to reconnoiter and draw antiaircraft fire if there was any and see how accurate it was.

A break in the weather came on 25 May, and the four aircraft proceeded as planned. Balchen circled the island at 5,000 ft. to check the various buildings and general layout of the camp below. He briefed his crews over the radio, then ordered the first bombing run on the base with the B-24s. Each carried ten 100 lb. bombs, and they flew over but did not drop them. When Balchen asked why they had not dropped, one of the pilots said he could not identify any buildings among the snow and rocks. Balchen told them to circle while he and Turner in the other B-17 flew in low toward a two-story house. The gunners opened up with incendiary bullets and set the house on fire. As they zoomed upward, Balchen noticed tracers from an antiaircraft battery, and the B-24s reported they then saw where their targets were. As they began to line up to make their runs, Balchen and Turner made a second attack on the antiaircraft guns, followed by the B-24s that dropped their bombs on the buildings and a ship in the harbor, leaving large, black plumes of smoke streaming skyward. The attack had lasted about 20 min. and seemed to have accomplished the mission. However, Balchen wanted to be sure. He returned on 21 July with two B-24s and found no signs of life. What the bombers had not destroyed the Germans did. The station was burned out and there was only a hole in the ice where the ship had been. The Coast Guard cutter *Northland* later dispatched its amphibian to the island and confirmed that there was nothing left.[17]

After Balchen returned to Iceland, he talked with the Reykjavik base provost marshal, who now had Ritter in the stockade. Ritter refused to talk to anyone. Balchen asked if he could speak with him because he could speak German. Permission was granted and Balchen interviewed him to see if he would get any information of value.

Ritter could speak Norwegian fluently so the conversation was not in German. He told Balchen the station at Sabine had been set up in August 1942 under Operation Holzauge and had not been discovered until the Danish sled patrol had found the uniforms at the trapper's cabin. He said he was an Austrian and a glaciologist, was interested in polar exploration, had been on a whaling ship, and had no interest whatsoever in the Nazi movement. He had been ordered to evacuate Sabine after the Eskimonaes raid.

Ritter, who had also served in the German army in World War I, confirmed that his mission was to supply long-range weather forecasts to the German Luftwaffe and to direct the Germans in their submarine warfare in the North Atlantic. The information was used regularly by Nazi merchant ships to enable them to run the gauntlet of the Allied navies and carry Axis supplies between Norway, Singapore, the East Indies, and Japan.

Ritter asked for some scientific literature and books on glaciology, which Balchen helped him get from Reykjavik. Ritter was later sent to a prisoner-of-war camp in the United States.

Another important German captured later on Sabine Island was Dr. Rudolf Sensse, who claimed he was a physician and was suspected to be a member of the Gestapo. For reasons never explained, he had been left alone on Sabine Island to fend for himself after Ritter's troops left for Germany. Apparently, he was apprehended when he left to look for Ritter. Balchen asked the *Northland* to proceed to Hansa Bay to look for Sensse and its crew took him into custody on 21 July 1943. Balchen flew cover for the cutter's landing.

Balchen and his B-17 crews remained in Iceland until September in case there were any attempts by the Germans to return to the east coast of Greenland. They never returned. The raid on Sabine Island was the northernmost U.S. bombing raid of World War II.[18]

Reflecting later on his wartime experiences in Greenland, Balchen wrote,

> Our war in Greenland was not a big war, as wars go. There were no major battles, no epic encounters of planes or tanks, no headlines in the home town papers. Loneliness doesn't rate a citation; they don't give medals for waiting. The casualties were not very glamorous: frozen lungs, a couple of missing fingers or toes, an amputated leg. There are no fields of crosses today to mark its battlefield: only a broken fuselage drifted deep with snow, a pair of crossed skis beside the trail, a forgotten dog sled lying forever at the bottom of a black crevasse.
>
> But it was an important war, for the knowledge of the Arctic that we gained, at the cost of these men who gave their lives on the Ice Cap, will insure the safety of tomorrow's aerial travel in the North.[19]

On 7 September 1943 General Arnold stopped at Keflavik, Iceland, on his way to England. Balchen met him and chatted about the work at BW-8 and the possibility of building other bases. Arnold nodded as Balchen talked, then said, "There's something else on your mind, isn't there?"

Balchen admitted he wanted to get into the fighting in Europe, possibly to help the Norwegian resistance movement. He said he had told himself when he became a U.S. citizen that some day he wanted to justify belonging to Norway and America. Maybe this would be his chance.

"General Arnold grinned and replied, 'You better come back to Washington and talk to Bill Donovan at OSS.'"[20]

A few days after Arnold left Iceland, Balchen received orders to turn over his command at BW-8 to a replacement. He flew from Keflavik to the Greenland Command headquarters at BW-1, where he was pleasantly surprised with a parade in his honor and a presentation of the Distinguished Flying Cross, an award that had been denied him several times previously. He arrived in busy wartime Washington, D.C., in late September 1943 for temporary duty at Army Air Force headquarters. He called his wife Emmy, then living in Arizona with their son, and they reconfirmed that their marriage could not be revived.

Left: Balchen family portrait. Dr. Lauritz Balchen holds oldest daughter Marie (Mia) and mother Dagny holds youngest daughter, also named Dagny. Bernt, then age four, poses shyly in front. Photo Balchen Papers, Library of Congress Manuscript Division.

Right: Bernt's official photograph after entering Norwegian Naval Air Force pilot training in 1920. He received his wings in September 1921. Photo from family album, courtesy Signe Balchen.

Members of the Norwegian Sparta Club with their wrestling and boxing awards in 1919. Balchen *(seated right)* won three first-place boxing and two wrestling championships. He also won awards as a skier and rifle marksman. Photo Balchen Papers, Library of Congress Manuscript Division.

Cmdr. Richard E. Byrd's Fokker *Josephine Ford* is off-loaded from the *Chantier* in the harbor at Kings Bay, Spitsbergen. Photo Ohio State University Archives.

Byrd's mechanics prepare the *Josephine Ford* for flight as a motion picture photographer records the scene. Tony Fokker insisted that his name appear prominently on the wings and fuselage so it could be seen in photographs shot from any angle. Photo Ohio State University Archives.

Commander Byrd *(third from the left)* with ground crew members before attempting the first takeoff from Spitsbergen. The takeoff was unsuccessful because the skis were improperly waxed. Photo Ohio State University Archives.

The *Josephine Ford* departs for the North Pole from Spitsbergen on 9 May 1926. The cruising speed of the aircraft and the winds aloft at that time show that they could not have reached the Pole, circled it, and returned in only 15½ hours. Photo History of Aviation Collection, University of Texas at Dallas.

Byrd *(center)* with Floyd Bennett on his left march amid ticker tape before large crowds to New York's City Hall. Photo History of Aviation Collection, University of Texas at Dallas.

After coming to the United States with Byrd, Balchen was hired by Fokker as a test pilot. He is shown here while working on the *America* before he was chosen for the 1927 flight to France. Photo courtesy Mrs. Audrey S. Balchen.

Balchen with the *America* while waiting for Byrd to make the decision to take off for France. Charles A. Lindbergh and Clarence Chamberlin, with Charles Levine, departed before Byrd and made successful transocean flights. Photo courtesy Mrs. Audrey S. Balchen.

Top: The *America*, while being test-flown by Fokker, nearly ended in tragedy as it crashed on landing. Bennett was seriously injured and was replaced by Bert Acosta; Balchen was named copilot. Photo History of Aviation Collection, University of Texas at Dallas.

Above: The *America* is readied for flight at Roosevelt Field, New York. Takeoff to Paris was delayed without explanation for many days as Byrd insisted he was not interested in competing for the Orteig prize. Photo Ohio State University Archives.

Top: Balchen ditched the *America* at night in the surf off Ver-sur-Mer, France, without injury to its four occupants. He flew the plane for nearly 40 hr. because Acosta was unable to fly on instruments. Photo Ohio State University Archives.

Above: French souvenir hunters strip the *America* after it is brought to the beach at Ver-sur-Mer. The wing, engines, and a few fuselage parts were returned to the U.S. Photo History of Aviation Collection, University of Texas at Dallas.

Top: Byrd, Noville *(on left)*, Balchen, and Acosta *(behind boy holding flag)* pose with villagers and schoolchildren at Ver-sur-Mer, France. Photo Ohio State University Archives.

Above: (From left) Commander Byrd, George Noville, French Premier Raymond Poincare, Bert Acosta, and Bernt Balchen in Paris. Photo Balchen Papers, National Archives (NARA).

Bernt Balchen *(left)*, with New York Mayor Jimmy Walker and Cmdr. Byrd, wait with Army and Navy officers to board the train to Washington, D.C., to receive the crew's congratulations from President Coolidge for the *America* flight. Photo Ohio State University Archives.

Balchen and mechanic substitute skis for wheels for performance tests on a Ford trimotor at Le Pas, Manitoba, March 1928. Floyd Bennett *(face obscured by propeller)* and crowd watch. Photo National Archives of Canada, courtesy Fred W. Hotson.

Top: (Left to right) J. R. Ross, Bernt Balchen, S. A. Cheeseman, and Fred J. Stevenson on their return from the airlift to Churchill in April 1927. The Fokker Universal, *City of Winnipeg,* was one of several used to pioneer airlifts in Northern Canada. Photo H. A. Oaks Collection, courtesy Fred W. Hotson.

Above: Bernt Balchen and Floyd Bennett *(left)* pose before one of the Fokker planes they tested and ferried to buyers. Bennett died of pneumonia during their effort to assist the crew of the *Bremen* on Greenly Island, Canada, in 1928. Photo courtesy Ohio State University Archives.

Herta Junkers, daughter of Dr. Hugo Junkers, manufacturer of the *Bremen*, arrived from Germany to aid the *Bremen* rescue party. She bids goodbye to James C. Fitzmaurice, copilot of the *Bremen*, while Charles J. V. Murphy, reporter *(with goggles)* and Balchen look on. The Ford trimotor was loaned by Edsel Ford to make the rescue flight. Photo G. Couture Collection, courtesy Fred W. Hotson.

Balchen in the *City of Toronto* used by Western Canada Airways. The passengers rode in the enclosed cabin and the pilots rode in an open cockpit. Photo H. A. Oaks Collection, courtesy Fred W. Hotson.

Balchen landed the rescue Ford on the ice at Greenly Island to assist the *Bremen* crew: Baron Guenther Von Huenefeld, Hermann Koehl, and James Fitzmaurice. They were eventually flown to New York for a ticker-tape parade. Photo courtesy Fred W. Hotson.

Top: Pilots, mechanics, and others in the aviation section of Byrd's first antarctic expedition met for this photo before leaving the United States. Balchen *(on right with arms folded)* was in charge. The other pilot was Dean Smith *(walking behind the group on right).* Photo History of Aviation Collection, University of Texas at Dallas.

Above: The Ford trimotor was named *Floyd Bennett* to honor the pilot who had flown Byrd during the Donald B. MacMillan Expedition to Greenland in 1925 and on the North Pole attempt in 1926. Photo Collections of Henry Ford Museum & Greenfield Village.

After crossing the edge of the polar plateau, Ashley McKinley took this photo looking backward to show the route the plane had taken up the glacier. Photo History of Aviation Collection, University of Texas at Dallas.

Lincoln Ellsworth *(left)* and Balchen in winter flying gear before leaving for antarctica in 1933. The plane was storm-damaged on the first trip and the expedition returned to the United States for repairs. The second trip was terminated because of bad weather. Ellsworth completed a third attempt with a Canadian pilot and crash-landed 25 mi. from Little America. The plane can be seen today at the National Air & Space Museum. Photo Smithsonian Institution.

Balchen supervises the tie-down of the *Polar Star* for the trip to Norway to meet the expedition ship *Wyatt Earp* that would take them to antarctica. Photo Balchen Papers, National Archives (NARA).

Amelia Earhart and Balchen at Washington Airport in 1932 before her historic solo flight across the Atlantic. Photo Smithsonian Institution.

Top: Balchen *(center),* then an Army Air Force captain, with his original cadre at Bluie West 8, the secret air base constructed at Sondrestromfjord, Greenland, in 1941. The base was a refueling point for combat aircraft being ferried to England under the Lend–Lease agreement. Photo Library of Congress.

Above: Balchen in front of a Navy PBY Catalina that had just landed on a small lake formed by a dimple in the ice, 12 mi. from a downed aircraft. Balchen led a party on skis over the treacherous crevasses to reach the crew and lead them to the PBY. The lake disappeared just after the aircraft took off. Photo courtesy Mrs. Audrey S. Balchen.

To lighten the load of a rescue plane, four men remained behind to ski 80 mi. across the ice cap to a base. Digging in to ride out winds up to 150 MPH and struggling through drifts and sastrugi, they made the trip in 10 days. *(Left to right)* Sgt. Hendrik D. Dolleman, Col. Bernt Balchen, Capt. Harold L. Strong, and Sgt. Joseph D. Healey are shown at the end of their journey. Photo U.S. Air Force.

Balchen in his winter parka, 1928. Photo Bernt Balchen file, History of Aviation Collection, University of Texas at Dallas.

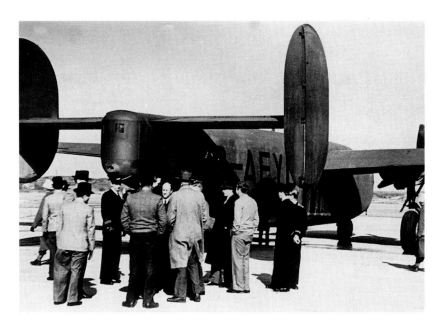

Top: American crew members in civilian clothes gather around an unarmed B-24 with British identification markings at the beginning of the secret airline operation into neutral Sweden code-named Operation Sonnie. The mission was to transport Norwegian soldiers and American airmen to England. Photo courtesy Cecil F. Grove.

Above: Carpetbagger crews load materials aboard a B-24 to be dropped to Norwegian resistance forces during Operation Ball. Photo courtesy George A. Reynolds.

Balchen *(standing forefront)* poses with his Operation Where and When officers at Kallax, Sweden, in 1945. The unit of ten C-47s became known as the "Ve Do It" Squadron. Photo courtesy Thomas C. Wahrmund.

Col. Gustav von Porat *(left),* Swedish air base commander at Kiruna, assisted Balchen by providing aircraft to airlift injured personnel. Although Sweden was neutral, they considered such flights as acts of mercy. Photo courtesy Richard Sizemore.

Top: Balchen *(second from left)* with two Swedish officers and a Russian officer *(right)* at a Russian base in northern Norway, January 1945. Photo Balchen Papers, Library of Congress Manuscript Division.

Above: A Grumman SA-16 rescue amphibian of the 10th Rescue Squadron rests on its hull after landing on T-3, an ice island in the Arctic Ocean. Balchen pioneered belly landings on ice and snow in Greenland during World War II. Photo U.S. Air Force.

Top: Dog team and handlers aboard a 10th Rescue Squadron C-47 en route to the crash site of a Lockheed F-80 fighter, April 1951. After landing, the dogs hauled the sledge *(in background)* 30 miles. Photo U.S. Air Force.

Above: Balchen and Gen. Frank A. Armstrong, commander of the Alaskan Air Command, examine a silver Viking ship model presented to Balchen to commemorate his 1949 nonstop flight in a C-54 from Fairbanks, Alaska, over the North Pole to Oslo, Norway, and then nonstop to Washington, D.C. Photo courtesy Mrs. Audrey Balchen.

Balchen is sworn in at the Pentagon as a regular Air Force colonel in October 1951 by Brig. Gen. G. P. Disosway. The appointment was a result of congressional action in view of his contributions to aviation in general and his achievements in arctic exploration. Photo U.S. Air Force.

Air Force Chief of Staff Gen. Hoyt S. Vandenberg *(right)* listens intently as Balchen briefs him on the progress made at Thule Air Base, Greenland, in 1952. Balchen was the project officer for the farthest north air base, which he had visited and visualized as an ideal site for aircraft operations in 1942. Photo U.S. Air Force, courtesy Ted R. Sturm.

The first commercial flight over the North Pole was made in November 1952 from Los Angeles to Copenhagen, Denmark, by Scandinavian Airlines System. Shown on arrival were Hjalmar Riiser-Larsen *(center)*, Norwegian Secretary of Defense, and Bernt Balchen, formerly copresident of the airline. Photo courtesy Mrs. Audrey S. Balchen.

Top: (Left to right) Gen. Curtis E. LeMay, commander of the Strategic Air Command; Balchen, Arthur Godfrey, Secretary of the Air Force Harold E. Talbott, and William Randolph Hearst Jr. flew to Thule Air Base, Greenland, on 31 December 1953 to celebrate the New Year with the men stationed there. Photo U.S. Air Force, courtesy Ted R. Sturm.

Above: Balchen receives the prestigious Harmon Trophy from President Eisenhower at the White House on 10 November 1953. The ceremony was attended by many aviation representatives, including Jacqueline Auriol *(right),* who received the award for France. Photo Abie Rowe/National Park Service records at the National Archives (file 79-AR-2211).

Top: Balchen and Dr. Ralf Stinson *(right)*, pilot of *My Gal Sal*, a B-17 that crashed on the Greenland ice cap in 1942, fly to the site in October 1964. Stinson gave one of his sons the middle name of Balchen in tribute for his rescue. Air Force photo courtesy Mrs. Audrey S. Balchen.

Above: Balchen at work on a watercolor of an arctic scape based on sketches and notes made previously on the scene. He often flew with sketch pad, paints, and water in his flight suit and then made larger paintings at home. Photo Library of Congress.

Adm. Richard E. Byrd *(left)* and Col. Bernt Balchen meet in 1953 at Kitty Hawk, North Carolina, for the 50th anniversary of the Wright brothers' first flights. This was to be the last face-to-face meeting between the two, and the occasion of a serious confrontation. Photo Ohio State University Archives.

11 · Operations Sonnie and Ball

Balchen was assigned temporary duty in the Army Air Force's Air War Plans division in the Pentagon under Maj. Gen. Laurence S. Kuter. During a conference about his Greenland experiences, Balchen suggested the possibility of establishing Army Air Force units specifically dedicated to arctic search and rescue. He had previously proposed this to the Greenland Base Command in the summer of 1942 and the idea had been circulating around the Army Air Force headquarters since.

Because Balchen personally brought up the idea again, General Arnold approved the activation of three rescue squadrons in 1944: one in southern Greenland, one in Presque Isle, Maine, and one in Great Falls, Montana, which was later moved to Alaska. These squadrons were the first Air Force flying units dedicated solely to air search and rescue.

Balchen wanted to be involved more directly in the war and told General Kuter he heard there was a need to establish an air transport service between the United Kingdom and Sweden to provide better contact with the British and American legations there. This concept had already been considered in London as a means to transport to England machines and parts manufactured in Sweden. The British had been using for this purpose Mosquito bombers and aircraft with civilian markings only at night, and the Norwegians had been running a courier service between the two points in transport aircraft only during adverse weather. The losses in personnel and equipment had been heavy. "From reliable British sources," a report said, "the statement was made that, of all the trips they make, this was the worst" and "most hazardous in every aspect."[1]

Balchen believed such a service was feasible with American planes and properly trained crews, and he expressed his interest in taking part. He checked with his friends in the Swedish and Norwegian embassies in Washington, D.C., and found that the resistance groups in Norway were getting better organized and needed supplies of guns, ammunition, clothing, radio equipment, and explosives. At Arnold's suggestion, Balchen met with Maj. Gen. William J. "Wild Bill" Donovan, prominent attorney and World War I Medal of Honor recipient, who was head of the Office of Strategic Services (OSS) and led its worldwide espionage, sabotage, and covert operations. Balchen told Donovan what he knew about German activities in Scandinavia and repeated his desire to help out any way he could to assist the Norwegian resistance forces.

General Kuter had not responded to Balchen's comments about the Britain–Sweden courier idea but brought the subject up later in a discussion of clandestine missions of dropping saboteurs and supplies inside areas occupied by the Germans. Balchen reminded Kuter that he would like to lead such an effort in Norway. He was immediately given a thorough top secret briefing about subversive activities in Europe and the need for more extensive intelligence collection. The suggestion of using Balchen's unusual background for such a venture made its way to General Arnold's office, and Balchen was called in to see him again in late November 1943.

Arnold asked Balchen what position he would like to have if he were to approve such an effort. Balchen replied that he would prefer to work directly with the Norwegian resistance effort because of his knowledge of Norway and his ability to speak the language. During the discussion, Gen. Barney M. Giles, Arnold's chief of staff, interrupted with a message from Gen. Ira Eaker, commander of the Eighth Air Force in England. Eaker asked if Balchen were available for an assignment to his headquarters in Britain. Arnold turned to Balchen and asked what he thought. Balchen said it suited him just fine. Arnold nodded approval and wished him good luck.[2]

Orders were issued for Balchen to proceed from Washington, D.C., to England. While in New York awaiting transportation he met Clyde Pangborn, who was still ferrying aircraft for the British Royal air force ferry command. Pangborn was en route to Montreal to pick up a C-47 to ferry to England. Balchen's orders authorized him to proceed "by any means possible," so he flew to Montreal with Pangborn to help him get the aircraft, and the two flew to Newfoundland where they were grounded by zero ceiling-zero visibility weather for 18 days. There were 185 combat aircraft waiting to cross, about 100 of them badly needed B-17s. They decided to go by way of the Azores and finally delivered the C-47 to Prestwick, Scotland. Balchen arrived in London on 22 January 1944 and reported to Gen. Carl "Tooey" Spaatz, head of the U.S. Strategic Air Forces, who asked Balchen to see an OSS officer at the American Embassy for his assignment. There Balchen met Georg Unger Vetlesen, his old friend, who was also working with the OSS on Scandinavian operations.[3]

After Vetlesen briefed Balchen on clandestine activities in Norway and Denmark, Balchen returned to General Spaatz's office. Spaatz said they had a request from the Norwegian government-in-exile to evacuate from Sweden to England 2,000 young Norwegians who were to go to the flying school at Little Norway. In addition, several hundred American Army Air Forces crew members interned in Sweden were awaiting transportation to England. Sweden, at great risk for violating their neutrality, had agreed to release them. Balchen was asked if he could carry out such an evacuation and when he said, "Ve do it," Spaatz said Balchen could write the directive himself. Balchen thus became the representative of the commanding general for the U.S. Strategic Air Forces in Europe and was "authorized to render decisions on all matters pertinent to the conduct of this operation."[4]

Balchen was transferred from General Spaatz's personal staff in January 1944 to the European division of the Air Transport Command (ATC) and he was directed to make whatever arrangements were necessary to establish and operate air routes between the United Kingdom or Iceland, and Denmark, Sweden, Norway, Finland, and Russia.[5] He immediately visited his old compatriot Riiser-Larsen and other Norwegian friends such as Trygve Lie, then foreign minister, and Oscar Torp, prime minister, and told them about his very welcome assignment.

It was never really clear why Hitler invaded Denmark and Norway in April 1940 and left Sweden alone. It was no doubt partly a result of the fact that Sweden had a large machine industry that required coal—and this coal came from Germany. Sweden had large resources of timber and wood pulp for papermaking, which had a ready market in Germany. Norway, on the otherhand, was a seafaring nation, and its ties looked westward rather than toward Germany. As the war progressed, the Swedes became more and more inclined to help their occupied neighbors to the east and west. It was a tremendous advantage to Norway and Denmark and to the Allied cause for Sweden to be able to provide a safe haven to more than 70,000 Scandinavians who would otherwise have wound up in German concentration or forced-work camps. In addition, there were thousands of people there from Latvia, Estonia, Lithuania, Poland, and Germany who had fled from the Nazis and the Soviet Union.

Sweden's willingness to violate its neutrality was an extraordinary chance to return the American airmen to duty who had made emergency landings in Sweden after their bombing and fighter missions. However, to make it appear to all nations that it was truly neutral, the Swedish government approved the entry of American planes into the country, as well as those of the Germans.

The directive that General Spaatz authorized to begin Balchen's clandestine airlift missions was dated 27 January 1944 and the evacuation of the Norwegians was originally to be completed in 90 days. It was given the code name Operation Sonnie, which was thought to be derived from the name of Sonja Henie, famous Norwegian American ice-skating star.

Five B-24 bombers of the Eighth Air Force were converted into a cargo–passenger configuration by having their armament removed, 35 bench-type passenger seats installed, and a radar navigational aid added.

In August 1944 the 801st Bomb Group, which had been flying missions to drop spies and saboteurs into the occupied countries, was deactivated and redesignated the 492nd Bomb Group. The Carpetbaggers, as they were called, consisted of four squadrons. Seven bomber crews were assigned initially to Operation Sonnie. None were told what their mission was to be, but they were experienced in working under OSS orders, so most assumed they would be doing the same sort of work. The aircraft used for this mission were to be painted dark green and have all military markings removed.

To comply with Swedish requests, all crew members were given American passports with visas for Sweden, Finland, and the Soviet Union. They were to wear only civilian clothing. Balchen, along with 60 men, visited the Selfridge Department Store on Oxford Street in London one morning and ordered two complete suits for each man, all different and all with labels removed. The clerks were surprised and asked for ration coupons. Balchen had none and asked the manager to call American Ambassador John G. Winant, as well as verify their status with Scotland Yard, which the manager did. No ration books were needed and the outfitting of the men went forward without comment from the store clerks.

While these preparations were being made, Balchen had difficulty with the British authorities who had to give permission to fly into and out of Great Britain and operate into Sweden. A number of wrangling discussions were held with the British general staff and air ministry, who disputed the arrangements and the effrontery of the Scandinavians in making such a request outside of their normal government channels.

The squabble dragged on for six weeks. When there seemed to be no solution, Balchen went to Foreign Minister Lie and asked if Lie could break the stalemate. Lie, with King Haakon VII and Crown Prince Olaf, had lunch with Prime Minister Winston Churchill and Anthony Eden, British foreign minister, in late March 1944. The Norwegian monarch had hardly been seated when he abruptly asked Churchill why the British government refused to permit the Americans to fly to Sweden. Churchill said he knew nothing about it. He turned to Eden who, embarrassed because he knew about the situation and had taken no action, said he would see to it that the Balchen operation could begin right away.[6]

Two days later Balchen and his converted B-24s flew to Leuchars, near the eastern coast of Scotland, the British base commander, and Norwegian air force Col. Finn Lambrechts, who had been chief pilot for DNL, the Norwegian airline. The base belonged to the RAF coastal command that operated Consolidated PBY Catalinas on antisubmarine patrols and attacked enemy convoys in the North Sea and along the coast of Norway. In addition, the base supported the Norwegian Underground and provided courier service between Leuchars and Stockholm with two Lockheed Lodestar transports that had been purchased by the Norwegians. Since the British forces and Balchen's men were doing the same type of top secret work, they shared the operations map room and facilities at Leuchars.

At this time Lt. Col. Keith N. Allen, a former airline pilot, was assigned to Balchen's unit as executive officer, and Balchen thought he was one of the finest instrument pilots he had ever known.[7] He was a man of very few words, and Allen proved to be a courageous individual who won the admiration of every person working on Operation Sonnie. Also among the first to be assigned was Capt. David Schreiner, Lt. Robert C. Durham, a navigator, and Lt. Glen Cupp, all of whom had completed many Carpetbagger missions dropping leaflets, saboteurs, and supplies to resistance units in France.

When he was asked by the British air ministry officials how he was going to fly the dangerous route through enemy-held skies into Sweden, Balchen said he wanted to fly only in bad weather, preferably at night, to conceal the aircraft well into Norway and Sweden. It meant much flying on instruments, but with radar in all the planes it would not be too difficult to navigate.[8] Radio codes and frequencies had to be agreed on for identification purposes over two points, Ytter-Malung in west-central Sweden, and the other at Goteborg on the southern route. Coded warnings were arranged to help them dodge German border patrol fighters detected by Swedish radar.

Ship movements out of any Norwegian port were promptly reported to Stockholm by Norwegian underground radio, and Stockholm relayed the information to London. The positions of enemy convoy or flak ships moving along the coast were known before any aircraft were dispatched. The Germans had night fighters based near Bergen, Stavanger, Oslo, Gossen, and Trondheim, which were continually watched.

> As a matter of fact, the information for our special flights was so good that other intelligence officers came to us for information. We knew where every gun was on the Norwegian coast, where every German division was stationed, how many planes there were on every field and what type, when they usually landed and took off and what bombers or transports went through Bergen or Oslo or any other important field.[9]

Balchen, Allen, Schreiner, and Durham, plus three other officers, and three enlisted men made their first B-24 flight to Stockholm's Bromma airport on 31 March–1 April 1944. They planned the route to fly over enemy-occupied Norway to Sweden at night, entering a corridor into Sweden 20 mi. wide reserved by Swedish air officials for commercial traffic so that Swedish antiaircraft batteries would not fire on them.

The flight was made without incident. The unmarked, dark green B-24 was parked next to a German DC-3, which had been seized from KLM, the Dutch airline. They were met by the American military and air attachés, who briefed the crew on what they could expect during their stay in Stockholm. Everyone exchanged their uniforms for civilian clothes before leaving the plane and told to debark and get inside a room in the terminal while the DC-3 was being loaded. Balchen wrote,

> As I walked from the ship towards the designated door in the passenger terminal, I saw a man I knew who was working as a press attaché in the German Embassy in Stockholm and whom I knew to be affiliated with German Intelligence. His name was Dr. Grassman. I walked up to him and said, "Guten Tag, Dr. Grassman. Wie gehts bei Ihnen zu Hause?" (Good morning, Dr. Grassman, how is everything at home?)

The doctor recognized who I was and was so flabbergasted that he started to stutter and did not reply.[10]

Balchen stayed in Stockholm for a few days to make himself known at the American Legation, coordinate with the Norwegian authorities there, and talk with the civil aviation authorities to make landing and routing arrangements. He also got in touch with his old friends in the Swedish air force to let them know about the evacuation plans.

Balchen could not discuss everything he was going to be doing with the U.S. legation, however, because of their responsibility to help Sweden preserve a neutral appearance. Because there would be liaison with the OSS and Norwegian underground, Balchen could not even tell his executive officer or crew members about talking with underground representatives. It was an interesting setup, Balchen said, but "loaded with dynamite" because of Sweden's professed neutrality.[11]

Balchen and his crew soon found that they were being followed everywhere in Sweden by German Gestapo agents and had to avoid giving them any cause to provoke an international incident that would reflect negatively on the Americans' status in a neutral country. Although the American Legation officials tried to keep tabs on Balchen and knew he was operating with some kind of government approval, they were reluctant to inquire. The OSS operatives within the legation knew what he was doing but officially paid no attention to his presence.

Balchen made a courtesy visit to Herschel V. Johnson, the American minister to Sweden, and told him that he was going to evacuate the 2,000 Norwegians and that he would need quarters for his crews and passengers. He also told Johnson that he was going to meet old Swedish and Norwegian friends who had nothing to do with the evacuation program. This was to convince Johnson not to be concerned that he would be meeting a lot of people who had no connection with Operation Sonnie. Johnson warned Balchen not to make any contacts that would embarrass the State Department and threatened to have him deported if he did. Balchen replied, "Don't worry, Mr. Minister. You'll never catch me."[12]

There was one requirement that Balchen had to comply with. Carl Jungberg, head of the Swedish Air Authority and an old friend, said Balchen had to have civilian numbers on his aircraft. Balchen contacted authorities in England and numbers were furnished. Jungberg did not specify what size or color they were, so they were painted black on the dark green fuselage and in very small print.[13]

Commercial licenses were also needed for certain crew members, so on their return to London certificates were typed out for the pilots and radio operators who satisfied those requirements.

It was important that Operation Sonnie have a facility at Stockholm to get the planes under cover for maintenance and for fueling. Balchen turned to another old friend, Capt. Carl Florman of ABA, the Swedish Airline, who not only found hangar space on Bromma airport but also helped with hiring local personnel and renting two apartment houses and hotel rooms. In time accommodations were found for as many as 250 internees at a time when they were in Stockholm ready to be flown out. An internment camp was set up at Mullsjo in Sweden's lake country until the time came to be transported to Stockholm for their flights.

Balchen contacted Lt. Gen. Bengt Nordenskiold, chief of the Swedish air force, Karl Ljungberg, director of the Swedish Air Ministry, and Sven Grafstrom, secretary to the foreign minister, who promised their cooperation in any future operations with which Balchen was involved. Balchen then turned to another old friend, Dr. Harry Soderman, chief of the Criminal Institute in Sweden, who had helped set up police training camps for 12,500 Norwegian youths who had escaped from Norway. The Swedes had provided uniforms, arms, and equipment and trained the youngsters as "police soldiers" or ready reserve. Soderman was in continual touch with the Norwegian underground and briefed Balchen on the serious problems faced by the resistance fighters.

Soderman put Balchen in touch with the Norwegian resistance leaders in Sweden and their radio operators so that Balchen could obtain information about German fighter-interceptor activity and antiaircraft batteries in Norway that might interfere with his flight operations. He also obtained radio codes and call letters for use when his flight crews needed to communicate with the Norwegian resistance forces.

There had been other forces at work supporting the underground before America entered the war. The British Overseas Airways Corporation (BOAC) had been operating its airline into Sweden and Douglas Grey, chief of BOAC's Swedish office, gave Balchen office space to use as his headquarters. A ticket office was set up in the Hotel Stockholm for the ticketing of the internees. The Germans did their ticketing through the Swedish airlines, which were flying to Berlin and other German cities.[14]

Operations to evacuate the Norwegians from Sweden to England began immediately and during April Capt. David Schreiner made seven flights with nearly 40 passengers on each run. "It was anything but a luxury ride for those boys," Schreiner said. "I just packed them in like sardines but nobody complained. They had been waiting for two years to get out."[15]

Balchen's agreement with the Swedes included a stipulation that he and his pilots would always file flight plans in advance. Because the Lufthansa manager was a known Nazi agent, it was accepted that the manager would relay the flight plans to the German fighter interceptors and anti-aircraft batteries along the route that Balchen's planes declared they would fly. Balchen had his crews file fake flight plans that satisfied the Swedish civil aeronautics authorities.

Sweden's neutrality had its strange, sometimes comical outcomes. When one of the Sonnie B-24s blew a cylinder head on one of its engines in Stockholm, Balchen jokingly asked Florman to see if he could borrow a cylinder from the Germans. The German Lufthansa representative said he would see what he could do. An undamaged cylinder was taken from a crashed Liberator in Germany and flown to Stockholm. It was installed in the B-24, which flew back to Leuchars. The next day a replacement cylinder was flown to Stockholm and given by the Swedes to the Germans with thanks from the Americans.[16]

The American military airline operation to Sweden matured under Balchen's leadership. He developed operations procedures as if for a civil airline. Scarce commissary supplies were hauled in as well as communications and air navigation aids, such as radio range stations and beacons and weather reporting instruments. Not only did it help the American and Swedish air operations at the time, but Balchen planned it all with postwar civil aviation in mind.[17]

Also acting under the guise of operating as a commercial airline, the British RAF had been using Mosquito bombers to drop supplies to the resistance units in Norway, where an estimated 40,000 men were hiding in the woods to avoid being taken captive by the Gestapo. Those who were living in the forests needed to be organized and trained to be better able to assist the force fighting from the outside. They needed equipment, weapons, food, clothing, and medicine, which were dropped to them in the winter—but there was one hitch. Although the British Royal air force had sole responsibility for supplying the underground during the first years of the war, the RAF refused to send their aircraft on drop missions during the summer months when there is light almost all day and night. A lack of equipment for planes, harsh winter weather conditions, and higher priority for other occupied countries further decreased the number of drops.

Repeated requests to the RAF from the resistance forces for increased assistance were to no avail. The Norwegians in Sweden asked Balchen if
there was anything he could do about it when he returned to London.

On his next trip to London, he met with General Spaatz and told him
of his success in getting Operation Sonnie started, and then mentioned
the plight of the Norwegian underground. He proposed that he be permitted to fly the paradrop missions that the British found too dangerous.
Spaatz was dubious. "That would be one hell of a risky business," Spaatz
said. "If the RAF doesn't want to do it, do you think it can be done?"
Balchen assured him that he could do it.

"Dammit," Spaatz replied. "Every time I ask if you can do something,
you say, 'Ve do it.' I'm going to call you Ve Do It because no matter what
we tell you, you say you can do it, and so far you've carried it out.'"
Spaatz called in Gen. Frederick Anderson, told him to give Balchen what
he wanted, and wished him good luck.[18]

Balchen immediately shared the good news with Vetlesen. Vetlesen set
up a meeting with OSS and Allied counterpart representatives and
painted a dark picture of conditions in Norway. Without immediate help,
he said, the resistance units would have to be disbanded and get out of
the country. It would be a loss to the sabotage and other subversive actions in Norway, which had caused the Germans to keep large numbers
of troops there instead of on the battlefields in France. The Allied representatives at the meeting, especially the British, were not convinced, because the RAF had concluded that flying over occupied Norway dropping supplies and people had become entirely too risky. Twenty-three
RAF aircraft and crews had been lost in these operations. It was one
thing to drop men and equipment into the rolling hills of France at night
but the mountains and uncertain weather of Norway—plus the fact that
these drops were made mostly in daylight among prowling Luftwaffe patrols—was a far different matter.

Balchen, however, said he was convinced he could do it despite the
risks, and that he was ready to start immediately. Col. J. S. Wilson, one
of the British officers in charge of the Norwegian section of the British
Special Operations Executive (SOE), asked Balchen if he knew anything
about Norway. Balchen replied that he knew Norway quite well. Still in-
credulous, Wilson approved the American operation, wished Balchen
good luck, and reminded him that he had been warned.[19]

There was no more opposition from the British, and Balchen was off
and running with a new and more dangerous mission. It was given the

code name of Operation Ball, presumably because the missions would require that the ball machine gun turret in each B-24's belly be removed. About 10 B-24s were assigned. The crews were also furnished from the four squadrons of the 801st/492nd Bomb Group, all veterans of many drops in France.

Some additional aircraft modifications were required, which included painting the aircraft black and removing much excess weight, including the oxygen system, bomb sights, and all guns except those in the tail and top turret. Eureka-Rebecca radar sets were installed that made drops through the clouds possible into large areas. A new development, called an S-Phone, was used on later sorties. It was a direct radio–telephone contact with the "reception committee" on the ground.

The bomb bays were left intact to carry special preloaded metal containers with the supplies requested by the underground. Each load consisted of about 3.5 tn. of weapons, ammunition, communications equipment, food, clothing, and medical supplies in 12 containers loaded in the bomb bay. The holes remaining, after the ball turrets were removed, were padded and called "Joe holes." Through them, "Joes," the anonymous American, British, and other Allied military and civilian agents would parachute into the occupied areas at night from altitudes of about 500 ft.; supplies—not so easily damaged—were dropped from about 400 ft. Several women, referred to as "Janes" or "Josephines," were also dropped.

The speed of the planes for the drops was to be kept as low as possible with wheels and flaps down. The flights would be most often flown down in the valleys below the tops of mountains to avoid radar detection. All drops would be coordinated with Norwegian sabotage agents and none were to be committed unless authorized by the London OSS headquarters.

The routine for the agents was that on the afternoon before their flights they were to be brought to the Leuchars airfield by car from London and placed in quarters away from the air crews. They would be searched thoroughly to ensure that they did not retain any items like a London bus ticket, British coins, or an American cigarette that would identify them as belonging to the Allies. Each agent would then don a baggy jump suit fitted with a number of pockets to carry a dagger-like knife, concentrated rations, a flashlight, a first-aid kit, bundles of radio parts, and maps. A rubber cushion was placed in the seat of the suit and rubberized cloth was wound around the agent's feet to help absorb the landing shock. Knee-high boots and a rubber crash helmet completed the rig. As in the drops in France, none of the aircraft crews ever knew who the saboteurs were. They were hurried aboard in the darkness at the end of the runway just before takeoff and sat quietly in the aft fuselage awaiting the signal to jump.

Balchen soon had two operations in motion simultaneously from Leuchars: the armed black B-24s heading to Norway and the unarmed dark green ones destined for Sweden. Although those Sweden-bound were presumed to be empty, except for occasional passengers, they often carried arms, explosives, and radio equipment, also destined for the underground. The passengers on the return flights usually shared space with boxes containing Swedish ball bearings and other critical items. When these flights landed in Sweden, mostly during the small hours, and the Swedish police approached, Balchen and his men were to say the code word, *"Flygvapnet,"* which means "air force." A police guard would be promptly placed around the aircraft; later, a truck would appear and the cargo would be whisked to the basement of an apartment house that Balchen had rented. It would be stored there until it could be trucked secretly across the border to Norway. Not a single ounce of this material was ever lost.[20]

When he was satisfied that everything was ready, Balchen scheduled himself to fly the first official mission, code named Hatlock I, on 22 June 1944. Before takeoff he was invited to a special dinner at the Leuchars officers' club. King Haakon and Crown Prince Olaf were special guests. Balchen had a quiet chat with Prince Olaf and at 2200 told him he would have to leave for Norway. He asked the prince to ask his father if he would like to send a message to the reception committee. The king nodded and wrote a note of greeting and reassurance and handed it to Balchen, who excused himself and was airborne by 2300.

Balchen took his old Carpetbagger crew with him—Captain Schreiner, navigator Bob Durham, relief pilot Bob Withrow, and the standby crew he used on his original flight to Stockholm. The weather was partly cloudy and they could see the ground easily in the Norwegian summer dusk. They were within sight of a Nazi airfield outside Bergen but no interceptors rose to meet them. The supply drop was to be made near Bollhoe in preparation for the next operation against the enemy's heavy water facilities. As they approached the drop zone, they could see the lights on the ground from the reception committee. The B-24's wheels and flaps were lowered to reduce the speed and the bomb bay doors were opened for the drop.

The reception committee on the ground made the previously agreed on signals with a flashlight and the containers were dropped. Figures could be seen running to them, removing the parachutes, and quickly hauling the containers away. In one of them was the king's message and a message from Balchen that he signed and included in all future drops he made in Norway. It said, "This is the American Air Forces under my command. We are with you and will come with more when you need us. Enclosed in the container you will find a small gift from the American boys to the boys in Norway." It was usually packages of cigarettes along with reading materials, which were always welcome.[21]

Twelve containers were dropped that night after the flashlight code signals were verified. Balchen and his crew returned to Leuchars in time for the parade for King Haakon and Crown Prince Olaf the next day. There were 20 B-24s lined up on the field, most shiny black and the rest green, along with their flight crews. The king asked Balchen if he had delivered the message, and when told that he had the king expressed his appreciation for what he was doing for Norway. At lunch after the inspection of troops, Balchen was handed a radio a message from the reception committee at Bollhoe. It said, "Thanks for goods. All received. Thanks for the message. Thanks to the Yanks." It was shown to the king whose look of deep appreciation did not need any comment.[22]

Balchen's next two drops were equally successful. After the third drop at Holtaalen near Trondheim in bright daylight, he decided to return to Scotland by first flying to eastern Norway toward the Swedish border where the Germans were reportedly building a large airfield. The crew took photographs that verified that a large field was being built but was far from operational. The Norwegian underground, stimulated by the knowledge that the Americans were going to make drops regardless of the daylight, tightened their organization and became adept at communicating their needs to Balchen's Carpetbaggers through OSS channels.

In view of the seriousness of resistance needs in Norway, Balchen turned his full attention to developing Operation Ball. Thousands of details had to be carried out in complete secrecy. Once the communications net was firmly established, the resistance units would radio requisitions for guns, ammunition, clothing, food, and other supplies, plus special materials for sabotage operations. Because no two requests were the same, every drop had to be packed and marked especially to satisfy a particular request. This was done at the OSS packaging stations near Birmingham, where they were sealed and attached to colored parachutes. A special operations room was set up at Leuchars similar to that used by the OSS in London, where maps displayed vital information such as the location of German antiaircraft batteries and airfields. Balchen picked up much of the information for the maps on his visits to Stockholm.

As most drops were made during the twilight or during daylight hours of the Norwegian summer, the crews could generally see the delivery points and the reception committees on the ground. Positive identification of the drop zones was made either by fires or smoke. Balchen's preliminary flights refined the procedures his pilots would follow in subsequent missions.

Before being assigned to drop missions, the Liberator crews trained extensively for two weeks in night and instrument flying. The radio operators took advanced Morse code classes and were trained in the use of the liaison transmitter for ground-controlled navigation steers. The crews consisted of pilot, copilot, navigator, engineer, radio operator, and tail gunner.

With the initial missions completed successfully, Operation Ball slowly settled into a routine, interrupted only by severe weather. George M. Philbrick, a ball turret gunner, had been assigned to the Carpetbaggers as a gunner in the top turret position part-time and as a dispatcher. He explained what his role was on these sorties:

> As dispatcher, part of my job was to check all the gear for the jumpers as well as the containers in our bomb bay area. Our bombardier flew in the plexiglass nose watching for the Morse code light signal from the ground. We had a red, amber and green light hookup from the nose to waist area where I spent all my time while in the target area. I would get the red light as we approached the target area and then the amber; within seconds, I'd get the green light to drop. We tried to drop supplies and people on the first pass and leave the area as soon as possible. We had no contact with the people we were dropping until they were on our plane as it was about to take off. Destination orders were opened over the English Channel.[23]

Earl Zimmerman was a radio operator on one of the Ball missions and was assigned to a make-up crew. He tells about one of his flights:

> The green light was always given by Colonel Balchen. About supper time, he wandered from the hangar, hands in pockets, staring at the darkening sky and said in a thick Norwegian accent, "Ve go tonight,

boys." Our ships were prepared, we were briefed, chowed down, waited for total darkness and took off.

We crossed the coast of Norway at 8,000 feet and immediately search lights picked us up. However, prior to takeoff we had been given the enemy color of the day by Norway's clandestine radio. The Very pistol had been loaded with those colors and it was fired instantly. The lights winked off and we continued on our way.

Our flight plan was to make a 360-degree turn at three different locations to confuse enemy radar on the real drop zone. Approaching the first turn area, we saw a very bright flame pass across the plane's nose. It was very disconcerting as no one could figure out what it was. We went to [the real] drop zone, saw the correct light pattern on the ground, got the right radio code and made a successful drop.[24]

A. L. Sharps, a gunner on one of the Ball crews, commented on their leader and the missions he flew:

I still recall him as the best flier, the best navigator, and the most deadly soldier I ever knew. Balchen had a built-in compass in his brain which worked when the regular compass went crazy.

We did not fly under cover of darkness, for that far north it doesn't get dark in July and August. We flew at fifty feet altitudes and ducked in and out of fjords. Canisters were dropped at [approximately] 100 feet and agents at 400 feet.[25]

The drops always included newspapers and the latest magazines from the United States that reached England, such as *Reader's Digest, Life, Time, Collier's,* and the *New Yorker. Life* had especially good photo coverage of the Normandy invasion, and Balchen happened to be able to get many copies that had the date two days prior to one of Balchen's missions over Norway. They were dropped to a site near Oslo and Balchen heard later that copies were soon on the tables of the largest hotels in the city. The German Gestapo was furious.[26]

Col. Robert W. Fish, editor of *They Flew by Night,* a collection of Carpetbagger stories, commented,

Subordinates and associates found Col. Balchen an easy man to talk to, for he had no "side." He treated everyone from private to general as an equal. Yet beneath the quiet, unruffled exterior, it was easy to sense a steel core of the man. And for an untried operation—flying unarmed transports over enemy territory or dropping war materials to the underground—this combination of velvet and steel was especially desirable.

Leadership for those Carpetbagger projects required a unique working balance between the many conflicting interests of all countries concerned. These were the U.S., Great Britain, Norway, Sweden, and to a lesser degree, Russia and Iceland. Col. Balchen knew every important Norwegian and Swedish government official plus leaders of the underground personally. To an unusual extent, he had the confidence of Scandinavians of all classes and positions. This was a priceless asset for an operation in which informal understanding meant everything.[27]

Interspersed with the Ball missions, Balchen flew to Stockholm in mid-summer 1944 to check on his Sonnie responsibilities. The Americans were wearing their uniforms (Sweden was by now unconcerned about this) on the two Swedish flying fields that were being used openly and Balchen arranged to use five more. While the word came from the Norwegian underground that they were having trouble with the drop signals. A person-to-person meeting was necessary, so Balchen made a trip to Oslo to get the matter straightened out.

Balchen found that it was not difficult to get into Norway. He took an auto to a spot near the border, walked through the woods over the border, was met by another car, and drove into Oslo to meet his contact. He felt strange being in the city and not be able to tell anyone he was there. He saw several friends on the street but could not speak to them and did not dare to call his mother or sisters for fear of reprisals. He came face-to-face with an acquaintance who paled and whispered, "Get the hell out of here!" Balchen left hurriedly for Sweden.[28]

Returning to London immediately with the information he sought, Balchen had a meeting with Air Marshal Sir Trafford Leigh-Mallory, head of the British strategic forces, who wanted to discuss Balchen's clandestine missions to Norway and Sweden. Balchen explained that more than 1,000 Norwegians had been evacuated out of Sweden to England by that time and that 10 Norwegian drop missions had been completed without any losses. The British had made more missions than that since the invasion of Norway in 1940 but had lost 25 supply planes. Leigh-Mallory asked Balchen what he knew about Norway. Balchen explained that he was a native of the country and was acquainted with the problems of flying in Norway. Not impressed by Balchen's response, he said he doubted Balchen's ability to sustain operations that his own men had said were too dangerous. He asked when Balchen was last in Norway.

"I was there yesterday, Sir," Balchen replied.

The British air leader stared at Balchen incredulously a long time, then said, "Well, I give up. Good luck to you."[29]

From that time on, Balchen had no problems with any British interference in his Ball operations. All subsequent American missions to Norway were clearly left in Balchen's hands.

On 13 June 1944 a powerful A-4 German rocket without a warhead had crashed in Sweden. It had been launched on a test flight from Peenemunde, a site on Usedom Island in the Baltic Sea, and had veered off course. It had exploded several thousand feet in the air in southeastern Sweden, and pieces were scattered over some 60 mi. The Swedes were furious but kept the incident secret and hid the location of the main pieces. A joint British–American team of scientists operating under the code name of Project Big Ben was sent immediately to Sweden to collect the fragments and attempt to determine the missile's characteristics.

The pieces that were needed for further study were too large to get into a B-24, so a C-47 was borrowed from another unit in England. Its identification marks were painted over, the seats were removed, and Keith Allen, Bob Durham, Lt. Robert Withrow, and Borge Langeland, a navigator from the Norwegian air force, took the C-47 to Sweden and returned with the missile parts to Farnborough, where scientists were analyzing the German missiles.

The experts were elated at what they had to study, because the A-4 was the prototype for the V-2 ballistic missile and gave the Allies their first clues about the size, range, technology, and military capability of what was then the most advanced rocket vehicle in the world. Although no defenses could be devised against it, the major advantage was in knowing how the giant weapon was constructed and its damage potential. Balchen's clandestine airline had enabled the secrets of the Germans' ultimate weapon to be revealed before its first flight against England.[30]

During the first week of August 1944 Balchen assigned himself an early morning Operation Ball drop to Sundungen. He owned a house at Holmenkollen, a few miles north of Oslo, and was curious to see what it looked like. It was a beautiful morning with unlimited visibility. He flew even with the windows of the house and could see that everything seemed undisturbed. After the war, his neighbors told him that they had been awakened by the sound of the engines of the black bomber and saw the American star on its side. They knew who it was.[31]

It was to be a year before Balchen would be able to see peace restored to his native country and visit his old neighborhood openly. The Norwegian population was living under the rule of the Germans but led by Vidkun Quisling, a Norwegian fascist leader who had been minister of defense from 1931 to 1935. He had founded the fascist Nasjonal Samling party and had helped the Germans prepare for their conquest of Norway in 1940. They installed him as premier in 1942, but the general population considered him a traitor.[32]

While the legal Norwegian government was in exile, loyal Norwegians who remained in the country tried to maintain the governmental institutions and conserve the country's natural resources as best they could. They quietly resisted the Quisling-led government and attempted to slow down the usefulness of the country's industries to the Germans.

Balchen knew Quisling before the war but never thought that his political party was of any real consequence. Balchen believed it was made up of opportunists who thought that following Quisling during the German occupation was a way to achieve favors and recognition.

The vast majority of the Norwegian people revered King Haakon VII, who had been chosen king when Norway separated from Sweden in 1905. He became a symbol of the resistance to the Nazis and administered the government-in-exile in London. There were many high officials in Norway who assisted the king by secretly helping the resistance forces. Three examples were Chief Justice Paal Berg, Superior Court Judge Gunnar Schjelderup, and Gunnar Jahn, director of the Bank of Norway. Balchen had contacts with them as well as individuals inside the police force and industry to gain information during the occupation. There is no doubt that these men, if detected, would have been executed. Some were flown in and out of Norway on the shuttle service from Sweden; all of them used pseudonyms in their travels.

One of Balchen's most valuable Norwegian contacts was Jens Christian Hauge, a lawyer whose underground name was Edvard Lange. He was the top leader in Milorg, the name of the resistance organization, and after the war became Norwegian defense minister. Several times Hauge was able to get out of Oslo by donning a diving suit and hiding in the water tenders of the locomotives on the Oslo–Stockholm railroad.

One night at a meeting in London with Balchen and Vetlesen, Hauge, half joking, said, "What do you think about kidnapping Quisling?" He said he could get him if Balchen could get him out of Norway. Balchen looked at him and said, "Ve do it!"

A plan took form immediately. Balchen would get a PBY from the U.S. navy and land on a lake near Oslo. He would then take him back "alive and warm" to Scotland.[33]

Balchen went to London and asked General Spaatz for permission to launch the kidnap operation. Spaatz was dumbfounded, but permission was granted. A few days later, a PBY flying boat landed at Leuchars with a crew that had no clue what their mission was going to be. Their immediate job was to practice night landings on water and then wait until the signal was received from Norway to make the pickup.

After working out details, Balchen and Hauge decided that there was a man much more dangerous and ruthless than Quisling. His name was Wolfgang von Fehner, chief of the Gestapo in Norway. The code name of Sea Otter was assigned to a new plot to kidnap von Fehner, and three saboteur groups in Norway were chosen to help carry it out. The actual kidnapping was to be done by Hauge, but he missed the opportunity by only a minute when von Fehner suddenly changed his itinerary.

Assassination of other high Nazi officials was also considered; chief among them were Josef Terboven, chief commissar and chief of the state police, and General Marthinsen, ranking German officer. However, Marthinsen was shot from ambush by some of the resistance force. In reprisal for his death, German soldiers went into the Oslo streets, randomly picked out ten Norwegians, and shot them. The plans to kidnap Quisling, von Fehner, or have anyone assassinated were promptly abandoned.

One of the unusual Operation Ball missions was the requirement to determine the condition of the *Tirpitz,* Germany's great 45,000 tn. battleship. Allied air forces had been trying to sink it for weeks, but in September 1944 it was still afloat at its Norwegian anchorage at Altenfjord. Photo reconnaissance had not yielded sufficient information about its condition. Allen, Schreiner, and their crew volunteered to drop two agents as close to Altenfjord as they dared. Their B-24 was modified with additional gas tanks in the bomb bay. The flight from Britain to the drop area and return was more than 2,600 mi. and took 16½ hr. They completed the drop, marking it as one of the longest combat missions flown during World War II. The position and condition of the *Tirpitz* was reported to England, and it was subsequently sunk while at anchor in Tromsofjord on 12 November 1944.

Carpetbagger missions into France ended 16 September 1944, when all of the country was liberated. The final mission for Operation Ball was flown on 27 September 1944. Balchen and his Carpetbagger crews had flown 166 Ball missions into Norway, of which 141 were successful drops. The others were abandoned because of weather, disturbances on the ground, interference by the Germans, or improper signals. They were not without tragedy. Three airplanes crashed and 18 crew members were killed. None of the planes were lost to enemy fire.[34]

Even though Operation Sonnie was to last only a few months until the 2,000 Norwegians trainees were evacuated from Sweden, it was clear in December 1944 that others should be evacuated. Balchen recommended that the airlift should continue for at least another year.[35]

Balchen's extensive efforts on Operations Sonnie and Ball received praise from the U.S. military attaché in Stockholm, who recommended him for the Legion of Merit for his distinguished service. The recommendation was approved.

> Operating under adverse weather conditions, flying unarmed and exposed constantly to enemy attack, Colonel Balchen completed, from March to December 1944, one hundred ten roundtrips between the United Kingdom and Sweden with the loss of only one aircraft. In addition to the Norwegians, over nine hundred American internees and evacuees and nearly one hundred fifty [individuals] of other nationalities were safely evacuated. Numerous important diplomatic and army officers were transported as well as large amounts of strategic freight. Beginning his second assignment, known as the "Ball Project," on 17 July 1944, Colonel Balchen as Command Pilot completed the first mission. Carrying out all operations during the night at low altitudes, using modified and camouflaged bombers to avoid detection by the enemy, his group undertook sixty-seven missions by 23 September of which forty-one were successfully completed. Agents and supplies were dropped within an area of 100 yards square. Colonel Balchen's successful efforts contributed materially to the prosecution of the war effort.[36]

At this time Balchen received a radio message from General Donovan in Washington: "If you are available would you be willing to come with

OSS to be on my immediate staff to deal with all our problems and increasing activities with air forces here and in the various theaters in which we operate?"[37]

Balchen replied that he was engaged in important operations that required his presence. He said he was interested in the offer but hoped he could be of further use in Scandinavia.[38] Balchen had good reason to turn down a new assignment. As the Allied forces pushed across France, there was great concern that Hitler would take a stand in Norway and increase his forces there. The Allied counter-strategy was to disrupt the German lines of communication, interfere with their troop-resupply system, and continue to reduce the industrial capacity within Norway by sinking their shipping, blowing up their bridges, and sabotaging their radio facilities.

12·Operation Where and When and the Sepals Project

To meet the continually changing war situation as the Allies pressed eastward into Europe in the winter of 1944–1945, administrative adjustments in the Scandinavian operations were necessary. Balchen's Carpetbaggers were assigned to the 1409th Base Unit and transferred from Leuchars, Scotland, to Metfield, England. One of the 1409th's first assignments was to transport top officials of the Norwegian government-in-exile from Britain to Sweden. Stockholm then became the center of activity for American, British, Norwegian, and Swedish contingents as they geared up for more aggressive covert actions against the Germans. Balchen was assigned as commander of the 1415th Base Unit, with headquarters at Stockholm and subunits at several bases from Bromma to Kirkenes on the Norwegian border.

Swedish troops were placed at strategic locations around the country; hundreds of displaced Danes were standing by in Sweden to sail home and attack the Germans. British and Norwegian naval units were gathering off Norway's west coast to forestall any German mass movements by sea.

At this time Brig. Gen. Alfred A. Kessler, Jr., was assigned as air attaché to Sweden. He had previously been in charge of shuttle bombing arrangements with the Russians, whereby Americans bombed targets deep inside Germany, landed in Russian territory, refueled, rearmed, and bombed more targets on the return to England. If the Germans should make a last-ditch stand in Norway, it was possible that similar shuttle bombing of German bases in Norway might take place on runs between England and Sweden. However, because Kessler was assigned to the State Department as an attaché, officially he had to maintain a neutral stance. Balchen had been warned by Kessler's predecessor to comply with instructions for military intelligence officers and refrain from transacting business directly with members of the Swedish Foreign Office or cabinet members. If they requested that he visit them, Balchen was to report the facts to the American minister prior to responding to the request. Balchen felt that his directives from General Spaatz, the top U.S. Air Force commander in Europe, superseded any such directives from the American Legation.[1]

Two new but related undertakings, code-named Operation Where and When and the Sepals Project, were formalized and Balchen was put in charge of both, with headquarters in Stockholm. Operation Where and When's mission was to transport supplies to the Norwegians from Swedish bases with C-47s and enable them to attack German targets on the ground in Norway. Working with the collaboration of Gen. Bengt J. Nordenskiold, chief of the Swedish air force, Balchen became the central figure for air operations with the basic objective of driving the Germans out of Norway.

Ten C-47s with five-man crews each and ground personnel were assigned from the Air Transport Command for Operation Where and When. This group became known as the "Ve Do It Squadron." The Where and When operation had several objectives. The planes were to be used to transport Norwegian police troops from Swedish bases to various places along the Norwegian–Swedish border and then provide them with supplies. The squadron was to fly food and war materials to areas where the occupying Germans had been displaced. And it was to help the Norwegian government-in-exile gain control over the territory that the Russian army had liberated in the north so that the Soviet Union could not annex the area and gain access to seaport bases along the Atlantic coast.

The Sepals Project was a program of sabotage to defeat German last-stand operations in northern Norway. In the spring of 1945 there were three sabotage teams in Norway, designated Sepals I, II, and III, each consisting of about 15 men. The American OSS had its Sepals team in northern Norway, and two British SOE teams operated in the southern and central parts of the country.

Balchen was directed to undertake dropping operations to a series of Norwegian guerrilla bases located near the Swedish– Norwegian border, but was instructed to undertake no drops at points within occupied Norway or at points not previously cleared with the military air attaché in Sweden.[2] This order was issued to satisfy the State Department's official stance in regard to Swedish neutrality. Balchen ignored it.

Balchen's Sepals mission was to have the C-47 crews carry and drop

OSS saboteurs, equipment, and supplies to blow up bridges, railway lines, and harbor facilities in Norway. Drops of a variety of necessities from fishhooks, building materials, and components of prefabricated houses to hay and oats for farm animals were also to be made to areas around Finnmark, where the devastation by the Germans was greatest.

Balchen actually had the Sepals Project in operation in October 1944 without the American Legation knowing about it. By the New Year he had established saboteur bases in three different places in Sweden as well as a base in northern Sweden at Peskijarvi, where there was a large amount of sabotage supplies to be moved in by road and railroad on the other side of the border. There were so many supplies accumulating that even with the men and the unlimited funds there was not enough transportation. A Swedish mountain artillery unit staged "maneuvers" in the area in the latter part of October, and all the supplies were carried over the mountains close to the Norwegian border.[3]

The following letter illustrates how some missions were originated informally. It was written by Norwegian Maj. John Giaver, with whom Balchen had designed the Balchen–Giaver sledge, a unique combination of sledge and tent used in antarctica:

> I have lately amongst other duties been engaged in bringing in supplies to the population of West Finnmark from Sweden. During the first month we are planning to take in about 90 tons over Karesuando with reindeer; for the following months we are planning about 70 tons per month. It would be so much easier and simpler in every way to take these supplies in by plane and drop them at Kautokeino and Karasjok. . . . I know that your help in this matter is very much needed . . . and I am certain that you would more than gladly like to transport in food for about 4,000 people. There is also a group of about 200 people in the mountains inside Revsbotten in Kvalsund who are starving. At Soroya, there are about 2,000 up in the mountains and a couple hundred at Kvaloy. I cannot reach these people alone on account of the Germans leaving troops on the coast and also operating patrols. Can something be done from air? . . . Planes equipped with skis can be landed on the rivers at Kautokeino or Karasjok. There is also a small flying field to the north of Kautokeino. I expect this field is mined.[4]

The letter had been sent to England and relayed to Balchen in Sweden. He approved the mission and the supplies were delivered.

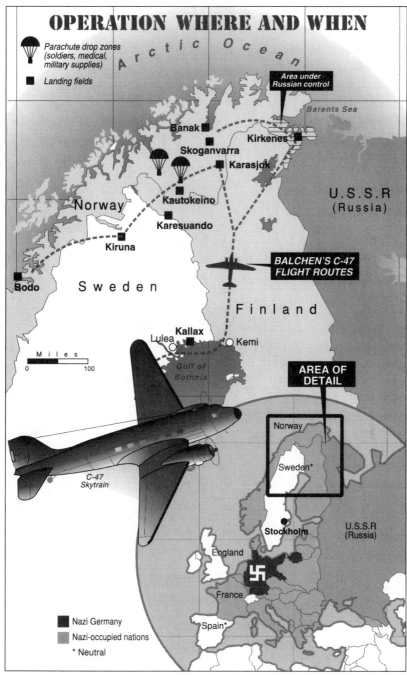

Map 3.

The Operation Where and When arrangements in far northern Norway did not go smoothly. Various objections were raised by the Soviets in the area they controlled. They especially objected to having Norwegian troops there for security reasons and issued a decree that they could not possess radios or firearms. Balchen ignored the order and supplied them anyhow. The Russians did not trust the Norwegians, and Balchen was often called in to negotiate.[5]

The arrangements were finally agreed on in mid-December 1944, and Balchen checked the facilities at the Vasteras, Bromma, and Kallax airfields on 19 December to receive the C-47s. After several days of weather delays, the planes departed for Sweden from Metfield under the command of Capt. Charles G. Hollyman.

The first group of Norwegians was loaded on 29 December at Vesteras airport and flown to Kallax airport near the Swedish town of Lulea. Onboard were a complete field hospital, 25 heating stoves, 14 nurses, 28 physicians, and medical specialists. Flying in clear weather in two formations of five planes each, with Balchen as copilot for Hollyman leading the first flight of five, they were escorted by Swedish fighters. Although such a formation of planes with American markings was unusual and Sweden was still officially neutral, the Swedish press was so sympathetic to the Allied cause that not a word about the move was published.

The first incursion task into Norwegian territory was to fly 19 tn. of equipment and 37 Norwegians north from Kallax to Kirkenes, where Balchen and his men arrived in midday darkness on 12 January 1945. With the exception of a few Russian patrols, it was the first Allied unit to land in occupied Norway. Evacuating German troops had burned the town and only two houses remained standing. The coal storage facility had been set on fire the previous November and it was still burning. Russian and Norwegian troops began to occupy the town under different conditions, with the Russians, poorly equipped, living in the snow, while the Norwegians lived in arctic tents supplied by the Swedes. In their retreat, the Germans continued to destroy everything habitable or useful as they made their way westward through Finnmark. When pursuing Norwegian ski troops started their movement westward from Kirkenes in March, supplies were dropped to the ski patrols in the field using Swedish-made paper parachutes.

The initial request for assistance had been for the transport of a total of 160 Norwegian "police troops"—the young soldiers trained in Sweden—who were fully equipped for prolonged winter operations, plus a field hospital. However, the requests were frequently amended, and Balchen's planes eventually hauled 1,442 soldiers and 1,100 tn. from Kallax to Kirkenes, then more tonnage to Kantekeino, Banak, and Bodo, as the Germans retreated down the Norwegian coast. When Balchen flew over Bodo, he saw that the buildings were flying Norwegian flags and all the Norwegian ships in the harbor had broken out the Norwegian colors. Hundreds of men, women, and children, newly liberated from their German oppressors, were marching down the main street, something they could not do for five years.

The Where and When flights had many communications difficulties because of Russian interference and translation difficulties. Information from Kirkenes was transmitted in Russian to Kallax; then translated into English by Norwegian interpreters before being transmitted to the American C-47s. All the Russian stations operated on the same frequency and caused much confusion. There were no radio navigational aids, so letdowns through the overcast were not recommended.[6]

Eventually 12 field radio stations were in place, most of them dropped by parachute. In addition to communications equipment, everything from blueberry soup, potatoes, bales of hay, and cigarettes were dropped. When an administrative officer lost his glasses in the snow and was helpless without them, new glasses were bought in Lulea and dropped to the "customer" near Karesuando a day after the loss.

The 10,000 paper parachutes, developed by the Swedish air force, proved very efficient and were used on most of the drops. Some supplies, such as hay for horses, could be dropped free-fall in steel-banded small bales. But one delivery Balchen made almost ended disastrously when the static line did not release a heavy generator and the parachute got caught in the tail surface of the plane and hung there for nearly a half hour, making the C-47 difficult to control.

Balchen wrote,

We were just about ready to abandon ship. Both of us pilots had all we could do to keep the ship on an even keel. The generator swinging back and forth gave a terrific jerky motion to the plane. We considered several ways to get rid of it, among other things to shoot off the shroud lines with a sub-machine gun. But it finally went off and took the whole de-icer boot with it. We found later there was some dislocation of the whole tail surface but we were able to repair it and continue our operations.[7]

One of the nagging administrative entanglements that Balchen had to deal with was the requirement by the Russians that all of his flights had to have a manifest containing the names of all passengers on the C-47s during the Norwegian operations. The complete list had to be supplied to the Russian field officer at the Kirkenes airport *before* the aircraft arrived or the plane would be denied landing permission. The Norwegian air attaché in Stockholm was concerned about this, but Balchen had a solution. He told a Norwegian liaison officer to get a telephone book, write out a random list of names for those who would be arriving two days later, and submit it to the Soviets. He did and it satisfied the requirement.[8]

As the Norwegians continued to press westward, an advancing ski patrol arrived at Kautokeino, a small Sami settlement in the mountains near the border of Norway and Finland. The Germans had decided to hold the main road down the coast of Norway. Balchen's friend, Dr. Harry Soderman, had gone into the area and reported that the patrol confronting the Germans there had run out of ammunition and medical supplies, and there were casualties. Help was needed as soon as possible.

Balchen decided he would use one aircraft and land on the frozen river where the Norwegians had marked a suitable landing area. En route he learned that a German paratrooper unit had landed on mountain ridges nearby. He made a pass over the marked landing area and as he lined up for the approach the Germans opened fire. He landed anyhow and sank immediately in deep, hard-packed snow that brought the plane to a stop in only a few feet. He unloaded the plane but was concerned about getting off because of the deep snow. There was only one thing to do: He marshalled about 150 Norwegian troops to make a runway on the ice during the night and by morning had a 1,000 ft. strip cleaned off.

The takeoff was difficult. There was a stiff cross-wind and the plane barely had enough airspeed to lift off. Balchen nearly stalled and had to make a turn in front of the German firing line. The enemy troops opened up with small arms fire but did not hit the C-47 as it clawed for altitude. Balchen's only comment in his notes: "It was quite an experience."[9]

In early spring the Norwegian ski patrols took over for the Russians and continued to push south after the retreating Germans, who were burning everything behind them and setting land mines and booby traps in the roads and bridges. On 3 May at Karasjok, a small Sami settlement, some Norwegian troops were demining the road between Finland and Skoganvarra. As they were loading the defused mines in a truck, one of them exploded and set off about 50 other mines. Twenty-two men were killed and nine others severely injured. Balchen contacted Norwegian authorities in Stockholm and found there was a field hospital available. Two Norwegian doctors in Stockholm—Col. Carl Semb, chief of the Norwegian medical service, Dr. Hjalmar Waergeland—and Ella Krogh, a nurse, volunteered to fly to the scene with the hospital equipment from Sundsvall, a city north of Stockholm. The plan was to fly the equipment to Karasjok and parachute it in, along with the doctors and the nurse, something the doctors and nurse had not been told beforehand.

Arriving at Kallax where a parachute training school had been set up to train Norwegian troops, they were given instruction and reboarded for the flight to Karasjok. The only building left standing in the burned out city was the church where the injured were sheltered. Radio communication was established with an agent on the ground and the two doctors and the nurse jumped. Supplies were dropped in front of the church and in an hour and a half the medical trio was performing operations. All the injured were saved but had to be evacuated for further treatment.[10]

Balchen had no aircraft with short landing and takeoff capabilities, but the Swedes did at Kiruna, 190 mi. away. He radioed Col. Gustav von Porat, commander of the base, and asked if two Fieseler Storch planes could be sent, even though it meant a neutral nation would be assisting a warring nation in that nation's territory. An immediate okay was received from Gen. Bengt Nordenskiold, chief of the Swedish air force, who considered the mission an act of mercy, not an act of war. The Storches were dispatched and landed on a large cake of ice in the river. The casualties, doctors, nurse, and their hospital equipment were rowed over to the ice and flown to Kiruna, where they were picked up in C-47s and flown to Boden.

The Russians, controlling the base at Kirkenes, were hated by the Norwegians almost as much as the Nazis. They stole personal effects, especially watches, from the Norwegian barracks, in spite of consequences that were brutal. Thieves were shot on sight by their superiors if caught in the act and were left lying where they fell.

Balchen saw some Russian soldiers clearing an airstrip with a bulldozer and warned the colonel in charge that the field had been mined by the retreating Germans. He paid no attention to Balchen and a few minutes later the bulldozer and soldiers were blown into the air by a violent explosion. The Soviet colonel shrugged his shoulders and told Balchen it was nothing to worry about. "We have plenty of men, and we can always get more bulldozers from America."[11]

The weather was also a constant enemy, and weather reporting and forecasting were woefully deficient. An American meteorology officer was ordered to Kallax and held a daily weather briefing at 0515. Balchen always attended when he was on the base and, after listening attentively, would thank him for the briefing. Often Balchen would say, "But we are now in the Arctic regions and the weather should be like this. . . ." After one meeting at which Balchen's forecast was found to be accurate, the meteorologist apologized and said, "I studied meteorology at the Massachusetts Institute of Technology for four years and then have had experience during the war, but now I'm at my wits' end. He is always right, in his considerate way."[12]

One of the notable sorties by the Carpetbaggers was Operation Rype (Norwegian for ptarmigan, a small grouse). On 24 March eight black B-24s were dispatched to drop agents and supplies on frozen Lake Jaevsjo in the mountains near Trondheim. Only four of the planes dropped anywhere near the target; one dropped 50 mi. inside Sweden, and three were forced to return to England. The leader of the 16-person group was Maj. William E. Colby, later to become director of the U.S. Central Intelligence Agency (CIA). Their mission was to destroy a railroad bridge. They blew it up and left their American-flag shoulder patches to show who had done it, in the hope of protecting the local populace from German reprisals. The possibility of such retaliation was very real. The German Reichskommisar for Norway, Josef Terboven, wanted to shoot 10,000 Norwegians for the sabotage because the bridge was to be used by the retreating German troops. Fortunately, the war ended before he could carry out the threat.[13]

The B-24 Sonnie-type flights under Balchen's command continued between England and Stockholm, carrying passengers and freight. By April 1945 there were eight C-87s, eleven B-24s, and three C-54s on the Metfield–Stockholm runs. Balchen issued strict instructions to the crews about following his flight plans to avoid contact over Norway with German fighter interceptors and antiaircraft batteries. He wanted the pilots to fly in the clouds and take circuitous routes that he designated through German-controlled air space to avoid detection and minimize the danger to the crews. Lt. Robert H. Fesmire, a B-24 pilot, objected strenuously to Balchen's order to avoid shortcuts over Norway. Instead, on his first two flights to Stockholm, Fesmire flew a shorter route recommended by his unit's intelligence officer. Balchen found out about this and before Fesmire's third flight to Stockholm, Balchen told him his flight paths over Norway were foolish because of the risks to himself, his crew, and his plane. He prepared a flight plan for Fesmire and sternly ordered him to use it.[14]

Fesmire, a self-confessed maverick, did not realize that Balchen's orders were based on his own many flights on instruments over that same route. Balchen knew well the dangers and also was better informed than the intelligence officers of the units assigned for these missions. His Norwegian underground contacts kept him abreast of where the German flak batteries and fighter units were located.

Lt. Thomas C. Wharmund, one of the Operation Where and When C-47 pilots, tells of his experience when he deviated from a flight plan Balchen had specified:

We had to depend entirely on [his] decisions and preflight briefings [because] he alone had access to intelligence reports, weather, German aircraft, Russian contacts, etc. On one return flight from north Norway, a Norwegian officer on board persuaded me to divert to Hammerfest. He had heard that the Germans had retreated from Hammerfest and was confident they had but wanted to prove it. I knew I had no authority to divert from the briefing procedure but he made it sound so very important to his men, so I gave in. We sneaked in very low for a good look and confirmed Hammerfest was deserted by the Germans. This was supposed to be kept secret to protect me. But, somehow, Col. Balchen found out. At the next day's briefing he stated: "There will be no more deviations from the flight plan." He did not mention my name or look at me. I knew how serious my violation was and was very relieved at his tolerance and compassion. His briefings were informal—not like in the movies—and I consider myself very lucky.[15]

The official Swedish report of Operation Where and When, translated into picturesque English, tells about Balchen from the Swedish point of view:

Balchen had a personality that many learned to appreciate. He was not easily accessible but appeared polite and correct to everybody, high-ranked or low-ranked and in an unaffected way. He took the regulations and rules very easy and enjoyed to joke, but thought sometimes the air missions were too long and tiring. Ever since he was a little child he was used to an athletic and outdoor life style and took all opportunities he could to get some exercise. When he landed at Kallax he usually turned the kick-sleds [controls] over to the pilot, jumped out of the plane at the end of the runway and went by foot to the chancellery [operations] building.

On one occasion he caused some excitement when he on a dark winter night headed out alone on a skiing trip in the desolate landscapes. The American crew had landed at a temporary airport and bivouacked in tents, and the guard duty was held according to Finnish methods, since there was a danger that German ski patrols were in the neighborhood. The camp's patrol guards marked out a course around the camp that was regularly inspected. If there were any tracks that crossed the course they could be sure that they would get unwanted company and they could set alarm. At this time they noticed ski tracks and the alarm was set. After some excitement they found that Balchen was missing. After a while he returned, strengthened by some exercise, but he was probably scolded for the venture![16]

The Swedish report also described some of the items that were transported to Kirkenes or dropped to the villages in northern Norway.

They transported big iron stove-heated tents, which the Swedish Red Cross had received from the Finnish military authorities, and they also received prefabricated houses and furniture that could be transported in the airplanes. Groceries and clothes were requested by the often-homeless population, that during long periods of time had escaped to caves and holes in the earth. They flew everything, big things as well as small things. It could be everything from houses and tools, machines and spare parts to needles and fish hooks.[17]

The clandestine Sepal C-47 missions increased, as did Balchen's Where and When flights when the spring brought better weather. More drops of arms, ammunition, and explosives were needed for increased sabotage operations. Many drops were made during April and early May along the Norwegian–Swedish border inside Norway to get supplies in place for the resistance forces behind the German lines. Balchen told of a C-47 drop he made to a Norwegian ski patrol located on one side of a small lake, with Germans dug in on a promontory on the other side:

> I came in over a hilly terrain, the clouds were down on the hilltops; there was about a 200–300 foot ceiling and snow squalls, so we were rather confined for maneuvering. In order to drop the supplies I had to make a letdown behind and over the German lines to the Norwegian contingent. I could not make a drop parallel to the lines because we were down in a valley and the tops of the mountains were up in the clouds. It was the last time we were subjected to enemy fire. We got a couple of holes in the tail surface, that was all. It was more difficult not to hit any of the mountain peaks than to face the enemy fire.[18]

The German surrender was announced on 7 May 1945, and the Allied buildup of troops in Norway proceeded slowly. Small advance parties of British and Norwegian troops reached Norway on 9 May, followed by American troops of the 1st Airborne Division and a Norwegian parachute company. On 12 May three British cruisers arrived in Oslo with more troops and Norway's Crown Prince Olaf, chief of the Norwegian armed forces. King Haakon delayed his arrival until 7 June as a symbolic gesture, because it was five years to the day that he had been forced to flee the country.

On the day that the Germans officially capitulated, Balchen was in the air on a flight to Banak and picked up fragments of Churchill's speech announcing victory over the radio. The field at Banak had an 8,000 ft. runway covered with wooden trestles and had been used by the German aircraft to harass the convoys going between the United Kingdom, the United States, and Murmansk. Norwegian ground troops had worked hard to get the runway ready but it was pockmarked with bomb holes and mines were everywhere. Only 2,500 ft. of the runway had been cleared. When one of the planes landed behind Balchen, the pilot rolled into the mined area but nothing happened. Later a mine detector showed that two telemines were located between the wheels of the plane when it turned toward the parking area.[19]

One of Balchen's first postwar actions took place on 13 May, five days after the capitulation. He was asked by Dr. Soderman to have his planes fly 50 tn. of food and medical supplies to Bodo, one of the German strongholds in northern Norway. The purpose of the trip was to provide immediate relief to 20,000 prisoners of war, including a large number of Russians that the Germans had used to build a railway. Men from a Sepals mission had landed there the day before and arrested members of the Gestapo without difficulty.

Balchen arrived over the field around noon and saw a large group of Junkers JU-88s and Messerschmitt 109s lined up on the runway. He tried to contact the tower on the international frequencies but received no answer. He asked the other pilots to circle while he landed to see what the reaction would be. As he taxied in, a small car with a "Follow Me" sign led him to the taxi strip. The ranking field officer, who knew who Balchen was, introduced himself and offered help. Balchen told him to turn on his radio. Balchen called in his other planes, which were parked efficiently by the Luftwaffe personnel as if they did this for American planes every day.

German drivers took Balchen and his crews into town to the Grand Hotel where Dr. Soderman called a conference of city officials to inform them of his mission. They had just begun the meeting when they heard noises outside. A large procession of Norwegians was marching down the street carrying the national flag and cheering. On the square a Norwegian flag was on one mast and an American flag next to it; shortly afterward, a Swedish flag was raised on another pole to honor the Swedish Red Cross.

Several thousand people carrying Norwegian flags filled the streets and moved toward the square. For the first time in years, voices singing the national anthem filled the air. Armed resistance force members with white arm bands had already taken charge of the roads and the railroad leading into the city.

"Adhering to protocol, we made a formal call on the German military who were interned in their barracks with guards from the resistance units posted outside," said Col. Bjoern Roerholt, Balchen's chief of communications. "The Germans were sitting around silently and were likely in their own way as relieved that the war was ended as we were. We returned to Lulea that same night, Balchen very pleased with that day's operation. . . . He always had an uncanny ability to pop up where his skills were most needed. He was universally popular—a charming man of good will."[20]

Although there was much joy at the cessation of hostilities, Balchen could not savor the exhilaration of victory for long. During the war, the Germans had started a project to build a continuous railroad track along

Norway's entire coast to Kirkenes. Several thousand Russian POWs and a large number of Yugoslavian prisoners were put to work by the German Wehrmacht and imprisoned in about 150 camps.

Seven of Balchen's planes were dispatched with food and medicine; components of wooden prefabricated houses were flown in to replace tents. But now he was confronted with a new, unanticipated problem. Many were very sick with dysentery, skin rashes, and infections from starvation and unsanitary conditions. Mortality rates were high. Balchen saw one camp of about 400 prisoners in which 130 of them had been moved to a building called the *Vernichtunghaus*, which meant they would be left there to starve. About six or seven died that night. Outside was a pile of corpses.

The Germans were given responsibility for feeding the prisoners with German rations. In one camp with about 2,000 prisoners, six died during the night from overeating. Some of the Germans who did not need hospital care were expelled from the hospitals, and the German doctors were ordered to take care of the POWs.

Balchen sent a report about his findings to Allied headquarters in Oslo. There were about 60,000 to 70,000 people in all the camps, and their survival and transportation to their homeland would be an operation of major proportions. A meeting was held with Col. General Shcherbakov, commander of the Soviet arctic army, who was told that the Allies wanted to return these men to his control. Shcherbakov professed not to know what they were talking about. He said,

> We have a policy that all Russian voluntary and deported workers on a prisoner-of-war status are not wanted back in Russia before we have considered this more completely. Furthermore, the prisoner-of-war policy is this: a Russian soldier is not allowed to be taken prisoner; therefore, he will only face court-martial and a long prison term when he is returned to his homeland. I am not interested in them. They have served their purpose as far as we are concerned. You can do anything you want with them; we are not interested in them at all.[21]

Balchen was appalled and did not believe what he was hearing. Speaking in German, the general reiterated contemptuously: "*Sie sind verbraucht!*" meaning "used up" or "expended." They had surrendered; therefore they were not Russians any more.

This cruel standoff was reported to Allied headquarters in London and to Washington, and it took more than six weeks before the Russians gave the order to move the former prisoners back home. Many had been in Norway for three or four years and had become very friendly with the local population. Balchen learned later that none of them ever communicated with the Norwegians they had made friends with. They were either imprisoned or died. One man who escaped from a slave labor camp in northern Norway had gone home later to Russia voluntarily and was sentenced to 12 years of hard labor.[22]

"But the thing that shocked me most was the way they let Russian laborers fend for themselves," Balchen reported in a magazine account.

These men had been dumped there sometime in the spring of 1944 and told to make themselves homes. The only possible way they could get shelter was to dig into a clay bank with their hands. The front of the bank was pock-marked with holes where men had clawed their way into the clay to find some shelter from the rain and sleet and wind of the arctic. They had a few bits of wood to shore up the sides and roof, and where they needed protection they covered the entrances or roofs with turf. They had no heat, no way of cooking except with empty tin cans, and no sanitation facilities.

It must have been horrible in the summer, for anybody who has been in the north knows how punishing the mosquitoes and flies can be. But in the fall, when it rained and sleeted, it must have been even worse. In a space ten by fifteen feet, at least twenty men would cram themselves, hoping to keep from freezing to death by mere physical contact. They were sick, suffering from scurvy and all sorts of filthy disease. At least fifty percent of them died. We found their bodies, and even their skeletons, for if their own people did not bury them, the Germans let them lie where they fell. Helping to drive out the Germans who destroyed that area was worth all the dangerous flying we did.[23]

The Norwegian government-in-exile had a far different homecoming in Oslo from the Russians. On 7 June Balchen flew to Oslo and enjoyed what he felt was the proudest event in his life: seeing King Haakon VII welcomed back on liberated Norwegian soil by the largest parade in its history. Hundreds of resistance fighters marched proudly in uniforms and with arms and equipment, which had been supplied by Balchen's planes. They saw Balchen and his men on the hotel steps in the American uniform and shouted, "Thanks, Yanks!"

"My throat is so tight I cannot answer." Bernt recalled. "Now I know in my heart that it is possible to love two countries."[24]

At the Grand Hotel in Oslo a few days later, Balchen met a Luftwaffe general he had seen in the elevator during his clandestine visit a year before. Balchen had been wearing civilian clothes then but was in his American uniform now and the general stared in surprise. *"Ist es moglich?"* (Is it possible?) Bernt assured him it was. *"Es ist fantastisch!"* he said, as he stormed away.[25]

Balchen visited his mother and sister Mia, who were surprised to learn that he had been in the city during the war but of course understood why he could not contact them. Dagny and her family, living some distance away, was in fair health and had not suffered any confiscation of personal valuables. His own house, rented to Norwegians for the duration, had not been damaged nor had any items been stolen. His medals from his athletic victories were still in a safe deposit box in the local bank and keepsake items that had been hidden in the basement were undisturbed.

Balchen could spend little time celebrating. The Where and When missions had to continue because of the dire need for help in restoring medical care to destitute villagers. During the next few weeks, Balchen made many supply flights between Kallax and several Norwegian fields. The Swedish Red Cross workers, under the leadership of Count Folke Bernadotte, were the primary care givers who brought the situation under control. Balchen's "Ve Do It" planes transported more than 100 doctors, nurses, and medical specialists, and 240 tn. of food, clothes, and medicines to areas in acute need. The squadron also transported German officers to Germany who were wanted by the Allies for interrogation in connection with their war activities.

Although the Supreme Command of the Allies was formally dissolved on 14 July 1945, British and American forces remained in Norway to disarm and repatriate the German troops and their former prisoners-of-war from other nations. Balchen's group at Kallax made transport runs through June and July and left Sweden on 8 August 1945. The last Russian POWs finally left Norway on 25 September 1945, although there was an uneasiness that many of them would revolt and refuse to go home. There was also great concern that the Red Army might try to remain in possession of the area in eastern Finnmark it had liberated, but this never occurred.

Before Balchen's units left, Brig. Gen. Earl S. Hoag flew to Stockholm from England to hold an awards ceremony for the Ve Do It Squadron.

Balchen was awarded four Oak Leaf Clusters to add to the Air Medal previously received. All were awarded for outstanding missions he performed between 7 January and 22 April 1945.

Major General Donovan, head of the OSS, wrote this personal letter of commendation to Balchen for the Sepals missions:

> With the cessation of hostilities, it is but right and fitting that the Office of Strategic Services should express to you its sincere appreciation of the outstanding cooperation you have given. Your supply drops have been one of the outstanding operations of the war, and you have transmitted intelligence of inestimable value to the Supreme Commander, Allied Expeditionary Forces.
>
> This headquarters is fully cognizant of the fact that the operations you have been called upon to fulfill have been both difficult and hazardous, and, on many occasions, above and beyond the call of duty. Your command has at all times reflected credit both upon the Air Force and upon the American spirit that is so deeply engendered in your officers and men. You have carried out a task which at no time has had a precedent in the annals of American air history.[26]

Wilbur H. Morrison, noted historian, commented in his book about the World War II aerial campaign against Germany in Norway: "Only an experienced all-weather pilot like Balchen could have trained such a group of young aviators to the degree of flying skill required to perform such difficult tasks. Few other World War II organizations ever achieved such perfection in flying techniques, and no one will dispute that the group's expertise was due to this extraordinary pilot."[27]

Balchen returned to his native land a national hero. He was honored for his war service later when he received the highest honors from the three major Scandinavian nations: King Haakon presented him with the Royal Order of St. Olav, Grand Commander's rank; he received the Royal Order of the Sword, Knight Commander, from Sweden; and the King Christian X Medal of Liberation from Denmark.

It can be said without dispute that the missions flown under Balchen's direction and guidance were truly remarkable. His personal "Ve do it" style of leadership was rarely duplicated anywhere else during the war, and the missions he directed were accomplished successfully only because of his personal flying skills and unique character. He served his native and adopted countries with uncommon loyalty and valor.

13 · From Airline Copresident to Squadron Commander

American forces in the Pacific were making a determined final drive toward Japan in the spring of 1945. Many in the Allied forces were being shifted from Europe to the Far East. But all that changed in August 1945 with the atomic bombing of Hiroshima and Nagasaki, Japan. Thousands of Americans were immediately separated from the armed services. As an Army Air Force reserve officer, Balchen knew he might have little chance of remaining on active duty. Given the opportunity, he wanted to become a regular Air Force officer. If that was not possible, there was that unfinished airline business in Norway.

In 1943, before going to England, he had met in Washington, D.C., with Per A. Norlin and Tore Nilert, Swedish friends who were involved in the plan to form an international airline. While Norlin's primary job was to represent the Swedish airline (ABA) in the United States during the war, he maintained contacts at home so that efforts to start air operations between the United States and Scandinavia after the war would not be wasted. His task was complicated by disagreement among the Norwegians on whether DNL should be a government monopoly or an independent entity. That question seemed resolved when DNL applied for a concession to operate as a government monopoly and the Norwegian government-in-exile approved the concept. Balchen felt strongly that the work started in 1936 with the bilateral agreement between the United States and Norway was binding on Norway. Furthermore, as far as he knew the agreement that the three Scandinavian airlines (including DNL) had made was also still in force.

Meanwhile Norlin had come up with an idea for the future. He suggested that some of the sizable number of B-17 Flying Fortresses interned in Sweden might be loaned, leased, or sold to Sweden to be converted to passenger transports for long-range operations. To carry out this plan, a new privately financed Swedish company was formed and named Svensk Interkontinental Lufttrafik (SILA) for international flying, with ABA becoming the regional airline.

According to the official history of the Scandinavian Airlines System (SAS), when Norlin met with General Arnold in Washington, D.C., and discussed the prospects of a route between Scotland and Moscow, Arnold suddenly said, "If you Swedes will release the Allied pilots you hold prisoner, you can have the Flying Fortresses. Or let us have three airports in South Sweden from where we can bomb Berlin and you can have 50 C-54s."[1]

As a result of this conversation, the American crews were eventually released and in June 1944 ten interned B-17s were sold to SILA, the Swedish airline, for $1 each and sent to the SAAB plant near Linkoping for conversion into passenger planes. By the end of the war, three had been converted and delivered to SILA for flights between Stockholm and New York. As for a consortium among the three nations, there were now grave doubts. DNL had no money and no aircraft; DDL, the Danish airline, had some money, a small staff, and one aircraft; and SILA now had some war-battered B-17s, but its finances were in fair shape. It was obvious that none of them could afford to start an international transatlantic airline on their own.

During his final days in Norway, Thomas and Rudolf Olsen asked Balchen to consider returning to his native Norway to finish the work he had begun with DNL. When Balchen was asked how much it would cost to start a Norwegian international airline, he came up with a figure of 120 to 150 million kroner ($24 to $30 million at that time). This amount was for airline operations only. The government would have to pay for airports and air navigational aids. The Olsens felt it was beyond their means, as well as the Norwegian government's.

The Swedes decided to establish an international airline presence alone. On 27 June 1945 one of SILA's converted B-17s arrived at La Guardia Field, New York, on a token flight from Stockholm with the promise of a start of weekly flights. These developments spurred Balchen and others into action to ensure that the Norwegian DNL airline would begin as a free enterprise, not as a government-operated carrier. However, when the Olsens and Thomas Falck found that they could raise only 35

to 50 million kroner—not the 120 to 150 million that Balchen had calculated—he told them that he would not return to Norway to help operate a government-financed airline.[2]

Balchen left Norway in September 1945 and reported to the Pentagon in
October. He met with Gens. Carl Spaatz, Frederick Anderson, and James
H. "Jimmy" Doolittle to discuss his experiences in Norway. The conversation got around to what remained of aviation facilities there, and
Balchen reviewed the bases that the Nazis had built and their state of
readiness for military and civil operations. After studying the international political situation and intelligence reports about the apparent intentions of the Soviet Union, all four agreed that an armed conflict with
the Soviet Union might develop. Balchen was asked what he thought
would be needed in Norway if that were so. Balchen's response included
a reference to the airport at Sola near Stavenger, which had potential for
development but needed extensive improvements. It could be defended
on very short notice by sea forces until antiaircraft and ground defenses
could be established; it would be difficult for ground forces to attack because the lines of communications were very few, and the surrounding
countryside would be difficult to cross. It had the capability to take heavy
plane traffic, and runways could be extended for future jet operations. It
would be a key location in a future conflict and would offer convenient
air access by American bombers to any target in the Soviet Union.[3]

　　After this discussion, Balchen said he wished to remain on active duty.
He received orders to report to the Army Air Forces Research and Development Office at Wright Field, Ohio, and then was to be transferred to
Ladd Field, Alaska, to work on cold-weather tests of equipment and aircraft. However, before he departed he received a radiogram from Rudolf
Olsen: "Can you arrange being released from Army soonest possible as
you are urgently needed here now for reorganization of the civil aviation
in Norway."[4]

　　Balchen immediately discussed the offer with General Spaatz; present
were Generals Anderson, Doolittle, and Ira Eaker. Balchen told them
about his previous experience trying to organize Norway's national airline and asked for advice. General Spaatz confided that Balchen's return
to Norway would fit into the future plans of the U.S. Air Force and recommended that he accept. His mission, to be kept secret, would be to see
if he could persuade the Norwegian government to make the necessary
improvements so that the Sola airport could be used for future possible

U.S. air operations by heavy aircraft. Balchen would be given at least 18 months' leave and then be returned to active duty. Spaatz then promised that, on return, he would be recommended for promotion to brigadier general. This promise of promotion was a welcome incentive and was later confirmed in conversations with Balchen by General Doolittle in Washington, D.C., in August 1956 and by General Anderson in November 1956.[5]

Balchen accepted the offer and was relieved from active duty on 10 December 1945. He immediately traveled to Norway as a civilian.[6]

Balchen's first task on returning to Norway was to learn what had developed economically and politically since he had left the previous fall. After the Germans had capitulated, the Norwegian air force, under Maj. Gen. Hjalmar Riiser-Larsen, had quickly established minimal airline operations to meet the country's internal air transportation needs. About a dozen Douglas C-47s and a few Lockheed Lodestars were acquired, along with 11 captured JU-52 float planes.

Balchen conferred with the Olsens and Falck, and they decided that a new, private Norwegian national airline could be started from a foundation financed by 25 million kroner ($5 million), of which 5 million to 10 million kroner would be borrowed from the government. The balance was to be furnished by the five largest Norwegian steamship companies, along with private stockholders. The Norwegian Storting (Senate) approved the formation of Det Norske Luftfatselskab (DNL) in February 1946 as Norway's national airline.

Thomas S. Falck, Jr., was elected chair of the board of DNL; Balchen was to be a copresident with Per M. Backe, a lawyer with no experience in air transportation or administration. Balchen was to be able to concentrate on the technical details and airline operations, and Backe would be in charge of personnel and financial matters. Balchen was not pleased and felt that such a divided responsibility was inefficient and bound to cause internal management difficulties.[7]

The summer of 1946 was difficult. The only airport facilities were those left by the Germans, which were not designed for passenger handling. Further, there were few personnel available with any airline experience.[8] Meanwhile, airline consortium discussions were being held between Sweden, Denmark, and Norway. After weeks of sometimes acrimonious negotiation, an agreement was finally reached at 0300 1 August 1946, the birth date of the Scandinavian Airlines System (SAS). Balchen and Falck signed for DNL.

The capital, equipment, and the operation were to be divided as nearly as possible between Denmark and Norway, which were to receive two parts each, and Sweden, which was to receive three parts. Denmark and Norway were to provide two DC-4s each and Sweden three, to initiate transatlantic service. Orders were placed for Boeing Stratocruisers for later addition to the fleet. Personnel were to be recruited on the same 2:2:3 ratio, and each country would have similar shares of the maintenance and overhaul business. There was adequate hangar and workshop space available for the training of flight and ground crews in Sweden. An SAS directorate was established to give each of the nations equal representation, and the position of chair would be rotated annually. Norlin was elected the first president of SAS.

Balchen devoted the following months to studying the requirements to be met for Norway to serve future air needs of the country and participate in SAS. He had a detailed plan ready for presentation to DNL's board covering the estimated size of the company, hiring policies, and finances. Unfortunately, his plan was not considered by the board of directors immediately and it became quite clear that the dual presidential arrangement would not work. Falck was executive president of a shipowner's association and also president of his own ship company and thus had too much responsibility to do a good job with the airline. The decision-making process was slowed down to such an extent that Balchen could see it would take a long time to get approval for his projects. He recommended that both positions be advertised but only one person appointed president of DNL and SAS's Norwegian region. The board agreed; a single position was declared vacant by the board and both men were asked to apply for it.[9]

Meanwhile, SILA completed 24 roundtrips across the Atlantic with the B-17s. An SAS route-proving flight was made on 16 September 1946 with a DC-4, and an official inaugural flight took place the next day with a refueling stop at Gander, Newfoundland. Balchen was aboard, along with airline executives and high officials of the three governments.

Early in 1948 Gen. Carl Spaatz, the U.S. Air Force's first chief of staff after it had become a separate service, inquired about Balchen's status and about his wish to return to active duty.[10] Balchen replied that he felt more had to be done to accomplish his Air Force mission in Norway and requested more time. Spaatz responded, saying he regretted Balchen had not been able to fully accomplish what he set out to do but suggested he raise the subject again in September 1948. By that time, Balchen had been able to see that work on the Sola airport was in progress and requested that he be recalled to active duty about October 1948. Meanwhile, the DNL board appointed Major General Riiser-Larsen as president.

Balchen's legacy to his native country was a master plan for DNL with a forecast of anticipated traffic and costs as the company expanded. He also recommended development of an airways system for the country that included navigational aids and airfield development. Time would reveal that his cost estimates were amazingly accurate and that his basic plan was a sound one.

During his busy months in Norway, Balchen had found time to be active in the Norsk Aero Club and had been elected its president, which gave him a platform to develop and crystallize his thoughts about the influence of air power on world affairs. The Polar Club of Norway was another of Balchen's interests. It was an outgrowth of the Linge Company, the organization of trained commandos that had been the focal point of OSS operations in the country during the war and was the nucleus of men and women trained in the tactics and techniques of guerrilla warfare.

Balchen's activities were closely watched by the Soviets. In August 1948 an article in the Soviet newspaper *Literaturnaja Gazeta* (reprinted in a Swedish communist publication) revealed Balchen's plan to adapt Scandinavian airfields to American military specifications and falsely reported he had large debts:

The Metamorphosis of a Colonel

Colonel Bernt Balchen has for three years been the chairman of the board of the Norwegian civil aviation company. At government expense he constructed the big airfields designed for heavy American planes. The airfield construction he designed at Sola near Stavenger was going to cost 400 million kroner. His building activities were so extensive as to spread to Sweden. Under his influence the Swedish company Aerotransport, which equally belongs to what is called "civil aviation," began to build a large airfield outside Lulea at the Gulf of Bothnia. And then it was Finland's turn: Captain Florman, the head of ABA, got it into his head that the airfield at Malmo near Helsinki did not correspond to what he called "current demand." He therefore declared that he was willing to make available means for the expansion of that airfield—that is, for reconstructing it with a view to being suitable for American bombers.

With an eagerness which is in no way typical of the Norwegians, Mr.

Balchen tried to prove that a great service would be rendered to humanity by anyone contributing to the creation of an airline from the La Guardia air field near New York via one of the Greenland bases, Keflavik on Iceland, Sola in Norway, and Lulea in Sweden to Helsinki in Finland.

The eager Colonel grew extremely popular in the Scandinavian military press. But some time ago this active champion suddenly retired and disappeared from Norway in an altogether unknown direction. He left behind debts of roughly 50 million kroner which the Norwegian state has now to pay.

Soon enough, however, Mr. Balchen was traced. The Danish newspaper *Berlingske Tidende* discovered the Norwegian colonel in no other place than the very U.S. Department of Defense. He now heads in that department a special bureau for "Northwestern Arctic Area."

In the last analysis, there is nothing extraordinary to be found in this fact. The American military agent Balchen has simply fulfilled his mission in Scandinavia. He has built airfields at the order of the U.S. Army and he has adapted Norway to the demands of the U.S. "polar strategy." And now he "coordinates" the defense of the Nordic countries with the plans designed by the American militarists.[11]

Balchen said he felt honored that so much news space was devoted to him by the communist press and found it interesting that his orders to return to active duty had not been published yet. "They made a good guess," he said. "Not good enough, but close."[12]

What was very accurate was that the airport at Sola had been improved so that it was able to accept B-29 and B-50 heavy U.S. bombers immediately, and by the summer of 1948 would be able to accommodate the very heavy six-engine Consolidated B-36 intercontinental bombers then coming into the Air Force inventory. The Norwegian Storting had approved the 10-year plan Balchen had proposed and authorized additional funds for the construction of maintenance facilities, workshops, and hangars. The action by Norway's governing body to support DNL, participation by Norway in SAS, and the improvements at Sola meant mission completed for Balchen.

The time in Norway had brought Balchen closer to his family. He had been able to spend time with his sisters and his mother—a wonderful cook who passed on her skill and recipes to a receptive, developing gourmet. He became reacquainted with Inger Engelbrethsen, a representative for a Norwegian publisher who had previously interviewed him in connection with a book translation. His divorce from Emmy was final, and Balchen and Engelbrethsen were married in February 1948.

When his pending departure from Norway was announced, Balchen received invitations to lecture in Oslo, Stockholm, and Copenhagen. He emphasized the importance for the Scandinavian nations to direct their attention to the development of the arctic routes to the Far East and the West Coast of the United States. He also encouraged the governments to consider the strategic potential of the arctic for defense and the value of joining other nations in military preparedness against the growing threat of world domination by the Soviet Union.

On 1 October 1948 Balchen gave his final lecture to the Norwegian Engineering Society in Oslo. Attending were King Haakon, members of the Storting, air ministry, shipping companies, and board members of DNL. He reviewed the history of aviation briefly and traced Norway's civil aviation progress since World War II, followed by the projected consolidation into SAS of the three nations' airline systems. He commented on the "rhythmic economic cycle" that could be expected and displayed logarithmic air traffic curves derived from various American and English studies and applied them to his predictions for Norway. He concluded with his estimates of the facilities, equipment, and capital that would be needed. His thoughtful presentation was greeted with a standing ovation.

Balchen was invited to a private audience with King Haakon and Crown Prince Olaf on 4 October 1948. They thanked him for his work, wished him luck, and said they hoped he would return soon to Norway.

"It was a feeling of anticipation of the new work ahead and also sorrow at leaving our friends that we saw the lights of Norway become obscured by the clouds as the SAS plane carried us to the United States," Balchen said. "My dreams of many years (about establishing an international airline) were now a reality, and it could have been a lifetime job."[13]

A week later, Balchen took his oath of office for active duty at the Pentagon. He reported first to Maj. Gen. Lauris Norstad, deputy chief of staff for Operations. After a cordial visit with him, Balchen met Maj. Gen. Joseph H. Atkinson, commander of the Alaskan Air Command who asked Balchen if he liked to hunt and fish. Balchen replied, "I'd rather hunt and fish than eat," which was exactly what Atkinson wanted to hear. He explained that he needed someone to set up arctic survival training and develop techniques for air search and rescue in the arctic. Balchen volunteered as soon as the general finished talking.

The assignment of Balchen to Alaska was part of a master plan to counter the aggressive moves of the Soviet Union in the arctic. A few days after he retired in June 1946, General Arnold made a statement for the press that reflected what all airmen know. "Study your globe," he told Americans, "and you will see the most direct routes [between the Soviet Union and the United States] are not across the Atlantic or Pacific, but through the Arctic." He warned that if a third world war broke out, "Its strategic center will be the North Pole."[14] The resultant policy for the Air Force leaders who followed Arnold was to increase its knowledge of arctic operations, learn what the Soviets were doing there, and train American forces to survive and fight in subzero conditions.

By the time Balchen returned from Norway, Gen. Hoyt S. Vandenberg had replaced General Spaatz as the Air Force chief of staff. He may not have been told of the promise of a promotion for Balchen when he succeeded in his secret Air Force assignment in Norway. General Spaatz had left no written record of such a pledge. Balchen did not inquire, thinking that a promotion would come in due time after he had settled into his new assignment. He was pleased to be back in an American uniform with an exciting task ahead.

Bernt and his wife arrived at Elmendorf Air Force Base near Anchorage on 11 November 1948. He was immediately assigned as commander of the 10th Rescue Squadron with the responsibility for air search and rescue operations for the entire territory of Alaska and north of Alaska to the North Pole. This included not only all military aircraft and personnel but also civil aircraft, lost hunters and fishermen, and other types of emergencies.

The 10th had been originally activated in March 1946 with detachments at Elmendorf, Ladd Field in Fairbanks, and at Adak in the Aleutians, along with subdetachments at Shemya and Cold Bay. About 45 aircraft were assigned, including PBY Catalinas, C-47s, and four-engine C-54s and B-17s.

Over the next two years after Balchen's arrival, the 10th Rescue Squadron would be involved in a life-saving rescue operation on an average of 1 every $2\frac{1}{2}$ days. The first major rescue in which Balchen was involved occurred not in Alaska but in Greenland. A C-47 had crashed on the ice cap on 9 December 1948 with 12 stranded airmen. A B-17, dispatched from Goose Bay, Labrador, was wrecked during an attempted landing at the crash site. Two CG-15A gliders towed and released at the scene were to have been snatched off the ground by a C-54 with the survivors aboard but were damaged. The men were all safe but marooned there until help could arrive.

Additional aircraft were sent to BW-1: two C-47s equipped with skis and JATO (jet-assisted takeoff); a CG-15A glider was being towed from a base in Georgia; another glider was to be towed from Goose Bay, Labrador; plus a Fairchild C-82 carrying a small ski-equipped Cessna. The Navy aircraft carrier *Saipan* with helicopters aboard was en route to Greenland from off the coast of Nova Scotia, intent on making the rescue.

The Air Force was embarrassed by this fumbled rescue and a message was sent to Alaska asking for Balchen's assistance. He and copilot Lt. Col. Eugene O. Strouse made the 4,300 mi. flight to Goose Bay in a C-54 with 12 passengers. On arrival Maj. Gen. Caleb V. Haynes, commander of the Northeast Air Command, gave Balchen *carte blanche* to take over the operation.

Balchen did not believe ordering a large armada of aircraft to the scene was necessary. When he learned there was a ski-equipped C-47 and Lt. Col. Emil Beaudry, an experienced ski-flier, based at BW-8, and a PBY with JATOs at BW-1, he felt that was all that would be needed. The weather was ideal for one or the other aircraft to land at the crash site. Balchen decided to take off immediately for BW-1 and see for himself.

As he headed for BW-1 in the winter darkness, the base radioed that it was closed because of a dense fog. Balchen immediately changed course for BW-8, his former Greenland base. As he approached, he heard Beaudry report that he was en route in the C-47 to the crash site and would soon land at the scene. Balchen contacted him and arrived overhead in time to watch as Beaudry took all the passengers aboard and blast off easily with a jet-assisted takeoff. He proceeded to BW-8 to congratulate Beaudry.

A message was received from Goose Bay that everyone connected with the rescue was to proceed to New York and Washington, D.C., for receptions. Balchen declined because he felt he had no part in the operation; besides, there was a rescue operation developing in Alaska that he wanted to monitor. He made an extensive report on his return to Alaska about the excessive number of aircraft and personnel assigned to the rescue and commented that a land party equipped with dog teams could have easily reached the crash site. He had found the terrain at the scene was also ideal for ski or flying-boat operations. Although he said glider snatches seemed feasible, they required further development of equipment and techniques under arctic conditions. He added that helicopter operations from a Navy carrier could not have been accomplished with any reasonable safety, speed, or efficiency.

For future planning and guidance, Balchen's report of the episode reviewed the mistakes that were made in attempting the rescue. He complimented the B-17 crew for their ability to use the material at hand to construct comfortable shelters and set up a camp.[15]

Another aspect of this experience was the difficulty Balchen had in getting weather forecasts on his flights between Alaska and Goose Bay. There was no weather information available en route, so for safety reasons he had landed twice, which added many miles and much time to the flights. He wanted to see action taken to improve weather reporting over Canada so that aircraft could get accurate forecasts, not only for military operations but also future commercial flying between Alaska and Europe.

Balchen was now thoroughly convinced that much needed to be done throughout the Air Force to increase search and rescue capabilities in the arctic. He found that there were few directives or instructions on elementary techniques for arctic aircraft operations such as ski-flying and how to heat an engine in cold weather. He found that the Arctic Indoctrination School that had been established at Nome could be much improved with emphasis on teaching air crews to survive in the huge, widely varied Alaskan area with its tundra, forests, rugged fjords, glaciers, mountains, and barren areas. The solution was to require all flying personnel assigned to Alaska to undergo a rigorous course that would be more physically demanding than any other before. He put a policy into effect immediately for all flyers in his command: All flying crews were to go on a hike once a week to keep them in shape.

"The first time was in April [1949] and we made only a three-mile hike," Balchen recalled.

About 25% of them came home with blisters on their feet and all tired out. They had no packs. By September, the crews were then in the kind of condition that I wanted to see them in. I took them out for a 20-mile hike with 30-pound packs. All of them completed it and none complained. Once a month they stayed out, summer and winter, down in the Aleutians, up in the mountains, in the timber, in the Arctic, and they came to like it. My ground rescue crews stayed out 26 weeks of the year, half of them were out all the time, and on call; the rest were on standby for rescues.[16]

The necessity for this kind of training was enhanced by the ever-growing threat of military moves against the United States by the Soviet Union. In 1947 the Strategic Air Command (SAC) had developed an ambitious operational schedule for the training of long-range B-29 and B-50 bomber crews. To hone the command's combat capabilities, SAC flew "maximum effort missions" simulating bombing runs over various American cities, and long-range good-will missions to Europe and South America. Many of SAC's flights were made over the arctic regions and enabled the crews to experience the problems of cold-weather flying, such as rapid ice buildup on aircraft, ground fogs, and difficulties of navigation and communications.

Balchen initiated an intensive training program for his own rescue crews, especially those flying ski-equipped C-47s. Nearly 100 practice landings were made on the polar pack ice more than 250 mi. north of Barter Island, and experiments were conducted with helicopters and gliders. Training in arctic grid navigation was given for conducting search patterns over the vast polar ocean and making evaluations of an ice surface for possible landings.

The flight to and from Greenland for the earlier rescue had made Balchen realize that there was no coordination for search and rescue between the Alaskan Air Command, the Royal Canadian air force, and the Northeast Air Command. In the event of hostilities, all three would be involved in guiding aircraft through their respective air space, finding cripples on their way home after an attack, and rescues. He recommended active liaison among the three, along with the Canadian civil aviation authorities.

Balchen increased the number of practice landings on the pack ice. These landings were so successful that he recommended to Gen. Nathan F. Twining that a station should be set up on the polar pack ice and remain there for awhile to make meteorological and ice floe studies. Twining gave his approval, and on 20 February 1951 eight men were landed on an ice floe 115 mi. north of Barter Island. They stayed until 9 March when the ice floe split in two and the party had to be hurriedly evacuated.

The 10th Rescue Squadron supported many other scientific parties on the ice pack from a base on Barter Island. These were from the U.S. Hydrographic Office and Cambridge Laboratories, which made acoustical and seismic soundings, gravity observations, and studies of ice movements. By the time Balchen left Alaska in 1951 he had established precedents of training and cold weather operations that gave the Air Force valuable experience and information to counter what Soviet expeditions had been doing secretly in the arctic for many years.

Much was happening on the world scene during Balchen's tour in Alaska. On 25 June 1948 the Russians had halted all passenger and freight ground and water traffic to and from Berlin, but three connecting air corridors remained open. The result was the Berlin airlift, which saved the Germans in the Allied zones of the city from starvation. This Cold War episode was a proving ground for air transport operations and had given air and ground crews unprecedented experience in weather flying, air traffic control, aircraft maintenance, and operational procedures. The fact that the airlift was necessary proved that the United States and the other Western powers had a dangerous potential adversary. This was felt even more strongly when the Soviet Union exploded its first atomic bomb in August 1949.

Before dawn on 25 June 1950, thousands of miles east of Berlin, communist North Korea attacked South Korea. The so-called police action threatened to develop into another worldwide conflict. If war with the Soviet Union came to the United States, there was no doubt it would come by air over the northern polar region. Additional bases would be needed farther north of the Arctic Circle than BW-8 at Sondrestromfjord, Greenland, and Goose Bay, Labrador. The most important base to be established, in Balchen's view, was the site of the United States–Danish weather station at Thule, which had the potential for a large base that Knud Rasmussen had told him about many years earlier.

Balchen immediately planned more experiments with aircraft that would add greatly to the U.S. Air Force's knowledge about arctic operations. In August 1949 he made a landing on Taku Glacier, near the Juneau ice field, in a C-47 with a special retractable ski-wheel landing gear, bringing in equipment and supplies to a group of scientists. It was believed to be the first successful glacier landing ever made with such a large, heavily loaded aircraft. He repeated the feat on a glacier at Mount Logan at an altitude of 19,850 ft.[17]

Balchen realized that a search and rescue organization had another potential that could be developed as a corollary mission. That was for teams of trained individuals who could infiltrate enemy-held territory and sabotage enemy installations in the arctic areas, much as the World War II operation he had been a part of in Norway. He also foresaw the need for the 10th Rescue Squadron to train personnel for evacuation and evasion missions that might be required in time of war.[18]

Though the concept had the support of Generals Twining and Armstrong, it was not so easy to sell it to Washington, D.C. However, Balchen's report reached the desk of Gen. Curtis E. LeMay, commander of the SAC, who asked Twining to lend Balchen temporarily to advise the command on setting up such an organization. This led to the concept of forming units that would establish caches of supplies in remote arctic areas for SAC and rescue crews should the former bail out or crash land in arctic areas after attacking targets in the Soviet Union.

Balchen discussed with his two Alaskan bosses the possibility of the B-29 flights to the North Pole being extended to proceed to Norway and return via the Pole. This would provide an opportunity to see how a weather forecasting system would work over this route. Balchen was thinking not only of the military value but also the benefit for civil aircraft operations. To prove the point, Balchen requested permission to fly nonstop from Fairbanks to Oslo by way of the North Pole and Thule in a transport type of aircraft, such as the long-range Douglas C-54. Such a flight would prove its feasibility, show the need to improve communications and weather forecasting, and evaluate the general conditions of the polar ice pack. Permission was granted in September 1949 by General Vandenberg.

Balchen had decided to fly to the Pole and on to Norway via Thule because he wanted to refresh his memory about the area since he was last there in 1942. The group, including Brig. Gen. Frank Armstrong, departed Ladd Field near Fairbanks on 23 May 1949 on a flight plan that called for about 15½ hours flying time. As they approached the Pole, Balchen took the controls and felt a strange sense of exhilaration as he reflected on his 1929 flight at the other end of the globe. He made two circles around it and proceeded to Thule where he saw the area where he had recommended to General Arnold in 1942 that a long permanent runway could be constructed.

The historic nonstop flight of 3,980 mi. ended at the Oslo airport, where Balchen was surprised to be greeted by Crown Prince Olaf, Prince Harald, and a cheering crowd of 50,000 Norwegians. As Balchen was entering the flight time in the Form 1 as commander of the flight, the crew chief asked, "Colonel, weren't you the pilot on the South Pole flight?"

Balchen nodded affirmatively and said, "Ja. Why do you ask?"

The sergeant said, "Then doesn't this flight make you the first man to *pilot* an airplane over both poles?" On thinking about it for the first time, Balchen told the sergeant he believed he was right.[19]

Balchen received orders to return by flying nonstop from Norway to New York and then to Washington, D.C., to prove that those two vital cities could be bombed by the Russians if they established bases in Norway. Balchen explained at a Washington, D.C., press conference the importance of the flights to U.S. national defense, which were believed to be the longest nonstop flights made by a C-54 up to that time. By using that type of transport plane, Balchen had shown that civil aircraft could soon be making such trips just as easily. To do so safely, however, they would place new demands on the military search, rescue, and survival capabilities because commercial aviation could never support the necessary cost of such operations. Civilian airliners were poorly equipped to land anywhere in the arctic regions. Passengers of both genders and all ages fly in ordinary street clothes and have no training in survival. Airline operators could not be expected to take care of these contingencies by having all the survival necessities on board in case of a forced landing. The answer in Balchen's mind was for the Canadian and U.S. governments to provide a thoroughly equipped and trained organization to be ready to give immediate assistance to downed aircraft and perform the quickest evacuation possible.[20]

After the press conference, Balchen received a telephone call from Admiral Byrd requesting that he come see him immediately in his Pentagon office. It was their first meeting in many years but instead of a cordial greeting, Byrd asked gruffly about the flight and Balchen's flying proficiency, apparently to find out if he had actually piloted the C-54. Balchen was surprised at the question but showed him his Air Force green instrument card, proving that he had been personally flying regularly in instrument weather conditions and had received a flight check just before the flight. Byrd then asked who had given him permission to make the trip. Balchen told him it had been approved personally by General Vandenberg. No expressions of congratulation were offered and Balchen left Byrd's office mystified at the unexpected interrogation.[21]

During the winter of 1949–1950 and into the spring, the 10th Rescue Squadron tested many items of equipment and new techniques that Balchen initiated. One of the most promising for searching was adoption of the Eureka and Rebecca electronic devices used by Balchen in Norway and Sweden during World War II. The set in an airplane sends out a signal that triggers a responder on the ground and the one in the plane then shows the pilot the direction and distance from the responder.

By the spring of 1950, more than 100 landings had been made on pack ice with a ski-wheel (combination of a ski and a wheel) C-47, and it was found that JATO was rarely necessary. A number of helicopter and glider landings, both on wheels and skis, were also made with only one major accident to a glider. Also evaluated extensively was a pickup system whereby a glider could be snatched from the ground after rescuing survivors. The apparatus, known as the Skyhook Aerial Retrieval System and invented by Robert E. Fulton, had been perfected before Pearl Harbor by All-American Aviation, a Pennsylvania airmail operation. It featured a grappling mechanism that could snatch mail bags from a transfer line stretched between two poles set 50 ft. apart.

To evaluate newer equipment, Balchen asked for Northrop C-125 tri-motored aircraft to be assigned and also large Piasecki helicopters for experiments with heavy loads under arctic conditions. His specifications for the ideal fixed-wing aircraft for arctic operations included a short landing capability, a range of 3,000 mi., short take-off run with JATO, large cabin space for equipment and supplies, and adaptability for wheels, track gear, skis, and floats. He developed requirements for the design of arctic hangars and heated shelters and pushed for ski research on large aircraft.

It was the question of whether or not the polar ice cap could be used for the landing and takeoff of heavy aircraft that occupied much of Balchen's time. One of the training missions he planned was to have a plane fly out about 500 mi. north of the Alaskan coast, land at a place unknown to search parties and have them attempt to locate it. However, as in Greenland during World War II, he found he was involved more and more with directing or participating in many actual rescues. One of the latter involved a C-47 that was en route from Point Barrow to Fairbanks and had run out of gas. The pilot crash-landed in the winter darkness on the frozen Stewart River in Canada's Yukon Territory and radioed his predicament to Fairbanks. The temperature was around −50°. The six men aboard were injured and would probably not survive for more than a few hours with the clothing and survival equipment they had with them. Within two hours of receiving the message, a C-54 towing a ski-equipped glider was en route to the scene. The C-54 flew over the wreckage and the glider was cut loose and landed within a few yards. The glider crew loaded the injured men aboard and erected two poles on the river ice with a line stretched between them that was attached to the glider's tow cable. The C-54 made several trial low passes over the poles and then snatched the glider into the air. The C-47 crew was quickly on the way to a hospital.

The glider rescue crew, all experienced survival experts, remained behind and erected temporary shelters to settle in for a long stay. They repaired the C-47, attached skis to the main gear, smoothed out a runway on the river ice, and one month later flew it back to its base.

On 13 June 1950 Balchen's squadron was directed to establish and operate an experimental base on the polar ice pack approximately 200 mi. north of Barter Island prior to 15 August 1950. The base was to be maintained on a year-round basis, to be followed by other ice island stations for the purposes of having bases for search and rescue, support advanced bases, and provide airlift for scientific investigations. The experimental landings on the ice pack blazed the trail for later landings on T-3, a great slab of ice 120 ft. thick, 9 mi. long by 4 mi. wide that had broken off from Ellesmere Land and was floating in an eddy of the Beaufort Sea.

T-3 later became known as Fletcher's Ice Island after Lt. Col. Joseph O. Fletcher, who was appointed as project officer for Project Icicle in late 1951. Much valuable scientific information was gained in this project. Teams of scientists, transported and supplied exclusively by air, remained there for more than two years and drifted nearly 1,700 mi. before the station was abandoned in 1954. Snow compaction techniques were used to create runways that were as smooth and hard as concrete until they became slushy during the summer months. The real heroes of the first experiments were the pilots of the 10th, especially Lt. Col. Eugene O. Strouse, who made the first ice island landings.

After his historic over-the-Pole flight to Oslo, Balchen realized more than ever that Alaska and the arctic had assumed an importance that air crews could most readily understand. Balchen prepared a paper that he used as a basis for many talks on the importance of the arctic for military and commercial usage. It was important to note, he said, that the large industrial and commercial centers, which in time of war would become the prime targets for the strategic air forces of the countries involved in an armed conflict, are all situated between latitudes 35° and 50° north. As military and civil aviation progressed, a network of weather, radar stations, and emergency landing fields would be required in the arctic areas.[22]

In December 1949 Secretary of the Air Force Stuart Symington visited Alaska, and Balchen briefed him on his ideas of defense in the arctic regions and suggested the establishment of a base at Thule on a high priority basis. Balchen made many recommendations, including formation of a joint USAF–RCAF search and rescue organization; scheduling of reconnaissance flights and landings on the polar ice packs; and establishment of scientific stations on the ice islands to report the weather. He advised that studies should be made of ice thickness; direction and velocity of pack ice and ocean currents; depth soundings, electronic investigations, and radio propagation studies. One of the most urgent suggestions was the procurement and assignment to the arctic bases of aircraft equipped with track gear, floats, skis, and JATO that would be dedicated solely to search and rescue work in subzero conditions. Downed aircraft had to be located quickly and rescue aircraft with highly trained crews experienced in high latitude navigation available on a full-time basis. He recommended that three search-and-rescue bases be established to provide continual coverage for the area north of 83° degrees latitude to the North Pole and beyond: one at Barter Island off the extreme northeast corner of Alaska; another in the Canadian Archipelago; and the third on the gravel plateau at Thule. Although Symington was leaving office in April 1950 he passed on Balchen's recommendations with approval to his successor, Thomas K. Finletter.[23]

To allow him more time to prepare studies of arctic problems, Balchen was transferred as commander of the 10th Rescue Squadron to the headquarters of the Alaskan Air Command as special advisor to the commanding general. At the same time the 10th Rescue Squadron was transferred to the Air Rescue Service and placed under the Military Air Transport Service (MATS).

Finletter visited Alaska in late 1950 where Balchen briefed him on the value and urgency of establishing the base at Thule. Finletter was greatly impressed with his knowledge, foresight, and concern about the lack of progress toward preparations for a possible war that could come across the Arctic Ocean to North America from the Soviet Union. When the secretary returned to Washington, D.C., he sent a top secret memorandum to the Air Force chief of staff stating that he was not satisfied that the SAC had made sufficient provisions for alternative staging bases. Finletter endorsed the three locations that Balchen had recommended be built up in the arctic regions and said a thorough study should be made of "the feasibility and desirability of construction, operating and protecting bomber staging bases at these locations, together with an estimate of construction costs." He added, "Plans would have to be made immediately if we are going to get the bases in operation by the end of the next construction season in the summer of 1951."[24]

After the Finletter briefing Balchen was transferred to the Pentagon in January 1951 to serve as special assistant on arctic problems to the director of Installations. He was assigned to a desk in a crowded office in the basement.

During his months in Alaska, Balchen had carried on a cordial correspondence with Admiral Byrd and voluntarily kept him apprised of the arctic projects he was engaged in. The letters from Byrd showed no indications that he harbored any animosity toward Balchen. Meanwhile, Balchen had applied for a regular commission in the Air Force and when he had not heard anything, asked Byrd to see what was happening to his application. Byrd found that Symington had proposed a bill for the Senate (S. 3314) to provide regular status for Balchen and Brig. Gen. Joseph F. Carroll, head of the Air Force's Office of Special Investigations. In April 1950 Byrd informed Balchen that the bill had received favorable consideration from the Armed Services Committee of the Senate and mentioned that "My brother, Harry, was acting chairman of the committee at that time."[25] In a later letter, he cautioned Balchen that "No bill, however meritorious, ever goes through without someone to guide it. There are hundreds of worthy bills that do not see the light of day. Therefore, if you have anyone here who is helping with this bill, please let me know."[26]

Balchen sought recommendations to obtain a regular commission from radio commentator Lowell Thomas, Pan American Airways executive Sam Pryor, and others who wrote letters to influential members of Congress on Balchen's behalf. Robert C. Reeve, president of Reeve Aleutian Airways, wrote to Oregon senator Warren G. Magneson and Rep. Henry M. Jackson and suggested that a bill be introduced only for Balchen. Symington testified before the Senate Armed Forces Committee on behalf of Balchen and Carroll. The hearing was chaired by Senator Byrd. In defending Balchen's nomination, Symington told the committee that Balchen had so much more ability and experience than anyone else, it would be a loss to the country if he were not given a regular commission.[27]

However, Sen. William Knowland of California objected, and the bill was "passed over" on the Senate floor. Knowland believed both of the officers' positions should be nonmilitary and if they could not be replaced by civilians that an overhaul of officer personnel structure in the Air Force was needed. Senator Byrd did nothing to support Balchen's nomination.

The bill was dead for that session of Congress and it appeared that the main objection was not Balchen's background but that of General Carroll, former special assistant to the director of the FBI during World War II who had joined the Air Force in 1948. Commissioned directly from civilian life, Carroll had only two years' active military service and none of it in combat.

For those wanting Balchen to be appointed as a regular officer, the solution appeared to be that suggested previously by Reeve: A bill might be passed if it were introduced only for Balchen. This was done by the Senate Committee on Armed Services in the next congressional session as S. 1220 with the following explanation:

> It had been Colonel Balchen's intention to apply for integration into the Regular Air Force under the terms of Public Law 281 of the Seventy-ninth Congress. According to information furnished the committee he was specifically requested not to request integration at that time so that he could perform the mission for which his special qualifications made him particularly desirable. After carrying out the mission satisfactorily he returned to active duty as a Reserve officer on October 11, 1948. He has continued on active duty since that time.
>
> Colonel Balchen is one of the outstanding experts of the world in the field of cold-weather operations and techniques. He has rendered invaluable service to the Air Force in Arctic training and polar combat operations. The Air Force states that his knowledge of cold-weather flying is unique and indispensable.[28]

The summary for the bill also pointed out that Balchen's case was an exception because appointments as regular officers were normally in the grade of second lieutenant.

> However, this is a case of a highly qualified officer who has had many years of service in the Reserves of our country and a great many more years in the military service of Norway. He was fully qualified to be integrated into the Regular Establishment under our integration program at the end of World War II. The fact that he did not become a Regular

officer at that time was because of the specific request made on him to conduct a special mission in the interest of the United States. The committee does not believe he should be penalized for that action. Furthermore, the committee does not intend to establish a precedent by its action in this case. It feels it is a well-justified exception which is necessary to correct an obvious injustice to an outstanding member of our military organization.[29]

General Vandenberg, who had become Air Force chief of staff in April 1948, and Finletter testified on Balchen's behalf before the Senate and House Armed Services Committees. Secretary Finletter told the House committee that Balchen was the foremost living expert on the subject of cold-weather air operations and techniques. He reviewed Balchen's career and noted that he had served on active duty continuously since 5 September 1941 with one exception: "This was a period during which he performed a special mission for the Air Force which required that he serve in a civilian capacity." He added that when Balchen had said he wanted to be integrated into the Regular Air Force in 1945, "He was specifically requested by the Commanding General, Army Air Forces, not to request integration at that time so that in the national interest he could perform this mission for which his special qualifications made him particularly desirable."[30]

After unexplained delays, the bill was passed by both houses and signed by President Truman on 27 August 1951. Balchen's appointment as a colonel in the Regular Air Force was backdated to 2 April 1948.[31]

During Balchen's Alaskan tour, Clayton Knight, aviation artist and writer, and Robert C. Durham, who had served with Balchen in the World War II Scandinavian operations, collaborated on a Balchen biography titled *Hitch Your Wagon.*[32] It received favorable reviews; however, the publisher declared bankruptcy soon thereafter. Eric Sevareid, former war correspondent and radio commentator, wrote a review that highly praised the man and his achievements:

> This is the life story of Bernt Balchen, whom many would place in that distinguished pioneering roster but who, by grace of history's sense of timing, was handed the airplane as his instrument and the polar skies as his laboratory. A more natural, more gifted flier never lived, not even

Lindbergh, and perhaps no working pilot has contributed more in airplane design, flying techniques, the conquest of weather, polar geography, airline organization or even the winning of World War II.[33]

Capt. Eddie Rickenbacker, top American fighter ace of World War I, also
reviewed the biography and called Balchen a "phenomenon" who "seems
to have been chosen by fate to dare and do what no man before him had
ever accomplished." To try to cover his life in a single book "is like trying to contain, in a cheesecloth bag, the stratospheric winds that range
his polar world."[34]

Hans Christian Adamson, a Danish-born journalist, commented in a
review that "There is much about Balchen and his present mission for the
United States Air Forces in the Polar North that cannot be told, so much
a part of the country's security has he become. . . . [He] is one of the
brightest yet least publicized stars in that brilliant constellation of flying
men who, by their incredible feats and boundless faith, piloted the world
into the fabulous Air Age."[35]

Balchen was honored by the Explorers' Club in New York with the club's
much-prized and seldom-awarded Gold Medal in January 1951. Lowell
Thomas told his radio audience that night,

> Balchen, foremost of polar airmen, has been working with that re-
> markable Air Force outfit which performs endless exploits of picking
> up castaways in the northern wilderness. Mighty important—consid-
> ering those North Pole flights which our B-29s now make on regular
> daily schedule for weather observations. Suppose a plane on the North
> Pole run should be forced down on the Arctic ice pack. It hasn't hap-
> pened, but the Tenth Rescue Squadron is prepared for such a crisis.[36]

Meanwhile, Balchen's many recommendations were being studied in the
Pentagon as he worked in the basement. He was named the Air Force
project officer for Operation Blue Jay, a top secret undertaking to build a
giant air base at Thule. The recommendations that Balchen had first
made in 1942 to General Arnold and later to other Air Force leaders had
finally been turned into action.

14 · "The Most Unpleasant Years of My Life"

Balchen went from Alaska to Washington on temporary duty in December 1950, where a group known as the Glover Committee was meeting to make an evaluation of recommendations for the construction of arctic air bases. Air Force Undersecretary Carroll McCone asked Balchen "to study the matter of Northeast Air Bases" and "give consideration to all possible bases in that area."[1] Balchen turned in a detailed report, stating, "From my knowledge of the areas in the northeast high latitudes where an air base could be constructed, maintained and supplied with certainty, Thule is the only area that should be considered."[2]

Secretary Finletter pushed the secret project vigorously and the Army Corps of Engineers began preparations for the massive undertaking. Balchen accompanied the first engineering survey party, code-named Operation Blue Jay, to Thule in February 1951 and they arrived during the worst weather that could be expected in the region. Temperatures were down to –40°, and winds reached a steady velocity of 95 to 100 MPH for several days.[3]

Winter weather in 1951 lasted longer than the Greenland natives could remember. Not until mid-June could the initial construction force of 7,500 sail from Norfolk, Virginia. None of the men knew their exact destination before sailing. They were all recruited from the cold states, and had passed rigorous health, mental, and aptitude tests. By the time Baffin Bay was open to sea navigation in July, about 3,000 other construction workers had already been airlifted to the site by Air Force transports in one of the most outstanding arctic air operations of all times.

The main force workers arrived by sea transports on 9 July. By the first week in September the last of the cargo ships was unloaded and departed before being caught in Baffin Bay ice. In fewer than 62 days between 1 July and the end of August 1951, a giant air base began to rise from Thule's frozen flats. More than 300,000 tn. of equipment had been brought to Greenland by plane and ship.[4] The construction that followed was truly a momentous triservice project. In addition to barracks, fuel storage tanks, office buildings, warehouses, heated hangars, taxi ways, and the aircraft parking apron, a 200 × 10,000 ft. runway was completed. Many construction firsts were accomplished, including the erection of large buildings on the permanently frozen ground, the world's largest salt water distillery, and the second tallest radio tower. The sparse information released by the Air Force offered nothing but that "some rehabilitation and construction work" was being carried out at Thule under the NATO defense program. The first flight took off secretly from the new runway on 11 September 1951. However, with hundreds of construction workers returning to the States when their work was completed, word leaked out and a major story appeared in the *New York Herald Tribune* on 13 October 1951. The headline read, "U.S. HAS TOP-OF-WORLD AIR BASE, COULD BOMB ANY PART OF EUROPE." The existence of the base could no longer be denied.[5]

The "secret" label that had been kept on the construction phase of the base was challenged by the American press when it was learned that "Moscow Molly," a Soviet propaganda broadcaster, had tried to disrupt the morale of base workers. In radio programs beamed to the base, she said the families of the construction crews were in dire straits because they had not been paid. The allegations were untrue and typical of the anti–United States propaganda of the era. The veil of secrecy was officially lifted in the fall of 1952, and Balchen accompanied 36 journalists from Washington, D.C., to Thule. An awed American public learned about the base and something of its strategic and commercial importance in a *Life* magazine feature and in an article in *Reader's Digest.*[6]

Although most news commentators and observers applauded the development of the base, Maj. Alexander P. deSeversky, internationally known pilot, aircraft designer, and author of *Victory through Air Power,*[7] saw it as a "half billion dollar blunder." He added, "As a staging or refueling point for offensive action against the Soviet industrial vitals by our heavy bombers, it is money and effort down the drain."[8]

There is no record that deSeversky visited Thule; his description, far from precise, pronounced it "a place of ice, fog, snow, cold, dark, and

150-mile gales, where men at times can work only an hour or two a day. Ships are jammed and ice-locked in its harbor, providing a perfect target for hostile aircraft." He concluded that building the base was not only a monumental mistake but "to the extent that it may give us a false sense of safety it is not merely a waste of effort but a positive danger to security."[9]

Construction of the major runway enabled heavy four-engine C-54 and C-124 aircraft of the Military Air Transport Service (MATS) to land almost year-round and the excellent harbor enabled Military Sea Transport Service (MSTS) ships to offload supplies until Baffin Bay was closed to navigation in the fall. All major construction was completed by the fall of 1952. The capability to transport so many building materials by air had cut down the construction time by at least a year.

Balchen made many trips from Washington, D.C., to Thule, Europe, and Alaska. However, the trips were not always directly related to the work there. In a clandestine role as an intelligence gatherer, he went to Finland to make "an evaluation of the covert capabilities in that country for the protection of downed airmen and other intelligence matters in the event of the outbreak of war with the Soviet Union," according to a source in the Executive Office of the President.

> He also volunteered a strategic evaluation of the Scandinavian concept of defending Scandinavia in offensive operations on the Scandinavian peninsula, which was supplemented by a later evaluation of Soviet capabilities against northern Scandinavia.
>
> In connection with a trip to Scandinavia, Colonel Balchen obtained highly classified information from Swedish military leaders with regard to certain estimates of capabilities. He also undertook special conversations with Norwegian and Swedish officials, all of which have been made available to Air Intelligence and, through channels, to the CIA.[10]

It was on a trip to Sweden in November 1951 that Balchen ran afoul of the American ambassador. Balchen, acting on top secret orders, made the trip without contacting the ambassador in advance and met with civil and military officials. The ambassador became highly incensed when he learned about the visit but, as in many of his World War II visits, Balchen was in and out of the country before the ambassador's staff could locate him. The ambassador refused to approve a follow-up visit eight months later unless he checked in at the embassy first. Balchen complied but did not reveal the intelligence purpose of his visit.

On his return from the last of these trips, he prepared a complete operational evaluation of the defense of the Scandinavian Peninsula and Denmark in the event of war with the Soviet Union. He drew excellent maps and made extensive recommendations if attacks should come from the north, south, or east by air, naval, or ground forces. The study was forwarded to the Air Force's planners for inclusion in contingency war planning. He also prepared an extensive top secret study of the Soviet Union.[11]

The base at Thule was only one step in a massive program to build a protective radar fence across the arctic areas to be known as the Distant Early Warning (DEW) Line. Balchen became heavily involved in the planning and kept a log of meetings he attended. An important one was held on 8 September 1952 with Secretary of the Air Force Finletter; Danish ambassador to the United States Henrik de Kauffmann; assistant Secretary of State for the Greenland department Eske Brun; and SAS chair Georg Unger Vetlesen. Finletter said he intended that Thule would also be used as a stopping point for civil aircraft and that he would back any plans to speed up the process for SAS to use it for their Far East and West Coast routes—an announcement that surprised and greatly pleased Balchen and Vetlesen.

The Scandinavian governments were quick to see the value of Thule as an ideal stop for SAS aircraft on the polar route to America's west coast and Alaska. Plans were made to build seven radio stations on the route from northern Norway across Greenland, Baffin Island, and the North Canadian wilderness. Meanwhile, SAS ordered 14 long-range Douglas DC-6B airliners, and planned to fly the first two planes from the Douglas plant at Santa Monica, California, over the arctic Great Circle route to Scandinavia, with stops at Edmonton, Canada, and Thule.

Formal requests were filed on 3 October 1952 with the U.S. Civil Aeronautics Board to operate between the Scandinavian cities, Los Angeles, and San Francisco. This was granted, but the international situation had grown more tense, and despite Finletter's promise the Air Force had to deny permission for any landings at Thule for security reasons; the route for SAS flights was changed to land at Sondrestromfjord (BW-8), Greenland.

On 19 November 1952, SAS chief pilot Povl Jensen took the *Arild Viking* DC-6B from Los Angeles over the arctic route carrying reporters and ambassadors to the United States from Norway, Denmark, and Sweden. Balchen was aboard as an official Air Force observer. Twenty-six hours, six minutes later Jensen landed at Copenhagen, Denmark, on the first transarctic commercial flight and the first flight to use the polar route in the winter months.

In December 1952 Balchen prepared a memorandum proposing an alternate plan for a Distant Early Warning Line to be located farther north, which would be less expensive to build and would give earlier warning of an attack than the proposed trans-Canada line. In January he flew to Thule with Air Force Secretary Harold Talbott. While en route Talbott asked Balchen what projects he thought were most important in the arctic. Balchen responded that among them was his recommendation about having the DEW Line built farther north. Talbott was interested in this because of Balchen's estimated lower cost, as well as strategic advantage. He instructed Balchen to give him a copy of his original memorandum, which had not been forwarded by Balchen's superiors, who disagreed with his concept. When Maj. Gen. Roger M. Ramey, director of operations, heard of this conversation, he reprimanded Balchen for daring to discuss the arctic and the DEW Line with Talbott. Ramey said he did not share Balchen's viewpoint on these matters and on the arctic's potential for defense.[12]

Balchen lost the argument for a DEW Line farther north but continued his liaison with the other services and civilian contractors on the Thule project from his desk in the Pentagon, with the title of Assistant for Arctic Activities. In July 1953 he was informed that he would be assigned to the DEW Line project as it was planned to cross Canada, an assignment that was going to last about three years. He would remain in Washington, D.C., working under a colonel who previously never read nor paid attention to Balchen's studies and recommendations.

Brig. Gen. James C. Jensen, deputy for Operations and Plans, proposed the possibility of extending the DEW Line eastward to tie it in with the Scandinavian early warning network. Balchen was sent to Norway to seek permission from the Norwegian government to let the United States establish warning sites on its territory. He returned two weeks later with an official affirmative answer from the government of Norway.

But a surprise awaited Balchen when he returned to his Pentagon desk. General Ramey told him that he would have no further connection with arctic operations. Orders were issued transferring him to the 3500th Recruiting Wing in Dayton, Ohio. Before the move, however, he was sent on a nationwide recruiting tour. In New York during the trip, his orders were canceled and he was informed that he would go to the antarctic on temporary duty for five months with the Navy. Again there was an unexplained cancellation and he was ordered to make another trip to Norway "on an urgent classified matter," which he completed but never divulged.

Balchen was baffled and very unhappy with the cold-shoulder treatment he was getting at the Pentagon. For reasons he could not fathom, he was frozen out of later important discussions on DEW Line developments and any other subject dealing with the arctic.[13]

Fortunately, Balchen had talents to draw on to reduce the frustration and stress he felt. One outlet was his hobby of cooking, particularly fish and game. He and his wife coauthored a cookbook published in Norway in 1951 titled *Bernt Balchen's Oppskriftsbok (Recipe Book).*[14] When in Alaska he had made a number of wood carvings, of which polar bears were the favorite subject. At his home in Alexandria, Virginia, he produced beautiful watercolor paintings, making use of his stored memories and detailed pencil and watercolor sketches made throughout his career in the arctic and antarctic, in Scandinavia and Alaska.

On 6 January 1953 the Grand Central Art Galleries in New York City put on an exhibition of 75 of Balchen's watercolors in a show called "The High North." Sponsors included Gen. Jimmy Doolittle, Thomas K. Finletter, Arthur Godfrey, Eddie Rickenbacker, Lowell Thomas, Juan Trippe, and William Randolph Hearst. On opening day 500 people visited it. Reviewers who were given a preview found it an interesting paradox that a man who was the world's foremost arctic expert and war hero was a serious, sensitive, accomplished artist. The *New York Times* described the exhibit as "a collection of watercolors in which the forbidding northlands have been interpreted by a scientific eye. The midnight blue sky, stark, subtly colored Thule, Greenland; the Alaska flats; the Yukon where the colors are unbelievable; the huge Kodiak bears, the eroded icebergs, and the magnificent play of the Northern Lights are just a few of the Colonel's subjects."[15]

Bill Davidson in a *Collier's* magazine article wrote, "His watercolors enable the viewer to see through Balchen's eyes the rescue of flyers lost in the Arctic; establishment of U.S.'s northernmost air base at Thule; a parachute drop, and dozens of other perilous undertakings."[16]

This first show in New York was so successful that all of the paintings were sold. Dr. Laurence Gould, then president of Carleton College, invited Balchen to place his works on display there. Balchen took out sketches and color notes from his files and painted 41 large pieces. Another show was held in Chicago, followed in 1954 and 1955 by repeat exhibits at the Grand Central Art Galleries. Today Balchen paintings and sketches are highly valued and collected. They are found in private collections and those of several universities, the Explorers and Wings Clubs in New York City, the Toledo Museum of Fine Arts, the San Diego Aviation Museum, the Air Force Museum in Ohio, and the Air Force Art Collection, as well as the National Air and Space Museum in Washington, D.C.

The question of who was responsible for having Balchen effectively eliminated from his assignment as an arctic specialist and denied a promotion to star rank was focused by Balchen on Admiral Byrd and his brother Harry, then the senior senator from Virginia. Documented proof is hard to come by but the genesis for Byrd's growing animosity toward Balchen can be said to date from the early 1920s when Gen. Billy Mitchell was campaigning to establish a single, independent air force. Byrd, as a young retired naval officer, was able, with the help of his brother's political clout, to play a key role in fighting Mitchell's concepts, including his forecast of the role of the arctic in a future war. The fight was against the "battleship admirals" who had enlisted his help to quash Mitchell and the "conspiracy" against the Navy. Most naval officers at the time could see no reason to have even a special Bureau of Aeronautics, and the ranking admirals grew testy about what they called "absurd fancies of young flying radicals." Byrd and other naval pilots saw the crusade by Mitchell as taking aviation away from both the Army and Navy. "So we—a group of young flyers—began to organize," Byrd wrote. "I volunteered to write a bill to present to Congress for the creation of a Bureau of Aeronautics in the Navy Department."[17]

Byrd bragged about his ability to lobby inside the Navy and the halls of Congress, and showed that he had the political connections to lobby for legislation when such independent actions by military officers were prohibited. It was this brashness and political cunning that was to be called on later after Byrd became world famous for his polar flights and was widely considered a world authority on arctic matters.

The opportunity came after World War II when the question arose again: Should there be a separate air force under a Department of Defense? Once again there was a "Revolt of the Admirals" as they fought the Army's "fly boys." But they lost this time, and the U.S. Air Force came into being officially on 18 September 1947. The fight then became one for appropriations, and it was a battle between funding new Air Force aircraft, especially the giant six-engine Consolidated B-36 long-range bomber, versus a new super aircraft carrier that the Navy wanted as a first step toward having its own strategic nuclear bombing capability.

This stand was stated by Fleet Adm. Chester W. Nimitz in a 1948 report. He said,

> Offensively, it is the function of the Navy to carry the war to the enemy so that it will not be fought on United States soil. The Navy can at present best fulfill the vital functions of devastating enemy vital areas by the projection of bombs and missiles. It is improbable that bomber fleets will be capable, for several years to come, of making two-way trips between continents, even over the polar routes, with heavy loads of bombs. It is apparent, then, that in the event of war within this period, if we are to project our power against the vital areas of any enemy across the ocean before beachheads on enemy territory are captured, it must be by air–sea power; by aircraft launched from carriers; and by heavy surface ships and submarines projecting guided missiles and rockets."[18]

When the "police action" in Korea began in June 1950, the appropriations battle accelerated. All three services needed the wherewithal to fight the ground, sea, and air war, while forward-thinking air strategists realized that the real threat was not North Korea but the Soviet Union. Funds were needed for the radar defense wall that people such as Balchen knew was essential. When Balchen was being shunted aside from all connections with his area of expertise, there had to be a reason. In speeches, he was effectively calling public attention to the vital importance of arctic bases for defense where Navy aircraft carriers could have only a secondary role. Was there a connection?

Sen. Harry Byrd had become one of the most powerful legislators in the U.S. Senate at this time. As a member and later chair of the Armed Services Committee in the 1950s he was able to block appropriations for the Air Force. It is impossible to know how much influence he had on keeping Balchen from promotion and in effect pushing for an early retirement. But there is evidence that Richard Byrd played a significant role. Unbeknownst to Balchen, a long series of covert attempts on Byrd's part to belittle his activities and honors had begun in 1950. Byrd asked Ashley C. McKinley, the photographer on his first antarctic expedition and then an Air Force colonel assigned to the office of the Chief of Naval Operations for Polar Projects, to find the information in the material that Balchen had previously written for Byrd about his ice landings in Alaska. Byrd wanted this information, without attribution, inserted into a Navy report he was going to make about Greenland because "when it comes to Greenland, you [McKinley] and I are the only ones who have the 'picture whole.'"[19]

This memo marked the start of surreptitious attempts to counter the favorable publicity and reception that Balchen was getting for his talks on arctic defenses. Byrd seemed to take any praise of Balchen as an affront to his own reputation as an arctic expert. He was again demonstrating his paranoia by projecting his personal conflicts to the supposed hostility of others. The focus of this paranoia on Balchen became increasingly evident as the months progressed.

There had been no lengthy, substantive meetings between Byrd and Balchen after the first antarctic expedition. Their next meeting after the strange talk following the over-the-Pole C-54 flight was at Fort Myer, Virginia, in March 1952 for the funeral service of Dr. Francis D. Coman, the physician on Byrd's first two antarctic expeditions. They exchanged brief greetings but nothing else.

The following month, Byrd learned that the Associated Press was planning a story about the transatlantic flight of 1927. He was concerned that Balchen might make statements that would be counter to his views of the flight and wrote a memorandum to McKinley, then on duty at the U.S. Navy headquarters in Washington, D.C., instructing him to have Balchen call him. "It's a pretty long time to remember facts," he wrote, "and he and I should not give separate interviews without checking with each other."[20]

Reader's Digest ran a laudatory article about Balchen by Francis and Katherine Drake in January 1953. It mentioned that Byrd's chances of reaching the North Pole in 1926 would not have happened "had not Amundsen generously loaned him the services of 26-year-old Bernt Balchen, Norway's ski champion.

The husky young redhead rapidly constructed a more serviceable type of ski which enabled Byrd to take off first and achieve a historic triumph."[21]

Apparently Byrd took offense at this statement, and he or Mooney contacted members of the 1926 expedition and asked them to write letters "correcting" it. The Byrd files at the Byrd Polar Research Center, Ohio State University, contain a five-page analysis refuting this quote, giving credit for repairing the skis to "Lt. Cmdr. George Noville, E. J. De-mas and Thomas J. Mulroy, assisted by Floyd Bennett and Capt. Parker." An unsigned statement by T. L. Sullivan said, "If Balchen had made it possible for Byrd to reach the Pole first, it would have been a betrayal of Balchen's commanding officer, Amundsen." Additional unsigned notes were attributed to M. J. Brennan, captain of the *Chantier*, Demas, and Noville.[22]

John Davies, a reporter for *Newsweek* magazine, learned of the cold-shoulder treatment Balchen was receiving in the Pentagon and wrote an article titled, "Will the Air Force Fire a Great Arctic Expert?" He out-lined Balchen's career briefly, gave him credit for the construction of the base at Thule, and added,

> But this fanatical believer in the importance of the Arctic has stepped on some high-ranking toes. Today he has almost nothing to do with Air Force operations in the Arctic. He hasn't visited Thule in almost a year. Where Finletter consulted him frequently, he hasn't been near the front office in months. Some of the new civilian service chiefs may not even know that while they worry about transpolar air attack one of the great experts on the region is sitting in the basement unconsulted.
>
> Passed over for promotion, Balchen will have to retire next year be-cause of his age, length of service, and time served in his present rank. A promotion to brigadier general would save his services for the Air Force, but the chances seem slight. Like Rear Admiral Hyman Ricko-ver, whose uphill battle for the atomic submarine nearly cost him his job, Balchen has discovered that the promotion systems of the armed services make little allowance for the extraordinary, highly trained spe-cialist. USAF officials deny any prejudice against him; it's just that there are many others in the USAF who know the Arctic.[23]

The public reaction to the article was immediate. The story was picked up by newspapers across the country and letters from people Balchen had never met poured into congressional and Air Force offices in Washington, D.C. In a letter to President Eisenhower, U.S. Sen. Edward J. Thye of Minnesota urged that Balchen be retained on active duty and promoted immediately. He volunteered to sponsor legislation to make it possible.[24]

Mrs. Norman Potosky, a concerned private citizen of Aniak, Alaska, expressed her opinion in a letter to the Secretary of the Air Force that was shared by other Alaskan citizens: "Col. Balchen has that rare and slightly old-fashioned quality of being able to inspire men to do, and want to do, far more than they believe themselves capable of." She doubted that there were very many Air Force personnel who "also know" the arctic as well as Colonel Balchen. "Search for Bernt Balchen's equal if you will," she said. "you will not find one. Request a duplicate? There is none."[25]

All similar letters were transmitted to the Air Force staff for response, and a standardized answer was sent to all inquiries:

> The Officer Personnel Act of 1947 provides for the elimination from the active list and retirement of permanent colonels on the fifth anniversary date of appointment in that permanent grade in the Regular Establishment, or thirty days after the date of completion of thirty years of service, whichever is later. In the case of Colonel Balchen, he will not complete five years in the permanent grade of colonel until October 1956. Therefore, at this time he is scheduled for retirement on October 31, 1956.[26]

South Dakota Gov. Sigurd Anderson wrote to Sen. Francis Case of Minnesota asking if anything could be done to give merited recognition— long overdue—to this outstanding American military figure. "There are a great many Minnesotans," he wrote, "that wonder why it is that a person who has such ability as does Colonel Balchen, and who has made so many contributions, does not receive recognition by being promoted to a higher rank."[27]

Balchen was unaware of the letters being written on his behalf. No written record existed of the promised recommendation for promotion that he had been given verbally on his return to active duty in 1948, and those who had made it were either retired or dead. However, Balchen learned from a general on the selection board that his name had been forwarded by the Air Force seven times for promotion to brigadier general but had been disapproved by unknown forces on Capitol Hill.

It was the *Newsweek* article that had infuriated Byrd most, and it was soon after on 13 October 1953 that Balchen had his next and last face-to-face talk with Byrd. Both had been invited to attend an aerial pilgrimage to Kitty Hawk, North Carolina, to commemorate the 50th anniversary of the Wright brothers' first powered flights. While they waited at Bolling Air Force Base, Washington, D.C., for air transportation, Balchen walked over to pay his respects to Byrd. The admiral immediately pulled out a clipping of the *Newsweek* article and bluntly asked where the reporter had gotten the information. Balchen said it had come from former Secretary Finletter and General Spaatz, because they were shocked to learn about the treatment he had been getting in the Pentagon. Byrd asked what he was doing and Balchen told him he had not worked on any arctic projects since November 1952. "It appeared to me that this was not news to him," Balchen said in a memorandum of the encounter.[28]

They traveled by air separately to Kitty Hawk and after arriving Byrd took Balchen aside from the rest of the group to speak to him again. Balchen described the encounter:

> He opened up with this: "I am going to let you know right away that the publicity you have been getting and are getting has got to stop. I am demanding and I am ordering you to stop it at once and forever. I am going to keep you responsible for this in the future. You can stop this and you <u>will</u> stop it if you and I are going to be friends. If you do not take care of this immediately, I am going to see that this is done. Many of my influential friends have been looking at this for a long time and are tired of this thing and of the way you are taking credit for a lot of things that you never did and are getting recognition which you do not deserve or have the background to receive; you can include me in this, too. Do not ever believe for a moment that I will stand for being stepped on by you."[29]

Balchen was stunned and confused as Byrd continued his diatribe. Byrd cited his close association with President Eisenhower, which he said gave him access to the White House at any time. He reminded Balchen that he was the one who had brought him to the United States, took him with him across the Atlantic, and it was only because of his kindness that Balchen was chosen for the South Pole flight, because Dean Smith was just as good a pilot. He added that he had held up approval of his regular commission and could have stopped it. Because he claimed he had easy access to the White House, Byrd said he could influence Balchen's future in any direction he desired. He then said that the Air Force had a case developing against Balchen he could stop if Balchen wanted him to.[30]

Balchen's reply was that if the Air Force had anything legitimate against him, he was willing to take the consequences. Byrd then asked if Balchen knew that he had worked for two years in the arctic (this was untrue) and Balchen said it was certainly news to him. Byrd said he had written a book about the strategic value of the arctic and that he and he alone was responsible for Thule Air Base being in existence. "I had no comments to make," Balchen reported. "The whole thing was so absurd."[31]

"Such was my last conversation of any length with this magnetic but in many ways inscrutable personality," Balchen noted in his autobiography.

It was a deeply saddening end to a long association.

Did the saddening outburst at Kitty Hawk go back, in some way, to those adventurous years? Or did the growing public recognition of my own work somehow disturb this man whose personality seemed composed of such conflicting elements? It was inconceivable to me that there should be any need for concern on this score on Byrd's part, for his position was assured for all time.[32]

Three days after the encounter Balchen was called in to Air Force chief of staff Gen. Thomas D. White's office to talk about the *Newsweek* article. General White said that he and Byrd were old friends and that Byrd had complained to him a number of times about Balchen getting too much publicity, which was detracting from his own public position. The general said it was clear to him that "Byrd's days were over years ago" and assured Balchen that he would let him know if the Air Force had any criticism about his work.

"I said that Byrd's accusations and attack on me were absolutely without foundation," Balchen wrote in a memorandum of the meeting, "that I at all times have given him full credit that is due him. That I owe a lot of gratitude to Byrd as he took me over here; he took me across the Atlantic and across the South Pole and therefore gave me my start over here. For this I am forever grateful to him and have done my best to show this."[33]

Balchen also sent a note to Byrd the same day telling him that he had related their conversation at Kitty Hawk to General White. He said, "I believe that after you have given more thought to this matter, you will realize that I have never said or done anything that could have been detrimental to you. Quite the opposite."[34]

Balchen was heavy hearted about the episode at Kitty Hawk. Someone had overheard Byrd's tirade against Balchen, and it was reported, sensationally and inaccurately, in the nationally syndicated column of Drew Pearson:

Bernt Balchen once flew Admiral Byrd across the Atlantic. But the other evening Byrd backed Balchen into a corner and shouted angry threats at him largely because Balchen has been getting recognition for his flight research over the North Pole. Byrd flew into a rage accusing Balchen of stealing the limelight and threatened to see, no, to use, political connections to wreck his AF career if he continued, in effect, to get his picture in the paper. Balchen flushed an angry red but friends interceded before things got out of hand.[35]

Balchen never commented on Pearson's column but had no doubt that it angered Byrd even more. He wished the unpleasant confrontation at Kitty Hawk had never happened.[36]

The award of the prestigious Harmon International Trophy to Balchen by President Eisenhower on 10 November 1953 increased the hostility that Byrd felt toward Balchen. The prize was established in 1926, is one of the most prized aviation awards, and is given by the president from a grant established by Col. Clifford B. Harmon (1866–1945), pioneer American balloonist and aviator. Balchen's award (for the year 1952) was given "for outstanding service to the advancement of aviation in connection with Arctic operations, Arctic exploration, Arctic rescue and Arctic pilotage, including many polar flights."[37]

Shortly thereafter Byrd learned that there was speculation in a news report that Balchen was to be promoted to brigadier general. In a rambling letter to McKinley, he wrote that he and Balchen had broken diplomatic relations and he had been fighting for his reputation. He complained that there was a leak in McKinley's Washington office. "By leak, I mean there is someone that does not have a favorable attitude towards me," he said. "In your office they are all loyal to you, but there is a traitor there to me. I am not sure yet just who it is." He added, "I have some friends who have been working for me. And General White has been, I am told, completely informed of Balchen's conduct plus his disloyalty to everyone with whom he has been connected."[38]

The Kitty Hawk meeting was not the last Balchen would hear from Byrd. Byrd called Balchen's home in Alexandria late at night and accused Balchen of continually demeaning him in the speeches he was making. Byrd said he was instrumental in getting Balchen out of arctic work in the Air Force.[39]

After one of these calls in November 1953, Balchen sent Byrd a note saying he was "shocked and surprised at the accusations you made at Kitty Hawk and again when you called me the following Saturday night and at the airport in New York. However, I hope that these most unpleasant occurrences are now over."[40]

Byrd followed immediately with a scathing response, accusing Balchen of

utter ruthlessness which shocks me beyond measure. . . . If some friend
of yours helped you to write these letters, he must indeed be a bitter
enemy of mine to join you in such ruthlessness.

It is an infinite pity that my friendly request to you to try to prevent
misstatements of fact about me and my associates should bring about
such arrogance and vengeance. Perhaps you and your friends feel that
I have become a weakling, with no ability to defend myself? If there is
a possibility that you have not meant what you said, then I would like
to find out about that.[41]

Balchen decided he had had enough. He wrote a final letter:

Your letter of November 13th has me completely nonplussed. I do not
know what you are driving at. All I can say in answering it is to repeat
and to stress what I have said before, that I have never said or done
anything that could have been detrimental to you, or to your associates. I have always expressed my gratitude for what you have done for
me in the past. This is my final say in the matter.[42]

Before retiring as Air Force chief of staff in June 1953, Gen. Hoyt S. Vandenberg called Balchen to his office and told him that Byrd had visited
him and complained of a remark that Balchen had made in a talk given
at the Circumnavigators Club in New York—that he believed Lindbergh
had contributed more to aviation than any other flyer then alive. Byrd felt
that *he* deserved that distinction and asked Vandenberg to order Balchen
to be more careful about making such broad statements to his detriment.

"General Vandenberg relayed that information to me with a big wink,"
Balchen said, "but I didn't take it lightly. Both the admiral and the senator
were men of enormous influence and I figured I would hear from them
again."[43]

Added to the recognition given to Balchen with the Harmon Trophy
was another accolade that undoubtedly infuriated Byrd. It was an honorary degree of Doctor of Science from the University of Alaska awarded
in May 1954 as an outstanding aviation pioneer, organizer, and "leader
of innumerable exacting missions."[44]

The Byrd files at Ohio State University reveal that one of the individuals
who led the Byrd campaign to vilify Balchen was James E. Mooney, long-

time associate of Byrd and a top civilian in the Navy's Antarctic Affairs Division. He visited Balchen in his Pentagon office and proposed that Balchen consent to use his name on an article to be written by a professional magazine writer that would depict Byrd as a great flyer, navigator, and explorer. It would not only tell how Byrd reached the South Pole but also the North Pole. In return, Balchen would receive the proceeds from the sale of the article and a guarantee from Byrd that he would be promoted to general.[45] Balchen declined the offer but would not have been surprised that, if he had accepted, such a promise could be fulfilled by the political machinations of the admiral and his brother.

A series of letters between Mooney and Byrd during the 1953–1954 time period reveal that Mooney directed an intensive campaign to discredit Balchen with Byrd's continuing encouragement. Either Byrd had him on a monetary retainer or Mooney was so devoted to Byrd that he voluntarily spent much personal time and effort writing to Byrd's known supporters, asking them to point out the misconceptions and errors in the favorable publicity that Balchen was receiving. Mooney reported to Byrd that he had several "successful" meetings with General White and Col. Arno Luehman, Air Force director of Information, in which he told of supposed falsehoods that Balchen was spreading around. He composed letters for friends and former associates of Byrd to send to the news media and influential politicians detailing alleged inaccuracies in news stories about Balchen and his reported contributions to arctic knowledge. He researched books and articles about Balchen and had Byrd supporters, such as E. J. Demas, Capt. M. J. Brennan, and Lt. Cmdr. George O. Noville agree to sign or approve favorable statements about Byrd's North Pole and Atlantic flights. He asked them to refute the accuracy of the articles about Balchen in the magazines, especially that Balchen had been a moving force behind the planning, development, and construction of the Thule air base.

"As far back as 1925 Admiral Byrd brought to the attention of the American people the importance of the Arctics [sic] to military and civil air transportation," Mooney wrote in a 14-page paper rationalizing why Balchen did not deserve the credit he was getting in the news media. "If any names are to be singled out with respect to the Thule air base and predictions about the use of aircraft in the Arctics [sic], that of Admiral Byrd ranks on top."

Mooney added,

There is a growing feeling that the omission of facts, giving of half truths and implications contained in the public press leave the uninformed reader with an entirely erroneous impression. It is not alone the omissions, but more important, it is the strong implications that the success of many of Admiral Byrd's outstanding undertakings were entirely dependent upon, and in some cases, directed by Bernt Balchen. . . . It is time the American people knew the facts and that insidious and erroneous half-truths be brought into the open in the true light of accomplishments.[46]

A copy of a note written in a third-person style and sent by Byrd to Mooney, apparently to be used as talking points when contacting people who could rebut the pro-Balchen images, stated,

Ever since Balchen has been working with Americans he has been a traitor to those with whom he has worked. First of all, he betrayed Amundsen at Spitsbergen when he left him and went over to the Byrd camp because he wanted to come to the United States.

Secondly, after the South Pole Expedition, after Byrd had given him honors and befriended him in every way in the United States and on the Expedition, he deserted Byrd and went to Europe to try to get Ellsworth to form an expedition to beat Byrd back to the Antarctic. He went down to the Antarctic twice with Ellsworth and did not make a single important flight of exploration; and afterwards betrayed Ellsworth and said the most derogatory possible things about him. Now Balchen is ready to betray the Air Force if the Air Force doesn't do what he wants."[47]

Mooney responded that there appeared to be no question that "some malice and planned program are afoot to try and damage your reputation. Now whether B.B. is the sole instigator using others in a sinister movement, or whether others are using him, is to be determined, and we shall make that determination."[48]

Mooney delightedly reported to Byrd three weeks later that Balchen was not getting Air Force support for promotion to brigadier general.

The facts are no major person in the Air Force is interested in his problems, and it is taken for granted that he has received special attention thru [sic] legislation to get where he is today as regards to advancement in the Air Force. I have been informed that there is no movement afoot to promote Balchen, nor is there any attempt on the part of major officers to be so interested on his behalf.

Further, Admiral, I am now in a position should any steps be made for Congressional initiation of a plan to have Balchen made a B.G. over the heads of the military establishment, that it will be squelched.[49]

Mooney followed this with a special delivery letter that included the following: "I checked further on the Balchen matter as regards Senatorial support for a B.G. I just can't find any beyond what was indicated previously, namely Senator Thye, and in looking into this and from what I learned he had been "caused" to make that support, and I think it was cursory and not fundamental with him."[50]

In December 1953 Balchen was invited to fly to Thule with Secretary of the Air Force Harold E. Talbott, Gen. Curtis E. LeMay, commander of the Strategic Air Command, William Randoph Hearst, Jr., and Arthur Godfrey and USO entertainers to celebrate New Year's Eve with the men. It was an opportunity for LeMay to see how much the base had progressed and he was impressed. He turned to Balchen and said, "Here's a place I can fight from!" It was a supreme compliment coming from the tough, nononsense commander of the Air Force's strategic bomber force.[51]

The trip to Thule had been well-publicized, and Mooney sent Byrd a Walter Winchell column written in his typical staccato style: "Col. Bernt Balchen who flew Godfrey to the Arctic (and Byrd to the South Pole) and led the Norwegian Underground. Senators will demand to know who is keeping him from promotion (He's the world's No. 1 flier)."[52]

Although Balchen was not taking part in the staff work at the Pentagon, he continued to be in demand for speaking engagements and interviews as the threat from the Soviets loomed ever stronger in the wake of the stalemated truce arrangements at Panmunjom, Korea. He told one audience,

We cannot escape the fact that this is an air age we are living in now . . . . The development of long-range aircraft has completely changed our world. Places that are the farthest apart by ordinary geography are much closer by air over the Pole. The day when we could overlook blank spaces on our maps is finished. All military targets anywhere in the populated part of the globe above 35 degrees north latitude are reachable. The Arctic is no longer a cold spot but the "hot spot" on this planet.[53]

Honors came Balchen's way again in 1954. He received the Charles H. Johnson Medal for extraordinary heroism and humanity from the Norsemen Lodge in Norway. Later in the year he received the Adventurers' Club Medal in New York. In 1954 Erik Bergaust, a Norwegian American writer, proposed they collaborate on a book that would tell of Balchen's predictions of the future in aviation and space over the next 50 years. Balchen agreed. In a question-and-answer style, Balchen made unprecedented predictions that ranged from the future of jet aircraft, helicopters, and supersonic travel to rocket and atomic propulsion, and space flight. In retrospect, his predictions, although conservative in some cases, proved remarkably accurate. In more than 200 pages of text, Balchen discussed convertiplanes, supersonic jetliners, "electronic brains" (computers), flights to the moon, and space stations. Most of his predictions came true long before the 50 years from 1954 when the book was published.[54]

Without explanation, Balchen was placed on temporary duty with the National Science Foundation in Washington, D.C., on 1 November 1954. He was to assist in the planning for U.S. activities in antarctica for the International Geophysical Year (IGY) of 1957–1958. The IGY was an effort by a dozen nations to set up a system of research by means of simultaneous and consecutive expeditions and fixed observatories. He was to retain his basement office in the Pentagon and be available to the Air Force for consultations when needed. He had little interest in the IGY assignment because he felt it was less important than the threat of the Soviet Union to start a shooting war with ballistic missiles.

The following months were difficult for Balchen, because nothing had changed in the Pentagon. He felt abandoned by his coworkers, the civilian appointees, and the general officers who had replaced those he had worked with previously. He expressed his unhappiness in a letter to a retired friend who had formerly worked with him on arctic projects and had asked about the DEW Line and Thule:

I do not know very much of the planning of the DEW Line as I am— and have been for nearly two years now—kept entirely out of any AF projects that have to do with the Arctic. For a year and a half I sat around and did not do one single thing, except giving some lectures once in a while. I am at present assigned to the Third International Geophysical Year, National Science Foundation, where I am assisting in setting up their Antarctic planning. Just marking time for my retirement, which can go into effect around May 1956.

Regarding the question about Thule and who told Finletter about it, here's what I have to contribute: In October 1950, Mr. Finletter came to Alaska. He told me then that he had talked with Stuart Symington about the Arctic defenses and that he had read a report that I had written in January the same year about the overall Arctic problem, in which Thule was one of the main support bases for an Arctic network of stations. He asked me at great length about Thule.

Mr. Finletter later made the statement to Ambassador Kauffmann of Denmark and C. B. Allen of the *Herald Tribune,* that it was solely on my recommendation that he decided to go ahead with Thule in spite of strong resistance from the Air Force staff. Credit for discovering Thule and making the decision for Mr. Finletter has been claimed by numerous of our present explorers and others. I do believe that I am the only one who has suffered the consequences of recommending this base at a time when it was not popular to do so in the AF. I don't believe that it makes much difference who talked to Finletter about this. It was his decision and his responsibility after the decision was made. There are lots of flag wavers on the bandwagon today, and there would have been more if the concept had received the recognition that it warrants for the defense of our country.[55]

By now it seemed certain that Balchen was not going to be promoted to brigadier general so that he could remain on active duty for an additional five years instead of having to retire by law on 31 October 1956. He learned from a Pentagon source that Senator Byrd had blocked his promotion seven times "for personal and special reasons," which apparently required no further justification.[56] The possible reason rested in Senator Byrd's power to steer military appropriations as he saw fit. Sacrificing one Air Force officer was an easy price to pay to steer funds to favored Navy projects.

When a writer interviewed Balchen in 1955 and asked, off the record, who was really obstructing his promotion, he responded, "Dick Byrd."

When asked why, he said, "Because he didn't fly over the North Pole and he knows I know it." When he was queried later if he would permit a newspaper article to be written about that remark, he said, "No. I don't want to destroy Byrd as a hero to American schoolchildren."[57] In later years, when asked the same question, Balchen would reply, "The truth will come out. It will be long after I'm gone."[58]

Increasingly unhappy that he was not using his time constructively, Balchen asked for a transfer out of Washington, D.C. In a letter to Harry Bruno, he expressed his desire to be transferred to an intelligence assignment where his intimate knowledge of the Scandinavian countries, their leaders, and their languages could be put to good use.

> The most important thing to me is not, however, a promotion, but to be allowed to work again. During the last year and a half I have just been marking time, almost without a thing to do, and even my public appearances on behalf of the Air Force have been on a "quota basis," with an allowance for me to give one public address per month. It is my firm conviction that I could still contribute some to the defense of our nation if allowed to work during the short time of service that I have left before my mandatory retirement in 1956.[59]

Balchen's normal three-year Pentagon tour was completed in the fall of 1954 and he received orders to join the 3500th Recruiting Wing at Wright-Patterson Air Force Base, Ohio. His duty would be to conduct a nationwide recruiting campaign until his retirement. "It is impossible for me not to look upon the arrangement with some bitterness," he wrote to a friend, "but I do welcome the chance to keep busy, at least, and will then work for this cause until my retirement."[60]

Without explanation, the orders were revoked and he was told he was going to be assigned to the antarctic with the Navy on an ice breaker for five months. However, no orders were ever issued. Instead, he was sent on a two-month trip to Canada, Greenland, and Iceland as an advisor on the siting of radar stations.

Col. Hubert Zemke, a World War II fighter ace, then on duty with Balchen at the Pentagon in the Directorate of Operations, was determined to see if he could prevent any further misuse of Balchen's talents and experience. He wrote a personal letter to Lt. Gen. Glenn O. Barcus, commander of the Northeast Air Command (NEAC) in Newfoundland, asking if a position for Balchen could be found there until his retirement "without going through the labyrinth of service messages."

"I have tried to keep this man busy," Zemke said.

> In the meantime he has been called upon continually to give lectures, appear on TV programs, help in recruiting, etc. Frankly, the Air Force is wasting him. Bernt is an outdoor man and a doer, not a political Pentagon desk officer.
>
> The net result is that he has become despondent. In an attempt to retire, he was turned down and told he could retire in October 1956. When brought into the Service by Generals Spaatz, Vandenberg and Mr. Finletter, the story was different. These people have gone and his story is lost. In the meantime it is expected that he ride out his last tour doing menial staff work as best can be dug up.
>
> For a man of his accomplishments and specialized ability, this is wrong. Based on his war-time record, the Air Force must certainly have something more in store. When his Washington tour ended last Fall I made a recommendation that another Arctic assignment be made. Nothing was found. The situation has boiled down to where he remains in my outer office with a quasi-loan status to the International Geophysical Year being his mainstay for service existence. Monthly he is sent on odd lectures and occasionally a bit project of some sort arises.
>
> If you would be receptive to taking Colonel Balchen as a Special Assistant on Arctic Affairs, I am certain I can arrange such transfer.[61]

General Barcus was delighted with the prospect of having the world's foremost arctic airman as a special assistant on his staff. Orders were issued transferring Balchen to Newfoundland in September 1955.

Grateful for Zemke's intervention, Balchen prepared for his last Air Force assignment: Pepperell Air Base near St. Johns. He left his cramped office in the Pentagon basement with a feeling of relief but deeply disappointed that he had been unable to contribute his knowledge and experience in meeting the problems the Air Force was having in the north. It was some consolation that he would be able to catch up with the latest technological developments on the DEW Line, visit Greenland, and observe military and commercial aviation operations in Scandinavia. Now, perhaps, he could once again make some meaningful contributions to the Air Force.

In Balchen's final months in Washington, D.C., Admiral Byrd never let up on his caustic verbal attacks on Balchen. Byrd continued to call Balchen at his home in the middle of the night to vent his fury at some imagined insult to his reputation that he attributed to Balchen. These attacks left Balchen completely mystified, and Balchen did not deem them worthy of a reply. In a thank-you letter to Zemke, Balchen said his years in the Pentagon "were the most unpleasant years of my life."[62]

15 · An Autobiography Raises a Storm

Balchen reported for duty at Pepperell Air Base, Newfoundland, in the fall of 1955 to be special assistant to the commanding general of the Northeast Air Command (NEAC). Lt. Gen. Glenn O. Barcus immediately gave him free rein to seek out problem areas and recommend improvements to enhance the command's defense mission. Balchen visited the units in its area of responsibility and checked on the command's arctic and survival training program, where improvements were needed. He collaborated with Air Force Capt. Theodore R. Sturm to write an arctic survival manual for the crews of the Strategic Air Command. He also spent time on the Greenland ice cap observing the latest snow-compaction experiments. He studied the logistics and communications security problems of the command and served as the Air Force consultant to the U.S. Army's Sea Ice and Permafrost Research Evaluation (SIPRE) project. Much time was spent on projects that sought to test the bearing strength of the ice covering arctic lakes and bays, and he kept abreast of the reoccupation of the T-3 floating ice island, then about 300 mi. from the North Pole.

He recognized the importance of good relations between military and civil aviation, and in an effort to make communications among them more viable, as well as help predict future requirements for military and civil operations, he visited Canada, Denmark, Sweden, and Norway to confer about joint defense measures with top officials and make recommendations. Most of his military missions to Scandinavia were top secret and his intelligence assignments concerning the Soviet Union's Cold War activities have still not been released.

In February 1956 Balchen traveled to Bemidji, Minnesota, to evaluate dual-purpose ski floats intended to lift a heavy cargo plane from either land or water. June and July found him aboard the Norwegian sealer *Norsel*, a ship that had been leased to the Air Force for a high-priority mission to establish electronic shore stations on the east coast of Greenland. Under Balchen's direction the ship penetrated the pack ice more than two months earlier in the season than ever attempted at such an extreme northern latitude to accumulate data that President Eisenhower personally specified he wanted available by August 1956. Next Balchen represented the Air Force at a North Atlantic Treaty Organization (NATO) symposium in Brussels on cold weather operations.

The day 31 October 1956, Balchen's mandatory date of retirement, came all too soon for him. He received many expressions of gratitude for his unique contributions to U.S. arctic defenses. In a formal ceremony, he received the highly coveted Distinguished Service Medal. The citation noted that Balchen's

firm leadership, extensive background and selfless devotion to duty were instrumental factors in the successful accomplishment of several major projects of vital significance to the defense of the entire North American continent. His profound understanding of intricate Arctic conditions and the zeal with which he overcame the challenges of his numerous responsibilities materially contributed to the betterment of international relationships between the Canadian and Scandinavian Governments and this country.[1]

Gen. Nathan F. Twining, then Air Force chief of staff, wrote Balchen and noted that he had

rendered expert advice on the development of concepts, procedures and programs pertaining to the Arctic that has been consistently utilized by other agencies in planning projects and operations of national and international interest. As the individual primarily responsible for the pioneering and development of the Air Base at Thule, Greenland, you contributed immeasurably to the Air Force mission.

The Air Force is proud to have had you as one of its leaders and I hope your future undertakings continue to evidence that brilliancy of execution that has marked your endeavors during your past career.[2]

Fellow officers, saddened to see him retire, gave Balchen a fine farewell dinner. He had been an inspiration and mentor and a delight to listen to when prodded to tell of his own experiences, which invariably included valuable advice on arctic survival.

Shortly before retirement Balchen had been contacted by Corey Ford, who had collaborated with him and Oliver La Farge in writing *War below Zero: The Battle for Greenland*, published in 1944. Ford asked Balchen if he would be interested in collaborating on an autobiography.

Balchen decided he would do it. The book, to be titled *Come North with Me*, was placed under contract to the E.P. Dutton Company. It was to consist largely of material from Balchen's diaries, logbooks, and notes meticulously written through the years. Writing started early in 1957. Because his conclusions about the Byrd North Pole flight would be the most controversial part of his book, Balchen reviewed his records on weather conditions and timing of the flight noted at Spitsbergen in 1926 and the detailed flight records made during the two-month tour in which he and Floyd Bennett had flown the *Josephine Ford*. Based on this data, he again carefully calculated the estimated speed of the Fokker on the North Pole flight. He then had a Fokker aeronautical engineer, who had worked on the plane in 1925–1926, check the company flight test records to confirm or reject his calculations. They were confirmed.

Just before the Balchen autobiography was completed, Admiral Byrd, who had been in deteriorating health, died in his sleep on 11 March 1957 at age 68. He was buried with full military honors at Arlington National Cemetery. Obituaries credited him as being one of the last great figures of polar aviation. His gravestone bears an engraving of the Congressional Medal of Honor, the nation's highest military award, given to him for the North Pole flight. A larger than life statue of him in arctic wear was erected by the National Geographic Society on the boulevard leading to the cemetery.

Balchen was momentarily hesitant about including in the book his conclusion that Byrd had failed to reach the North Pole. But his reluctance was overcome by the painful memory of Byrd's unrelenting harassment, the Kitty Hawk encounter, and the blocking of his Air Force career. He told Ford that he had decided to tell the story as he knew it to be once he was out of uniform, because Byrd had not done so during his lifetime. He had hoped the revelation would be through a scientific investigation by a polar institution of some kind, but none had come forward.[3]

Balchen's resolve to reveal the facts about the North Pole flight, as well as the evidence of Byrd's efforts to wreck his career, was strengthened by new evidence of Byrd's unbridled hostility toward him, which he learned about soon after Byrd's death. It dated as recently as Balchen's receipt of the Distinguished Service Medal—an honor Byrd clearly did not want him to receive. The manager of the Lexington Hotel in New York, a favorite Byrd haunt, told Balchen about Byrd's reactions during a three-day time period spent with George Noville, when they expressed very uncomplimentary remarks about Balchen at the bar and in the lobby. It was reported that both men were wearing their uniforms at the time; this made them stand out and be noticed by everyone there, especially because there was no war on.[4]

The completed manuscript was delivered to the publisher in the early fall of 1957. When a Dutton editor made what seemed to be arbitrary changes —none of which had anything to do with Byrd—Ford refused to do any more work on the book. The changes seemed relatively minor in Balchen's opinion, so he approved them. Unbound galleys were made available for review in February 1958. Some were obtained by Byrd loyalists.

Supporters of Admiral Byrd who had great self-interest in sustaining his heroic image immediately joined with family and friends to stop its publication or have deleted anything that was less than totally flattering to Byrd. Robb Oertell, who had been one of Byrd's North Pole expedition officers, was among them. In October 1957 he called Harry Bruno, who was well-known in New York public relations' circles and who was Byrd's former publicist and a good friend of Balchen's, asking him to warn Dutton not to include anything about Byrd's North Pole flight in the autobiography. Bruno ignored the request, confident that neither Balchen nor the publisher would comply.

The *Saturday Evening Post* had wanted to publish an article on the North Pole flight with emphasis on Balchen's calculations and analysis, as did *Look* magazine. In view of these objections and fearing reprisals, both publications dropped their plans, an extraordinary turn of events and a measure of how powerful Byrd's friends were. Ben Hibbs, editor of the *Saturday Evening Post,* wrote Balchen that "I fear that if we were to publish the article, Byrd's friends—perhaps aided and abetted by the Navy—might well raise such a rumpus that we would find ourselves in an untenable position and might have to end up publishing an article in defense of Byrd. And that would be a bitter pill to swallow, feeling as I do about Byrd."[5]

Meanwhile Noville, Harold June, and other Byrd backers poured over the galleys trying to find some basis for a law suit. Byrd's son, Richard E. Byrd III, called Dutton's president, Elliott B. MacRae, and warned him not to publish the book under threat of legal action on unspecified charges, followed by a similar warning from Noville's lawyer. Others joined in, including Charles J. V. Murphy, ghost writer for Byrd's books and articles, who had been in touch with Senator Byrd. The senator reportedly engaged Edward P. F. Eagan, a noted New York lawyer, to lay the groundwork for a lawsuit. Eagan wrote to MacRae and enclosed a collection of letters and statements from six "witnesses," whom Eagan had apparently assembled—crew members on the *Chantier*, Byrd's polar expedition ship—with their reasons for backing Byrd's claims on the flight. None of these were airmen; they had joined the ship as young volunteer adventurers.

Word that Balchen was revealing his flight analysis leading to the conclusion that Byrd could not have reached the Pole spread quickly to a wide range of people who felt impelled to comment in Byrd's favor to the publisher or to Balchen, such as Paul A. Siple, Adm. Arthur W. Radford, Angier Biddle Duke, and others. Mrs. Arthur H. Sulzberger, wife of the publisher of the *New York Times,* joined in to object strenuously. Siple who had been on Byrd's first and subsequent antarctic expeditions, wrote a three-page letter to Balchen asking him to "reconsider and delete the charge that Byrd didn't fly over the North Pole and the Kitty Hawk remarks at any cost before the book is released. Whatever controversies you and Byrd may have had should remain buried," he wrote.

> I doubt that dollar profit from a book can ever offset the damage you can do to yourself. . . . Please, Bernt, if it is humanly possible, withdraw your negative remarks about Byrd and alter them to positive words of eulogy. You will be loved much more by your friends if you show gratitude and understanding instead of trying to tear down Byrd for the sake of trying to build up yourself.[6]

The opposition was terribly troubling to Balchen, and he sought advice from Laurence Gould. He had great respect for Gould, who was second in command on the first Byrd arctic expedition. Gould was concerned about the fallout, which he thought would be detrimental to Balchen. He wrote a long letter to Balchen pleading with him to remove the portions of the manuscript unmasking the admiral. "Psychologically, this would be the worst possible time imaginable to expose the shortcomings of Admiral Byrd," he said.

> People would inevitably say that you had waited until he was dead to do so. Let things rest awhile and possibly what goes on abroad about the North Pole flight will emerge in publication.
> I am quite sure that the National Geographic Society with all of the power it has—and I have discovered it is very great—would immediately rise to denounce you as a detractor of Byrd. I am not sure but that the Navy, much as they hated him, would likewise rise to his defense.
> Even though everything you have said in the book is true, still it is a better part of wisdom—in my humble opinion—to delete everything directly critical of Byrd.[7]

The pressure on Dutton continued to build. Balchen's friend Col. Walter Wood of the Arctic Institute was informed that a number of people with extensive means were uniting to try to publicly refute his findings. During a meeting at the Dutton office with Balchen in mid-April 1958 a telephone call was received from Harold B. Miller, a retired admiral, then an official at Pan American Airways, who stated that Byrd's son, Richard E. Byrd III, was spreading the word that the Byrd family was planning to sue Balchen and the publisher. On the same day MacRae received an official letter from U.S. Marine General G. B. Erskine, assistant to the Secretary of Defense, stating it was

> not in the best interests of the country to destroy the dignity of two of our pioneer aviators by what would appear to be bickering in public; and that such action would accrue to the benefit of no one and to the detriment of all concerned.
> Such action would make distressing commentary on our American way of life that the reputations of two men who have led the way should be subject to what will universally be considered belittlement, when both men would otherwise remain figures of unsullied reputation in the permanent light of history.[8]

Murphy called on Lowell Thomas, hoping that Balchen's influential friend would dissuade the publisher from printing the galley material. Thomas reacted with anger that an experienced journalist with Murphy's reputation would make such a request and heatedly ordered him to leave his office.[9] In hindsight, it is strange that no pressure was exerted by anyone at this time to have Byrd's North Pole flight records brought to light and analyzed by qualified experts, at least as far as is known.

The question of whether to cancel publication or make extensive revisions was debated vigorously by the Dutton staff. But the print order was not cancelled, and 8,600 copies rolled off the press. Pressure continued to mount with calls and letters from prominent movers and shakers. Dutton's lawyers advised that the book in its initial form should not be released; either cancellation of the contract or an extensively revised edition was recommended. Company officials reluctantly decided to give in. All copies of the original printing were ordered destroyed. A Dutton editor would rewrite the manuscript, deleting material that offended the Byrd clique.

Rather than bear the expense of a lawsuit or have the book cancelled altogether, Balchen approved the numerous revisions to the original text. Byrd's supporters (Balchen's friends called them "Byrd Watchers") had won the battle.

Following are excerpts of deleted material from the first printing of *Come North with Me*. The principal complaint of the "Byrd Watchers" centered on references to Byrd in connection with the North Pole flight and to Balchen's revelations regarding personal encounters with Byrd and some of his associates. Pages 66 and 67 of the original edition noted the conversation between Floyd Bennett and Balchen at the completion of the *Josephine Ford*'s nationwide tour when they were thinking about making an Atlantic flight of their own:

My eye runs over the instrument gauges, and automatically I note down the speed and fuel consumption for the last time. I start to slip my log book into my shirt again, but something in the back of my mind keeps bothering me. I run over the data I have compiled on the tour, and frown, and check the figures carefully on my slide rule, once more. There must be a mistake. "Tell me," I ask Bennett, "what do you get for our average cruising speed?"

Bennett takes his own log out of the leg pocket of his coveralls. "Let's see. About seventy miles an hour."

"So do I. There's something here that doesn't quite jibe," I ponder. With ski landing gear on, the speed couldn't be more than sixty-eight, could it? Well now, my diary says you were gone fifteen and a half hours from Kings Bay to the Pole and back. Figuring roughly,

1,550 miles round trip, that would be averaging better than a hundred miles an hour."

"We had a tailwind, though."

"But you had to buck that wind all the way back to Spitsbergen." I shake my head. "Our figures must be way off, because you put your turning point a couple hundred miles short of the Pole."

"We're both cockeyed somewhere," Bennett shrugs. "Well, it doesn't matter now. We won't be flying this bucket across the Atlantic or anywhere else. You'll be working in the Fokker factory, and I'll be looking for a job."[10]

From pages 301–302, this material was expunged:

What is important, what is not? Take the strange contradiction in Commander Byrd's record of his North Pole flight. According to his own figures, the *Josephine Ford* was in flight 15 hours and 30 minutes and spent 13 minutes (sometimes Byrd put the time a minute longer) circling the Pole—which leaves a total of 15 hours and 17 minutes to fly 1,340 nautical miles (1,542 statute miles. The distance sometimes varies a few miles in different estimates). This means the average cruising speed would have had to be 87.2 knots (100.3 mph). From actual test data—plus my little pocket slide rule that Byrd despised—I compute that with the ski installation the best cruising speed that could have been squeezed out of the plane would have been no more than 74 knots (85.1 mph).

In Byrd's stated time of 15 hours and 17 minutes, he could therefore have traveled a maximum distance of only 1,131 nautical miles (1,300.7 statute miles), and the farthest North Latitude he could have reached was 88 degrees 15.5 minutes, or 104 nautical miles (120.2 statute miles) short of the Pole. All his life I waited for Admiral Byrd to give some explanation of the discrepancies in his log. To the best of my knowledge he never did, at least not publicly.[11]

There were other revisions that extensively altered the original text—some to improve the flow, others to purify Byrd's image. They dealt with the flight of the *America* to France, life in antarctica, Byrd's personnel management style, his paranoia about loyalty. Most important was that all references to Balchen's rationale of why Byrd could not have reached the Pole were expurgated, including these consolation paragraphs that were the last words in the original manuscript:

Is the difference in miles between 88° 15.5′ north latitude and the Pole important, after all? Even if Byrd missed the Pole by a hundred miles—which would make Amundsen the first human being in history to reach both Poles—this is not what matters. Byrd dreamed a big dream, and that he may have failed to achieve it does not make his dream less big. A great man is always a little strange, different from the rest. With some understanding of the conflicts that must have gone on in his mind, the secrets that he carried locked in his heart, he becomes more human to us, and therefore his achievements become greater still. Byrd's effort broke through the psychological barrier that existed in men's minds, and he led the way for others to fly to the Pole. His importance lies in this vision he had, the concept of tomorrow's air age, and he belongs to the great company of pioneers who helped to usher in the new era of polar flight.[12]

Although it had been the publishing company's decision to destroy the books, Balchen was asked to share the cost of printing the destroyed copies, amounting to $6,033.76. One half of this amount would be added to the royalty advance of $5,000, which Balchen and Ford had shared. Therefore, there would be no royalty payments until the total authors' earnings had exceeded $8,016.88.

The revised version of *Come North with Me* was released in July 1958 to mild reviews. Balchen's conclusions about Byrd's failed North Pole flight that advanced publicity promised were, of course, not included in the revised version. For this reason, it is believed that some periodicals may have decided not to review it.

The *New York Times*, a Byrd champion through the years, assigned Orville Prescott to write a review. He wrote a scathing critique that may have influenced sales negatively. He said Balchen was not a good writer, which "is hardly surprising in an outdoor type who has been a crack skier, proficient boxer and expert mechanic as well as a flier and soldier. If Mr. Balchen was aided by a ghost writer, which I suspect, the ghostwriter's performance was inadequate."[13]

A review by John K. Hutchens in the *New York Herald-Tribune* was more complimentary:

> The quality he most admires in men, says Col. Bernt Balchen, is the old pioneer spirit that takes obstacles in its stride—and as his vigorous au-

tobiography attests, the tougher the obstacle, the longer the stride, the happier the colonel. That he himself is full of that spirit, right up to his fifty-eight-year-old, frequently frostbitten ears, no one is on record as denying. Nor does the eminent aviator, soldier-explorer and part-time water-colorist offer any evidence to the contrary. That's fair enough, isn't it, or can you think of any good reason why the first man to pilot a plane over both poles should beat shyly around a bush in his own backyard?[14]

Men who had served with Balchen or who knew firsthand of the perils he had faced and the lives he had saved were enthusiastic about *Come North with Me*. Treasured in Balchen's files, among many letters of this nature, was one from Navy Capt. A. Y. "Dick" Parunak, the Navy PBY pilot who had participated with Balchen in a classic World War II rescue operation on Greenland. He wrote, "It is truly a fascinating story. It takes me back to our short, but busy duty in Greenland—and to our 'Greenland Salvage Co.'. . . You have been most modest in telling of your life. From what little I saw of it in working with you I am afraid the average reader will not comprehend the vast amount of planning and courage which went into your exploits."[15]

The book did not enjoy best-seller status, possibly in part because it did not reveal the facts about the North Pole flight. It would remain for others to hope for the release of Byrd's records and analyze them after both men were gone. Balchen revealed his feelings in a letter to his friend Dean Smith, who was writing his own autobiography, which contained many revealing insights on Byrd:

> For many years, I thought Byrd himself would tell the truth about his flight. Then I forgot the whole thing, but after the war while I was in Washington with the Air Force and Byrd tried everything to make my life miserable, I remembered it and started to collect data, fully intent on giving out the story as soon as I was out of uniform. Byrd must have known all along that I knew the truth, and this must have been the reason for his behavior. My big disappointment was that he passed away before I was able to get it out.[16]

The American public did not have any doubts about Byrd's claim. Any uncertainty expressed publicly by a few was dismissed as "sour grapes."

Encyclopedias and history books list the epic North Pole flight at the top of the list of his life achievements. Children in school are told the Byrd story without question.

Balchen learned just as his autobiography was completed that Gosta H. Liljequist, a highly respected Swedish meteorologist, had become interested in the Byrd flight while spending the 1957–1958 winter in Spitsbergen. After studying Byrd's writings and available facts, Liljequist made an extensive analysis of the weather observations extending from Spitsbergen to northern Russia and along the Siberian and Alaskan coasts reported for the period before and during the flight. In a detailed article titled, "Did the *Josephine Ford* Reach the North Pole?," published in the May 1960 issue of *Interavia*, a highly regarded Swiss aviation magazine, Liljequist analyzed the North Pole flight claim. He concluded,

> To have reached the Pole, the plane would have had to have a tail wind of about 15 knots as an average for the outward flight and the wind would also have had to change direction and increase to about 22 knots from the Pole to Kings Bay on the homeward flight. . . . The fresh winds could have occurred only during the first half of the homeward flight, in which case they would have had to reach at least 40 to 50 knots from the north. Such a northerly gale should have made itself felt at Spitsbergen soon afterwards, but it did not. The whole of the Arctic was covered by an anti-cyclone, and 40 to 50 knots close to this high pressure area is highly improbable.[17]

Sverre Petterssen, a meteorology professor at the University of Chicago, had been the forecaster at the Norwegian weather-reporting facility at Tromso in 1926, and had supplied weather information for the Amundsen flight. At Balchen's request in 1958 he restudied the daily synoptic charts for the period 8–11 May 1926, prepared by the Norwegian Forecast Center and the U.S. Weather Bureau. His analysis showed that there had been a very light tailwind on the poleward portion of the flight, but he could not substantiate Byrd's claim in his report to the National Geographic Society of a tailwind of 23.5 MPH on the return flight.[18]

When Dean Smith's memoirs, titled *By the Seat of My Pants*, were published in 1961, it had a frank appraisal of Byrd, his personality, and his desire for dramatic publicity and commercial success at any cost, which he observed on Byrd's first expedition to antarctica:

The expedition was Byrd's own show: he was producer, director and star. For him to realize the maximum profit from his show, and for him to have a following that would enable him to stage subsequent productions and star in them too, it was important to be constantly brought before the public's eye in a manner befitting his role and with care that no one steal his scenes. This constant concern for building his reputation was particularly necessary for a man like Byrd, who lacked most of the specialized skills that would have helped him: he was not a scientist, a practicing aviator or an experienced mariner; nor was he blessed with outstanding physical abilities. Only a complete dedication to his purpose could overcome his handicaps; his lifelong success was a measure of his determination.[19]

Smith's book did not incur the wrath from Byrd supporters that Balchen memoirs did. Smith admitted he was aware of Balchen's sad experience and had "sharply edited" his comments about Byrd in his original manuscript, "partly from fear, it is true, but largely because I had no desire to write an exposé and thus discredit the entire [antarctic] expedition and some of the excellent work done despite Byrd."[20] However, Smith did make a detailed report of his experiences with Byrd, including the theft of his personal diary, which he believed Byrd had somehow managed to acquire. "The diary was an opus of some magnitude," he wrote in his memoirs. "Since I had written with no thought of publication, it was an unexpurgated account, criticizing freely and even bitterly anyone whose behavior I did not like or understand."[21]

The doubts about Byrd's North Pole claim reached a crescendo on publication of a book in April 1971 titled *Oceans, Poles and Airmen*[22] by Richard Montague, an experienced aviation reporter for the *New York Evening Post* and *New York Evening World*. He opined that "perhaps [the claim] was accepted originally with a little too much haste. Apparently the committee of experts never considered the speed of the plane and distance flown in relation to the time Byrd spent in the air." He added that Byrd's claim seemed to be "the biggest and most successful fraud in the history of polar exploration."[23] Without any source attribution, he quoted Floyd Bennett, apparently erroneously, as having told Balchen that early in the flight an oil leak had developed and Byrd immediately ordered a return to within sight of Spitsbergen. At that point, although the leak stopped, Montague claimed that Byrd had ordered Bennett to fly back and forth over the north coast of Spitsbergen for 14 hours.

The portion of Montague's book about Byrd's doubtful claim received continuing press coverage, particularly in Norway. While Balchen was recovering from major surgery in the hospital in December 1971, he was interviewed by Vern Haugland, Associated Press aviation reporter. Balchen flatly declared that the admiral lied in claiming he had made the first flight over the North Pole. "Byrd's whole fame was based on that story—based on a fraud," Balchen said. "Floyd told me the whole story." Balchen confirmed that the plane had a cruising speed (with skis) of 67 MPH and carried enough fuel for about 20 hr. of flying. He added, "They were out for 15½ hours, and to negotiate the distance Byrd claimed, they would have had to make a cruising speed of 105 miles an hour."[24]

A reporter for a business magazine later asked Balchen about his assessment of the North Pole episode. Balchen replied that he wished the question had never been revived. "After all," he said, "Bennett is dead. Byrd is dead and cannot defend himself. This will hurt his widow, a fine woman, and others. And what good can it do?"[25]

Interest in aviation circles about Byrd's claim continued. When Balchen addressed a convention of the Canadian Aviation Historical Society in June 1971, he was asked about Byrd. He responded,

> He had the uncanny capability of picking his men. Administration— no! Leadership—no! He was vain and uncertain of himself. It is written in Montague's book that he perpetrated the greatest fraud in the annals of exploration by not going to the North Pole at all—but not being as far north as Amundsen in 1925. This deception made him a tremendously unhappy man—knowing that it was the feat on which his whole reputation was made.[26]

When Balchen recovered from surgery in 1971, he was invited to speak at a banquet at the Henry Ford Museum at Dearborn, Michigan. He had been asked to tie his speech in with the three airplanes that were a part of his life and then in the museum's collection—the *Bremen, Josephine Ford,* and *Floyd Bennett*. However, he later received a letter from Dick Hagelthorn, an admirer of Balchen's and member of the club, apologetically canceling the invitation because they "could not welcome a man who was denigrating the collection."[27]

Balchen responded, "It is too bad that it had to come to this. . . . Perhaps one day an independent commission of some sort will be set up to investigate the facts and set the record straight once and for all."[28]

London's *Sunday Times* published an analysis of the Montague book in August 1971 and concluded that

> it now seems probable that the career of Admiral Richard Byrd, one of the most decorated heroes of American polar exploration, was founded on a deception of simple but enormous scale. . . . Byrd's subsequent career, particularly in the Antarctic, was to raise frequent questions about his ethics. Those who worked with him found, growling under the mantle of a modest public hero, a careerist whose appetite for the limelight was insatiable. His undoubted courage and his imagination . . . could run leagues ahead of his exploits and he was not averse to claiming for himself the discoveries of his subordinates. Powerful men sustained his reputation at home—his own brother Harry Flood Byrd who died in 1966, was a senator.[29]

The National Geographic Society received a letter of concern about the Montague allegations from a member in January 1972 and George Crossette, chief of Geographic Research, responded. "Officially, the Society has no comment on this subject. Until new evidence that Admiral Byrd did not reach the North Pole can be presented to and accepted by the scientific community, his recognition as the first man to fly over both poles will have to remain."

As an afterthought, Crossette added, "Speaking as an individual, I have known Bernt Balchen personally and have no reason to doubt his word although I have not discussed this issue with him."[30]

Capt. Finn Ronne, a veteran of nine antarctic expeditions, was another who doubted Byrd's claim. In a 1979 autobiography Ronne revealed that Isaiah Bowman, former president of the American Geographic Society (AGS), told him a secret in 1949 on the condition that Ronne would keep it to himself as long as Bowman lived:

> Upon Byrd's return from the Arctic in 1926, I had doubt that he ever flew over the North Pole. I asked to see his compilation and what navigational aids were used to prove he had reached 90 degrees north. Byrd always gave evasive answers and said no one should question his integrity. But he had no proof of having passed the northernmost point

of Ellsworth and Amundsen the year before. I got the answer to my suspicion when Byrd returned from the Antarctic in 1930. Byrd visited the AGS and after lunch we went for a walk. . . . It was raining that afternoon and with raincoats on we kept walking and talking for almost two hours around the blocks of Broadway and 156th Street. By that time I managed to break down Dicky Byrd, and the time it took to do so was worth it. Byrd confessed . . . that he had not reached the North Pole, but had missed by about 150 miles.[31]

Bowman never disclosed his secret to anyone else because Byrd was such a national hero that he felt no one would believe him. Besides, he had no documents to study. They were kept from public scrutiny by the family for many years after Byrd's death.

Still another researcher who concluded that Byrd's Pole attempt was not successful was David Roberts, who wrote an article, published in the October 1981 issue of *Outside* magazine, titled, "Heroes and Hoaxers: Byrd's Polar Flights of Fancy." It was followed by a book in 1982, *Great Exploration Hoaxes*. Roberts argued that Gilbert Grosvenor, president of the National Geographic Society, had deliberately doctored the official report about the five-day study that the society's experts had made before awarding Byrd its prestigious Hubbard Medal. The time period of the study was originally reported as having taken place between 23 June and 28 June 1926. However, the award to Byrd was made on 23 June—the day the study was to have begun. Grosvenor adjusted the dates so that the September 1926 issue of *National Geographic* would show the study was *concluded* on 23 June.

"Obviously, then," Roberts wrote, "the certification was an after-the-fact effort if it took place at all; and the NGS was not about to embarrass itself by withdrawing credit from the man to whom it had just given its highest award."[32]

Although the National Geographic Society had been steadfast in its refusal to admit it may have erred in giving credit to Byrd for the North Pole flight, the September 1978 issue of *National Geographic* magazine noted in a review of assaults on the Pole: "Recent critics have questioned the limits of the plane's performance, but neither Byrd nor Bennett is alive to reply."[33] An accompanying map with a drawing of the flight route of the *Josephine Ford* shows a turnaround short of the Pole. This is the closest admission to this day that the Society may be backing down from its long-time stand.

Nothing changed as a result of the reports of doubters who received brief mention in the world's periodicals. But serious doubts persisted in the minds of those who are troubled by the simple logic of it all. One of those was Dennis Rawlins, an independent scholar in Baltimore who specializes in navigation studies and publishes a journal on navigation and astronomy. In delving into the records of Robert E. Peary's claim that he had reached the North Pole on the surface in 1909, Rawlins had been instrumental in showing that it had not been possible. In 1995 he was commissioned by the Byrd Polar Research Center at Ohio State University to analyze the diary entries of the disputed Byrd claim, which were found in the large collection of historical materials documenting Admiral Byrd's life and career.

A breakthrough came about when a PBS television crew asked to see Byrd's records and the university's archivist Dr. Raimund E. Goerler located Byrd's original record of the flight, which had been previously overlooked. Goerler found that the 1926 records were written on unused pages of Byrd's 1925 diary, along with notes about his 1925 trip to Greenland and the Atlantic flight of 1927. When Rawlins carefully studied this new material, he found that there were "multiple and nontrivial" disagreements between Byrd's polished report to the NGS and the original diary version. He said, "they leave little doubt that Byrd knew . . . that he had not succeeded."[34]

The reason for the relatively recent discovery is that the 1926 diary had been available only since 1994, when the Byrd collection was finally cataloged and made available to the public. The diary had been misfiled in a box labeled "artifacts" and had been ignored because of this filing error. Prior to the acquisition of the Byrd papers between 1985 and 1990, the family and others had kept the collection, including the 1926 diary and other important documents, under tight security.

Because the diary showed calculations on the distance traveled and the elapsed time, plus the sextant observations of the sun, Rawlins said in an interview with *New York Times* reporter John Noble Wilford, "If he shot the sun, he had to know that he had not quite reached the pole. And it's in the diary that he used the sextant to shoot sun angles."[35]

Wilford added,

One page [of the diary] records critical moments in the flight. One of the engines develops an oil leak at about 9 A.M., Greenwich time. Byrd, using 85 miles an hour as the average air speed, does some arithmetic on the page, arriving at 722 miles covered since takeoff. Byrd writes, "20 miles to go to pole."

These calculations were, however, dead reckoning, an imprecise form of navigation. Based on a 7:07 A.M. sextant reading, the last one recorded in his diary and presumably a more accurate indicator of his true position, Byrd was actually about 150 miles farther south than he reckoned. This sextant reading was changed in his final report to one that was consistent with his claim to have reached the pole.[36]

In his report to the university, Rawlins stated a blank was found in the diary where something had been erased but was still legible. It was a question by Byrd to Bennett: "How long were we gone before we turned around?" The reply, written below the erased question is "8½ hours."

"This is not the sort of question one expects from a navigator who has been keeping track of times and distances," Rawlins wrote. "It also sounds like the turnaround was pretty sudden. And it doesn't feel like the words of someone who has just reached a great goal and lingered there for 13 minutes of circling."[37]

"The calculations of Byrd's on-the-record North Pole flight critics roughly correspond," according to Robert N. Matuozzi, a manuscript librarian at Washington State University, who was a member of the Byrd archival team and author of a master's thesis on Byrd. "Bernt Balchen put Byrd and Bennett no further than 88 degrees, 15.5 minutes N; Liljequist put them at 88 degrees, 36 minutes N; and Rawlins put them at 87 degrees, 75 minutes N. Ironically, Balchen's and Liljequist's calculations turn out to be more generous than Dennis Rawlins's most recent finding!"[38]

There are other discrepancies in Byrd's report of the flight that should not go unreported. Byrd stated in *Skyward* that he had reached the pole at 0902. He described circling the Pole several times and for reasons never explained did not drop some small American flags as he had planned.

The diary states that they were a few miles short of the Pole at 0915. However, in a radio message to the Navy three days after the flight, he stated that they arrived at the Pole at that time. In his final report Byrd said he departed the Pole at 0915, after having circled it for 13 minutes.

These new findings of doubt about Byrd's North Pole claim were noted in two Public Broadcasting Service television programs in 1997 and 1999. One was titled, "Richard Byrd: Alone in Antarctica" for the *Adventurers* series.[39] The other was "Alone on the Ice" for the *American Experience* series.[40] Several of Byrd's former associates on his first antarctic expedition were interviewed for both productions. On the 1997 video-tape, Eugene Rodgers, author of *Beyond the Barrier,* and Robert Matuozzi related their observations based on their studies of Byrd's files. Rodgers credited Byrd for being an expert fundraiser but noted that he was insecure, afraid of flying, and was motivated to carry out the fraud because he was in great debt for the North Pole expedition. Matuozzi said paranoia had developed in Byrd as a result and reiterated that he was not always truthful in his claims. Matuozzi stated that Byrd was a troubled and complex man who had perpetuated a public myth and found he could not always control all the circumstances around him.[41] In the 1999 production, it was noted that the National Geographic Society had "verified" Byrd's claim after awarding him its gold medal.[42]

News of the discovery of Byrd's North Pole flight diary with its altera-tions and erasures rated headline coverage in May 1996 newspapers throughout the United States, Canada, and Europe. A growing number of qualified observers now want the record corrected on the North Pole flight to give proper credit for a momentous achievement to those who rightfully earned it.

16 · The World's Polar Consultant

yrd and the North Pole matter had to be put aside after Balchen's retirement as he focused on a new life. Although out of uniform, strong ties to the military remained as he was appointed a special consultant to the Air Force chief of staff on arctic affairs. He regularly gave lectures on arctic construction and survival procedures at the Air Force Institute of Technology's Civil Engineering School, Wright-Patterson Air Force Base in Ohio, and participated in Project North Star, which included flights to arctic bases in Alaska, Canada, and Greenland, and seminars for deans and faculty members of U.S. engineering schools. In addition to the engineering aspects, the talks reviewed the development of aviation in the arctic and its strategic importance for the defense of North America. These trips also afforded Balchen a chance to see old friends in Alaska and to indulge in one of his favorite sports, salmon fishing.

Many professional organizations and corporations were well aware of the vast extent of his interests and knowledge and took advantage of his availability with continual requests for guidance and advice. Knowing of his background in forestry, a Swedish steamship company asked for his guidance on proposals to develop timber and mineral resources in Labrador and Newfoundland. Sikorsky Aircraft Company wanted his input about helicopter requirements for arctic work; the government of Iceland asked for his assessment of air facilities. Others who sought his counsel included Hughes Aircraft Corporation, General Dynamics, and Page Engineering Company, the latter concerning arctic construction. Electric Boat Company and Canadair, divisions of General Dynamics, also asked Balchen's advice on various projects. In 1957 he accompanied Lowell Thomas, Sir Hubert Wilkins, and Adm. Donald B. MacMillan on an aerial photographic flight to the North Pole in connection with the International Geophysical Year.

As the great diversity of his scientific knowledge became even more widely known, Balchen was contacted by airlines operating in the arctic environment. He accepted the vice presidency of Resort Airlines, a nonscheduled airline operating internationally under U.S. Defense Department contracts. Later, he joined the board of directors of Wien Alaska Airlines and worked with SAS in training their personnel in grid navigation for the polar routes.

Honors were still coming Balchen's way. In June 1957 the first Outstanding Aviator Award from the National Pilots Association in Washington, D.C., was presented to him by General Doolittle. General Spaatz spoke on behalf of President Eisenhower, who sent a letter to Balchen saying, "For a full generation your name has ranked high among the pioneers of air exploration and adventure. . . . It seems strange that it has taken so long for those responsible to class you as the 'outstanding aviator of the year.' On the other hand, the award this evening is surely an additional tribute to your vital and continuing role among the leaders of world aviation."[1]

Drawing on Balchen's pioneer work on a transarctic route, SAS inaugurated a polar route to Tokyo with simultaneous flights in each direction on 24 February 1957 in Douglas DC-7Cs. It was a major event for SAS and for aviation because it would cut the east–west time to the Far East from 52 to 27 hr. It became the first airline in the world to operate a round-the-world service over the polar regions without a change of aircraft, a dream that Bernt Balchen had since before World War II.

The Balchens purchased their first house in the United States at Chappaqua, Westchester County, New York, in April 1957. Balchen had been attracted to this area in 1930 when he joined the Campfire Club of America—a sportsmen's club set in acres of woodlands and lakes, founded by Theodore Roosevelt and other notable sportsmen and well-known for its collection of trophies representing every wild animal species in North America. There he was able to enjoy his hobbies and expertise in trap and skeet shooting and fly casting. Sketching, painting, photography, and woodworking in his professionally equipped workshop were among his spare-time activities. There was also his extensive library of books on exploration, history, biography, and art, which had followed him in many moves. A son was born to the couple on 26 December 1958.

Balchen was 59. He was named Lauritz after Balchen's father. Laurence M. Gould was the boy's godfather.

Balchen joined General Precision Laboratories, an electronics company headquartered at Pleasantville, New York, in 1959, as a consultant. Later, he was named special assistant to the company president and traveled extensively in the United States and Europe. As he participated in sales and market planning for their wide range of projects, his ability to speak the Scandinavian languages and German proved especially useful in translating technical materials for the company's sales and scientific personnel. His high-level military and government contacts in the United States and Europe were invaluable to the company.

With a rapidly burgeoning international military interest in the arctic, which was provoked by the continuing Soviet missile threat, Balchen strongly advocated the concept of an Apogee Intercept Defense System (AIDS) that promised to provide the United States with a capability to intercept and destroy missiles while in flight toward the United States. To accomplish this, forward radar stations in Alaska, Norway, and Germany would be required for detection, acquisition, and initial tracking of Soviet-launched intercontinental ballistic missiles (ICBMs). The Air Force invited Balchen to join a group to make an inspection of a number of air bases in the arctic areas of Greenland and Alaska in 1960 to judge suitability.

Balchen had become firmly convinced of the value of the AIDS strategy while viewing an antiballistic missile defense system demonstration at Thule in 1961. General Precision Laboratories was enthusiastic about the idea, and Balchen joined a team of scientists and engineers to determine how the concept could be turned into reality; the team submitted a feasibility report to the Department of Defense in June 1962.

One project that developed as a result was Project Iceman, a proposal to place intermediate range ballistic missiles (IRBMs) in Greenland. In addition to being able to reach Soviet targets as far south as the Black Sea and all of Siberia, Balchen pointed out in a detailed company memo that "such a system would also have the important function of attracting the Soviet nuclear threat away from the populated areas of the U.S. to the non-productive wastes of the Greenland Ice Cap, an important factor to consider in nuclear survival."[2]

Balchen also participated in a study of European air traffic control to put all the European countries under a common system to prevent air traffic saturation should an emergency arise. Balchen gave briefings to the

Scandinavian military and civil aviation decision makers on airborne navigation systems and radar systems. Of special concern was the possibility that in the event of hostilities, the entire European airways system would be pervaded by military aircraft and cause chaos for both military and civil air operations. Having established a personal rapport previously with Thomas K. Finletter who had been appointed ambassador to NATO, Balchen contacted him directly to ask for a proper forum to discuss the General Precision proposal for an integrated air traffic control system.

He participated in developing aircraft to fight forest fires, and worked to improve navigation and radar systems. He continued to advise civilian educators, scientists, and Defense Department officials on arctic construction.

Balchen also worked on a number of military weapons systems, including sabotage equipment, remote control detonation, Doppler radar-triggered time-delay fuses and bomb devices, aerial delivery systems, parachute-drop techniques, operational procedures for fighter–bomber weapons delivery, electronic beacons for clandestine and rescue operations, infrared detection systems, passive responders, and an ammunition firing system for which Balchen obtained a patent.

A concept that Balchen initiated was an electronic system for trail marking for the benefit of ground troops in the arctic and in the jungle. A flashback to his World War II experiences came with his recommendation that paper parachutes be adopted by the Air Force for use in dropping supplies to troops or in air rescue situations. He cited the economic and operational advantages of paper parachutes over the widely used and more expensive nylon types. Based on his recommendation, the Air Force tested samples and marketing was effected through General Precision Laboratories.

In 1963 Balchen flew to Oslo and Copenhagen to discuss the use of aircraft simulators to train F-104 jet fighter pilots. A previously submitted proposal by General Precision to both governments had been ignored and Balchen was asked to investigate. Knowing personally the high-ranking principals who made the decisions in both countries, he was able to get the proposal approved, the contracts signed, and the funds allocated.

Balchen was invited to participate in the first round-the-world flight over both Poles in November 1965. The invitation to take part in "the last great adventure of the air" as Lowell Thomas called it, was extended by Col. Willard F. Rockwell, board chair of Rockwell-Standard Company. Besides making the flight an aviation "first," the primary purpose was scientific, to fly highly instrumented scientific packages around the world over both Poles in a short period of time at a relatively constant altitude. Scientists onboard would have the opportunity to conduct many studies with particular emphasis on cosmic-ray absorption and high-altitude meteorology, including clear air turbulence.

A long-range Boeing 707 was leased from the Flying Tiger Line and named *Pole Cat*. Two veteran TWA pilots, Capts. Fred L. Austin and Harrison Finch, initiated the project and, with the help of the Explorers Club, brought it to reality. The flight originated in Honolulu on 14 November 1965 and flew over the North Pole to London, then to Lisbon, Buenos Aires, and over the South Pole to Christchurch, New Zealand, and on back to Honolulu. The 26,500 mi. flight was completed in 62 hr. 27 min. elapsed time and 51 hr. 27 min. in the air. Eight point-to-point world speed records were established.

The national news media followed the flight closely, and Balchen was delighted to be included as an official observer with the ten scientists. Having been the first to pilot an aircraft over both Poles, he was invited to share the controls over them again. As a bonus, he was able for the first time to see the Balchen Glacier in antarctica, which Byrd had named for him in 1931.

Balchen experienced a personal life change when he and Inger separated in 1964 and were divorced in June 1966. On 30 November 1966 Balchen married Audrey C. Schipper of Chappaqua and New York City, a graduate of Columbia University and market research director for Fairchild Publications in New York. They were married in New York at a gathering of family and long-time friends.

Balchen joined Canadair in August 1966 as a marketing advisor for their aircraft, with focus on developing sales in the Scandinavian countries and northern North America. Later that year he became a consultant in the Engineering and Program Development Department of General Dynamics Corporation, an association that continued through 1971. His projects included liquid natural gas tankers; ice breakers for the U.S. Coast Guard; new epoxy plastic materials for possible use in the construction of submarines; improved vehicles for over-snow operations in the Navy's Operation Deep Freeze; and a seagoing electronic weather system that would take current, temperature, salinity, and pressure measurements at various depths that could be interrogated by radio. He continued to speak to industry and civic groups, always focusing on the potential that the arctic region presented for defense and commerce.

Balchen at this time became increasingly aware of the possibility of an energy crisis with U.S. reliance on foreign supplies of oil. He was called on as a consultant by Hercules Oil, Phillips Petroleum, and Moran Towing companies while planning was being carried out to extract oil from Alaska and transported by pipeline from Prudhoe Bay in the far northern part of the state to Valdez. His basic concept was to have oil, gas, and minerals from the Alaskan fields transported to the East Coast by specially built tankers and cargo ships that would be led through the ice packs by rugged, dedicated icebreakers throughout the year. He presented detailed statistics to show that such a plan would be more economical and less a threat to the environment than a pipeline.

Balchen was one of the founders of the International Aviation Snow Symposium established in the early 1960s by the northeast chapter of the American Association of Airport Executives. At an annual meeting airport managers and pilots study snow and ice control problems at large and medium hub U.S. civilian airports and exchange ideas. The Colonel Bernt Balchen Award was established in 1975 and is awarded annually to honor the airport that has the most successful snow and ice control program as judged by pilots.

One of the most important speeches of Balchen's consulting career was given in March 1968 at the Long-Range Polar Objectives Conference in Easton, Maryland. He reviewed the history of aviation in the arctic and remarked that it had powerful resources lying beneath its icy surface that could be exploited. He had observed during his many years flying over it that the arctic pack ice was thinning and that a large portion of the Arctic Ocean within the arctic rim might become an open sea within a decade or two. Several specialists agreed that there was progressive shrinkage of the ice and if further in-depth scientific investigation proved they were right, the riches of the region would be accessible by ships.

Balchen's belief that there were hidden riches in the arctic actually came about 30 years before when he saw oil slicks on the ice and surface indications of iron ore. Later surveys by the Canadian government uncovered high-grade iron ore estimated at more than 100 billion tn. To tap these resources, Balchen pointed out, would require a combination of submarines, huge surface tankers, ice breakers, and land-based equipment such as snow-traveling cargo trucks. All were within the state of the mechanical and naval arts at the time.

According to Walter Sullivan in a *New York Times* article, "The warning [about the increasing temperatures in the arctic] sounded by Colonel Balchen has stirred up enough excitement in Washington for the Navy to ask Dr. Norbert Untersteiner of the University of Washington to prepare an assessment of trends in the pack."[3] Although there was opposition to and disbelief about Balchen's observations and predictions, there is agreement now among scientists that the carbon dioxide and ozone content of the world's air has risen during the past century, and smog, dust, and ash from volcanoes has tended to reduce the solar heat from reaching the surface. Balchen sparked the first public acknowledgments by the scientific community of what today is called *global warming* and is now on the world's agenda of major environmental concerns. Balchen received continuing press coverage in the United States and Canada for his views and predictions about global warming. To counter his critics, he noted that ice over the Arctic Ocean had decreased in depth from 43 ft. in 1893 to 12 ft. during the International Geophysical Year 1957–1958, and decreased to an average of 6 to 8 ft., winter and summer, over an area of as much as 5 million square miles. He explained that the ice heretofore had provided the Arctic Ocean with a relatively cold surface, which had caused the stationing of a high pressure area over the arctic area the year round.

This Arctic high pressure deflects the cyclonic systems originating over the North Pacific to a more southerly pass across the agricultural areas of the U.S. and Canada. Calculations indicate that if the pack ice were to disappear, the Arctic Ocean surface temperature in the coldest months would be about 42 degrees Fahrenheit, and the pack ice would not form again.

Mid-latitude climates would be 20 to 25 degrees warmer than now, and low latitudes 10 degrees cooler in winter. The cyclones of the Northwest Pacific would be deflected northward into the Arctic Ocean and form a low pressure system. The moist air from these lows would dump a great amount of snow over the Arctic and sub-arctic land areas. Annual snowfalls would increase another eight to 10 feet in these areas.[4]

Balchen was reappointed as a consultant to the Air Force in 1970. Despite signs of failing health in 1972, he was determined not to let up or admit any pain. He was able to make three trips to his beloved Alaska for the Air Force that year. One trip was to participate in marking the 15th anniversary of the first transpolar flight by SAS (from Copenhagen to Tokyo); the second, marking the 25th anniversary of the Air Force's Alaskan Command; then participation in the annual Project North Star trip to arctic bases. That spring he took his wife Audrey along on a flight to Norway, marking an inaugural direct SAS flight from New York to Horten. There was an opportunity to visit old friends and show his wife sites that meant so much to him in his early life and during the war. Particularly important to him was a visit to the place in Oslo where "his boys"—members of the Norwegian resistance—had been executed by the Germans. He was welcomed everywhere as a national hero.

Balchen's health deteriorated in 1973. In July, a United Airlines DC-8 jet circled the earth during a two-week charter trip with 156 students aboard "A Classroom in the Sky." Capt. William S. Arnott, three other captains, and their crew members, knowing of Balchen's illness, had named the plane *Bernt Balchen* because it was going to fly over both Poles, representing "his polar world for which he is famous in American aviation history." In September Balchen was admitted to Northern Westchester Hospital, Mt. Kisco, New York, because of sudden severe back pain, where doctors found a vertebrae had broken as a result of metastatic bone cancer. Word of his serious condition was sent to his friends all over the world. Visitors included the president and executives from SAS who came over from Scandinavia. Charles Lindbergh sent a handwritten letter noting the times they were together in Alaska. Senator Hubert H. Humphrey and James A. Farley, President Roosevelt's former postmaster general, also sent letters of concern and warm wishes.

On 17 October 1973 Bernt Balchen's stout heart gave out and the world's greatest polar airman was gone. Funeral services were held over a period of three days—21–23 October. The first at a funeral home near his residence brought a gathering of family, friends, and business associates. A traditional "farewell to a brother" tribute was conducted by a Sons of Norway Lodge, whose members had traveled from Brooklyn. New York representatives of the Explorers Club, Masons, and American Legion raised their banners near the casket. On it, an associate from the first Byrd Expedition to antarctica placed a special wreath.

At noon the following day in the Protestant Chapel at New York's JFK International Airport, the second service took place. The chapel was filled to overflowing with representatives of the U.S. Air Force and the governments of Norway, Sweden, and Denmark. In addition to industry executives and pilots from SAS, individuals from the organizations close to Balchen attended, including the Quiet Birdmen and the Explorers and Adventurers Clubs. Eulogies were delivered by Eigil Nygaard, consul general of Norway, Berent Friele, SAS board chair, and Lowell Thomas.

Balchen was buried at Arlington National Cemetery on 23 October 1973: It would have been his 74th birthday. More than 100 associates and admirers in the military and aviation industry and members of the diplomatic and government services joined with his family to witness the ceremony with full military honors. In one of the cruel ironies of their relationship, Balchen was buried next to the grave of Adm. Richard E. Byrd.[5]

As the ceremony proceeded, a four-engine C-54 with red wing tips and tail, the colorful markings of the Air Force's Air Rescue Service, flew overhead at a low altitude, circled, and then headed west. Jerry Hannifin, aviation reporter for *Time,* asked several Air Force officers where the plane had come from. No one knew. He checked with the Federal Aviation Administration, the control tower at Washington National Airport, and the Pentagon. All denied any knowledge of a C-54 having permission to fly over the cemetery at that time. Several months later, it was found that some former Air Force pilots at Wallops Island, Virginia, a NASA research facility, had made a C-54 "photo flight" in the area that day. They had served in the Air Rescue Service and thus paid their last respects to their former leader.

Gen. John C. Meyer, commander of the Strategic Air Command, wrote Audrey Balchen, saying that he could not forget Balchen's saving his life after he had crash-landed a B-17 on Greenland during World War II.

A letter from a retired Air Force colonel was typical of those who served with Balchen in Alaska. He said that they had hiked, fished, flown, and took pictures of wild flowers together, and he watched while Balchen painted and carved scenes on wood from nature's album of the world he loved—the far north.

In the November 1973 issue of *Inside SAS,* the president of the airline wrote,

The ranks are thinning out among the pioneers of aviation. . . . Now Bernt Balchen is gone. With his death Scandinavia and international aviation have lost a unique figure, a colorful and individualistic airman and officer who came to mean a great deal for SAS in the early years . . . especially for SAS's pioneering efforts in Arctic aviation. . . . He was a legend in his own lifetime. Balchen had an all-around personality. He loved outdoor life. He was an outstanding food expert; a competent painter. But first and foremost he was a pilot, and among people in the business he is considered one of the 10 greatest pilots the world has known. The key to his success was that everything he attempted was always planned. . . . He was a good, personal friend to many of us. He will be greatly missed.[6]

More honors had been planned for Balchen before his death, including his induction into the National Aviation Hall of Fame at Dayton, Ohio, in December 1973. Gen. George S. Brown, Air Force chief of staff, made the induction presentation posthumously. It was acknowledged by Audrey Balchen with a poignant speech dramatized by showing one of his arctic flying boots—"a large boot to fill," she said.[7]

Balchen was also inducted into the Aviation Hall of Fame of New Jersey at Teterboro where his long career is featured. In 1974 he was installed in Canada's Aviation Hall of Fame at Edmonton, the only non-Canadian to be so honored, in recognition of his pioneer cargo flights to Fort Churchill, Hudson Bay, in 1926. Also in 1974 the Alaska Geographic Board named an 11,140 ft. peak in the Alaska Range "Mount Balchen" in recognition of Balchen's contributions to geographic knowledge and his love of the state.

The Wings Club in New York dedicated the Bernt Balchen Room in a ceremony in October 1975 during which Norway's King Olaf V presented a granite fossil plaque from Spitsbergen, engraved in Balchen's memory. It was displayed among a collection of his remarkable water-color paintings of arctic regions, which were on loan from the Corcoran Art Gallery in Washington, D.C. Some of them are still there. During the same month, Balchen's memory was honored with his investiture in the International Aerospace Hall of Fame in San Diego, California. A permanent exhibit devoted to the Greenland rescue operations in World War II was opened at the Air Force Museum, Dayton, Ohio. The National Air and Space Museum in Washington, D.C., received a collection of Balchen's Ellsworth expedition sketches and two arctic paintings, as well as military decorations and awards from France marking the *America* flight. Also included were the flying helmet and goggles used on the Ellsworth flights, which are on display near the Lockheed Gamma *Polar Star* Balchen flew on Ellsworth's 1935 antarctic expedition.

On 23 October 1975, the 76th anniversary of Balchen's birth, his widow Audrey was joined by Gen. George S. Brown, chair of the Joint Chiefs of Staff; Air Force assistant vice chief of staff M. L. Boswell; representatives of the governments of Norway and Sweden, of SAS, the American Legion, and friends at Balchen's grave site. An Air Force color guard stood by as a granite gravestone designed by Mrs. Audrey Balchen was dedicated by Chaplain Maj. Donald J. Harlin.

The honors and memorials were still not over for Balchen with this dedication. He was remembered in his native Scandinavia in 1979 with a tree planting and a stone marker at Kjevik Airport at Tveit, Norway, where he was born. This was supplemented in 1987 by a larger stone monument erected by the Sons of Norway and other national groups. An international air show, sponsored by the Royal Norwegian Air Force, was held near Oslo in June 1984 in Balchen's honor, the largest air show ever held in that country.

In Sweden and Norway there are several memorials erected to honor Balchen's Carpetbaggers and those who gave their lives to support the World War II effort. One monument, erected in 1944, is at Alingsas, Sweden, incorporating the twisted propeller of a crashed B-24 in which six crew members were killed. Memorial ceremonies were held by the Swedish Armed Forces in June 1995 and in 1997 at the Flygoperation Balchen Monument on the Kallax Air Base near Lulea, Sweden, to honor participants in the Where and When flight operations of 1944–1945. A life-sized bronze statue of Balchen is to be dedicated on the 100th anniversary of his birth—23 October 1999—in Kristiansand, Norway, sponsored by the Sons of Norway.

The honors that came during and after his lifetime testify that Bernt Balchen was a man of the world whose many contributions, quietly achieved, will continue to be recognized. In the words of his widow Audrey, "Forces of history, geography and time converged with his inborn talents, his physical strength, endurance, courage and stubborn will to propel him to a destiny of achievements spanning the ends of the earth, to unselfish acts of heroism on behalf of his fellow men, to contributions of renown, both in war and peace."[8]

Appendix • Bernt Balchen's Honors and Awards

Military (arranged in order of significance)
Distinguished Service Medal
Legion of Merit
Distinguished Flying Cross
Soldiers Medal with 3 Oak Leaf Clusters
Air Medal with 5 Oak Leaf Clusters
European Theater of Operations Medal with 4 Combat Stars
American Campaign Medal
World War II Freedom Medal

U.S. Nonmilitary (arranged chronologically)
Special Congressional Medal for Byrd Antarctic Expedition I
Harmon International Trophy
Outstanding Aviator Award, National Pilots' Association
Medal of Valor, City of New York
Silver Medal, Aeronautical Chamber of Commerce
Explorer's Club Gold Medal
Adventurers Club Medal
Charles H. Johnson Medal, Norsemen Masonic Lodge
Camp Fire Club of America Medal
Civil Engineering Center Accolade, Air Force Institute of Technology

Foreign Decorations (arranged alphabetically)
Aero Club de France Medallion
Brotherhood of Silver Wings (Northwest Territories, Canada)
Campaign Medal (Norway)
City of Paris Gold Star
King Christian X Medal of Liberation (Denmark)
Leif Erikson Award
Medal of Canada's Aviation Hall of Fame (Edmonton, Alberta, Canada)

Medal of Icarus (Canada)
Medal of the Order of Flight, City of Edmonton (Alberta, Canada)
Medal of the Order of Polaris (Yukon Territory, Canada)
Norwegian Campaign Medal
Royal Order of St. Olaf, Grand Commander's Rank with Swords and Stars
  (Norway)
Royal Order of the Sword, Knight Commander, 1st Class (Sweden)
Sons of Norway Award for Professional Achievement
Le Touguet Paris Plage Medal
Ville de Dunkerque, Republique Francaise Medallion

Honorary Degrees and Other Honors (arranged alphabetically)

Balchen Glacier between Phillips Range and Fosdick Mountain in Edsel Ford
  Range of Antarctica Named
Balchen Ryggen Mountain on Spitsbergen (Svalbard) Named
Balchen Mountain in Sor Rondan Mountains in Antarctica Named
Doctor of Science, Tufts University
Doctor of Science, University of Alaska
Enshrined in the Aviation Hall of Fame of New Jersey (Teterboro)
Enshrined in Canada's Aviation Hall of Fame (Edmonton, Alberta)
Enshrined in the International Aerospace Hall of Fame (San Diego, California)
Enshrined in the National Aviation Hall of Fame (Dayton, Ohio)
Mount Balchen in Alaska Range Named
Mount Balchen in Herbert Range, Queen Maud Mountains in Antarctica
  Named

Notes

Introduction
1. Personal communication, Walter J. Boyne, 14 March 1996.

1. Spitsbergen
1. Letter, Maj. Gen. Hjalmar Riiser-Larsen, Royal Norwegian naval air force, to Louis Ruppel, editor, *Collier's*, 30 January 1950, Bernt Balchen Collection, Air Force Historical Research Agency, Maxwell Air Force Base, Alabama, file 168.7053-85 (hereinafter cited as Balchen Collection, Maxwell AFB).
2. Richard E. Byrd, *Skyward* (New York: G. P. Putnam's Sons, 1928), 166.
3. Byrd's first article appeared in *National Geographic* in the fall of 1925. The National Geographic Society would provide him with funds, technical assistance, and help spread his fame throughout the world during the next three decades.
4. Byrd, *Skyward*, 168.
5. Byrd never mentioned the name Fokker in a detailed report to the National Geographic Society, probably because of this blatant advertising. It was referred to as "polar plane," the "Byrd plane," or the *"Josephine Ford."* In a letter to Ford, Byrd complained that Fokker "has written his name all over the plane" and would not let Byrd fly it unless allowed to do so. Byrd Polar Research Center, Ohio State University, box 99, file 3996 (hereinafter cited as Byrd Polar Research).
6. Byrd, *Skyward*, 176.
7. From page 5 of a 674-page dictated account by Bernt Balchen of his life from 1926–1949, copy in the Papers of Bernt Balchen, Manuscript Division, Library of Congress, identification no. 75922, container no. 3 (hereinafter cited as Transcript).
8. Transcript, 8
9. Transcript, 24. In his diary entry for 2 May 1926 Byrd wrote, "Took lunch with Amundsen who professes great friendship but gave Lt. Balchen (who is a peach and wanted to help us) orders not to come near us again." *To the*

Pole: The Diary and Notebook of Richard E. Byrd, 1925–1927, ed.
Raimund E. Goerler (Columbus: Ohio State University Press, 1998), 76.
However, Balchen never mentioned such an order; on the contrary, he said
he was encouraged by Amundsen to help Byrd in any way he could.

10. Bernt Balchen, *Come North with Me* (New York: E. P. Dutton, 1958), 35.
11. Balchen, *Come North with Me*, 41–42.
12. Transcript, 32.
13. Letter, Riiser-Larsen to Ruppel.
14. Transcript, 35.
15. Transcript, 40.
16. Transcript, 42.
17. Balchen, *Come North with Me*, 51.
18. Charles J. V. Murphy, *Struggle: The Life and Exploits of Commander Byrd*
    (New York: Frederick A. Stokes, 1928), 204–205.
19. Ibid.
20. Byrd, *Skyward*, 207.

2. The Lad from Tveit

1. Balchen, *Come North with Me*, 53.
2. Clayton Knight and Robert C. Durham, *Hitch Your Wagon: The Life of
   Bernt Balchen* (Drexel Hill, PA: Bell, 1950), 13.
3. From undated manuscript by Balchen for a speech titled, "Roald Amundsen," Balchen Collection, Maxwell AFB, file 168-7053-92. Amundsen
   bought his own airplane in 1912 and became licensed civil pilot number 1
   in Norway in 1914.
4. Balchen, *Come North with Me*, 19.
5. Knight and Durham, *Hitch Your Wagon*, 42.
6. Ibid., 51.
7. Ibid., 55.
8. Ibid., 54.
9. Ibid., 57.
10. Ibid.
11. John Lawrence, *Bernt Balchen: Viking of the Air* (New York: Brewer and
    Warren, 1931), 63–64.
12. "Roald Amundsen," Balchen Collection, Maxwell AFB, file 168.7053-85.
13. Ibid.

3. Introduction to a New World

1. Balchen, *Come North with Me*, 56.
2. Ibid., 57.
3. Murphy, *Struggle*, 213.
4. Ibid.
5. Richard Montague, *Oceans, Poles and Airmen* (New York: Random House,
   1971), 35.
6. Murphy, *Struggle*, 221.
7. Ibid.

8. Balchen, *Come North with Me*, 59.

9. Ibid.

10. Ibid.

11. Byrd, *Skyward*, 115.

12. The Fokker company declared bankruptcy in March 1996 but continues to manufacture spare parts and aircraft armament.

13. Lesley Forden, *The Ford Air Tours 1925–1931* (Alameda, CA: Nottingham Press, 1973), 2.

14. Balchen, *Come North with Me*, 64.

15. Ibid.

16. Montague, *Oceans, Poles and Airmen*, 48.

17. Transcript, 58. The dictation from which the transcript was made took place in 1949; this appears to be the first instance Balchen expressed his doubts in a written record that the Fokker reached the North Pole in the time it was gone from Spitsbergen.

18. Balchen, *Come North with Me*, 69.

19. Ibid., 70.

20. Ibid., 71.

21. Knight and Durham, *Hitch Your Wagon*, 101.

22. Letter, Edsel Ford to Byrd, 7 October 1926, Byrd Polar Research Center, box 181, file 6539.

23. Ibid.

24. Balchen, *Come North with Me*, 86.

25. Byrd, *Skyward*, 236. Photos taken two weeks later do not show a cast.

26. Ibid., 236.

27. Anthony H. G. Fokker and Bruce Gould, *Flying Dutchman* (New York: Henry Holt, 1931), 257.

28. Ibid.

29. Jack Huttig, *Summer of Eagles* (Chicago: Nelson-Hall, 1980), 11.

30. Transcript, 102.

31. Ibid., 106.

32. Ibid., 105–106.

33. Balchen, *Come North with Me*, 95.

34. Ibid., 95.

35. Ibid.

36. Knight and Durham, *Hitch Your Wagon*, 112.

37. Ibid., 115.

4. The Flight of the *America*

1. Balchen, *Come North with Me*, 98.

2. Byrd, *Skyward*, 239.

3. Ibid., 240.

4. Fokker, *Flying Dutchman*, 260.

5. Balchen, *Come North with Me*, 99.

6. Byrd, *Skyward*, 241–242.

7. Transcript, 111a.

8. Montague, *Oceans, Poles, and Airmen,* 121.
9. Balchen, *Come North with Me,* 103.
10. Ibid., 109.
11. Ibid., 111.
12. Byrd, *Skyward,* 258.
13. James E. Mooney, *Air Travel* (New York: Scribner's Sons, 1930), 238–239.
14. Balchen, *Come North with Me,* 115.
15. Knight and Durham, *Hitch Your Wagon,* 126.
16. Byrd, *Skyward,* 269–272.
17. The village established a Musée America–Gold Beach museum to honor these two historic events.
18. P. J. Philip, "Down off Shore at Ver-sur-Mer, Normandy," *New York Times,* 3 July 1927.
19. Ibid.
20. P. J. Philip, "Balchen Stands out as Hero," *New York Times,* 3 July 1927.
21. Ibid.
22. Ibid.
23. Knight and Durham, *Hitch Your Wagon,* 128.
24. Balchen, *Come North with Me,* 123.
25. Undated telegram from Mr. and Mrs. Fokker, Closter, N.J., Byrd Polar Research, box 26, file 1092.
26. An example is a radiogram addressed to Balchen in Paris, dated 1 July 1927, from Rodman Wanamaker expressing "the deepest gratefulness to Providence that you have been given the privilege to bring to France the good heart and welcome spirit of America." Byrd Polar Research, box 36, file 1574.
27. C. B. Allen, "How American Honors Her Heroes of the Air," *Outlook and Independent,* 7 January 1931.
28. Fokker, *Flying Dutchman,* 260. Fokker gave Balchen a bonus of $500 for the flight. The America Trans-Oceanic Company paid him $675 for the period 23 June–23 July 1927. Byrd, in addition to unspecified compensation, received a new Lincoln automobile from Edsel Ford. Balchen received $1,000 from the *New York Times* for exclusive worldwide rights for newspaper publication of his story. Byrd Polar Research, box 26, file 1092.
29. Byrd, *Skyward,* 263.
30. Ibid., 337–338.
31. Fokker, *Flying Dutchman,* 262–263.
32. Undated copy of citation from city of Hoboken, NJ, Byrd Polar Research, box 36, file 1577.
33. Letter, Grover C. Whalen to Balchen, 28 July 1927, Byrd Polar Research, box 26, file 1091.

5. Tragedy and Prelude to Triumph
1. Letter, "To Whom It May Concern," signed by Byrd, 27 July 1928, Byrd Polar Research, box 26, file 1577.
2. Balchen, *Come North with Me,* 129.

3. Letter, Byrd to Edsel Ford, 3 September 1927, Byrd Polar Research, box 37, file 1639.

4. Balchen, *Come North with Me*, 136–137; Knight and Durham, *Hitch Your Wagon*, 139.

5. Transcript, 142.

6. Fred W. Hotson, *The Bremen* (Toronto: CANAV Books, 1988), 125; Balchen, *Come North with Me*, 139.

7. Balchen, *Come North with Me*, 140.

8. Ibid., 141.

9. Ibid., 142.

10. Ibid., 144.

11. Associated Press wire story, 26 April 1928, Balchen Collection Maxwell AFB, file 168.7053-83.

12. Transcript, 158.

13. Ibid.

14. *Washington Star*, 4 May 1928. The *Bremen* was returned to Germany for repairs, later placed on display in New York's Grand Central Station and then the Smithsonian Institution, before being donated in 1936 to the Ford Museum in Dearborn, Michigan. In 1997 it was obtained by a group of German industrialists and returned to Germany for permanent exhibition.

15. Eugene Rodgers, *Beyond the Barrier* (Annapolis, MD: Naval Institute Press, 1990), 157.

16. Byrd, *Skyward*, 305.

17. Dean C. Smith, *By the Seat of My Pants* (Boston: Little, Brown, 1961), 185.

18. Transcript, 167.

19. Ibid., 173.

20. Ibid., 176.

21. Balchen, *Come North with Me*, 163.

6. To the South Pole

1. Transcript, 196.

2. Rodgers, *Beyond the Barrier*, 94.

3. Transcript, 200.

4. Smith, *By the Seat of My Pants*, 197.

5. Ibid., 198–199.

6. Balchen, *Come North with Me*, 174–175.

7. Balchen wrote on the title page of Diehl's book, "I carried this book with me on the flight across the South Pole, November 29, 1929." Balchen Collection Maxwell AFB, file 168.7053-17.

8. Transcript, 223–224.

9. Norman D. Vaughan, *With Byrd at the Bottom of the World* (Harrisburg, PA: Stackpole Books, 1990), 86–87. All members of the expedition signed a statement declaring that they would wait at least two years after their return before publishing any books about their antarctic experiences.

10. A description of the sled is contained in a letter from Balchen to Leland L. Barter, 24 August 1970, Balchen Collection, Maxwell AFB, file 168.7053-83.

11. Russell Owen, *South of the Sun* (New York: John Day, 1934), 152–153.
12. Transcript, 225b.
13. Balchen, *Come North with Me* (first printing), 180 (on microfile at Maxwell AFB). This was published only in the first edition of the book that was destroyed by the publisher. However, a few review copies were distributed in advance of the announced release date. The expurgated text of the original version is published in Richard Montague's *Oceans, Poles and Airmen* (New York: Random House, 1971), 289–300.
14. Transcript, 225i.
15. Balchen, *Come North with Me* (first printing), 181.
16. Smith, *By the Seat of My Pants*, 192.
17. Ibid.
18. Rodgers, *Beyond the Barrier*, 142.
19. Ibid., 145.
20. Transcript, 232.
21. Translation of undated paper from Norwegian by Carl O. Petersen, Balchen Collection, Maxwell AFB, file 168.7053-237.
22. Balchen, *Come North with Me*, 186.
23. Balchen, *Come North with Me* (first printing), 186.
24. Smith, *By the Seat of My Pants*, 216–217.
25. Transcript, 235.
26. Ibid., 237.
27. Balchen, *Come North with Me*, 186.
28. Ibid., 190–191. Byrd also dropped a Norwegian flag to honor Amundsen and a Union Jack for Robert Scott, who reached the Pole after Amundsen in 1911.
29. Byrd, *Little America* (New York: G. P. Putnam's Sons, 1930), 341.
30. Transcript, 240.
31. Montague, *Oceans, Poles and Airmen*, 262. This was the first message sent by an American president to antarctica. It was forwarded to Little America through the *New York Times* radio station in New York City.
32. Transcript, 247–248.
33. Smith, *By the Seat of My Pants*, 230.
34. Quoted in undated rough draft of manuscript titled, "Making of a Hero: Richard Evelyn Byrd," by Andrew A. Freeman, p. 21, Balchen Collection, Maxwell AFB, file 168.7053-92.
35. Transcript, 248.
36. The *Floyd Bennett* was returned to the United States after Byrd's second antarctic expedition, 1933–1935, and is on display at the Ford Museum, Dearborn, Michigan. The Fairchild FC-2W *Stars and Stripes* was also flown on the second expedition. Much of it was later used to provide parts for another FC-2; however, a few parts are in storage at the National Air and Space Museum in Washington, D.C. The wreckage of the Fokker Universal *Virginia* was located in 1956 by a U.S. Navy survey party during Operation Deep Freeze. In 1994 Chris Rudge, a New Zealand aviation enthusiast, announced he wanted to dig it out and restore it to display at the

Christchurch, New Zealand, airport. He began negotiations with the Byrd family because, he said, they still owned it. No decision had been made at press time.

7. Fame and Misfortune

1. Balchen, *Come North with Me,* 193.
2. Knight and Durham, *Hitch Your Wagon,* 194.
3. Ibid., 195.
4. "Balchen Fought in Naturalization," *New York Times,* 21 June 1931.
5. Montague, *Oceans, Poles and Airmen,* 265; Knight and Durham, *Hitch Your Wagon,* 195; Rodgers, *Beyond the Barrier,* 253–254.
6. Balchen, *Come North with Me,* 195.
7. Rodgers, *Beyond the Barrier,* 253.
8. Transcript, 254.
9. Ibid., 255.
10. From undated notes believed written in 1930, Balchen Collection, Maxwell AFB, file 168.7053-21.
11. Ibid.
12. Balchen Collection, Maxwell AFB, file 168.7053-21. Byrd named a glacier in antarctica for Balchen in January 1932. It is about 10 mi. wide and located in the Edsel Ford Range.
13. Transcript, 256.
14. Enclosure to letter from Ernest L. Jahnncke, acting secretary of the Navy, to Balchen, 29 July 1931, Balchen Collection, Maxwell AFB, file 168.7053-83.
15. Letter, Byrd to Balchen, 13 October 1931, Balchen Collection, Maxwell AFB, file 168.7053-83.
16. Letter, Byrd to Balchen, 12 October 1931, Byrd Polar Research, box 37, file 1638.
17. Transcript, 261.
18. Ibid., 262.
19. "Balchen Fought in Naturalization," *New York Times,* 21 June 1931.
20. "Balchens Admitted to Citizenship," *New York Times,* 6 November 1931.
21. Mary S. Lovell, *The Sound of Wings* (New York: St. Martin's Press, 1989), 126.
22. Muriel Earhart Morrisey and Carol L. Osborne, *Amelia, My Sister* (Santa Clara, CA: Osborne, 1987), 88.
23. Transcript, 263.
24. Lovell, *The Sound of Wings,* 178–179.
25. Doris L. Rich, *Amelia Earhart: A Biography* (Washington, D.C.: Smithsonian Institution Press, 1989), 132.
26. Transcript, 264.
27. Lovell, *The Sound of Wings,* 185.
28. Telegram, Earhart to Balchen from Londonderry, Ireland, 22 May 1932, Balchen Collection, Maxwell AFB, file 168.7053-83.
29. Lincoln Ellsworth, *Beyond Horizons* (New York: Doubleday, Doran, 1938), 253–254.

30. Ibid., 371.
31. Letter, "To Whom It May Concern," signed by Ellsworth, 18 April 1932, Balchen Collection, Maxwell AFB, file 168.7053-83.
32. Richard Sanders Allen, *The Northrop Story: 1929–1939* (New York: Orion Books, 1990), 154–155.
33. Letter, Ellsworth to Balchen, 12 May 1932, Balchen Collection, Maxwell AFB, file 168.7053-83.
34. Transcript, 267.
35. Ibid., 271.
36. Ibid., 275.
37. Ibid., 277.
38. Ellsworth, *Beyond Horizons,* 277–278.
39. Transcript, 292.
40. *Natural History,* June 1935 (a publication of the American Museum of Natural History, New York), 402.
41. Donald Dale Jackson, *The Explorers* (Alexandria, VA: Time-Life Books, 1983), 98.
42. Ellsworth, *Beyond Horizons,* 296.
43. Ibid.
44. Ibid., 298.
45. Transcript, 299.

8. Prelude to War

1. Transcript, 308.
2. Ibid., 309.
3. Knight and Durham, *Hitch Your Wagon,* 225.
4. Ibid.
5. Ibid., 227.
6. Balchen diary, 1937, Balchen Collection, Maxwell AFB, microfilm 30915.
7. Balchen, *Come North with Me,* 332; Knight and Durham, *Hitch Your Wagon,* 231.
8. Transcript, 332.
9. Ibid., 332a.
10. Ibid., 332b.
11. Anders Buraas, *The SAS Saga* (Oslo, Norway: Scandinavian Airlines System, 1979), 26.
12. Balchen diary, 1939, Balchen Collection, Maxwell AFB, microfilm 30195.
13. *Little Norway in Pictures* (Toronto: S. J. Reginald Saunders, 1944), 22.
14. "To Whom It May Concern" letter, signed by Wilhelm Morganstierne, Minister of Norway to the United States, 27 May 1940, Balchen Collection, Maxwell AFB, file 168.7053-83.
15. Transcript, 341.
16. Early in 1941 a decree was issued by the Norwegian government-in-exile calling all Norwegian nationals throughout the world between the ages of 18 and 35 to report for military service in England or Canada. A second

training center was established at Muskoka Airport near Huntsville, about 120 mi. north of Toronto.

17. Transcript, 350.
18. Ibid., 351.
19. Transcript of Air Force oral history conducted at Rochester, New York, 22–23 October 1975, Air Force Historical Rsearch Agency, Maxwell AFB, file K239.0512-875.
20. Letter, Maj. Gen. H. H. Arnold, chief, Army Air Forces, to Capt. Bernt Balchen, 12 September 1941, Balchen Collection, Maxwell AFB, file 168.7053-83.

9. The Challenge of Bluie West 8

1. Henry H. Arnold, *Global Mission* (New York: Harper and Brothers, 1949), 98.
2. Memorandum for the chief of staff, Army Air Forces, subject: Greenland, Sondrestrom Staging and Defense Area, signed by Lt. Col. Claude E. Duncan, secretary of the air staff, July 25, 1941, Balchen Collection, Maxwell AFB, file 168.7053-83.
3. Report to the adjutant general, Washington, D.C., subject: survey of Greenland, Iceland, and England on extension of route survey, signed by Capt. Elliott Roosevelt, 21st Reconnaissance Squadron, Newfoundland Air Base, 8 September 1941, Balchen Collection, Maxwell AFB, file 168.7053-83.
4. Ibid.
5. Ibid.
6. Letter, Lt. Col. Claude E. Duncan, secretary of the air staff, 13 September 1941, Balchen Collection, Maxwell AFB, file 168.7053-83.
7. Transcript, 359.
8. Ibid., 362.
9. Ibid., 365.
10. Ibid., 366.
11. Ibid., 377.
12. From undated notes for talk by Balchen given to Air Force audiences, Balchen Collection, Maxwell AFB, file 168.7053-89.
13. Ibid.
14. Transcript, 383.
15. From *Egedesminde: The Last Flight of 19108* (a privately published book by Robert W. "Bill" Shelton, 1994), 25–29. Shelton returned to the village in July 1988 and unveiled a plaque dedicated to his crew and the aircraft. The plaque was fixed to a piece of the plane's wing and mounted on a large boulder in front of where the plane stopped—just 18 in. away.
16. Transcript, 390.
17. Stinson's crew members were assigned to other duties during the war and all but one survived. After the war Stinson became a physician, married, and had three children. He named one of two boys Leslie Balchen Stinson. Twenty-two years later, Balchen and Stinson flew over the wreckage. The

rescue and return flight were featured in a 1964 issue of *Life*. In 1995 sal-
vagers returned the wreckage to the United States for restoration and display at the Tillamook Naval Air Station, Oregon. An estimated 60 planes
remain buried somewhere on the Greenland ice cap.

18. Transcript, 402–403.
19. Dr. McBride also received the award. The Soldier's Medal is awarded to per-
    sons in the Armed Forces who perform a heroic act involving voluntary risk
    of life in a noncombat situation.
20. Transcript, 386.
21. Ibid., 408.
22. Ibid., 409b.
23. Personal correspondence, Herbert C. Stein, 8 August 1997.
24. Margaret Barret, "Many New Tributes Honor Air Pioneer," *The Reporter
    Dispatch* (White Plains, New York), 21 October 1975.

10. "War Below Zero"

1. Bernt Balchen, Corey Ford, and Oliver La Farge, *War below Zero* (Boston:
   Houghton Mifflin, 1944), 14.
2. Transcript, 388–389.
3. Balchen et al., *War below Zero*, 22.
4. Pat Epps, owner of an Atlanta air charter service, led several expeditions to
   Greenland and finally located all eight planes in 1988. One of the P-38s was
   retrieved and is being restored; the others remain buried under about 250 ft.
   of snow and ice.
5. Transcript, 417.
6. Pritchard and Bottoms were awarded the Distinguished Flying Cross
   posthumously.
7. Balchen et al., *War below Zero*, 70.
8. Balchen, *Come North with Me*, 243.
9. Ibid.
10. Ibid.
11. Undated letter, Balchen to Roy Rutherford, Cleveland, Ohio, Balchen Col-
    lection, Maxwell AFB, file 168.7053-83.
12. Transcript, 448.
13. Balchen, *Come North with Me*, 246.
14. Scrap book, Balchen Collection, Library of Congress (no file no.). In 1989
    Harry Spencer, copilot of the B-17, returned to the crash site but could not
    locate the aircraft. He left behind a small plaque to honor the men who lost
    their lives.
15. Balchen, *Come North with Me*, 248.
16. Transcript, 464–465.
17. Ibid., 468.
18. Balchen was awarded an Oak Leaf Cluster to the Air Medal for leading the
    missions against the German installations.
19. Balchen, *War below Zero*, 37.
20. Balchen, *Come North with Me*, 256.

11. Operations Sonnie and Ball

1. Letter, commanding officer, VIII Air Force Service Command, to assistant chief of staff, Eighth Air Force, 7 January 1943, Balchen Collection, Maxwell AFB, file 168.7053-93.
2. Transcript, 476–477.
3. Ibid., 478.
4. Directive signed by Maj. Gen. Fred L. Anderson, deputy commander, Operations, U.S. Strategic Air Forces in Europe, 29 January 1944, Balchen Collection, Maxwell AFB, file 168.7053-93.
5. Memorandum from commander, European Division, Air Transport Command, to Col. Bernt Balchen, 28 August 1944, Balchen Collection, Maxwell AFB, file 168.7053-93.
6. Balchen, *Come North with Me*, 263.
7. Ibid., 264.
8. Transcript, 490.
9. Bernt Balchen, "Our Secret War in Scandinavia," *Collier's*, 9 March 1946.
10. Balchen, *Come North with Me*, 264–265.
11. Balchen, "Our Secret War in Scandinavia."
12. Balchen, *Come North with Me*, 266.
13. Transcript, 501.
14. Capt. Eric Friedheim, "Scandinavian Carpetbagger," *Air Force*, August 1945, 28–29.
15. Ibid., 29.
16. Balchen, *Come North with Me*, 267–268.
17. Transcript, 514. As soon as hostilities were over in Europe in 1945, American Export Airlines, later named American Overseas Airlines, began operations into Sweden and other European countries north of the 50th parallel.
18. Transcript, 508–509.
19. Ibid., 511. Special Operation Executive (SOE) was formed soon after the collapse of Norway in 1940. Saboteurs were given training, and SOE worked with Milorg, the Norwegian resistance organization. A command structure was set up to help Milorg put the greatest possible pressure on the Germans. An office in Stockholm handled Milorg affairs.
20. Balchen, "Our Secret War in Scandinavia."
21. Transcript, 521.
22. Ibid., 524.
23. Personal correspondence, George M. Philbrick, 2 February 1997.
24. Earl Zimmerman, "St. Elmo's Fire," *They Flew by Night* (privately published, San Antonio, TX, 1990), 203, a collection of stories, edited by Col. Robert W. Fish, written by former members of the 801st/492nd Bombardment Group. The light pattern Zimmerman described was the positioning of lights on the ground that was the code for the day. The flame he described was a colored flare fired by the Germans. Knowing their flares for the day and firing them fooled the enemy into thinking they were Germans.
25. Ben Parnell, *Carpetbaggers* (Austin, TX: Eakin Press, 1993), 212–213.
26. Transcript, 528.

27. Fish, *They Flew By Night,* 206.
28. Transcript, 529.
29. Balchen, *Come North with Me,* 278.
30. Ibid., 280–281. Balchen was in London on 8 September 1944 when the first V-2 rocket landed on British soil.
31. Transcript, 533–534.
32. Ibid., 536–537. After the Germans capitulated in 1945, Quisling was tried for high treason and executed.
33. Transcript, 540–541.
34. Ibid., 564.
35. Memorandum for American Minister Herschel V. Johnson, subject: "AATS Operations between the United Kingdom and Sweden," 18 December 1944. The Royal Norwegian air force also had a transport service between England and Sweden during the winter months under supervision of British Overseas Airways. Balchen Collection, Maxwell AFB, file 168.7053-93.
36. Letter, Col. Felix M. Harrison, military air attaché, American Legation, Stockhold, to commanding general, European Division, Air Transport Command, 11 December 1944, Balchen Collection, Maxwell AFB, file 168.7053-93. During a flight from Stockholm to Oslo on an SAS-747 in 1972, Balchen was handed a business card from the pilot, Capt. Torleif Skogstad. On it was written, "Thanks for the ride on Liberator, 23/4 1944 Bromma-Leuchars. Except for you I wouldn't be sitting here now."
37. Message no. 85611 for Col. Bernt Balchen, 8 December 1944, relayed from Washington, D.C., Balchen Collection, Maxwell AFB, file 168.7053-93.
38. Reply to Message no. 85611, 13 December 1944, Balchen Collection, Maxwell AFB, file 168.7053-93.

12. Operation Where and When and the Sepals Project

1. Memorandum from Col. Charles E. Rayens, military attaché, U.S. Legation, Stockholm, to Balchen, 4 December 1944, Balchen Collection, Maxwell AFB, file 168.7053-33.
2. Letter, Col. Charles E. Rayens to Balchen, subject: "Sepals Project," 3 May 1945, Balchen Collection, Maxwell AFB, file 168.7053-33.
3. Transcript, 572.
4. Knight and Durham, *Hitch Your Wagon,* 306–307.
5. Transcript, 573.
6. Report of Kirkenes Operations, Kallax Air Field, to commanding general, EDATC, 31 January 1945, Balchen Collection, Maxwell AFB, file 168.7053-33.
7. Transcript, 585.
8. Ibid., 588–589.
9. Balchen, *Come North with Me,* 293.
10. Ibid.
11. Ibid.
12. Jan Waernberg, *Flygoperation Balchen,* 8, a report of Operation Where and When, undated, translated from Swedish.

13. Balchen, *Come North with Me,* 286–287.
14. Robert H. Fesmire, *Flight of a Maverick* (Nashville, TN: Eggman, 1995), 106.
15. Personal correspondence, 11 April 1997.
16. *Flygoperation Balchen,* 15.
17. Ibid., 16.
18. Transcript, 600.
19. Ibid., 602–603.
20. Undated manuscript in Swedish by Bjoern Roerholt titled, "Bernt Balchen: Polar Pilot and War Hero," 3. Translated into English by Ornunf Thune. Provided to author by translator.
21. Transcript, 605–606.
22. Ibid., 606–607.
23. Balchen, "Our Secret War in Scandinavia."
24. Balchen, *Come North with Me,* 295.
25. Ibid.
26. Letter, Maj. Gen. William J. Donovan to Balchen, 2 July 1945, Balchen Collection, Maxwell AFB, file 168.7053-93.
27. Wilbur H. Morrison, *Fortress without a Roof* (New York: St. Martin's Press, 1982), 232–233.

13. From Airline Copresident to Squadron Commander
1. Buraas, *The SAS Saga,* 35.
2. Transcript, 619.
3. Ibid., 619–620.
4. Radiogram to Balchen from Rudolf Olsen, 28 November 1945, Balchen Collection, Maxwell AFB, file 168.7053-36.
5. Transcript, 622.
6. Ibid.
7. Ibid., 625.
8. Ibid.
9. Ibid.
10. Ibid., 632.
11. Ibid., 639.
12. Ibid., 640.
13. Ibid., 641.
14. *Washington Post,* July 6, 1946.
15. Undated report by Balchen, "Greenland Mission," Balchen Collection, Maxwell AFB, file 168.7053-47.
16. Transcript, 646.
17. Robert C. "Bob" Reeve, early Alaskan bush pilot and founder of Reeve Aleutian Airways, was believed to be the first to operate an aircraft from a glacier. He supplied miners in the mountains near Valdez, Alaska, and was widely known as the "glacier pilot."
18. Transcript, 663.
19. Balchen, *Come North with Me,* 300.

20. Report to Commanding General, Alaskan Air Command, "Training of Evacuation and Evasion Units," 17 June 1949, Balchen Collection, Maxwell AFB, file 168.7053-59.

21. Undated chronology of events, 1927–1957, prepared by Balchen, furnished by Mrs. Audrey S. Balchen.

22. Undated Balchen manuscript titled, "Arctic Survival and Rescue Problems," Balchen Collection, Maxwell AFB, file 168.7053-57.

23. Report by Balchen titled, "Central Arctic Search and Rescue Organization," 20 January 1949, Balchen Collection, Maxwell AFB, file 168.7053-57.

24. Memorandum from Secretary of the Air Force for acting chief of staff, 2 October 1950, Balchen Collection, Maxwell AFB, file 168.7053-57.

25. Letter, Byrd to Balchen, 10 April 1950, Balchen Collection, Maxwell AFB, file 168.7053-21.

26. Letter, Byrd to Balchen, 25 May 1950, Balchen Collection, Maxwell AFB, file 168.7053-21.

27. Testimony on S. 3314, 81st Cong., 2nd Sess., 17 April 1950.

28. House of Representatives report no. 808 to accompany S. 1220, 82nd Cong., 1st Sess., 8 August 1951.

29. Senate report no. 211 to accompany S. 1220, 82nd Cong., 1st Sess., 4 April 1951.

30. Statement of Secretary Thomas K. Finletter before the Kilday Subcommittee, House Armed Services Committee on S. 1220, 82nd Cong., 1st Sess., 20 May 1951.

31. Letter, Col. H. C. Thorne, Jr., to Balchen, subject: "Appointment in the regular Air Force," 25 September 1951, Balchen Collection, Maxwell AFB, file 168.7053-83. Joseph F. Carroll received a regular commission later and was promoted to major general in 1950 and lieutenant general in 1960. In 1961, he became the first director of the Defense Intelligence Agency.

32. Knight and Durham, *Hitch Your Wagon.*

33. Eric Severeid, "Incredible Norseman," *New York Times,* 29 December 1949.

34. Undated reviews headlined, "Life of Bernt Balchen Is Thrilling Adventure Story," William Van Dusen Associates, New York, Balchen scrapbook, Balchen Collection, Library of Congress, box 75932.

35. Ibid.

36. Transcript of radio broadcast by Lowell Thomas, 19 January 1951, Balchen Collection, Library of Congress, box 75932.

14. "The Most Unpleasant Years of My Life"
1. Memorandum from Col. Harold C. Donnelly to Balchen, 13 December 1950, Balchen Collection, Maxwell AFB, file 168.7053-83.

2. Memorandum from Balchen to Carroll McCone, 20 December 1950, Balchen Collection, Maxwell AFB, file 168.7053-83.

3. From notebook used as a basis for informal talks, Balchen Collection, Maxwell AFB, file 168.7053-89.

4. Balchen, *Come North with Me,* 305.

5. C. B. Allen, "U.S. Has Top-of-the-World Air Base. Could Bomb Any Part of Europe," *New York Herald-Tribune,* 13 October 1951.

6. Bill Brinkley, "How We Built a Giant New Air Base at the Top of the World," *Reader's Digest,* December 1952. Condensed from *Life,* 22 September 1952.

7. Alexander P. deSeversky, *Victory through Air Power* (New York: Simon and Schuster, 1942).

8. Alexander P. deSeversky, "Greenland Air Base Blunder," *New York Journal-American,* 12 October 1952.

9. Ibid.

10. Letter, "To Whom It May Concern," from Edward T. Dickinson, vice chair, National Security Resources Board, 29 May 1952, Balchen Collection, Maxwell AFB, file 168.7053-83.

11. Report by Balchen titled, "A Preliminary Examination of Arctic Problems with Reference to the USSR," Balchen Collection, Maxwell AFB, file 168.7053-99.

12. From undated paper by Balchen titled, "Chronology of Meetings in Connection with DEW Line Discussions and Planning I Have Participated in Since 1952," Balchen Collection, Maxwell AFB, file 168.7053-80.

13. Ibid.

14. Bernt Balchen and Bess Balchen, *Bernt Balchen's Oppskriftsbok (Bernt Balchen's Recipe Book)* (Oslo, Norway: Steenshalle, 1951).

15. Sanka Knox, "Public to Discover Explorer Balchen Is an Artist," *New York Times,* 5 November 1952.

16. Bill Davidson, "Colonel Bernt Balchen's Arctic Art," *Collier's,* 17 January 1953, 54–55.

17. Byrd, *Skyward,* 102.

18. Adm. Chester Nimitz, "Future Employment of Naval Forces," *Vital Speeches,* 15 January 1948.

19. Memorandum from Byrd to Col. Ashley McKinley, 11 December 1950, Byrd Polar Research, box 51, file 2243.

20. Memorandum from Byrd to Col. Ashley McKinley, April 1952, box 51, file 2243.

21. Francis and Katherine Drake, "Bernt Balchen: Viking of the Air," *Reader's Digest,* January 1953, 35–39.

22. Rebuttal (unsigned) to *Reader's Digest* article concerning ski repair on the *Josephine Ford* at Spitsbergen in 1926, Byrd Polar Research Center, box 51, file 2275.

23. "Will the Air Force Fire a Great Arctic Expert?" *Newsweek,* 5 October 1953, 19.

24. Letter, Sen. Edward J. Thye to President Eisenhower, 28 October 1953, Balchen Collection, Maxwell AFB, file 168.7053-82.

25. Letter, Mrs. Norman Postosky to Secretary of the Air Force, 20 October 1953, Balchen Collection, Maxwell AFB, file 168.7053-82.

26. Letter, Maj. Gen. Robert W. Burns, assistant vice chief of staff, to Mrs. Nor-

man Potosky, 4 November 1953, Balchen Collection, Maxwell AFB, file 168.7053-82.

27. Letter, Gov. Sigurd Anderson to Sen. Francis Case, 23 April 1954, Air Force Historical Research Agency, Maxwell AFB, file 186.70532-82.

28. Memorandum from Balchen to Col. Arno H. Luehman, Director of Information, Office of the Secretary of the Air Force, 13 October 1953, Balchen Collection, Maxwell AFB, file 168.7053-83.

29. Ibid.

30. Ibid.

31. Ibid.

32. From original printing of *Come North with Me* that was destroyed, 301–302. These paragraphs were eliminated in the revised printing, which is discussed in some depth in Chapter 15.

33. Memorandum for record of meeting with Gen. Thomas D. White, 16 October 1953, Balchen Collection, Maxwell AFB, file 168.7053-21.

34. Letter, Balchen to Byrd, 16 October 1953, Balchen Collection, Maxwell AFB, file 168.7053-21.

35. Drew Pearson, *Washington Post,* 1 November 1953.

36. Balchen, *Come North with Me* (first printing), 303.

37. From citation for Harmon International Trophy, White House, 10 November 1953. Separate trophies are awarded for international and national achievements. The awards were suspended during World War II.

38. Letter, Byrd to Col. Ashley McKinley, 25 November 1953, Byrd Polar Research, box 51, file 2275.

39. Summary of diary entries for 1953, Balchen Collection, Maxwell AFB, file 168.7053-82.

40. Letter, Balchen to Byrd, 8 November 1953, Balchen Collection, Maxwell AFB, file 168.7053-21.

41. Letter, Byrd to Balchen, 13 November 1953, Balchen Collection, Maxwell AFB, file 168.7053-21.

42. Letter, Balchen to Byrd, 18 November 1953, Balchen Collection, Maxwell AFB, file 168.7053-21.

43. From rough draft of manuscript by Andrew A. Freeman titled, "The Making of a Hero: Richard Evelyn Byrd," Balchen Collection, Maxwell AFB, file 168.7053-83.

44. Personal communication, Mrs. Audrey S. Balchen, 20 September 1997.

45. Diary entry, 29 April 1954, Balchen Collection, Maxwell AFB, file 168.7053-82. Mooney had written a book titled, *Air Travel* (New York: Charles Scribner's Sons, 1930), that was grossly inaccurate and highly laudatory of Byrd.

46. James E. Mooney, 14-page untitled paper, Byrd Polar Research, box 51, file 2275.

47. Memorandum from Byrd to Mooney, 12 November 1953, Byrd Polar Research, box 51, file 2275.

48. Letter, Mooney to Byrd, 15 November 1953, Byrd Polar Research, box 51, file 2275.

49. Letter, Mooney to Byrd, 8 December 1953, Byrd Polar Research, box 51, file 2275.

50. Letter, Mooney to Byrd, 13 January 1954, Byrd Polar Research, box 51, file 2275.

51. Balchen, *Come North with Me*, 306.

52. "Walter Winchell of New York-Broadway," *Washington Post*, 6 January 1954.

53. Text of speech given by Balchen at Explorer's Club, New York, 13 February 1954, Balchen Collection, Maxwell AFB, file 186.7053-93.

54. Balchen and Bergaust, *The Next Fifty Years of Flight* (New York: Harper and Brothers, 1954), 190–192.

55. Letter, Balchen to Col. Albert E. Milliken, 3 January 1955, Balchen Collection, Maxwell AFB, file 168.7053-93.

56. Montague, *Oceans, Poles and Airmen*, 274.

57. Evelyn Moore Isakson, *Bernt Balchen: A Special Report on the Unique Career of a Great American* (Northridge, CA: Hollycrest Enterprises, 1972), 96–97.

58. Ibid.

59. Letter, Balchen to Harry A. Bruno, 24 November 1954, Balchen Collection, Maxwell AFB, file 168.7053-93.

60. Letter, Balchen to A. Walker Perkins, 5 September 1954, Balchen Collection, Maxwell AFB, file 168.7053-92.

61. Undated letter (ca. July 1955), Col. Hubert Zemke to Lt. Gen. Glenn O. Barcus, Northeast Air Command, Balchen Collection, Maxwell AFB, file 168.7053-92.

62. Letter, Balchen to Col. Hubert Zemke, 5 March 1956, Balchen Collection, Maxwell AFB, file 168.7053-92.

15. An Autobiography Raises a Storm

1. Citation for Distinguished Service Medal, U.S. Air Force, Washington, D.C., 31 October 1956. This medal is awarded for exceptionally meritorious service in a duty of great responsibility. When Balchen's Air Force flight records were closed out, they revealed that he had more than 11,000 hr. pilot time; an estimated 9,000 hr. were over arctic areas.

2. Letter, Twining to Balchen, 31 October 1956, Balchen Collection, Maxwell AFB, file 168.7053-89.

3. Letter, Balchen to Corey Ford, 5 June 1957, Balchen Collection, Maxwell AFB, file 168.7053-83.

4. From notes for speeches, undated, Balchen Collection, Maxwell AFB, file 169.7053-89.

5. Letter, Ben Hibbs to Balchen, 11 March 1958, Balchen Collection, Maxwell AFB, file 169.7053-83.

6. Letter, Paul A. Siple to Balchen, 30 March 1958, Balchen Collection, Maxwell AFB, file 169.7053-83.

7. Letter, Laurence M. Gould to Balchen, 12 April 1958, Balchen Collection, Maxwell AFB, file 169.7053-83.

8. Letter, Maj. Gen. G. B. Erskine, USMC, to Elliott MacRae, 14 April 1958, Balchen Collection, Maxwell AFB, file 169.7053-83.

9. From notes to speeches, Lotus Club dinner, 12 May 1958, Balchen Collection, Maxwell AFB, file 169.7053-83.

10. Balchen, *Come North with Me* (first printing), 66–67.

11. Ibid., 300.

12. Ibid., 301.

13. Orville Prescott, "Books of the Times," *New York Times,* 8 August 1958.

14. John K. Hutchens, "Book Reviews," *New York Herald Tribune,* 8 August 1958.

15. Letter, A. Y. Paranak to Balchen, 25 September 1958, Balchen Collection, Maxwell AFB, file 169.7053-83.

16. Letter, Balchen to Dean C. Smith, 9 March 1960, Balchen Collection, Maxwell AFB, file 169.7053-83.

17. Gosta Liljequist, "Did the *Josephine Ford* Reach the North Pole," *Interavia* (May 1960): 58–60.

18. Letter, Sverre Petterssen to Balchen, 2 September 1958, Balchen Collection, Maxwell AFB, file 169.7053-83.

19. Smith, *By the Seat of My Pants,* 191.

20. Letter, Dean C. Smith to Fred W. Hotson, 25 June 1974. Letter quoted by permission.

21. Smith, *By the Seat of My Pants,* 232.

22. (New York: Random House, 1971).

23. Montague, *Oceans, Poles and Airmen,* 283.

24. Vern Haughland, "North Pole Feat Called Fraud," *Washington Post,* 15 December 1971.

25. *Patent Trader,* 6 January 1972.

26. Fred W. Hotson, undated paper titled, "A Case for Historians." Used with permission of Hotson, former CAHS president.

27. Letter, Dick Hagelthorn to Balchen, 29 December 1971, Balchen Collection, Maxwell AFB, file 169.7053-83.

28. Letter, Balchen to Dick Hagelthorn, 15 January 1972, Balchen Collection, Maxwell AFB, file 169.7053-83.

29. Peter Dunn, "The Strange Flight of Admiral Byrd," *Sunday Times* (London), 7 August 1971.

30. Letter, George Crossette to Mrs. M. Gordon Knox, 17 January 1972, Balchen Collection, Maxwell AFB, file 169.7053-83.

31. Finn Ronne, *Antarctica, My Destiny* (New York: Hastings House, 1979), 134.

32. David Roberts, *Great Exploration Hoaxes* (San Francisco: Sierra Club Books, 1982), 132.

33. "First Solo Assault on the Pole," *National Geographic,* September 1978, 302.

34. Dennis Rawlins, "Raimund Goerler's Discovery and Its Revelations," a report directed to Raimund Goerler and Ken Jezck, 4 May 1996, Ohio State University Archives.

35. John Noble Wilford, "Did Byrd Reach the Pole? His Diary Hints 'No,'" *New York Times*, 9 May 1996.
36. Ibid.
37. Rawlins, "Raimund Goerler's Discovery and Its Revelations," 7.
38. Letter, Robert N. Matuozzi to Mrs. Audrey Balchen, 1 June 1996. Quoted by permission.
39. "Richard Byrd: Alone in Antarctica," PBS *Adventurer* series, 1997. Producer/director: Ken Kirby.
40. "Alone on the Ice," PBS *American Experience* series, 1999. Writer/ producer/director: Nancy Porter.
41. "Richard Byrd."
42. "Alone on the Ice."

16. The World's Polar Consultant

1. Letter, President Dwight D. Eisenhower to Balchen, 24 June 1957, Balchen Collection, Maxwell AFB, file 169.7053-83.
2. Memorandum from Balchen to D. W. Smith, General Precision, Inc., 6 October 1961, Balchen Collection, Maxwell AFB, file 169.7053-121.
3. Walter Sullivan, "Expert Says Arctic Ocean Will Soon Be an Open Sea," *New York Times*, February 20, 1969.
4. From undated interview notes sent to Balchen by Vern Haugland, Associated Press, Balchen Collection, Maxwell AFB, file 169.7053-83.
5. Apparently it was a random decision made by the superintendent at the cemetery.
6. "A Great Pilot Gone," by Knut Hagrup, *Inside SAS,* November 1973.
7. Acknowledgment speech by Audrey S. Balchen, National Aviation Hall of Fame, Dayton, Ohio, 14 December 1973. Used by permission of Mrs. Balchen.
8. Acknowledgment speech by Audrey S. Balchen, International Aerospace Hall of Fame, San Diego, California, 2 October 1976. Used by permission of Mrs. Balchen.

Bibliography

Balchen, Bernt (with Corey Ford and Oliver La Farge). *War Below Zero.* Boston: Houghton Mifflin, 1944.

Balchen, Bernt (with Erik Bergaust). *The Next Fifty Years of Flight.* New York: Harper and Brothers, 1954.

Balchen, Bernt. *Come North With Me.* New York: E.P. Dutton, 1958.

Bennett, Cora L. *Floyd Bennett.* New York: William Farquhar Payson, 1932.

Bowman, Gerald. *Men of Antarctica.* New York: Fleet Publishing, 1958.

Buraas, Anders. *The SAS Saga: A History of the Scandinavian Airlines System.* Oslo, Norway: Scandinavian Airlines System, 1979.

Butler, Susan. *East to the Dawn: The Life of Amelia Earhart.* Reading, MA: Addison-Wesley, 1997.

Bruno, Harry A. *Wings over America.* New York: Robert M. McBride, 1942.

Byrd, Richard E. *Skyward.* New York: G.P. Putnam's Sons, 1928.

———. *Little America.* New York: G.P. Putnam's Sons, 1930.

———. *Exploring with Byrd.* New York: G.P. Putnam's Sons, 1937.

Calitri, Princine M. *Harry A. Bruno: Public Relations Pioneer.* Minneapolis: T.S. Denison, 1968.

Carter, Paul A. *Little America: Town at the End of the World.* New York: Columbia University Press, 1979.

Clarke, Basil. *Polar Flight.* London: Ian Allan, 1964.

Cleveland, Reginald M. *America Fledges Wings: The History of the Daniel Guggenheim Fund for the Promotion of Aeronautics.* New York: Pitman Publishing, 1942.

Colby, William E. *Honorable Men: My Life in the CIA.* New York: Simon and Schuster, 1978.

Ellsworth, Lincoln. *Beyond Horizons.* New York: Doubleday, Doran, 1938.

Fokker, Anthony H. G., and Bruce Gould. *Flying Dutchman.* New York: Henry Holt, 1931.

Foster, Coram. *Rear Admiral Byrd and the Polar Expeditions.* New York: A. L. Burt, 1930.

Glines, Carroll V. *Polar Aviation*. New York: Franklin Watts, 1964.

―――. *Lighter-than-Air Flight*. New York: Franklin Watts, 1965.

―――. *The Compact History of the United States Air Force*. New York: Hawthorn Books, 1973.

Goerler, Raimund E., ed. *To the Pole: The Diary of Richard E. Byrd, 1925–1927*. Columbus: Ohio State University Press, 1998.

Gould, Laurence McKinley. *Cold: The Record of an Antarctic Sledge Journey*. Northfield, MN: Carleton College, 1931.

Green, Fitzhugh. *Dick Byrd: Air Explorer*. New York: G.P. Putnam's Sons, 1928.

Hamlen, Joseph R. *Flight Fever*. Garden City, NY: Doubleday, 1971.

Hatch, Alden. *The Byrds of Virginia*. New York: Holt, Rinehart and Winston, 1969.

Hegener, Henri. *Fokker―The Man and the Aircraft*. Letchford, Herts, England: Harleyford Publications, 1961.

Hotson, Fred W. *The Bremen*. Toronto, Canada: CANAV Books, 1988.

Hoyt, Edwin P. *The Last Explorer: The Adventures of Admiral Byrd*. New York: John Day, 1968.

Huttig, Jack W. *1927―Summer of Eagles*. Chicago: Nelson-Hall, 1980.

Jablonski, Edward. *Atlantic Fever*. New York: Macmillan, 1972.

Jackson, Donald Dale. *The Explorers*. Alexandria, VA: Time-Life Books, 1983.

Kirwan, L. P. *A History of Polar Exploration*. New York: W. W. Norton, 1959.

Knight, Clayton, and Robert C. Durham. *Hitch Your Wagon*. Drexel Hill, PA: Bell Publishing, 1950.

Lawrence, John. *Bernt Balchen: Viking of the Air*. New York: Brewer and Warren, 1931.

Leary, William M. *Aviation's Golden Age*. Iowa City: University of Iowa Press, 1989.

Leary, William M., and Leonard A. LeSchack. *Project Coldfeet*. Annapolis, MD: Naval Institute Press, 1996.

Lovell, Mary S. *The Sound of Wings: The Life of Amelia Earhart*. New York: St. Martin's Press, 1989.

Mason, Theodore K. *Two against the Ice*. New York: Dodd, Mead, 1982.

Miller, Francis Trevelyan. *The World's Great Adventure*. Philadelphia: Universal Book and Bible House, 1930.

Murphy, Charles J. V. *Struggle: The Life and Exploits of Commander Byrd*. New York: Frederick A. Stokes, 1928.

Montague, Richard. *Oceans, Poles and Airmen*. New York: Random House, 1971.

Owen, Russell. *South of the Sun*. New York: John Day, 1934.

―――. *The Conquest of the North and South Poles*. New York: Random House, 1952.

Rich, Doris L. *Amelia Earhart: A Biography*. Washington, D.C.: Smithsonian Institution Press, 1989.

Roberts, David. *Great Exploration Hoaxes*. San Francisco: Sierra Club Books, 1982.

Rodahl, Kaare. *North*. New York: Harper and Brothers, 1953.

Rodgers, Eugene. *Beyond the Barrier*. Annapolis, MD: Naval Institute Press, 1990.

Ronne, Finn. *Antarctic Command*. Indianapolis, IN: Bobbs-Merrill, 1961.

———. *Antarctica, My Destiny*. New York: Hastings House, 1979.

Roscoe, Theodore. *On the Seas and in the Skies*. New York: Hawthorn Books, 1970.

Roseberry, C. R. *The Challenging Skies*. New York: Doubleday, 1966.

Saunders, S. J. Reginald. *Little Norway in Pictures*. Toronto: S. J. Reginald Saunders, 1944.

Seth, Ronald. *The Undaunted: The Story of Resistance in Western Europe*. New York: Philosophical Library, 1956.

Siple, Paul A. *90 Degrees South*. New York: G.P. Putnam's Sons, 1930.

Smith, Dean C. *By the Seat of My Pants*. Boston: Little, Brown, 1961.

Steinberg, Alfred. *Admiral Richard E. Byrd*. New York: G.P. Putnam's Sons, 1960.

Vandegrift, John L., ed. *A History of the Air Rescue Service*. Orlando, FL: Military Air Transport Service, U.S. Air Force, 1959.

Vaughan, Norman D. *With Byrd at the Bottom of the World*. Harrisburg, PA: Stackpole Books, 1990.

Victor, Paul-Emile. *Man and Conquest of the Poles*. New York: Simon and Schuster, 1963.

Williams, Archibald. *Conquering the Air*. New York: Thomas Nelson and Sons, 1928.

Index